When
French Women
Cook

Other Books by Madeleine Kamman

MADELEINE M. KAMMAN

❀

When French Women Cook

A Gastronomic Memoir

❀

Foreword by
SHIRLEY CORRIHER

TEN SPEED PRESS
Berkeley · Toronto

*Ten Speed Press
Box 7123
Berkeley, California 94707
www.tenspeed.com*

*Distributed in Australia by Simon & Schuster Australia,
in Canada by Ten Speed Press Canada, in New Zealand by
Southern Publishers Group, in South Africa by Real Books,
in Southeast Asia by Berkeley Books, and in the United Kingdom
and Europe by Airlift Book Company.*

Cover design: Nancy Austin

Library of Congress Cataloging-in-Publication Data

Kamman, Madeleine M
  When French Women Cook
  Includes index.
  I. Cookery, French.   I. Title.
  TX 719.K27   641. 5'944   76–11582
  ISBN 1-58008-384-6

Originally published in the United States in 1976 by Atheneum.

*Printed in Canada
First printing, this edition, 2002*

1 2 3 4 5 6 7 8 9 10 — 07 06 05 04 03 02

Dedication

This book, in its own way a feminist manifesto, is dedicated to the millions of women who have spent millennia in kitchens creating unrecognized masterpieces, with a very special thought to Paul Bocuse's grandmother and mother, and to my Aunt Claire Robert, to whom I owe most of what I know, practice, and teach.

It is also dedicated to three men; to Alan for his understanding of my cooking disposition, to the memory of Samuel Chamberlain who shared with me all too short and precious moments reminiscing about the same France we both knew, and, last but not least, to my good wine and food-loving friend Monbousquet.

CONTENTS

FOREWORD

THESE ARE THE memories of a great chef and teacher. *When French Women Cook* is, like Madeleine Kamman, a classic and a treasure. The title refers to an earlier France, where, as Madeleine writes, "the stars in cooking did not go to men anxious for publicity, but to women with worn hands stained by vegetables peeled, parched by work in house, garden or fields, wrinkled by age and experience." For food lovers, here is an exceedingly rare opportunity to experience the rich French countryside of yesteryear—the joy of running down the beaches of Normandy to gather pails of mussels, the beauty of white crocuses and tiny blue flowers pushing up from the snowy earth of the Alps, the incredible excitement of finding a six-inch morel (who knew they could grow that big?), and the cozy warmth of the two brown-and-white Normandy cows in their stalls as the Camemberts drip in the cheese room next door. Brought to life through wonderful characters, enchanting stories, and astonishingly timeless recipes, here is Madeleine's France—the glorious France of days gone by.

Madeleine was born in Paris and, during her preschool years, had the good fortune to spend a lot of time with her great-grandmother, Marie-Charlotte. A skilled and artful cook, Marie-Charlotte let tiny Madeleine tag along on her marketing trips and train rides to gather mushrooms (in addition to the everyday hard work of making mattresses). Madeleine also tells of fun excursions—joyrides full of song and laughter—in her father's Peugeot to visit Henriette, a family friend in Normandy and the maker of a masterful apple tart with puff pastry crust, apple Bavarian cream filling, and topped with candied apples flambéed in Calvados.

There is the great darkness of World War II, when children were sent long distances to be safeguarded. Madeleine was dispatched to a children's home in the village of La Balme de Thuy, where she spent one day a week with the home's cook, Mimi, often dining on juniper berry—"treated" quail—compliments of Mimi's father, an irrepressible poacher. Their home in the Alps was a huge, old-fashioned greystone chalet with a sharply slanted roof, under which half of the first floor was allotted to the ten Tarentaise cows that produced the heat for the whole house. We then read of mischief with teenage Madeleine and her cousins, who pitch in to make wine for a neighboring vineyard and, in doing so, partake a bit and then share the alcohol-laced must with the chickens, who proceed to cackle all night and stop laying for two days.

With the invasion of Paris, Madeleine's family sought refuge in the Loire Valley at Château-la-Vallière, where Madeleine came of age while working in her great-aunt Claire's Michelin-starred restaurant, Hôtel des Voyageurs. Even when studying at the Sorbonne, Madeleine cooked there three months out of the year. And so it was that Madeleine came to understand perfection in the kitchen at an early age.

At first, it may appear that there are simply eight chapters here, each one dedicated to a woman who had a major influence on Madeleine's life. Then you realize that Madeleine, ever the master teacher, intentionally selected women from the various regions of France—Poitou, Auvergne, Normandy, Savoie, Touraine, Alsace, Brittany, and Provence. In doing so, she not only gives you their recipes, but exposes you to their wonderfully different foods and ways of life.

Though this book was written over twenty-five years ago, Madeleine was even then a recognized chef. Paul Bocuse proclaimed her restaurant, Chez La Mère Madeleine in Newton, Massachusetts, one of the finest in America and, indeed, it held a four-star Mobil rating and five stars from the *Boston Globe*. Madeleine has always been a daring leader. Her book, *The Making of a Cook*, which came out in 1971, was a landmark. It was the first time that a chef explained the science behind the dishes. Madeleine led the way for all the rest of us who now write as much about science as we write about food.

When French Women Cook is much more than a tour through the French countryside. It is also an introductory course in authentic, regional French cooking infused with the practical, resourceful insights and techniques of centuries-old methods and traditions. Each recipe includes the best season to prepare the dish, approximate expense, time required for preparation, appropriate accompanying wine and, best of all, remarks on ingredients that are a culinary education in themselves. We learn, for example, how to identify types of watercress and the amount to use of each variety, how to cut and clean squid, how to tell a female lobster from a male, how to tell if an oyster is alive, the best kind of salted cod to buy, which mushrooms may be substituted for those called for, and the best substitutes for genuine French ingredients.

The recipes themselves are truly exciting. Madeleine details how to make Alsatian spaetzele and her great-aunt Alwine's Kirsch Wedding Cake; both a triumph in their simplicity and relative ease. Some of the recipes make you want to drop everything and rush to the kitchen. Just imagine the Walnut Honey Cake—it calls for fine crumbs and ground walnuts instead of flour, a honey buttercream icing, and a garnish of walnuts dipped in caramel that shine like amber jewels. Other recipes—such as the marvelous pan-fried shrimp, which is quickly sautéed, covered, and steamed for 3 minutes, and served in a simple reduction sauce made with the pan drippings—are so contemporary you might think they came from a current magazine. This is cooking that fits right into our busy lifestyles.

Best of all, at every turn, there is Madeleine with the fascinating details that will make you successful: "Make a well in the flour, add the eggs and milk and mix until the mixture shreds from the whisk in heavy strands." Madeleine tells you how to correct flavors: "Lemon juice can neutralize saltiness or, if a dish or sauce is too acidic, acids can be tamed with salt." Here are the basics that these French women knew and we should, too—above 130°F, a butter sauce will break, how to repair a separated butter sauce, how to reheat a cold butter sauce. There is so much exciting knowledge and experience in these pages—exactly how to make a flaky short pastry, how to make a chiffonade of lettuce, how to produce a true brown veal stock.

Since this book's debut in 1976, Madeleine has won much-deserved honor upon honor. Her 1997 book, *The New Making of a Cook*, not only won a James Beard Award but also received the Beard Gold Medal as the finest cookbook of the year. She has received a Doctorate Honoris Causa from Johnson & Wales University, a Round Table for Women 1984 Pace Setter Award, citations from the Senate of California and the city of San Francisco, and a knighthood in the French "Ordre des Arts et des Lettres" awarded by the French Minister of Culture in 1991. From 1984 to 1991, American audiences were delighted with Madeleine's hit public television series, *Madeleine Cooks.* She is a member of the Escoffier Foundation Society and one of the Eschansons of Châteauneuf-du-Pape. In 1997, Les Dames d'Escoffier International presented Madeleine with the prestigious Grande Dame Award. Madeleine is so revered that the School for American Chefs was set up at Beringer Vineyards so that chef scholarship recipients, the brightest and best, could study with her.

The honors go on and on, but to me, Madeleine is a national treasure because of all that she has given to others. Madeleine has trained many of our finest chefs, top food writers, cooking teachers, and cooking school owners and, most important of all, many a family cook. Families across America enjoy wonderful meals because of Madeleine. Now we are so fortunate to be able to rediscover the making of this culinary canon through her own girlhood memories and treasured recipes.

Shirley O. Corriher, author of *CookWise*
February 2002

INTRODUCTION

I LEFT FRANCE during the early days of 1960 and the France I left, my France, does not exist anymore; it has disappeared, slowly receding into time past.

When I was growing up, French cities were small, French houses were just a story or so high, unstereotyped, all different and all blaring the individuality of their respective owners. Fields were mostly covered with blond wheat to make bread, not lush green corn to make plastics; wines were bought in barrels and took a long time to mature. The game one hunted for was really wild and I recall fondly the distinct smell of hare pelts and pheasant feathers. There was salmon, shad and eel in most of the rivers, crawfish to be gathered at dawn from homemade traps lowered into deep cool pools, trout to be observed flowing silkenly through the clear waters of alpine torrents. Mountains were climbed on foot, not in motorcars. The air smelled nice; clean, fresh, and permeated with the happy essences of bread baking, the nostalgic aroma of wood burning, or the earthy smells of cattle ruminating in nearby barns.

Where are you, my France, where Sundays were gastronomic celebrations, where dinner tables were islands for animated conversations around plates of nuts being cracked and picked by nimble fingers? Where are you, my France, where women cooked, where the stars in cooking did not go to men anxious for publicity but to women with worn hands stained by vegetables peeled, parched by work in house, garden or fields, wrinkled by age and experience. Where are you?

Nowhere but in the folds of my memory and, in the pages that follow, I shall woo you and recreate you, bring back to life your women so that you know, dear readers, that there was once a civilization that was human, tender, enjoyable and lovable.

Madeleine M. Kamman
Newton Centre, Massachusetts
March, 1976

Basic Ingredients and Cooking Techniques

ABOUT THE RECIPES

MOST OF THE RECIPES in this book have never been written down before. Those that have (Eugénie chapter, page 215) were written in such a form that the whole list of the ingredients and the way to combine them had, more or less, to be guessed from the general idea. When French people write down a recipe, it resembles in no way the organized American pattern. It is a general description of methods given succinctly most of the time, with proportions that are more often than not a little wacky. This is due to the fact that French people, mostly French women, cook without recipes. It is not rare to hear a French woman say: "What am I going to cook for dinner tonight?"

Her next step then is to go down to the stores lining the street where she lives to see what looks good, buy it, and before you know it, a lovely little meal is on the table, complete from soup to cheese and dessert.

In most of the households I knew when I was growing up, the stock pot to last the week was on the stove every Sunday. Whether the woman in the house worked outside of the home, or inside, there was a full meal on the table at noon and at night every day. My mother worked all her life and I fondly remember the lunches she put on the table for our family during the ninety minutes that her lunch hour lasted. At least once a week it included French fries peeled, hand cut, and fried on the spot and a bowl of lemony mayonnaise, mixed also on the spot and with an old wooden spoon at that, since Maman acquired her first electric mixer in 1965.

Claire's recipes were easy to remember since I cooked them with her in her restaurant; so were Magaly's, whose kitchen remains so hospitable to me. For Henriette's, Victoire's and Marie-Charlotte's recipes, I sat and bored my mother with millions of questions until I squeezed out of her all she remembered that could come to the rescue of my own memories. Loetitia and Mimi are great and willing talkers.

The difficulty of execution of the recipes is graded from simple to very difficult. Even the very difficult ones do not require more than a high school education for anyone to understand and execute. It is interesting to note that among all the women included in this book, only Magaly has a college education; the others never studied beyond junior high school.

When a recipe is labelled "easy," it is necessary for the cook to understand that "easy" does not always mean "quick." Some good food can be cooked rather quickly, but most dishes require time and care.

These recipes are designed for entertaining. With the paucity of truly excellent restaurants and the high cost of a meal in the few good existing ones, entertaining at home is becoming prevalent and many do not hesitate to invest time and money in producing a good meal at home. For at home, quality can be controlled and personal satisfaction can be gained from preparing something beautiful and tasty. With this in view, an indication of the cost of each recipe has been given from inexpensive to very expensive. Check through the book; some provinces cook more cheaply than others.

In the Poitou, for example, you will find quite a few relatively cheap dishes.

The length of time taken to execute the recipe will vary with each person. The times given here have been counted for hands with good experience in home cooking. Novice hands may be slower, professional hands will work faster.

Before you start cooking, please sit down, read, and understand the recipes. If you are not familiar with the techniques, refer to *The Making of a Cook* (Atheneum 1971 and Crown 1976). Before you go shopping make a list, then finally, get ready. That means: prepare your ingredients; peel, chop, or dice vegetables; have flour and liquid ingredients measured and lined up on a tray. The tray is a professional method which makes it possible, once everything is ready, to proceed in sequence without interruption. If the work is spread over two days, make a tray each day.

The important ingredients have also been given in grams, since we are supposed to work with the metric system soon. There may be slight variations between the cup system and the metric system and I suggest that the cook not worry about it, the variations being negligible to the final outcome of the recipe. May I suggest you use a measuring cup graded in avoirdupois (avdp.) on one side and in metric on the other; they are now available everywhere.

CHOICE OF BASIC INGREDIENTS

It is sometimes difficult to duplicate the ingredients of French provincial dishes in the United States. To obtain the true French taste from a French province, please pay attention to the comments given in "remarks on ingredients" which appear just before the list of ingredients of many recipes.

The following are indications as to the best basic ingredients to use:

BUTTER

In France there are *crus* of butter as there are *crus* of wine. The taste of the butter varies with that of the cream used to make it from province to province. Use the best possible grade of unsalted butter for all French foods. With the exception of the Province of

Brittany, which uses excellent lightly salted butter called *Demi Sel,* the whole of France uses unsalted butter. Purchase the best commercial brand of unsalted butter in a supermarket, and, for the recipes of Brittany calling for salted butter, lightly salted grade AA 93 score butter. Some so-called "lightly salted" butter in the U.S. is positively rancid: be particular as to grade AA 93 score.

Some local dairies in all states produce very good butters. Compare them with supermarket butters before you use them: check the color, the smell, the taste raw, the taste when cooked, and the amount of whey and solids lost when melting and clarifying the butter. It should be no more than 20 percent of the total weight when melted. Bear in mind that when a recipe calls for clarified butter, you need 20 percent more raw butter by weight from the start.

HEAVY CREAM AND SOUR CREAM

When cream is used in all French provinces, it is *crème fraîche;* the only exception to this is the *fleurette* or unfermented liquid heavy cream used to scallop potatoes in the *gratins* of the mountain regions of the Alps and the Jura. American heavy cream is in texture a good replacement for the fermented crème fraîche. Crème fraîche *cannot be made.* Crème fraîche can happen only by itself and its taste varies from region to region so that Normandy cream and Alps cream are considerably different.

Trying to make crème fraîche is a ridiculous waste of time since the taste you are dreaming of comes from the combination of the grass from meadows four thousand miles over the ocean, milk from breeds of cows that do not exist in the United States, and bacterial fermentations that cannot be the same in the U.S. as they are in France.

So do not waste your time. Use the heavy cream as it is in the United States, blending it with a bit of excellent sour cream.

To thicken American heavy cream, reduce it by cooking it down. Since it is too sweet after reduction, blend it with sour cream and if necessary, correct its taste with a few drops of lemon juice.

If you own a cow or a herd, you know how to skim raw milk to obtain heavy cream and also know how to let it ripen and thicken to crème fraîche. The taste of your cream will vary from summer to fall to winter with the type of fodder you are giving your animals.

The great problem with modern technological American heavy cream is the addition to it, in the last ten years, of multiple preservatives and stabilizers. These represent an advantage only to the manufacturers, certainly not to the consumer, and they do nothing for the taste or texture of finished dishes or cakes.

If the heavy cream is not too good, the sour cream is even worse and you will have to be discriminating when buying it. Read the labels for contents. There are a few brands of sour cream sold in the United States that are free of preservatives and additives. Do not use sour creams containing preservatives, stabilizers or added milk solids.

FLOURS

Use unbleached all-purpose flour. For whole wheat, rye and buckwheat flours, go to an honest health food store.

SHALLOTS

If you can possibly locate gray shallots, by all means use them; they are finer than the reddish ones. The red shallots lose so much reddish pigment in sauce bases that the bases turn rose; thus a "White Butter" in this country or the closest approximation one can get to it is often tinted rose instead of bright yellow with the carotene in the butter, as it is in France.

SPICES

The formula for the mixture of *quatre-épices,* the spice mixture used in French pâtés and terrines, varies from house to house. This one was used by Claire in her restaurant in Touraine (see page 172).

2 tsp. cinnamon   *2 tsp. grated nutmeg*
4 tsp. ground allspice   *4 tsp. ground coriander*
1 tsp. ground cloves

Mix all the spices well and store in a small well-sealed jar.

OILS

Follow the provinces. No other oil but olive oil can be used for Provençal food, for example. The olive oil there is rich and light green, sometimes very fruity. Use a good French imported olive oil or a first-class Italian Lucca olive oil. California olive oil can be a good replacement if not too green and fruity.

In most other places, one uses peanut oil, which in France is more highly refined than in the United States and does not taste so much like peanut butter.

Most mountain areas as well as the Poitou and Touraine use as much walnut oil as peanut oil, and occasionally in Alsace someone may still use a bit of *colza* oil to cook old onions and sweeten them, but it is rare.

MUSHROOMS

In the United States, for the last few years, cultivated mushrooms have come in two breeds, the white strain and the new "natural golden mushroom." The latter is far superior in flavor to the former.

The French woods, forests, and meadows in all the provinces are still full of marvelous wild mushrooms, some of which can be found easily in the United States. I have included those mushrooms in a number of recipes.

If you want to study mushrooms, start with these books: *The Mushroom Handbook,* by Louis C. Krieger, Dover Publications, Inc., New York; *The Mushroom Hunter Field Guide,* by Alexander Smith, University of Michigan Press; *The Savory Wild Mushroom,* by Margaret McKenny, University of Washington Press; *The Complete Book of Mushrooms,* by Augusto Rinaldi, Vassily Tyndalo, Crown Publishers, New York.

The last book is by far the best since it gives related and identical species information for Europe and the United States with very accurate detailed drawings in color of shapes and characteristics.

However, *be careful.* A mistake is easily made and can be fatal. Unless you have become an expert, do not eat mushrooms that you have gathered yourself without asking an authority to identify them for you. The species indicated in this book all taste very good and are all considered the choicest mushrooms from the forests of the world. It is wise to study mushrooms with a mycological group for several years to be sure. Mushroom studying appeals to children and can be a joy for the cook, or the photographer, and give the opportunity for numerous stimulating family outings. *Do not let children touch mushrooms with anything else but a wooden stick.* Please impress upon them the urgency of observing that rule. Once they know how to recognize a species that is edible and totally harmless, let them touch only that species. It will be a reward that they will enjoy and appreciate.

When you gather mushrooms, keep the different edible species in separate bags or baskets. Remove dirty roots and wipe caps of all leaves and twigs immediately after gathering. Wash mushrooms only if they are dirty and full of sand. Morels must be washed and chanterelles more often than not have to be washed, but if a large boletus appears free of dirt, wipe it with a barely moist cloth only. Commercial mushrooms rarely need more than a wiping with a damp cloth. Since a mushroom acts like a sponge and soaks up moisture, the less it is in contact with large amounts of water, the better.

To purchase dried mushrooms of the following species, write to Maison Chassain-Aldon, Saugues, Haut-Loire, France. They sell: dried *cèpes* (*Boletus edulis*), dried morels (*Morchella conica*), *mousserons* (*Marasmius oreades*), at various prices and mail to the United States. Morels are as expensive as in the United States, but boleti and *mousserons* cost half as much even with air-mail postage.

To dry your own mushrooms, slice them, thread them, and hang them to dry in a well-ventilated place.

WINE AND CIDER

I have strongly recommended using the wines of the provinces discussed here whenever they are available in this country. The varietals of California will never have the real *terroir* of the French wines since the soil of course is all-important. Furthermore, now that French country wines are easily accessible in this country at prices as reasonable as those of California wines, there is not one reason in the world not to use them.

The ciders present a problem, so look for Normandy imported *Sec* (dry) cider or English cider, which is close enough to the Normandy cider. Do not, under any circumstances, use American ciders; they are all too sweet for Normandy cooking. French Canada produces some cider very close in taste to the French product.

VINEGARS

French imported vinegars are available everywhere at reasonable prices. If you cannot locate them, you will never make a mistake if you use American cider vinegar.

BASIC PREPARATIONS

Basic preparations are stocks and pastries that will be used all along in this book as a base or a part of a recipe. Here are the basic recipes with a few comments on their value and how to prepare them in bulk and store them.

JUS DE VEAU BRUN
[Brown Veal Stock]

This stock is the essence of true French cuisine. There cannot be any true-tasting French cuisine made with anything coming out of a can. You can upgrade canned broth with unsalted vegetable broth to make a few things for your daily meals but you must understand that unless you prepare the dishes included in this book with the real thing, they will taste and look just as French as a dish of hominy grits.

All honest French cooks, whether at home or in restaurants, use that *jus de veau* which is the essence of French sauces, especially those lovely butter sauces which have for centuries been the base of the food of the women of France and have been readopted lately by the chefs, especially Fernand Point and all the younger chefs he trained who are still active today. There is absolutely no way to make a butter sauce with a canned stock. It does not contain enough natural gelatin, is too salty from the start, and results in nothing else but the loss of good butter.

The advantage of *jus de veau* is that it can be used for everything successfully because its texture is heavy and gelatinous and its taste good but neutral enough to allow the taste of chicken, beef or game to appear very firmly in a sauce in which it has been used. There are some instances in this book where *jus de veau* was not absolutely necessary for the success of the dish and in this case, I have indicated in the recipe: Brown veal stock or any other stock of your choice.

JUS DE VEAU BRUN
[Brown Veal Stock]

5 Quarts

For this stock, keep all bones and pieces of veal trimmed from roasts or chops. Use a thick braising pot.

5 lbs. veal shank (2½ kg)	*3 large onions*
2 to 3 lbs. veal trimmings and	*1 large leek*
bones (1–1½ kg)	*2 cups white wine*
2 TB butter (30 g)	*1 TB salt*
6 quarts warm water (6 litres)	*1 large bouquet garni*
4 carrots	

Brown the meats in the oven, and brown the vegetables in butter on top of the stove. Put vegetables and meats in a braising pot. Cover the pot and place over very low heat without disturbing for 20 to 25 minutes. Remove the lid and add two-thirds of a cup of wine. Raise the heat very high and let the stock evaporate until the meat juices at the bottom of the pot brown and caramelize. Perform the same operation, each time using two thirds of a cup of wine, twice more. Cover the meats with the warm water and bring to a boil. Add the salt and *bouquet garni*. Simmer a *minimum* of 6 to 8 hours. The longer it cooks, the better it tastes. Remember that it takes 12 hours to completely strip a piece of knuckle from its gelatin. Stop the cooking as soon as all the gelatin is rendered or the stock will acquire a bony taste. Add boiling water to the stock at regular intervals to maintain the level of the liquid. Strain and let cool at room temperature. Refrigerate and skim off the fat. The stock is ready to use. Brown veal stock keeps well in clean jars in the refrigerator. It also freezes very well. Do not keep frozen more than three months or loss of flavor will occur. The ideal would be not to freeze it—to always have fresh stock—but that would be unrealistic and too expensive for a regular household.

MEAT GLAZE
[Glace de Viande]

To obtain meat glaze reduce brown veal stock by three and a half; that is, you will obtain ½ cup meat glaze for each quart of brown veal stock reduced.

FUMET DE POISSONS
[Fish Stock]

I know that the temptation to use clam juice instead of fish stock is great, but fish stock is to fish dishes what *jus de veau* is to meat dishes. Whenever clam juice could be used without detriment to the dish I have mentioned it.

To make fish stock, please use good quality, very dry white wine, never Vermouth. It is better to make the fumet without wine than make it with cheap acid wine or Vermouth. You should use an enamel or stainless steel pot so that the stock will not turn gray.

Once the stock has reached the boiling point, do not let it cook beyond 35 minutes. If the stock is too thin, strain it and reduce it to concentrate it. Reducing while the bones are still in the pot results in a stock that tastes bony. Fish fumet freezes well, but it is preferable to make it fresh for every new dish.

WHITE WINE FISH FUMET	RED WINE FISH FUMET
1 large onion, sliced	*2 small onions, sliced*
½ very small carrot, sliced	*½ small carrot, sliced*
1 TB butter (15 g)	*1 small garlic clove*
½ cup mushroom stems and pieces (75 g)	*2 TB butter (30 g)*
4 lbs. fish heads and bones (2 kg)	*¼ cup mushroom stems and pieces (75 g)*
2 cups good dry white wine (2¼ dl)	*4 lbs. fish heads and bones (2 kg)*
8 cups water (2 litres)	*4 cups dry red wine (1 litre)*
Very small bouquet garni	*8 cups water (2 litres)*
½ tsp. salt	*Large* bouquet garni
6 white peppercorns	*½ tsp. salt*

Sauté onion and carrot (and garlic for red wine fumet) in the butter, then add mushrooms and fish bones. Cover the pot and let cook over very low heat for 15 minutes, or until fish bones fall apart. Add wine and water and bring briskly to a boil. Add *bouquet garni* and salt. Cook over medium heat for 30 to 35 minutes. Add peppercorns (white wine fumet only) during the last 10 minutes of cooking. Strain.

ORDINARY SHORT PASTRY

1½ cups sifted flour (180–200 g)	*1 tsp. salt (5 g)*
3 to 4½ TB chilled water (½ small dl)	*9 TB butter, chilled (125 g)*

Put the flour on the counter top; make a well in the center and put in it ½ tablespoon water, the salt and the butter cut into ½-inch cubes. Working with the tips of the fingers, rub flour and butter together until the mixture forms particles the size of a pea. In culinary jargon this is called *sabler*, which means "reduce to sand," but very rough sand. Now add the remainder of the water, ½ tablespoon at a time.

Mix it into the mixture with the tips of the fingers of both your hands extended down toward the counter in such a way as to form a natural pastry cutter; the palms face each other. Push the dough from left and right, throwing it up from the bottom and fluffing it about 2 inches above the counter top. The more water you add, the more difficult it becomes to break the lumps, until large lumps form that cannot be broken anymore.

Take the dough in one hand; using the dough ball as a mop, gather all the loose particles remaining on the counter. Put your right hand and wrist flat on the counter in front of the ball of dough. Leave your wrist on the counter, but extend your hand upward at a 45° angle with the counter. *Do not knead,* but with the heel of the hand slide the dough 6 to 8 inches *forward* only—not sideways—flattening nut-size pieces of it onto the counter. When all the dough has been used, reform all the pieces into a ball and repeat the same operation. This procedure is called *fraiser.* This action flattens the fat in extremely thin leaves between layers of flour, gives the pastry homogeneity, and, most important, develops just enough gluten to give the dough a certain plasticity for easy handling. This procedure is not kneading, which is reserved for yeast doughs. Shape the pastry into a circular 3-inch cake that is about 1 inch thick. Test it by poking your finger into it. If the hole remains, you may use the pastry within 15 minutes. The more that hole closes, the more gluten you have developed and the more the dough needs rest in the refrigerator.

When you roll out the pastry, you further flatten the fat into very thin sheets between the thin layers of flour. In the heat of the oven, the fat melts and is absorbed by the starches while the steam resulting from the boiling of the water contained in the dough applies pressure on the leaves of the baking dough and separates them from one another. The result is a flaky pastry.

PUFF PASTE

Read the recipe completely before you start to work. Work on a large amount of paste; it is easier. These ingredients will make a large 2-pound square of dough.

2 TB cornstarch (25 g)   *1¼ to 1⅓ cups water*
3⅞ cups sifted flour (475 g)   *(2¼–2½ dl)*
1½ tsps. salt (7½ g)   *2 cups (1 lb.) unsalted butter*
                    (500 g)

FLOUR AND WATER PASTE, OR DETREMPE

Put the cornstarch in a 4-cup measuring cup and sift enough flour on top to make a total volume of 4 cups. Pour the mixture onto the counter top and mix. Make a large well in the center and put the salt and ¼ cup water in it. Dissolve the salt in the water. Slowly bring some of the flour into the water with the tip of the finger. When the liquid looks like a crepe batter, start fluffing up the flour as for an ordinary pie crust (see page 13). Continue fluffing, adding the water tablespoon by tablespoon until the lumps of dough cannot be broken any more by the fingertips.

Gather all the lumps in one ball. Wipe all particles off the counter, using the dough ball as a mop. Holding the dough in both hands, break it open twice as you would a piece of bread. DO NOT KNEAD OR HANDLE IT ANY MORE, whether it is smooth or not. Cut a cross ½-inch deep in the top of the dough and refrigerate uncovered for 30 minutes.

PATON

After 30 minutes, remove the butter from the refrigerator. Let it stand at room temperature for 5 minutes; during those 5 minutes soak your hands in water as cold as you can stand it. Remove the wrappers from the butter and knead the butter with your bare hands until the water drips out of it and it has become soft enough for a finger to sink into it without resistance. Do not let the butter get oily.

Take the *détrempe* out of the refrigerator.

With the heel of the hand, gently pat the dough into a 9-inch square.

Flatten the butter into a 7-inch square. Put the butter on the *détrempe* with each corner of the butter square in the center of one of the sides of the *détrempe* square. Fold the four corners of the *détrempe* over the butter, edge to edge without overlapping; the points of the four corners of the *détrempe* square meet exactly in the middle, looking something like the back of an envelope. The dough and butter package is now a *paton*. Let it stand for 5 minutes, the rolling pin resting on it.

TURNS I AND II

Roll the *paton* 9 inches away from you and 9 inches toward you, keeping it 7 inches wide and never less than ½ inch thick. Do not bear down on the dough; roll the dough parallel (not perpendicular) to the counter top, in one or two decisive strokes.

If the *paton* becomes wider than 7 inches, block it on each side by placing the rolling pin parallel to the edge of the dough and tapping it gently. The edge will straighten up. Fold the dough in three. Now turn it by 90 degrees so that it looks like a book ready to be opened. With a bit of pressure applied with the rolling pin at the top and bottom seams, pinch the layers of dough together slightly to prevent the butter escaping. Roll out the dough again and fold it a second time exactly as described above. You will have given 2 turns. If the dough is less than 7 inches wide, tap it gently to flatten it a little. To keep track of the turns, punch 2 small depressions on the surface of the dough with a fingertip. Put the dough on a lightly floured plate, cover loosely with a sheet of foil, and put it to cool in the vegetable crisper of the refrigerator. Let the dough rest for 1 complete hour, or longer if you wish.

TURNS III TO VI

Finish the dough by giving 2 more series of 2 turns each, exactly as described above. The rest period, always in the vegetable crisper of the refrigerator, should never be less than 30 minutes. After turns III and IV, punch 4 small depressions on the surface of the dough. After turns V and VI, trace an X. That will remind you that the paste is finished and may be used.

ROLLING OUT, CUTTING AND FREEZING PUFF PASTE

Roll out the dough when it is deep chilled and very stiff. Cut the dough neatly, perpendicular to the counter top, so as not to produce stragglers that would prevent the paste from rising. After cutting patty shells or squares of dough, put them upside down on a cookie sheet. This keeps the baked product from being narrower at the top than at the bottom. Set the cutouts on a buttered cookie sheet rinsed under cold water. Use the same procedure when you cut the dough following a paper pattern. For a lovely color, brush the top of all pastries with an egg yolk glaze made of egg yolk mixed with 3 tablespoons of milk.

SEMI-PUFF PASTRY

2 cups sifted all-purpose flour	*1 tsp. salt*
(250 g)	*¼ cup water*
1 cup unsalted butter (225 g)	*(½ generous dl)*

Prepare a very small ordinary short pastry with all the ingredients. Chill 30 minutes in the vegetable crisper of the refrigerator. Then give two turns as for puff pastry. Chill another 30 minutes, still in the vegetable crisper of the refrigerator. Finish the pastry with another 4 turns given two at a time. Let the dough rest in the refrigerator in between each 2 turns for half an hour minimum.

PROPER TECHNIQUES

If you make a sauce bound with a roux, please cook the roux and skim the sauce, unless the directions in a recipe say differently. Otherwise, you will end up with a gooky, filmy sauce, heavy with flour proteins and having little to do with a true French sauce.

You may want to refer to *The Making of a Cook,* pages 139 and 140, where I explain the principle of butter sauces. Butter sauces are either built on a very reduced acid base (wine or vinegar reduction) or on a glaze base (any meat or fish glaze). The easiest way for a non-professional cook to bind these sauces is to keep the temperature of the base at 130° so that the butter emulsifies in the barely warm base. In professional kitchens where these sauces are likely to be made in larger quantities another, much faster and safer technique is used, that of bringing the acid or glaze base to a violent boil and emulsifying the butter by throwing it in chunks at the center of this violent boil. The pressure of the boiling process throws the butter in emulsion and keeps it there in perfect balance.

So all you have to remember is that either the temperature of the sauce should be no more than 130° or the sauce should be violently boiling. Anywhere in between, the sauce will break and separate.

Should a pure butter sauce separate, first bring back to a boil, then add more liquid (fish fumet if you have a fish sauce, *jus de veau* if you have a meat sauce), and keep one or two minutes at a violent boil to reinstate the emulsion.

If you have to reheat a cold butter sauce, put two tablespoons of the sauce in a pan and bring to a violent boil. Then, whisk the remainder, bit by bit, into the violently boiling sauce. Butter sauces taste best when freshly made and used as soon as finished.

PERSONAL TASTE AND SEASONING

Some basic recipes with unvarying proportions that are respected by all cooks have been established for centuries. They form the base of French cuisine and are the mother sauces, basic pastries, and doughs. There are some minor variations but everyone agrees generally on the ratios of butter to flour in all pastries, and the ratio of stock to flour or vice versa in the basic classic sauces. But there are millions of other recipes which can be called personal recipes written by many cookbook authors over several centuries. These personal recipes offer ideas on how to prepare a piece of meat or fish or combine eggs and flour to obtain cakes and desserts. It is important for the cook to understand that the cookbook writer is by no means God in the kitchen and that his or her taste does not have to be yours. If you think that a recipe has too much or too little of a spice or herb for your taste after you first try it, by all means use less or more the next time. You also may like more or less salt, a reason why I prefer to leave the final seasoning to the cook's personal taste. For example, salad dressings should have as much acid content as you find palatable. By all means, add or suppress vinegar or lemon juice as you please. Start with less acid to be sure; you can always add more; and if you really used too much acid from the start, rebalance the dressing by adding salt, oil, or even a bit of heavy cream.

Also bear in mind when you execute a recipe that the ingredients you will buy and use will be different from those used by the writer. Not any two stocks, creams, butters are ever completely identical; no two sauces will look the same, taste the same or have the same texture. So use your head and think of what can be done; if a sauce is too thin, then think of a starch slurry or a little *beurre manie;* if it is too flat, think of meat extract added in small quantities and very progressively or if it is possible, concentrate it by reduction. Give a thought to the fact that lemon juice neutralizes saltiness, and acids can be tamed with salt. In a word, use your head. The recipe writer proposed an idea to you; make the best of it, trusting your taste and intelligence in the execution of that idea in your own kitchen.

PROPORTIONS AND PORTIONS

To increase a recipe to serve a larger number of persons, use the following formula:

$$\frac{\text{New required number of portions}}{\text{Number of portions the recipe is for}} = ?$$

? × each ingredient = the new required amount of each ingredient.

Marie-Charlotte

POITOU AND PARIS

1934–1937

Here, Treasure, that's for you, a good Christian drinks no water." I was the treasure who at age six was handed a tiny glass of Pineau des Charentes from a special bottle Marie-Charlotte, my great-grandmother, just brought back from her native Poitou. In my inability to pronounce that unending Grand-Mère Marie-Charlotte, I called her Mimi Chérie.

She was great, that Marie-Charlotte. Transplanted to Paris after the phylloxera crisis had destroyed all her grape vines, she became a mattress maker to survive in the capital. She never quite adapted to the big city, and no sooner had she sewed a few mattresses and put a few pennies away than she was standing at the ticket counter at Montparnasse to buy a ticket to her native Bourdrie lost somewhere between Poitiers and Châtellerault. I only came to understand her migratory mood in 1960 when that mean stretch of Atlantic Ocean separated me from *La Doulce France*.

She was slight and small; her face was so creased with deep lines and her skin so dry that when she fell asleep on her chair after lunch —and she often did—I would shake her and wake her up in fright, asking whether she was dead. At which point the dead woman would come alive and, deep blue eyes all sparkling, toss me high up in the air, kiss me and fuss over me and I invariably ended up hugging her around the waist. To this day I remember the dusty smell of her black pleated skirt. She wore several layers of skirts, making sure that her top *gugle,* the ample black pleated skirt of the Poitou women, had no pockets so they could not be picked by those scoundrels in the Metro.

I was so much with her in my preschool years that I remember vividly all we did together.

During the week, I accompanied her often on her mattress-making adventures. She worked in all the tiny yards of the suburban houses called *pavillons* around Paris. It took a whole day to make a mattress, and since when we went home I was too tired to walk, I would be allowed to sit on the straddle seat of her wool card and be wheeled home in style.

On Sundays, we went to market in the morning. Market had replaced Mass ever since two of her sons had died in the Great War. She claimed high and wide that she would get into Paradise for she had earned it all through her life.

Marketing with her was an adventure, for she combed the market for expatriates from her own village or district and it was endless. All these women knew one another, all were still attached to that Bourdrie where they had been born and all of them sold the real food of the Poitou, trucked over by sons or husbands or mailed to Montparnasse in huge wicker baskets. All of them, having suffered through periods of restrictions, practiced that ancestral cooking of hard times known as *la Cuisine de Misère* to millions of French women. Practicing *la Cuisine de Misère* meant cooking something with nothing. It meant *adouber* a tiny piece of meat with more vegetables, more dumplings, more sauce to make sure that it would stretch to feed a whole family; it meant making a couple of eggs or a piece of cheese multiply into a pie to feed six people; it meant all kinds of calculations going on under those tiny white lace bonnets, so that it would taste good and cost close to nothing.

So things would accumulate in those two huge *filets* that she lugged home from the market. There was always a rabbit because if you were born in Poitou, well this was your meat, so cheap to raise you know, and with shallots and a few nice and sour *cornichons* there was nothing like it. Of course, there was nothing wrong with a good civet once in a while but it cost more because of the wine— whereas shallots grew anywhere, even in boxes on window sills, and *cornichons* were less than a penny a dozen if you pickled them yourself.

She had a knack for finding an old hen with a broken wing that no one wanted and transforming it into a *Poule Piquante,* an ancestral dish revived lately by some fashionable restaurants under the name of *Poulet au Vinaigre;* but a formula really so ancient that it goes way back to the times when meat needed a bit of help to be palatable. The shopping for the *Chabichous* bored me to death. All those goat cheeses were ceremoniously lined up on straw mats, the fresh ones neatly wrapped in lovely blonde sycamore leaves, and Mimi Chérie drove her compatriots rather crazy by tasting so many and always pouting in a disapproving manner. Said the seller, "Marguerite made it, you know the Marguerite that lives two miles from . . ." and a whole genealogy would follow. Good grief, Mimi Chérie, buy your cheese and let us go. . . . I pulled on her hand and skirt. . . . But . . .

The neat thing about it all was that at four o'clock that afternoon a nice big piece of *tourteau fromagé* would sit on a plate in front of me, fragrant with fresh butter, rum and orange flower water. That *tourteau fromagé*—I have tried and tried to make it on American soil, but never got there: the fresh goat cheese remains way over that stretch of Atlantic.

If buying the cheese was long, such was not the case for the butter. She knew who had it and where it came from. It was something to see the merchant cut a big chunk out of a 25-pound *motte* of yellow Charente butter with a piano wire. I loved that, for there was always a little piece of the nutty fat called *l'appoint* weighing ten grams or so that was my reward for being so good and so patient at the market. I ate it plain, biting through the cool piece of fat that melted deliciously in my mouth.

From the butter woman, we went to the old fellow who sold bread that had arrived from La Bourdrie that very morning. It came in all colors and had the most incredible names: *pain de méture*, dark, heavy and as dense as a Russian pumpernickel, and *pain de fournier*, a nice combination of light and dark doughs mixed beautifully into each other. She explained to me time and again that a *fournier* was a baker who, since he baked the breads made on all the surrounding farms in his big communal oven, made a living by keeping some of the dough for himself, shaping loaves of diverse colors and selling them for a profit.

The goods bought on Sunday were used at Sunday lunch and dinner and rarely later than Tuesday, since in those days refrigerators did not exist and things had to be kept cool in a little *garde-manger* fitted with a screen and located under the kitchen window. In the Sunday basket there was always a nice *cabillaud* to prepare with mayonnaise and a vegetable salad. Mimi Chérie jealously guarded the head of the fish, for the cheeks, well mashed with leftover mayonnaise and spread over a slice of bread generously rubbed with garlic, was her lunch for Monday noon.

In the winter months, besides the fish, there were always several quarts of mussels and live snails. The live snails fascinated me. Mimi Chérie would stuff them into red clay pots and cover them with a plate and a heavy weight to keep them put and force them to go to sleep and build their winter windows. One boring Sunday afternoon, I succumbed to the temptation to remove the weight. By seven o'clock, when we came back from some venture, the walls were decorated with the visible trails of climbing snails. I got spanked, hated live snails forever for doing me in, and felt vindicated when they appeared in soups or sizzling in pastry shells.

Mimi Chérie's apartment consisted of one huge, spacious room under the roof of a suburban apartment building. The building dated from 1870 and the stove was fitted in a corner under a large *cheminée à hotte,* an old stove exhaust hood, surmounted as in the countryside by a mantel on which rested ageless spice canisters and an old oil lamp. When company came, the whole kitchen area was separated from the living area by one huge chintz screen.

She had recreated her kitchen and *salle commune* from La Bourdrie. Along one of the walls were several rotund sandstone jars in which she kept salt pork and which she called her *salous*. Every so often, out came a nice side of pork which she washed and rubbed with crushed bay leaf to give it a good smell. There were several small barrels containing Pineau wine from La Bourdrie, vinegar, and Vespetro, her homemade liquor without which she could not fall asleep at night. She was a joy to watch when she sat majestically at the table eating *Chabichou* and *Calas,* those fresh walnuts in their green cloaks that took hours to be peeled and stained her fingers deep yellow.

Of her prize possession, her *diable,* an earthenware casserole in which she cooked practically everything, she always said, "C'est vieux, ça vient des Arabes," and it was old and indeed probably a descendant of the Arab *tajin.*

She had a wall full of shelves on which all fruit ripened. Strawberries, red and black currants, and raspberries acquired their final flavor there. In the fall, there were always several trays of a rose-and-grayish Marochelin grape that she traveled especially to La Bourdrie to bring back for me. There were also apples of all sizes and dimensions, Bosc pears for baking with honey and the juicy Comice pears which were never ripe before Christmas. And flowers, flowers everywhere. She grew them in a *lopin de terre,* a tiny garden behind the apartment building, and she loved dahlias and gladiolas as much as she hated the multicolored mums that people took to the cemetery on November First, All Saints Day.

On Sunday afternoon, we often took the train to Nanterre or Saint-Cloud. In both places there were tons of dandelions to pick to make soup or to scramble into eggs; but the most interesting and the scariest adventure had to be the picking of the mushrooms in the dark tunnels of Nanterre, which in those days produced a good deal of the cultivated mushrooms found in the Parisian market. Mimi Chérie picked and bought huge baskets for pennies and would go around, the dear old businesswoman, the whole of Sunday night reselling them in the neighborhood, so that we had our mushrooms and our train tickets for free.

Mimi Chérie, you dear little woman with the huge black skirt and the creased face, if you ever reached your Paradise and look down upon this earth, you know how often I think of you and make your Vermicelli cake or your Pétatou all gooey with chocolate for the two curlyheads who are your great-great-grandsons and who also like Pineau. . . . I made sure that they remained good Christians.

CREME DE PISSENLITS
[Cream of Dandelion Soup]

SERVINGS: 6 COST: inexpensive EXECUTION: easy

TOTAL PREPARATION TIME: 1 hour

BEST SEASON: June through October

REMARKS ON INGREDIENTS: The young early spring to early summer leaves of wild dandelions (*taraxacum*) are the best for this soup and need no blanching. The old, toughish, long leaves can be purchased in Italian markets almost all year round. These require blanching.

2 lb. (850–900 g) dandelions

½ cup unsalted butter (100–110 g)

1 small carrot, diced into ⅓-inch cubes

1 large onion, diced into ⅓-inch cubes

¼ cup flour (30 g)

1 quart scalded milk (1 litre)

Salt and pepper

1 cup excellent brown veal stock (2¼ dl)

1 cup heavy cream (2¼ dl or 225 g)

1 TB Dijon mustard

2 rashers thick sliced bacon, rendered and crumbled

6 slices French bread, ⅓ inch thick

1 clove garlic

Wash the dandelions very carefully. If they are old and tough, blanch them in boiling salted water. Cool. Squeeze them dry and chop them. If they are young and small, simply chop them very fine.

Heat 4 tablespoons butter in a large pot and sauté the dandelions until all water has evaporated. Reserve for later use.

While the dandelions cook, sauté the diced carrot and onion in the remaining butter until the onion is translucent; add the flour and cook 4 to 5 minutes. Bind with the scalded milk and bring to a boil. Add salt and pepper and simmer for 30 minutes to obtain a béchamel sauce.

Meanwhile, add the veal stock to the dandelions and let simmer until the vegetable is almost dry again. Strain the béchamel sauce into the dandelion mixture. Mix well. Put through the blender to homogenize.

Strain the soup into a clean pot. Mix the heavy cream with the mustard and add to the soup. Reheat without boiling. Render the bacon and crumble fine. Add it to the soup. Toast the French bread slices. Rub them with the garlic clove and cut them in ⅓-inch cubes, discarding the crust.

Correct the seasoning of the soup one last time and serve sprinkled with the garlic croutons.

LA TREMPINE DU GRAND-PERE ALEXANDRE
[Red Wine Soup]

SERVINGS: 6 COST: moderately expensive EXECUTION: easy
TOTAL PREPARATION TIME: 1 hour
BEST SEASON: Fall through early spring
REMARKS ON INGREDIENTS: This is better when executed with good homemade stock. The highly salted canned broth does not blend well with the reduced red wine.

1 bottle red wine, preferably a light Bordeaux or Cabernet-Sauvignon	Pinch of salt
	2 TB butter (30 g)
6 shallots, chopped fine	1 carrot, diced into ¼-inch cubes
6 white peppercorns, cracked coarse	2 onions, diced into ¼-inch cubes

1 rib celery, diced into ¼-inch
    cubes
6 mushrooms, diced into ¼-
    inch cubes
Salt and pepper
6 cups brown veal stock or

stock of your choice (1¼
    litre)
6 slices of French bread,
    toasted lightly
1 clove garlic

Empty the wine into a saucepan and bring slowly to a boil. Add the shallots and let simmer, uncovered, until reduced to 1¾ cups. Add the peppercorns and a pinch of salt and let simmer again until reduced to 1¼ cups. Reserve.

While the wine reduces, heat the butter. Add the diced vegetables and sauté them in the butter until limp. Salt and pepper lightly and add the 6 cups of stock. Simmer uncovered until reduced to 5½ cups. Blend the broth and the wine reduction and simmer together for 10 minutes. Correct the seasoning.

Rub the French bread slices with the garlic clove. Put one slice of bread into each soup plate and ladle the vegetable broth over it.

OEUFS BROUILLES AUX PISSENLITS
[Scrambled Eggs and Dandelions]

SERVINGS: 6 COST: inexpensive EXECUTION: easy
TOTAL PREPARATION TIME: 30 minutes
BEST SEASON: June through October
SUGGESTED WINE: Saumur, Rosé d'Anjou
REMARKS ON INGREDIENTS: Use the young leaves of wild dandelions. If only older leaves are available, blanch them first, cool them, and squeeze them dry before sautéing them.

½ lb. dandelion leaves,
    chopped fine (250 g)
½ cup unsalted butter (100–
    110 g)
2 oz. chopped boiled ham
    (60 g)

One dozen eggs
Salt
Pepper from the mill
¾ cup heavy cream (2
    small dl)
6 toast points

Wash and pat the dandelions dry; chop fine. Heat 2 tablespoons of butter in a large skillet. Add the dandelions and sauté them until they start losing their juices. Raise the heat high and evaporate the juices completely. Add the ham, toss to mix well and set aside. Clean the frying pan.

Beat the eggs until well mixed but not liquid. Add a dash of salt and pepper from the mill, beat in the cream. Heat the remainder of the butter in the same large frying pan and cook the eggs on medium low heat, stirring rather fast to obtain small creamy curds. When the eggs are half cooked, add the dandelions and ham mixture and finish cooking the eggs. Correct the seasoning and serve on toast points.

TOURTEAU FROMAGE AUX OIGNONS
[Goat Cheese and Onion Pie]

SERVINGS: 6–8 COST: inexpensive EXECUTION: easy
TOTAL PREPARATION TIME: 1½ hours
BEST SEASON: Late September, but can be done through the winter
   with Saint Saviol cheese.
SUGGESTED WINE: A Muscadet or any nice dry white wine
REMARKS ON INGREDIENTS: The preferred cheeses are, in order,
   Chabichou, Saint Maure or Valençay, but the Saint Saviol is
   also very good.

1 recipe for basic pastry, page 13
½ cup butter (110 g)
1 lb. silverskin onions, peeled
   (500 g)
¼ cup stock or water (½ dl)
Salt and pepper
4 oz. goat cheese (Saint Maure,

Valençay, Saint Saviol)
   (125 g)
½ cup sour cream (120 g)
2 eggs
Pepper from the mill
½ tsp. salt (2.5 g)
Dried or fresh thyme leaves

Preheat the oven to 375°. Make the pastry. Keep it refrigerated while you prepare the filling.

Melt 1 tablespoon butter in a heavy saucepan. Cut a tiny cross in the root end of the onions so they do not explode or burst open while cooking. Add onions to saucepan. Then add stock or water, salt and pepper and cover. Cook for about 15–20 minutes.

While the onions cook, cream the remainder of the butter, grate the goat cheese finely into it, and mix well. Add the sour cream, 2 eggs, pepper coarse ground from the mill, and ½ teaspoon salt. Blend well.

Roll out the pastry to fit a 10-inch quiche pan.

Remove the saucepan's lid and raise the heat under the onions. Cook until there is no liquid left in the saucepan.

Arrange the onions on the bottom of the pastry. Bake 20 minutes on the bottom shelf of the oven.

After 20 minutes, pour the cheese mixture on top of the onions, sprinkle with thyme, and continue baking another 15–20 minutes, this time on the upper rack of the oven until the top of the pie is light golden. Serve lukewarm with a good salad.

LUMAS AUX NOUZILLES EN PATISSERIE
[Snails in Pastry]

SERVINGS: 6 COST: expensive EXECUTION: time consuming
TOTAL PREPARATION TIME: 4 hours, marination and pastry included.
BEST SEASON: All through the winter months
SUGGESTED WINE: Saumur or Vouray Sec. Any dry white California.
REMARKS ON INGREDIENTS: Use the French canned snails for this preparation. Keep the canning juices.

3 dozen snails with their canning juices	4 cloves garlic, mashed
	4 shallots, chopped fine
½ cup dry white wine (1 small dl)	½ cup chopped parsley (100 g)

Salt   ⅓ cup hazelnuts (100–120 g)
Pepper from the mill   One half the recipe for puff
Nutmeg   pastry, page 14
½ lb. butter (250 g)

Empty the can of snails into a strainer placed over a saucepan. Put the drained snails into a glass or porcelain mixing bowl. To the canning juices of the snails, add the white wine, 2 mashed cloves of garlic, 2 chopped shallots, and 2 tablespoons of chopped parsley. Bring to a boil and pour over the snails. Let marinate 4 hours at room temperature.

Meanwhile, prepare the snail butter. Mash together the butter, remaining garlic, shallots and parsley, salt and pepper from the mill, and freshly grated nutmeg to your taste. Do not strain the butter for this country dish.

Place the hazelnuts in a cake pan and toast them in a 350° oven for 7–8 minutes. Remove them to a dry towel, rub well to remove the skins, and chop the hazelnuts fine (about ⅛-inch pieces).

Roll out the puff pastry ⅙ inch thick and cut six 2½-inch puff pastry patties, tracing lids with a 1½-inch plain round cutter. Bake patties and lids in a 425° oven until golden. Cut the lid of each patty out and empty its center of all moist pastry.

TO FINISH THE DISH:

Remove the snails from their marinade and cut them in half lengthwise. Set aside. Reduce the marinade over high heat to about 2 tablespoons. Heat about 2 tablespoons of the snail butter in a 9-inch frying pan. Add the hazelnuts. Sauté them in the butter until they are golden. Now add the snails and reheat them thoroughly. Then pour in the reduced marinade and the remainder of the butter. Toss steadily over high heat until the mixture bubbles.

Spoon 12 snails into each shell. Pour half the hot sauce into the shells, place the lids of the patties on, and spoon the remainder of the sauce over the lid. Serving burning hot!

PAIN DE FOURNIER
[Two-Dough Bread]

SERVINGS: 12 COST: inexpensive EXECUTION: semi-difficult
TOTAL PREPARATION TIME: 30 minutes, plus 3 days for the dough's
    rising and ripening

DARK DOUGH:
3 cups all-purpose white flour
   (375 g)
1½ envelopes yeast
1½ cups water (3 generous dl)
½ cup buckwheat flour
   (100 g)
½ cup corn flour (100 g)
½ cup rye flour (100 g)
½ cup whole wheat flour
   (100 g)
1 TB salt (15 g)
¼ cup walnut oil (½ dl)
1 cup walnut meats chopped
   fine (125 g)

LIGHT DOUGH:
3 cups all-purpose flour
   (375 g)
1 envelope yeast
1½ tsp. salt (7½ g)
3 TB walnut oil (½ small dl)
¾ to 1 cup water (¾ to 1 dl)
TO BAKE THE BREAD:
1½ TB butter to butter the
   baking sheet
Cornmeal
1 egg white
2 TB water

PROCEED THE SAME WAY FOR EACH DOUGH:
To 1 cup of the all-purpose flour and the yeast add just enough water
to make a soft ball of dough which will be a starter.

Immerse the starter into a bowl of water at 110° F and prepare
the bulk of the dough while it starts fermenting.

To prepare the bulk of each dough, mix the flours or the all-
purpose flour with the salt and, for the dark dough, the chopped
walnuts. Make a well in the flour, add the remainder of the water,
the salt, and the oil. Gather into a ball. Depending on whether the
dough is too wet or too dry add a little more flour or a little more
water.

By the time you have made the bulk of the dough, the starter will
have come floating to the surface of its water bath. Gather it on your

hand, letting the water drip between your fingers. Add it to the bulk of the dough and mix dough and starter thoroughly. Knead 10 full minutes until each of the final bread doughs looks smooth, satiny, and retains the imprint of a thumb well.

Brush the top of each dough with a bit of oil and let rise until double in bulk. Pinch down, then let rise a second time. Punch down, cover loosely with a plastic wrap, and keep refrigerated for three days. It takes at least that long to develop a fine flavor. Punch down each dough and mix both doughs together, kneading them into each other. Shape into four 1½-pound loaves. Grease and sprinkle a baking sheet with cornmeal. Set the loaves on the baking sheet, dock—or cut deep slashes into—the top of each loaf. Let prove again until double in bulk. Bake 15 minutes in a preheated 425° oven.

Mix egg white and water lightly. Brush over the surface of each loaf and bake another 10 minutes. Cool on a rack.

Excellent with all cheeses and with plain unsalted butter.

PETITS PAINS AUX GRATTONS
[Crackling and Walnut Rolls]

SERVINGS: 12 COST: inexpensive EXECUTION: easy
TOTAL PREPARATION TIME: 2 hours 15 minutes, plus 3 to 12 hours
    rising time

¼ lb. fresh pork fatback or   *1 tsp. salt*
  plain pork fat (125 g)   *2½ cups flour (275 g)*
  ¼ cup water (1 small dl)   *⅓ cup chopped walnuts*
  ⅓ cup and 3 TB milk   *(100 g)*
  2 TB honey   *1 egg yolk*
  1 envelope active dry yeast

Cut the fatback in ⅓-inch cubes. Mix with the water and melt slowly over medium low heat. The fat will melt and leave little cracklings floating in the melted lard. Remove the cracklings to a measuring cup. Add enough lard to make ¼ cup. Cool to lukewarm.

Heat the ⅓ cup of milk to lukewarm. Add the honey and mix well. Sprinkle the yeast over the milk and let the yeast bubble up.

Mix the flour and salt. Make a well in the flour. Add the yeast mixture, the cooled lard and cracklings, and the walnuts. Gather into a ball, gradually incorporating the flour with the moist ingredients. Knead 10 minutes or until the dough is smooth and elastic. Let rise until double in bulk. Punch down and shape into 12 balls.

Butter a cookie sheet. Set the balls on it and let them again double in bulk. Brush with the egg yolk well mixed with the remaining milk. Bake in a preheated 425° oven for 20–25 minutes.

MORUE DE CHATELLERAULT
[Cod as Prepared in Châtellerault]

SERVINGS: 6 COST: reasonable EXECUTION: easy, but do not overcook the cod

TOTAL PREPARATION TIME: 1 hour plus 12–24 hours to soak the
fish

BEST SEASON: Summer through late fall with fresh sorrel. Year
round with frozen or canned sorrel.

SUGGESTED WINE: Muscadet

REMARKS ON INGREDIENTS: Purchase good thick cod with grey skin
in an Italian neighborhood market. Do not use the boxed flaked
cod sold in supermarkets.

1½–2 lbs. salted cod (750 g–1 kg)	3 medium Maine potatoes (375 g)
1 lb. fresh sorrel or 12 oz. frozen or canned sorrel (500 g)	3 TB flour (25–30 g)
	1 large clove garlic
½ cup unsalted butter (100–110 g)	1 cup heavy cream (225 g)
	½ cup sour cream (120 g)
Salt and pepper	Freshly cracked pepper
	½ cup fresh breadcrumbs (100 g)

Soak the cod under a thin stream of running cold water for 12–24 hours. Clean and wash the sorrel, chop it coarsely. Heat 2 tablespoons butter in a deep *cocotte*. Add the sorrel and toss in the hot butter until the sorrel wilts. Add salt and pepper. Set aside.

Boil the potatoes in their jackets for about 30 minutes. While the potatoes cook, put the cod in a large pot containing a large amount of plain water; bring very slowly to a simmer. As soon as the water simmers, turn the heat off, cover the pot, and let stand 12–15 minutes. Remove the cod from the water bath, skin it, and flake it. Reserve the water.

Heat 4 tablespoons of butter in a saucepan, add the flour and heat. Bind with 2 cups of the cod cooking water. Stir over medium heat until sauce thickens. Correct the seasoning.

Rub a 2-quart baking dish with a clove of garlic. Butter it with 1 tablespoon of butter. Peel and slice the boiled potatoes.

Spread a bit of the sauce on the bottom of the dish. Then add a layer of flaked cod and potatoes. Top with a layer of sorrel. Repeat until all ingredients have been used.

Finally, mix the sauce and the two creams together and pour slowly over the dish to give the sauce time to flow through the fish and potatoes. Top with freshly cracked pepper and the breadcrumbs. Reheat in a 350° oven, but do not let bubble at length or the cod will get tough.

MERLU-COLIN POUR LE DIMANCHE
[Poached Haddock or Whiting for Sunday Dinner]

SERVINGS: 6 COST: moderately expensive EXECUTION: easy
TOTAL PREPARATION TIME: 2 hours
BEST SEASON: April through fall
SUGGESTED WINE: Muscadet, Saumur Sec, or any nice dry white wine
    from California

FISH AND COURT-BOUILLON:
*One 4–5 lb. haddock or 2 large
     whitings, 3 lbs. each*
1 gallon water (4 litres)
*1 bottle ordinary dry white
     wine*
1½ cups wine vinegar (3½ dl)
2½ TB salt (35–40 g)
3 onions, sliced thick
2 carrots, sliced thick
1 lemon, sliced
12 peppercorns
VEGETABLE GARNISH:
*2 carrots, diced into ⅓-inch
     cubes*
*1 white turnip, diced into ⅓-
     inch cubes*
*¼ lb. green beans, cut into ⅓-
     inch long pieces (125 g)*
¼ lb. green peas (125 g)
3 eggs

3 tomatoes
*6 small artichokes 2 inches
     in diameter*
*Parsley in bouquets and
     chopped*
1 lemon, sliced thin
MAYONNAISE AUX HERBES:
1 tsp. vinegar
⅙ tsp. salt
⅛ tsp. ground white pepper
1 egg yolk
1 TB Dijon mustard
*1½ cups oil of your choice
     (3½ dl)*
¼ cup cold court bouillon
1 TB boiling water
*1 TB each chopped chervil,
     parsley, tarragon, chives*
1 large shallot, chopped fine
Lemon juice

Clean the haddock; cut tail and fins off. Set aside on the greased rack of a fish poacher.

Put water, white wine, and vinegar in the poacher. Bring to a boil. Add the salt, onions, carrots, and lemon. Simmer 30 minutes. Add the peppercorns.

Immerse the fish in the boiling *court-bouillon*. Bring back to a bare simmer and poach 8–10 minutes per pound. Cool completely in the *court-bouillon*.

While the fish cooks, boil the carrots, turnips, green beans, and peas 5 minutes in salted water. Rinse under cold water and drain well. Hard boil the eggs. Blanch the tomatoes to remove their skin. Cut the tomatoes in half, empty them, and put them to drain upside down on a cake rack. Clean and pare the small artichokes; boil them 8–10 minutes.

TO PREPARE THE MAYONNAISE:

Put vinegar, salt, pepper, egg yolk, and mustard in a small bowl. Mix well with a whisk. Begin adding the oil gradually, drop by drop, whisking well. When ¾ cup oil has been added, add a tablespoon of cold *court-bouillon*. Continue adding the oil until there is no more. Add a tablespoon of boiling water. Refrigerate one hour. Add all the herbs. Gather the chopped shallots in the corner of a towel and squeeze the juices out. Add the shallots to the mayonnaise and as much lemon juice as you like. Correct the seasoning. Turn into a bowl and chill.

TO SERVE:

Remove the fish from the water bath and skin it. Slide it onto a platter, and generously surround it with parsley. Mix the vegetables with a bit of mayonnaise and fill the tomato halves with them. Alternate tomatoes and hard boiled eggs, cut in half, around the platter. Put 3 artichokes at each end of the platter. Sprinkle the fish generously with parsley. Serve nicely chilled with the mayonnaise.

MOUCLES A LA MIE DE PAIN
[*Mussels in Buttered Crumbs*]

SERVINGS: 6 COST: moderately expensive EXECUTION: easy
TOTAL PREPARATION TIME: 1¼ hours
BEST SEASON: October through March
SUGGESTED WINE: Muscadet
REMARKS ON INGREDIENTS: It is essential, due to the extensive water pollution in many beach areas, that you purchase the mussels from a fish merchant who sells shellfish from controlled areas. There are two styles to this dish, one dry, the other with a sauce built on the shellfish juices and cream. Both are given here.

TO STEAM THE MUSSELS OPEN:
1 cup dry white wine (2¼ dl)
1 large onion, chopped
3 shallots, chopped
¼ cup chopped parsley stems
6 lbs. mussels
6 peppercorns

FOR THE DISH:
½ lb. unsalted butter (225 g)
2 cloves garlic, mashed
½ cup chopped parsley
1 cup dry breadcrumbs
* (about 100 g)*
Salt and pepper
1 cup heavy cream

Place the dry white wine, onions, shallots, and parsley stems at the bottom of a large lobster steamer.

Scrub the mussels well, add them to the pot with the peppercorns. Cover the pot and steam the mussels until they open. Do not overcook them. The shellfish should remain barely poached so that they can finish cooking with the crumb mixture. Shell and reserve the juices.

TO FINISH THE DISH IN ITS DRY VERSION:
Heat 8 to 10 tablespoons butter in a large frying pan. Add the garlic and parsley. Fry until the garlic turns a very light golden color. Add the breadcrumbs and the mussels and toss well together. More butter may be needed. Cover the pan to mellow the breadcrumbs. Correct the salt and pepper and serve.

TO FINISH THE DISH IN ITS MOIST VERSION:
Prepare the dish in the same manner but after the addition of the breadcrumbs do not cover the dish. Add one cup each of the mussel juice and the heavy cream. Let simmer until the mussels are done and juices are well bound. Serve in soup plates.

CANARD AUX COEURS D'ARTICHAUTS
[Duck with Artichoke Hearts and Hazelnut Sauce]

SERVINGS: 8 COST: moderately expensive EXECUTION: medium difficult

TOTAL PREPARATION TIME: 3 hours

BEST SEASON: When California baby artichokes are in season, from November through the end of April. A winter dish.

SUGGESTED WINE: In spite of the brown sauce, use a Barsac or any other Moelleux or semi-sweet white wine. The artichoke taste damages red wines.

REMARKS ON INGREDIENTS: Use the smallest possible California artichokes. They are available in all Italian neighborhoods.

2 ducklings, 4½ lbs. each (2 kg each)

Salt and pepper

2 TB chopped celery leaves

SAUCE:

2 TB oil

Giblets of both ducks

5 TB butter (80 g)

1 carrot, diced into ¼-inch cubes

1 onion, chopped fine

4 TB flour (30 g)

Bouquet garni

1 tsp. tomato paste

½ cup dry white wine (1 generous dl)

1¼ quarts brown veal stock (1¼ litre)

8 toasted hazelnuts

VEGETABLE GARNISH:

6 dozen baby artichokes

Lemon water

3 quarts water (3 litres)

¼ cup flour (30 g)

¼ cup ordinary oil (½ small dl)

Juice of one lemon

PRESENTATION:

Lemon wedges

Parsley or watercress

TO ROAST THE DUCKS:

Preheat the oven to 325°. Remove the wing tips and set aside with the giblets. Keep the duck livers to use in a terrine (see index). Salt and pepper and add 1 tablespoon chopped celery leaves to the cavity of each duck and truss the birds. Put them to roast for 2½ hours. After the ducks have been baking for three quarters of an hour, prick the sides of the skin.

At regular intervals tilt the ducks forward to let the juices running into the cavity escape into the roasting pan. This will be the base for a good gravy.

TO MAKE THE SAUCE:

This sauce can be prepared several days ahead of time. Brown the duck wings and giblets in 2 tablespoons oil. Remove to a plate. Heat the butter, brown the vegetables in it, add the flour, and cook it until it turns nut brown. Add the *bouquet garni.* Add also the tomato paste mixed with the wine and 1 quart brown veal stock, and bring to a boil. When the mixture boils, add the duck giblets and wings. Simmer together for one hour, skimming off as much scum as possible.

Strain into a clean pot. Add the remaining brown stock and bring back to a boil. Simmer until 1½ cups of very clean, rather thick brown sauce are left.

Put one-third of the sauce in the blender container. Add the hazelnuts and blend until smooth. Add the remainder of the sauce and blend again to homogenize. Strain into a clean pot. Reserve.

TO COOK THE ARTICHOKES:

The artichokes may be prepared ahead of time. Remove the stems. Peel off the outer leaves until the artichoke heart is no more than ¾ inch to 1 inch wide. Cut the tip of the artichoke and trim the bottom so it looks nice and rounded. Keep the artichokes in lemon water until ready to use.

Mix the water and flour in a 4-quart pot. Bring to a boil. Add oil, lemon juice, and then the artichokes. Bring back to a rolling boil. Cook 12–15 minutes or until a needle passes freely in and out of the largest artichoke in the batch. Drain, rinse under cold water, and salt lightly. Keep ready to use. Add the artichokes to the finished duck sauce.

TO FINISH THE DISH:

When the ducks are done, empty the gravy into a 1-quart measuring cup. Let the fat rise to the top and with a baster remove the fat-free gravy from under the fat. Add that gravy to the artichoke sauce. Simmer together 5 minutes, no more. Correct the seasoning.

Cut the ducks into eight portions. Arrange them on a platter; spoon the artichoke ragout over the duck. Surround with bouquets of parsley or watercress interspersed with lemon wedges, for those guests who may enjoy squeezing a few drops of lemon juice over their portions.

For a starchy vegetable, use a chestnut purée or rice pilaf.

LAPIN AUX ECHALOTES ET AUX CORNICHONS
[Rabbit with Shallots and Pickles]

SERVINGS: 6 COST: moderately expensive EXECUTION: easy
TOTAL PREPARATION TIME: 1½ hours
BEST SEASON: Enjoyable year round
SUGGESTED WINE: Rosé d'Anjou, Muscadet, California Folle Blanche

4 TB *unsalted butter*	*Salt and pepper*
2 *dozen large shallots, peeled*	*1–1½ cups brown veal stock*
1 *young rabbit*	*6 small sour pickles, sliced*

Preheat the oven to 325°. Heat the butter in a large *sauteuse*. Toss the shallots in the butter. Sprinkle with salt and pepper. Add the pieces of rabbit; salt and pepper them. Cover with the lid of the *sauteuse* and bake about 40 minutes at 325°, basting at regular intervals with the juices in the pot. After forty minutes, raise the oven to 375°, uncover the pot, and add ½ cup of the brown veal stock and the pickles. Keep basting the meat with those juices. Do not turn the pieces of meat over; they should be browned only on one side. Add more stock if necessary. The browning will require 15–20 minutes. The sauce should be as thick as a glaze and lightly coat the pieces of rabbit.

Serve piping hot with *Rôties au Blanc de Poireaux,* page 45.

PIGEONS AUX RAISINS ET AU PINEAU
[Squabs with Grapes and Pineau]

SERVINGS: 6 COST: expensive EXECUTION: easy
TOTAL PREPARATION TIME: 45 minutes
BEST SEASON: Can be enjoyed year round but is more adapted to the
    fall months when the grapes are fresh and ripe
SUGGESTED WINE: A good solid and robust red wine
REMARKS ON INGREDIENTS: If you want to make Pineau yourself
    see the home way of doing it, page 54. Otherwise, use a Pineau
    des Charentes imported from France. Seedless grapes do not
    exist in France. The best results for this recipe were obtained
    with Emperor grapes.

6 squabs (12–16 ounces each)
4 TB butter
Salt and pepper
⅓ cup plus 2 TB Pineau (1 dl)
⅔ cup brown veal stock (2
    small dl)

1 cup peeled grapes (125 g)
1 tsp. arrowroot
1 cup heavy cream (225 g
    or 2¼ dl)
Lemon juice to your taste

Salt and pepper the squabs in the cavity; truss them. In order for the
squabs to fit better in the cocotte, cut the wing tips off first. Heat the
butter in the cocotte. Brown the squabs well on all sides. Drain the
browning butter off.

Heat ⅓ cup Pineau in a small pan and light it. Pour it, flaming,
over the pigeons. Close the pot lid and cook covered over low heat
for no more than 20 minutes. The squabs must remain rare so the
breast meat is tender and succulent. If you cannot face a rare squab,
continue cooking another 45 minutes to 1 hour, turning the birds
several times while they are cooking.

As soon as the squabs are done, remove them to a serving dish,
keep them warm, and proceed quickly. Add the veal stock to the pan
and reduce to a heavy glaze over high heat. Add the grapes; let them
heat in the glaze while you mix together the arrowroot and heavy
cream. With a wooden spoon, stir the arrowroot mixture into the

glaze until it thickens. Correct the seasoning by adding in the following order, the 2 remaining tablespoons of Pineau, salt, pepper, and lemon juice to your taste.

Note: The grapes should be heated to the core but should not be allowed to cook or they will lose their juices and flood the sauce. If you are not sure that you can manage this because you are too busy elsewhere, use unpeeled grapes. They will be able to wait a bit better.

Plan a rice pilaf to soak up the good sauce.

POULE PIQUANTE
[Poached Chicken in a Vinegar Sauce]

SERVINGS: 8 COST: inexpensive EXECUTION: easy
TOTAL PREPARATION TIME: 1 hour and 15 minutes
BEST SEASON: Can be made and enjoyed year round
SUGGESTED WINE: Rosé d'Anjou or a Grenache Rosé from California

Two 3½–4 lb. roasting
   chickens (1 kg 500 g each)
Fresh or dried tarragon
3 quarts chicken or veal stock
   (3 litres)
1 cup tomato purée (2¼ dl)
1 cup dry white wine (2¼ dl)
⅓ cup wine vinegar
   (1 small dl)
¼ tsp. dried thyme
½ bay leaf

2 tsp. dried basil
2 TB chopped parsley stems
1 onion, chopped fine
2 shallots, chopped fine
Salt and pepper
6 TB unsalted butter (75 g)
6 TB flour (60 g)
1 cup heavy cream (225 g or
   2¼ dl)
¼ cup chopped parsley

Salt and pepper the cavities of the birds. Add a good tablespoon of chopped fresh tarragon, or a good teaspoon of the same dried herb, and truss the chickens.

Tie a piece of parchment paper around the breast of each bird. Bring the stock to a boil. Add the chickens and bring to a second boil. Reduce to a simmer; cook 1 hour.

While the chickens cook, mix the tomato purée and white wine with the vinegar, thyme, bay leaf, basil, chopped parsley stems, 2 teaspoons dried tarragon (or 2 tablespoons fresh), the onions, the shallots and a good pinch of salt and pepper. Reduce all ingredients to 1 cup.

When the chickens are three-quarters done, remove 1 quart of broth from the pot. With the butter and flour, make a roux; cook it 5 minutes. Whisk in the stock and bring to a boil. Reduce to a simmer. Skim for about 20 minutes. Reduce the sauce to about 3¼ cups. Add reduction of herbs to the velouté and immediately strain into a clean pot.

Bring back to a simmer, add another two teaspoons of dried tarragon (or 2 tablespoons fresh) and simmer another 15 minutes. Finally, add the cream, reheat the sauce without boiling it, and add the parsley. Correct the seasoning. To serve, remove the chickens from the broth. Cut each into four portions of two legs and two breasts. Skin each portion and coat with the sauce. Serve with the salad of lamb's lettuce and beans on page 48.

MOGETTES A LA CREME
[Fresh Shell Beans with Cream]

SERVINGS: 6 COST: inexpensive EXECUTION: easy
TOTAL PREPARATION TIME: 2 hours
BEST SEASON: July through middle October

6 lbs. shell beans, fresh (3 kg)	2 TB fresh chervil or parsley,
Water	chopped
2 large sun-ripened tomatoes	1 cup heavy cream (225 g or
(200 g)	2¼ dl)
Bouquet garni	½ cup sour cream (120 g or
Salt and pepper	1 generous dl)
	3 TB unsalted butter (30 g)

Shell and wash the beans. Put them in a 4-quart saucepan or pot with enough cold water to cover them completely plus two cups. Bring to a boil.

Meanwhile, bring another quart of water to a boil, to blanch the tomatoes. Then peel, seed, and chop the tomatoes into even ¼-inch cubes. As soon as the beans are boiling, add the *bouquet garni,* salt, pepper, and tomatoes. Simmer until the beans are tender.

When the beans are ready, drain them. Reserve the cooking juices which, when blended with any leftover beans, can give you a nice little soup.

Put the chervil or parsley in a pot. Add both creams and blend well. Add the beans. Toss together and reheat without boiling. Finally, correct the seasoning and add the soft butter, cut in small pieces. Toss quickly to make it melt fast. Serve piping hot.

OIGNONS AU PAIN
[Onions in Bread Dough]

SERVINGS: 6 COST: inexpensive EXECUTION: semi-difficult; watch
the bread techniques
TOTAL PREPARATION TIME: 3 hours with the bread dough preparation
BEST SEASON: Winter

6 large onions	¾ cup lukewarm water
Salt and pepper	(2 small dl)
2 cups brown veal stock	2 TB walnut oil
(2¼ dl)	2 TB chopped parsley
3 cups flour (375 g)	1 garlic clove, mashed
1 envelope yeast (5 g)	½ cup fresh breadcrumbs
1 tsp. salt	3 TB butter (30 g)
	1 egg

Preheat oven to 350°. Peel the onions; cut a cross in their root. Salt and pepper them. Set the onions in a 1-quart round baking dish. Add 2 cups of stock and bake, basting the onions often with the braising stock until they are almost tender. It is essential that the onions retain their shape. Let them cool completely.

WHILE THE ONIONS BAKE, MAKE A SMALL
BREAD DOUGH AS FOLLOWS:

Make a well in the flour. Add half the water and sprinkle the yeast over. Let the yeast bubble. Then add a teaspoon of salt, the oil, and the remainder of the water, and gather liquids and flour together. Add more water if dough seems too dry. As soon as the dough forms a ball, knead it for 10 minutes. Cover it and let rise until double in bulk. Punch down and let rise again. Punch down again and let stand 15 minutes. The dough is ready for use.

Remove the center of each onion to a thickness of about ¾ inch. Mash it with the parsley, garlic, the breadcrumbs, and whatever stock is left at the bottom of the baking dish. The mixture should hold together and not be too soupy. Stuff the mixture into each onion and top with ½ tablespoon of butter.

Roll the dough out ¼ inch thick and cut six round pieces about 4 inches in diameter. Fit the pieces of dough around the onions so that the seam will be at the root end of the onion. Cut a cross at the top of each onion, using scissors to make a steam vent. Let the dough rise again for another 30–40 minutes. Beat the egg well; brush it all over the onions. Bake 25 minutes in a 425° oven.

ROTIES AU BLANC DE POIREAUX
[Leek Toast]

SERVINGS: 6 COST: inexpensive EXECUTION: easy
TOTAL PREPARATION TIME: 45 minutes
BEST SEASON: Fall and winter months, up to the end of March

1 clove garlic
6 slices of French bread
1 dozen leeks, white and light
*   green parts*
3 TB butter (30–35 g)
Salt and pepper
3 ounces slab bacon (100 g)

1 cup heavy cream (225 g or
*   2¼ dl)*
1 oz. fresh white goat cheese
*   (30 g)*
3 TB clarified butter (30 g)
Chopped parsley

Peel the garlic clove. Let the slices of bread stale at room temperature for 30 minutes. Slash the garlic clove well with a paring knife and rub each slice of bread with it. Set aside.

Clean the leeks, slice them into ⅛-inch slivers. Do not blanch them. Heat the butter in a large frying pan; add the leeks. Toss them in the butter. Salt and pepper lightly and cover. Let steam over low heat.

Meanwhile, chop the bacon into ¼-inch cubes. Render it and let it crisp well. Discard the fat. Add the bacon to the leeks. Remove the lid of the pan and raise the heat to evaporate all the moisture. Add the cream and let reduce until it coats the leeks. When this happens grate the goat cheese into the leeks and mix well. Add a good three or four turns of the pepper mill set to a coarse grind.

Brown the bread slices in clarified butter. Top with the leeks and a dash of chopped parsley. Serve very hot.

DIABLE DE POMMES DE TERRE
[Garlic and Potato Casserole]

SERVINGS: 6 COST: inexpensive EXECUTION: medium difficult to
    difficult

TOTAL PREPARATION TIME: 45 minutes to 1 hour

REMARKS ON INGREDIENTS: A *diable* was an earthenware pot, a
    copy of the old *tajin* as translated in poitevin. Nothing in this
    country resembles it. Use a potato Anna casserole or an alumi-
    num *sauteuse* that can be closed tightly.

Unsalted butter, at least ½–¾ cup	*4 medium potatoes, Maine*
(125–175 g)	*or Idaho (300 g or 1 lb.)*
6 cloves garlic	*Salt and pepper*
	2 TB chopped parsley

Rub the bottom of the chosen cooking vessel with at least 4 table-spoons of butter. There should be ⅓–¼ inch of butter all around the sides of the vessel.

Peel the garlic cloves without crushing them first; slice into paper-thin slivers. Peel and slice the potatoes into ⅛-inch slices. A slicer is useful here.

Arrange a first layer of potatoes on the bottom of the cooking pot in attractive concentric circles. From then on alternate layers of potato slices with layers of garlic slices. Salt and pepper the layers of potatoes. When the pot is filled with half the vegetables, sprinkle a heavy layer of parsley on the potatoes and continue building the cake until all the ingredients have been used.

Put the pot on medium heat. Cover the pot tightly and let cook well covered for 10 minutes.

Shake the pan back and forth often to keep the potatoes from sticking to the bottom of the pan.

Push the potatoes down to pack them well and continue cooking slowly and well covered. After about 25 minutes invert the cake either onto the lid of the potato Anna dish or on a plate. Be careful.

Add more butter to the pot. Place the unbrowned side of the potatoes in the butter and resume the slow, covered cooking.

The potatoes must cook without water; the garlic must disappear and melt. The thickness of the potato cake will be half of its original size when the cake is done.

Serve it with *Poireaux à la Vinaigrette* and a piece of goat cheese. It is a royal meal.

POIREAUX A LA VINAIGRETTE
[Braised Leeks with Vinaigrette Dressing]

SERVINGS: 6 COST: inexpensive EXECUTION: easy
TOTAL PREPARATION TIME: 1½–2 hours
BEST SEASON: September through April
REMARKS ON INGREDIENTS: Use leeks no more than 1 inch wide.
   Larger leeks often have a wooden core, especially toward the
   end of their season. Keep light green parts of leeks for stock
   making.

1 dozen leeks	*3 TB wine vinegar*
3 TB butter (30 g)	*¾ cup walnut oil (2 small dl)*
3–4 cups brown veal stock	*2 TB heavy cream (30 g)*
(2 small dl)	*1 TB freshly chopped chives*
Salt and pepper	

Preheat the oven to 325°.

Butter two rectangular baking dishes each with 1 tablespoon of butter. Butter two pieces of parchment paper each with ½ tablespoon of butter.

Cut off the roots and green tops of the leeks. Slice the leeks in half lengthwise almost all the way. Leave 1 inch near the root to keep the vegetable from falling apart. Wash thoroughly under running cold water, letting the water run generously between the leaves to dislodge all traces of sand.

Place the leeks in both baking dishes. Pour 1½–2 cups of stock into each dish. Salt and pepper lightly. Cover with prepared paper. Bake in a preheated oven until the leeks are tender and the stock is reduced to almost a glaze. Turn the leeks two or three times while baking. Cool to lukewarm.

While the leeks are cooling, mix the vinegar with salt and pepper. Whisk in the oil and cream. Correct the seasoning and add the chives. Pour half of the vinaigrette mixture into each dish and serve lukewarm.

SALADE DE MACHE ET DE MOGETTES
[Lamb's Lettuce and Fresh Bean Salad]

SERVINGS: 6 COST: inexpensive EXECUTION: easy

TOTAL PREPARATION TIME: 20 minutes

BEST SEASON: Winter

REMARKS ON INGREDIENTS: Lamb's lettuce is not easy to come by, but as a consolation I can vouch for the fact that it grows like weeds. If sowed in October, a nice big bed can be expected early to late March. That is, in the proper cool temperate climate. Romaine is an acceptable substitute.

1 clove garlic
½ lb. lamb's lettuce or one head
  of Romaine
1 TB wine vinegar
Salt and pepper
½ large red onion, diced

2 TB fresh chopped parsley
  (30 g)
1 TB Dijon mustard (15 g)
1 TB chopped chives (15 g)
⅓–½ cup walnut oil (1 dl)
1½ cups cooked leftover fresh-
  shelled beans (mogettes)

Slash the side of the garlic clove and rub the salad bowl with it. Let dry; discard pieces of garlic left on the surface of the bowl. Wash the lamb's lettuce or Romaine.

Prepare the dressing directly in the salad bowl by thoroughly mixing the vinegar, salt, pepper, onion, parsley, mustard, and chives. Gradually add the walnut oil. Taste for seasoning. Add the beans and toss well. Then, just before serving, add the greens; toss and serve without delay.

POIRES MORDOREES
[Golden Baked Pears]

SERVINGS: 6 COST: inexpensive EXECUTION: easy
TOTAL PREPARATION TIME: 1 hour
BEST SEASON: September through December with Bartlett pears; November through January with Anjou pears

6 Bartlett or Anjou pears
¼ cup water (small ½ dl)
¼ cup liquid honey
  (small ½ dl)

3 TB butter (45 g)
Lemon wedges

Wash the pears, cut ¼ inch worth of flesh at the base; remove the core completely. Do not peel the fruit.

In a baking dish, mix water and honey. Cut 6 slices of butter, one half tablespoon each slice. Put the butter slices in the mixture of water and honey; set each pear on a piece of butter. Bake in a 350° preheated oven for 45 minutes. Baste the pears with the baking syrup. Bake another 10 minutes. Remove from the oven. Cool to lukewarm.

Pour the cooking syrup into a small warmed pitcher. Each guest should help herself or himself to a pear, cut it in half lengthwise, mash the pulp with some of the syrup poured from the pitcher, and lemon juice to taste, squeezed from a lemon wedge.

PETATOU AUX NOUZILLES
[Hazelnut and Potato Cake]

SERVINGS: 8 COST: inexpensive EXECUTION: easy
TOTAL PREPARATION TIME: 2 hours
BEST SEASON: Year round if desired, but better during the cold
    months
REMARKS ON INGREDIENTS: Use the potatoes indicated in the recipe;
    others do not give the same result.

3 medium Maine or Long Island	*¼ tsp. salt*
potatoes (½ lb. or 250 g)	*¼ tsp. anis extract*
7 ½ TB unsalted butter	*¼ cup hazelnuts (100 g)*
½ TB flour	*3 oz. Swiss bittersweet chocolate*
3 eggs, separated	*(85–90 g)*
⅓ cup sugar (85 g)	

Preheat the oven to 325°.

Scrub the potatoes. Boil them in their jackets until tender. Butter a 9-inch cake pan with ½ tablespoon butter. Dust the pan with the flour. While the potatoes cook, mix egg yolks, sugar, salt and anis extract. Beat until a heavy ribbon forms when the beaters are lifted from the mixture.

Melt 6 tablespoons butter. Peel the potatoes while they are warm. Strain the potatoes through a conical strainer directly into the melted butter. Mix well. Beat the butter and potato mixture into the ribboned egg. Beat the egg whites until they are stiff enough to carry the weight of a raw egg in its shell without the latter sinking into the egg mass by more than ¼ inch. Mix one-quarter of the whites into the potato base first and then fold in the remainder.

Turn into the prepared cake pan and bake in a 325° oven for 50–55 minutes, until browned. The cake should rise very high, then shrink back into the pan and end up no more than 1 inch high. Unmold into a cake rack and cool.

Do not turn the oven off when the cake is finished. Raise the temperature to 350°. Spread the hazelnuts on a jelly roll pan. Bake them 8–10 minutes. Empty them into a towel and rub well to remove the skins. Chop coarsely. Mix the chocolate and 1 tablespoon butter in a double boiler. Spread it on the sides and top of the cake. While the chocolate is still soft, sprinkle with the chopped hazelnuts. Let cool.

This cake tastes better if allowed to "ripen" 24 hours.

GATEAU DE VERMICELLES
[Vermicelli Cake]

SERVINGS: 6–8 COST: inexpensive EXECUTION: easy
TOTAL PREPARATION TIME: 1¼ hours
BEST SEASON: Preferably in winter but good year round for children

1 cup hot water plus 2 TB (2½ dl)	1 cup heavy cream, scalded (225 g or 2¼ dl)
¾ cup sugar (200 g)	⅓ tsp. salt
6 TB unsalted butter (90 g)	10 cloves
5 oz. vermicelli (150 g)	Rind of one lemon, grated fine
	4 eggs, separated

Preheat oven to 325°.

Mix 2 tablespoons water with ¼ cup sugar in a small pan and bring to a dark caramel over medium heat. While the caramel cooks, fill a 4 to 6 cup soufflé dish with hot water from the tap. Empty the dish and wipe it dry. Immediately pour in the caramel, turning the mold in all directions so the caramel covers the bottom evenly. Let cool. Butter very heavily, with 1 to 2 tablespoons butter, the sides of the mold not covered with caramel. Reserve.

Heat 4 tablespoons butter in a 9-inch frying pan. Crush the vermicelli and toss them into the hot butter until half of them have turned brown. Add the remaining hot water and toss until the vermicelli are almost done. Add the scalded cream, ½ cup sugar, the salt, only the crushed buds of the cloves, and the lemon rind. Mix well. Beat the egg yolks vigorously; mix into the noodle base.

Whip the egg whites until they are stiff enough to carry the weight of a raw egg in its shell without the latter sinking into the egg white bulk by more than ¼ inch. Fold into the noodle base.

Turn into the prepared dish and bake in a preheated oven, without a water bath, for 35–40 minutes. The lack of a water bath will allow the crisp caramel bottom to build easily while baking. The contrast of the crisp top with the soft center is one of the pleasures of the cake.

Unmold the cake into a lightly buttered platter as soon as it is removed from the oven. Serve plain, with whipped cream or custard.

PETITES DARIOLES AUX NOIX
[Walnut Cupcakes]

SERVINGS: 12–14 COST: expensive EXECUTION: easy
TOTAL PREPARATION TIME: 2 hours
BEST SEASON: Winter, a great Christmas sweetmeat
REMARKS ON INGREDIENTS: If you use a walnut liqueur, use the
    Italian one.

*One double recipe ordinary
    pastry, page 13
1½ cup chopped walnuts
    (½ lb. or 250 g)
⅓ cup sugar (85 g)*

*6 TB unsalted butter (60 g)
2 egg yolks
3 TB dark rum or walnut liqueur
Confectioners sugar*

Preheat the oven to 375°.

Chop the walnuts fine. Mix them with the sugar. Cream five table-spoons of butter until fluffy. Add the yolks and the rum, beat until homogenous. Blend in the mixture of walnuts and sugar.

Butter two small muffin tins with the remaining butter. Roll the pastry out ⅛ inch thick. Cut 24 circles 3 inches wide and fit them into the muffin tins. Fill the muffins two-thirds full with the walnut paste. Bake in a preheated oven until the edges of the muffins are nice and brown. Unmold, cool on a rack, and sprinkle with confectioners sugar.

POUPELAIN DE MARIE-CHARLOTTE
[Marie-Charlotte's Huge Lemon Cruller]

SERVINGS: 6–8 COST: inexpensive EXECUTION: easy
TOTAL PREPARATION TIME: 1 hour
BEST SEASON: Fall through winter
SUGGESTED WINE: Pineau des Charentes
REMARKS ON INGREDIENTS: Candied angelica is not to be found in the United States with the exception of one or two stores in New York City. If you cannot find it, add 3 crushed anise seeds to the cream while it reduces.

1 cup water (2¼ dl)	1 cup heavy cream (2¼ dl)
¼ cup sugar (60–65 g)	Rind of one lemon
¼ tsp. salt	1 oz. angelica, chopped, or
9 TB butter (125 g)	3 anise seeds
1 cup sifted flour (120–125 g)	1½ TB dark rum (22½ g)
5 eggs	1 TB superfine sugar (15 g)
	Angelica, diced (optional)

Preheat the oven to 350°.

Put water, 2 tablespoons sugar, salt and ½ cup diced butter in a 2-quart saucepan. Slowly bring to a boil.

As soon as the mixture foams, remove the pot from the heat and add the flour. Stir steadily to form a ball. Return the mixture to the heat. Stir 1 minute only. *Do not dry* the paste as you normally would for regular cream puffs. You are keeping the paste wet on purpose. If the center remains wet, it will absorb the cream easily and finally taste like a pastry cream. Add the eggs, lightly beaten, one by one. Mix until smooth.

Grease a 10-inch quiche pan with the remaining butter and fill the pan with the paste. Bake in a 350° oven for 50–55 minutes.

Pour 1 cup heavy cream into a 1-quart saucepan. Add 2 tablespoons sugar, the rind of a lemon cut in long strips and lifted from the fruit with a potato peeler, and, if you have no angelica, the anise seeds. Stirring occasionally, reduce over medium heat to ½–⅓ cup. Add the rum.

As soon as the cake is done, it will look bloated like a giant cream puff. Cut the top off in one single layer so as to make a lid. While the cake is hot, spoon the cream into the soft wet center of the cake. Sprinkle with diced angelica if you have some and put the cake cover back on. Brush whatever cream is still on the sides and bottom of the pan onto the lid of the cake. Sprinkle with superfine sugar and broil one minute. The cake should be enjoyed lukewarm.

PINEAU
[*Fortified Aperitif Wine*]

REMARKS ON INGREDIENTS: Pineau is made at home with the following basic formula. To vary the flavor, try different wines and different spirits. The vanilla bean is optional, but often used in the home.

1 bottle wine of your choice (Rosé d'Anjou or Muscadet is good)	*10 oz. Cognac, Armagnac, Marc or plain 90 percent proof alcohol*
½ cup sugar (125 g)	*1 vanilla bean, uncut*

Heat the wine to about 140° and add the sugar. Turn the heat off and stir well to melt the sugar. Add the Cognac or other chosen alcohol and mix thoroughly. Store in one or two containers. Add the vanilla bean whole if you have one container, cut in half if you have two. Seal the containers tight. Wrap them in foil and store them in a cool cellar for one month. After one month, remove the vanilla bean and let stand a second month. The Pineau is ready to drink.

VESPETRO
[Digestive Liqueur]

SERVINGS: 16–20 COST: inexpensive EXECUTION: simple

REMARKS ON INGREDIENTS: The angelica seeds which should be used here are not easy to find. Angelica roots may be purchased from the San Francisco Herb Co. in San Francisco and Aphrodisia in New York City. All other seeds are on the spice shelf in all supermarkets. You may skip the angelica and use twice as many anise seeds but the liqueur will not be as refined. It will still be good, however.

1 quart Akvavit (1 litre)
One 2-inch-long piece of
angelica root
1 cup water (2¼ dl)
½ oz. coriander seeds
(14–15 g)

12 fennel seeds
12 anise seeds
1 lemon
½ lb. superfine sugar (250 g)

Empty the Akvavit into a large mixing bowl. Immerse the angelica root into a pot with no more than 1 cup water. Slowly bring to a boil. Simmer until only ¼ cup water is left. Add water and root to the Akvavit.

Put all the seeds into a small mortar or the blender and pulverize as much as possible. Empty into the Akvavit.

Peel the lemon with a potato peeler so as to lift only the yellow skin, add the strips to the Akvavit.

Squeeze the juice and add it to the bowl. Empty the sugar into the bowl and stir.

Cover and stir occasionally until the sugar has completely melted. This will require about five days at room temperature. Cover with a plastic wrap and store in the refrigerator for another five days. Finally, strain through a paper filter into two decanters or bottles and keep away from the light in a dark cupboard.

Victoire

AUVERGNE

Summer of 1939

DISAPPOINTMENT comes early in life. It came to me in June of 1939 after my dance teacher overworked and overpracticed my young legs so much that I collapsed in the middle of the entrance competition to the Paris Opera Ballet School. I was shipped to a distant old cousin of my grandmother's who offered to nurse me back to health, high up in her hamlet of La Vachellerie, where the volcanoes of Cantal meet with the mountain of the Margeride.

I was put on a train at the Gare de Lyon, entrusted to the others traveling in my compartment, and placed on the luggage rack to sleep. And so I was off, feeling lonely and sad, toward the volcano country of France—that far-away Auvergne which, to this day, remains so blissfully unspoiled. I was awakened by the pungent smell of *café au lait* mixed with steam and coal from the train engine. It was cool and the platform of the station at Clermont Ferrand was alive with a colorful crowd. A man offering hot beverages was pouring coffee from the right and milk from the left into huge bowls to make *café au lait* that travelers were buying from the train windows. They swallowed fast, burning their throats, for fear the train would start before they finished.

People left the train compartment only to be replaced by others in regional costumes, heavy blue denim smocks for the men, black dresses and white round coifs for the women. I recognized the familiar smells of the country. The pungent homey smells of cows, dairy products, whey, grass, manure were all there, mixed and blended, having steeped and seeped into these people's clothes for decades. They were not dirty people; they were people smelling of their profession.

I was feeling somewhat giddy when I stepped off the train at Langeac. I was swept off my feet by a little, old Arab-looking woman, with a hooked nose, two piercing, flaming eyes, and a few wisps of gray hair peeking from under her immaculate white muslin coif. She took one look at me and declared that I looked no bigger nor fatter than an *artisoun,* that I was "spindly," and looked much too pale to please her. I had some problems understanding. Victoire, of whom I had heard so much and whom I had secretly dreaded meeting, spoke more of the old Occitanian language of the region than she spoke French. As a result, we never communicated more than half and half in French. But communicate we did, with our eyes and hearts. I owe Victoire my love of the mountains and my love for nature. It took me weeks to realize that the name *artisoun* that Victoire had given me was the name given by the Occitanians to the tiny, incessantly wiggling, microscopic worms that dwell in the little blue cheeses of the region. When she felt really sorry for me, she called me *poutoune*—little love—and covered me with comforting *poutous,* as kisses are called in that part of France.

From Langeac we took the bus that goes to Monistrol d'Allier. We drove from village to village, and after passing through the ancient little town of Saugues, were deposited at La Vachellerie. In the center of this hamlet was Victoire's house. It was an old stone building, southern in style with a round tiled roof and an enormous grapevine climbing up all the way under the eaves. As we entered Pépé Gaston, Victoire's husband, gave me some more *poutous.* All I could do was stand there looking, my eyes opening wider and wider, at a world that I had no idea existed. There was a huge chimney, black with the smoke of centuries, in which a pine needle and wood fire burned bright. And something mysterious, something I had never seen before—a bread oven. Victoire had already baked bread before she picked me up: on the table were three huge loaves of dark bread, their fresh smell still permeating the atmosphere. The bread paddles used to send the loaves to bake in the depths of the oven were hanging above the mantel. There was a table covered with an electric blue and white checkered tablecloth loaded with fresh bread slices, butter, rich and yellow, a side of bacon, several *saucissons,* and a huge pot of *café au lait.* The room smelled of everything, smoke, bacon, garlic, cows, cheese and lentils cooking in a huge, iron pot buried in the ashes of the hearth.

"Courcouné, pouleta," called Victoire after breakfast. A flock of chickens quickly materialized in the yard—the *or*—in front of the house; mixed in were a few ducks and two of those huge, gray geese from the Périgord. These geese proved to be the meanest old things. Many times, as I sat at dinner, they came waddling under the table looking and pecking for crumbs. They pecked at my legs without hesitation in the process. I seemed to be the only one to mind them.

It became immediately apparent to me that Victoire's active life was divided between three loves, mushroom hunting, cooking, and lace making. For two months that summer, I was to be part of her old-fashioned world. I was to learn how to use what the forests, meadows and rivers have to offer to reduce expenses in a household. Victoire had two cows and also a small flock of six white and three black sheep. Every morning we left the house, cows in front, sheep in back, to go graze the animals. Hector, the old Labrador, was at a certain point entrusted with the care of the animals and Victoire and I went hunting for mushrooms. She was incredible at discovering a mass of *mousserons,* those little fairy-ring mushrooms which made such delicious and fragrant omelettes; they came twice that year, late in June and again in early September, two weeks before I was due to leave. The yellow chanterelles came later, around the second week of July. Victoire said that on waking up, she could smell the day when, after a short rain followed by a burst of heat, the chanterelles came out. She was right: we found baskets of them. She sold most of them to that little chef at the hotel in Saugues who always begged her to think of him; but she also kept some for us. Two culinary masterpieces issued from that day's collection. First, a beautiful salad. Victoire sliced the raw mushrooms, marinated them in walnut oil for an hour and finished the salad with some Verjus and a nice little *persillade* of garlic and parsley. Then, on the next day, she prepared huge *escalopes de veau aux giroles* of the whitest veal topped with a mass of chanterelles blended with *persillade,* and browned in rendered *ventrèche* fat.

It was Victoire who introduced me to the splendid but deadly bright-colored *Amanitae.* She explained to me in detail how to distinguish the rare and glorious *Amanita* of the Caesars from its deadly cousin the *Amanita muscaria.* Come August we were busy, for the *Boleti* came out and so did the ink mushrooms, the *Coprini comati,* which could grow shaggy and lovely one day and be reduced to black mush the next. The *Coprini* we ate, but most of the *Boleti* we sliced at night and strung with a thin needle and thread into long necklaces which we dried for use during the winter months. Victoire put them to hang and dry in her back pantry where bouquets of mint and verbena, strings of garlic and onions of all colors, hams and sausages and sides of belly bacon—that *ventrèche,* which resembles closely in taste the *pancetta* of the Italians—were already waiting.

She was one businesswoman, that Victoire with her mushrooms. One day after a week of rain, we picked close to one hundred pounds of *Boleti* between the two of us and Gaston. Victoire promptly sold them to the young Monsieur Chassain Aldon down in Saugues. To this day Monsieur Chassain Aldon—he is now an old man with a comfortable pot-belly—sells his dried *cèpes* all over the world.

Victoire was popular in Saugues and immensely respected. So, when she took me to lunch at the Hôtel to celebrate our *Boleti* fortune, we were treated like queens. The "young chef," as she called him, was most solicitous but, she confided to me, his trout *au lard* did not measure up to what it should be, and promised she would prepare some for me. Sure enough, the next day Victoire, her skirts gathered around her waistband, stepped knee-deep into a pool of cool water. She stood there quietly and patiently, her hands below water level. All of a sudden one hand came up holding a flapping dart of silver that soon slipped away onto the grass of the meadow where it lay panting for just a few minutes. I never learned to do it and never found out her secret, but she was a champion poacher. That night we brought six trout home for dinner. She cooked them *au lard,* and indeed they tasted better than the trout of "the young chef."

One week, Victoire and I took a long trip to see her brother in the mountains of Cantal. The whole time we were climbing she gathered those lovely purple thistles that botanists call *Carlina acaulis.* I thought that like my mother, she would make a flower arrangement with them, but no, she boiled them in a large kettle of water and removed their straw to obtain what resembled tiny artichoke bottoms. With these she made a lovely salad with walnut oil and Verjus. Victoire's brother was a man of means. As far as the eye could see he owned the mountains and many of the small, thatch-roofed, cheese-making chalets called *burons* in the Auvergne. Since childhood he had raised brown *Salers* cows, and from fresh tomme cheese, pressed with his own knees and fists, he had for years made Cantal cheese as was the custom on the *aygades,* those high pastures of the Auvergne, until at least 1925. With roots of yellow gentians, painfully collected, he made the bittersweet favorite drink of Auvergne, the Suze. He made a small fortune with the drink, and with the money had bought vines in Armagnac country.

True Occitanians that they were, Victoire and her brother never spoke more than half French. They spent most of their time remembering how their father could work in the old forge one day and bargain on the price of a calf for hours at the cattle fair the next. Victoire must have inherited his bargaining gift; there was no one like her to get a good price on something at the Saugues market on Sunday mornings after mass. She bargained for dried cod to prepare an *estofinado,* for a large piece of Fourme d'Ambert, for a live eel of which Gaston was fond and which she would cook with a pot full of leeks and a bottle of bluish country wine. Victoire, who cooked for Gaston and to fatten me, never sat down to take a meal. She stood in one corner of the huge chimney, her back well arched against the wall, and silently emptied a large bowl of soup. There was no way for me to escape fattening up, with all these *pachades* full of raisins and walnuts, the soups made with dried chestnuts, the nice dark bread full of buckwheat flour that Victoire spread with a quarter inch of the butter she had churned herself and stored carefully wrapped in chestnut leaves.

The summer progressed. When the leaves took on a pale yellow tinge, it was time to make jams in the huge copper kettle that hung over the flames in the hearth. When the grapes on the vine reached the right degree of semi-ripeness, she made the Verjus. She picked the first melting pear off her William pear tree to prepare a *mesclade* for me with a fresh white cheese she called Sarrassou and heavy yellow cream. Was that ever a treat. It was sweetened with a spoonful of heavy, dark mountain-blossom honey that the bees produced in a small round wicker hive located right under the window of my room.

Nothing was ever lost in Victoire's kitchen. If she had made a chard tart, the green would be chopped to go into that delicious meat loaf she called *pounti;* if she had melted butter to store for the winter, the *gappe* of milk solids would go into a *pompe à la gappe* or a *fougasse salée aux noix.* The leftover rice from a meal, together with dry bread, went into a *maoutsa,* a heavy, utterly delicious pudding with prunes, of course, the plentiful prunes that she dried from the Italian plum tree in her garden. Victoire of the nimble fingers could catch a trout or a rabbit with her bare hands. She could spin yards of lovely lace by intercrossing linen threads in multiple patterns as she sat in the semi-obscurity of a warm summer evening listening tight-lipped to the less-than-charitable chatter of her neighbors. How fast she was at filling sausage skins on the day old Gaston killed the pig! She prepared quite a *Saint-Pourqui* celebration for the houseful of people that processed the pig that everyone called *habillé de soie*—dressed of silk. There was *garrou en pistache* fragrant with garlic, huge pots of rabbit in walnut sauce, and that poor baby *pourqui* I felt so sorry for filled with verbena. Then there was a *pastissous,* made with the liver of the defunct pig, and beautiful walnut cakes and chestnut cakes covered with a thick layer of Menier chocolate.

Victoire died a very old woman about ten years after the happy memories I described here happened. Her steady head saved her from multiple worries during the war years, when she was hiding hunted resistance fighters in the recesses of her barn. She and her Gaston rest in peace in the cemetery in Saugues. The ancient house still stands in La Vachellerie while the wind rustles in the pine, walnut, and chestnut trees that surround it and while Marie-France, Victoire's granddaughter, cooks on an electric stove fitted into the fireplace and takes her children hunting for *Boleti* and chanterelles.

ae

SOUPE A L'AIL ET AU VIN
[Garlic Soup]

SERVINGS: 6 COST: inexpensive EXECUTION: easy
TOTAL PREPARATION TIME: 1 hour
BEST SEASON: For late fall, winter, early spring (all the R months)

2 heads (repeat, 2 heads or 40–50 cloves) garlic
3½ oz. pancetta (see page 66) (115 g)
3 TB flour (25 g)
5 cups warm jus de veau (Brown veal stock) or any stock or broth of your choice (1 litre)

½ cup dry white wine (1 generous dl)
3 egg yolks
Salt and pepper
¼ cup chopped parsley
1 cup grated Cantal cheese (125 g)
6 slices toasted light rye bread, crusts removed

Separate each clove of garlic from the heads and crush each with the flat side of a chef's knife blade. Do not remove the garlic from its skin. Peel and chop one clove very fine; reserve it for later use.

Cut the *pancetta* in ¼-inch cubes. Put in a cold 2-quart saucepan. Let render gently until the *pancetta* pieces have turned into small golden cracklings. Add the flour to the pot and cook it in the *pancetta* fat for about five minutes. Gradually whisk in the warm stock and bring to a boil, stirring constantly. When the mixture boils, add the garlic and let simmer 45 minutes.

Mix the dry white wine and the egg yolks in a 1-quart measuring cup. Gradually add half the soup to this mixture to gently heat the yolks.

Reversing the procedure, pour the warmed egg mixture back into the soup. Make sure that the soup reheats enough to show a few bubbles.

Put the reserved mashed clove of garlic and the parsley in a preheated tureen and strain the soup on top. Mix well and correct the seasoning.

To serve, place one slice of rye bread at the bottom of each plate. Top with as much grated Cantal cheese as desired and ladle the soup over the bread. Enjoy piping hot.

SOUPE AU PAIN NOIR
[Black Bread Soup]

SERVINGS: 6 COST: inexpensive EXECUTION: easy
TOTAL PREPARATION TIME: 1 hour
BEST SEASON: During all the R months

6 slices dark unseeded Jewish
   rye bread, crusts removed
1¼ cup milk (2½ dl)
2 TB butter (30 g)
2 onions, chopped very fine
   (100 g)
3 cups brown veal stock or any
   broth of your choice (7 dl)

⅔ cup sour cream (150 g)
⅓ cup heavy cream (75 g)
¼ tsp. well-crushed anise seeds
Salt and pepper
1 cup grated Cantal cheese
   (125 g)

Remove the crusts from the bread; soak the bread in the milk, then pour into blender container and blend on medium speed to obtain a smooth texture.

Heat the butter in a large, heavy saucepan. In the butter, sauté the onions until golden brown. Watch however, that you do not burn them. Add the broth. Bring to a boil. Add the bread purée and simmer together 30 minutes.

Mix both creams. Crush the anise seeds fine and add them to the cream mixture. Blend soup and cream mixture. Reheat without boiling and correct the salt and pepper carefully. Serve piping hot with a bowl of grated Cantal cheese.

ESTOFINADO
[Stockfish with Potatoes and Garlic]

SERVINGS: 6 COST: inexpensive EXECUTION: easy
TOTAL PREPARATION TIME: At least 12 hours to soak the salt cod
    plus 45 minutes cooking time
BEST SEASON: Good all through the late fall and winter months
SUGGESTED WINE: Any inexpensive, steely dry white wine you like,
    whatever its origin; the dish is potent in taste, so you can remain
    very plebeian in your choice.
REMARKS ON INGREDIENTS: For the best stockfish, go to your local
    Italian market and purchase the fattest, best-quality stockfish
    offered there. Stockfish sold in supermarkets should not be con-
    sidered.

1 whole side of stockfish (about 750 g)
6 small Maine potatoes (1 lb. or 500 g)
½ cup butter or lard (110–115 g)

4 cloves of garlic, very finely chopped
3 TB parsley, chopped very fine
½ cup sour cream (120 g)
¼ cup heavy cream (60 g)
Coarse-grated black pepper from the mill

Cut the stockfish into large pieces and place in a kettle containing a large amount of water. Place the kettle under the spigot and let one little stream of water constantly fall into the kettle so the water is continually renewed. Let the stockfish soak this way overnight. Drain, dry, and keep refrigerated until ready to use. If the fish is still too salty, let soak another half day.

Peel the potatoes and slice them in ⅛-inch-thick slices. Heat the butter in a large frying pan. Add the potatoes and sear them first over high heat. Then lower the heat and finish cooking them.

Meanwhile, place the stockfish in a large kettle of cold, unsalted water. Bring to a boil over medium heat. As soon as the water boils, remove from the heat, cover, and let stand 7–8 minutes.

Remove the fish from the water. Remove the skin and bones. Flake the fish; add the flakes to the potatoes. Raise the heat under the frying pan and stir to mix well. You will see the potatoes fall apart. Add the garlic and parsley and continue stirring until the garlic starts taking on color and flavor and the parsley turns slightly crisp. The contents of the frying pan should be a mess of falling-apart fish and potatoes, the latter by now a light golden color. Drain any excess butter if you desire, but the fish will be better if it remains in the pan. Mix the two creams. Turn the heat off under the frying pan and pour the cream mixture into the frying pan. Sprinkle with several shakes of coarsely grated pepper. Serve with a good fresh salad made with a tart dressing.

TRUITES AU LARD
[Trout Panfried with Salted Pork Brisket]

SERVINGS: 6 COST: reasonable EXECUTION: easy

TOTAL PREPARATION TIME: 1 hour with fresh trout

BEST SEASON: Anytime you can obtain fresh trout during the fishing season

SUGGESTED WINE: Any good dry white wine of any origin. The dish is somewhat powerful, so you can again be somewhat plebeian.

REMARKS ON INGREDIENTS: *Pancetta,* the Italian aged, cured and salted bacon, replaces the French aged *lard demi-sel* and can be purchased in all Italian grocery stores. Do not use frozen trout. If you cannot find freshly caught trout, use the hatchery trout sold in all supermarkets during Lent.

6 *trout, no more than 8 inches long*	*2 cloves of garlic, chopped fine*
1 cup milk	*2 TB parsley, chopped fine*
3½ oz. pancetta (*115 g*)	*2 TB butter*
Flour	

Clean the trout. To do so, cut the thin membrane that connects the belly to the underside of the head without cutting the abdomen open and remove the innards. They will lose less juice while cooking if you clean them. Wash thoroughly to remove all traces of the gelatinous algae on the skin. Soak the trout in the milk while you prepare the *pancetta.* Dice the *pancetta* into ¼-inch cubes. Put it in a cold large frying pan or an unheated electric frying pan. Let stand over low heat, stirring occasionally until the *pancetta* renders its fat and the *pancetta* cubes are reduced to tiny cracklings. Remove the cracklings to a plate and reserve.

Remove the trout from the milk; shake off excess milk and roll them in the flour. Pan-fry the trout about 4 minutes on each side in the *pancetta* fat. Meanwhile chop the garlic and parsley very fine.

When the trout are done remove them to a serving platter. Add the butter to the fat in the frying pan, add the garlic, parsley and *pancetta* cracklings. Stir until the garlic starts to color and the parsley starts to crisp. Spoon the mixture over the trout.

The best way to enjoy the trout is to eat both the skin and the meat at the same time.

ANGUILLES AUX POIREAUX
[Eel and Leeks in Red Wine Sauce]

SERVINGS: 6 COST: moderately expensive EXECUTION: easy
TOTAL PREPARATION TIME: 1 hour
BEST SEASON: Middle December to middle January when the eels
    are sold in great numbers in Italian neighborhoods
SUGGESTED WINE: The same as used in the preparation of the fish
REMARKS ON INGREDIENTS: The eels should be purchased alive. Ask
    the fish merchant to skin it for you and to give you the heads;

you will need them. If you do not like eel or the idea of it, prepare the same dish with bass or carp. Both are also excellent.

3 medium-size eels
2 onions, sliced thick
Bouquet garni
1 bottle of Médoc or Pauillac (other Bordeaux discolor too much)
2 TB lard or clarified butter
6 medium leeks (white part only)

Salt and pepper
1 oz. Armagnac, Cognac, or light Scotch
Meat glaze or commercial meat extract
4 TB unsalted raw butter
2 TB flour
Chopped parsley

Put the heads of the eels in a saucepan with the sliced onions and the *bouquet garni*. Add the wine. Bring to a boil and simmer 35 minutes, uncovered. Meanwhile, cut the white part of the leeks into ¾-inch chunks. Sauté them in the 2 tablespoons of lard or clarified butter until they take on a light golden color. Cut the eels in 2-inch chunks. Place on the bed of leeks. Salt and pepper lightly. As soon as the broth has cooked 35 minutes, strain it over the mixture of fish and vegetables. Heat the Armagnac or Cognac or Scotch in a small pan, light it and pour it flaming into the sauce pot. Cover the pot and simmer for 10 minutes.

Remove leeks and eels to a colander and be absolutely sure that they drain completely.

Raise the heat under the stewing pan very high and reduce the cooking juices to 2 cups. Taste the sauce; add meat glaze or meat extract to your personal taste to balance the acidity of the wine. You should not use more than ⅓ of a teaspoon or it will be detectable in the final taste of the sauce and this is not desirable. Put the butter on a plate, mash the flour with it to obtain a *beurre manié*. Turn the heat down so the sauce barely simmers and whisk in the prepared kneaded butter. Remove from the heat as soon as it has thickened. Correct the salt and pepper.

Put the eels and leeks in a pretty fireproof casserole or pot. Strain the sauce over both and reheat without boiling. The customary vegetable is steamed potatoes, but rice will do just as well. Sprinkle chopped parsley over the dish before serving.

FOUGASSE A L'HUILE DE NOIX
[Walnut Oil Salted Bread]

SERVINGS: up to 12 COST: inexpensive EXECUTION: tricky . . . knead well!

TOTAL PREPARATION TIME: 20 minutes; rising, 6 hours; baking, 25 minutes

REMARKS ON INGREDIENTS: Buy the French imported walnut oil from a store that sells a lot of it fast, or it is liable to be some-what rancid. Use all the skim accumulated from the making of clarified butter.

3 cups flour (375 g)	*1 cup walnut oil (2½ dl)*
1 envelope dried yeast	*1 cup skim from clarified butter*
2 tsp. salt (10 g)	*(gappe), lukewarm (200 g)*
⅔ cups chopped walnuts	*Water (about ¾ cup or 1¾ dl)*
(100 g)	*Kosher salt, as much as you like*

Take one cup of the flour, mix it with the yeast. Add enough water to make a ball of dough which is not too tough but not too soft either. Fill a large bowl with plenty of lukewarm water. With a knife, cut a cross in the ball of dough and immerse it in the water. It will immediately fall to the bottom of the bowl. When the ball comes floating to the top it will be ready to be added to the bulk of the dough.

In the meantime, put the remainder of the flour on the counter, mix in the chopped walnuts, and make a well. In the well, add the cup of *gappe,* ¼ cup walnut oil, and salt. Gather the flour to make the dough; if it becomes too tough add water, 2 tablespoons at a time. By the time your dough has taken shape the starter will be floating at the water level of the bowl. Gather it, all dripping, in your out-stretched hand. Add it to your dough and knead actively and happily for 10 minutes, no more. The dough is ready to rise when it keeps the imprint of the thumb and is not tacky anymore.

Empty and dry the large mixing bowl where the starter fermented. Rub it with another 2 tablespoons walnut oil. Roll the ball of dough in this oil. Let rise until double in bulk. Punch down and as you punch down add another ¼ cup of walnut oil; the dough will readily absorb it. Let rise a second time until double in bulk and as you punch down, add yet another ¼ cup of walnut oil. Let rise a third time until double in bulk. Punch down and roll out to fit a 14-inch–16-inch pizza pan. The pizza pan should be nice and dull, that means old and well used, or the bottom of the bread will not brown. If you do not have a pizza pan fitting this description, use a nice and black 17-inch x 13-inch jelly roll pan.

Let the dough rise to be as thick as a woman's thumb. Brush the bread with the remaining 2 tablespoons of walnut oil. With your index and middle fingers punch a series of two holes at a time in the bread at 2-inch intervals. Sprinkle with kosher salt and bake in a pre-heated 425° oven until it is a crisp golden brown. This bread deserves the best unsalted butter.

VERJUS

This is a condiment dating from the Middle Ages, if not from the Roman Age. It is ancient and not even made in France nowadays. I have seen it used not only by Victoire for everything (chicken, duck, in salads instead of vinegar) but also by Marie-Charlotte, who was not against drinking a small glass of it as a remedy for diverse health problems.

For alcohol, use if possible pure 90 proof ethyl alcohol. Should you be unable to find this, use imported Italian Grappa or Peruvian Pisco. Both work very well. Pisco is to be found in all serious liquor stores across the country. Victoire used Eau de Vie, the equivalent of the Italian Grappa, or sometimes Armagnac since she had an abundant source of it in one of her brothers. With Armagnac, she made the most fabulous Verjus, for which my mother secured the recipe given here.

2 *lbs. green grapes* (*berries only*), *as green and sour as possible but already juicy* (*1 kg*)	*Sugar* *Alcohol as described above or* *Armagnac* *Wine vinegar*

Select about 30 very large berries and prick them with a fork in 4 different places. Put the berries in a half-gallon jar.

Crush the remainder of the grapes. You can use a blender on medium speed but do not liquefy completely or you will be unable to strain out all the skins. Rinse and squeeze dry a large piece of cheesecloth. Line a strainer with the cheesecloth and strain the grape juice, squeezing well to extract all the juice. Measure it accurately.

For each cup (¼ litre) of grape juice obtained, measure ¼ cup (75 g) of sugar, 2 cups (½ litre) of alcohol and ½ cup wine vinegar (1 generous dl). Dissolve the sugar in the grape juice. Add the alcohol and vinegar; pour over the berries in the half-gallon container. Store in a cool place (60–65° F) for at least 2 months before using. It keeps forever, and is good in all chicken dishes, with ham, with ducks and so forth. A supply made with 1 quart of grape juice, 2 quarts of alcohol and 2 cups of vinegar lasts one year.

PASCADE DE CELEBRATION
[*Holiday Meat Pancake*]

SERVINGS: 6 COST: very reasonable EXECUTION: simple
TOTAL PREPARATION TIME: 45 minutes maximum
BEST SEASON: Year round but tastes best in the fall when all types of greens are available
SUGGESTED WINE: Any ordinary red wine of your choice
REMARKS ON INGREDIENTS: If all the greens are not available, use one cup of any of them.

¼ lb. pancetta, *diced into ¼-inch cubes* (125 g)

1 *clove of garlic, chopped fine*

1 *onion, chopped fine*

¼ *cup walnut oil* (*generous ½ dl*)

¼ *cup each dandelions, swiss chard, sorrel, and Boston lettuce leaves* (*green*)*, chopped fine*

½ *cup each buckwheat and all-purpose white flour* (60 g each)

3 *eggs*

½ *tsp. salt* (2½ g)

Freshly ground pepper from the mill

1½ *cups whole milk* (3½ dl)

¼ lb. *very coarse grated Cantal cheese* (125 g)

Render the *pancetta* cubes in a large 9-inch skillet. Add the garlic; toss for one minute. Add the onion; let sauté until golden. If needed, add one tablespoon of walnut oil and sauté the greens until they are wilted and have rendered their juices. Continue cooking until all the juices have evaporated. Remove to a plate and let cool.

In a bowl, mix the buckwheat and white flours. Add the eggs, the salt and pepper and stir until homogenous. Gradually add the milk to obtain a thin batter. Add the cooled mixture of greens to the batter.

Add another tablespoon or so of walnut oil to the skillet, heat it well and add the batter. Cook over medium heat, letting the liquid batter escape under the portions already coagulated on the bottom of the pan. As soon as the top looks dull and almost solid, turn the pancake over. This is best done by sliding it on a plate first. Then add a last tablespoon of walnut oil to the pan, and invert the pancake back into the frying pan to brown the second side. Let the second side of the pancake brown nicely. While this is happening, sprinkle the top of the pancake with the cheese. By the time the pancake has finished browning, the cheese will have melted. Serve piping hot with a nice salad and a walnut oil dressing.

GARROU DE VEAU EN PISTACHE
[Shank of Veal with Masses of Garlic]

SERVINGS: 6–8 COST: moderately expensive EXECUTION: easy
TOTAL PREPARATION TIME: 1½ hours
BEST SEASON: Fall to spring
SUGGESTED WINE: A Côtes du Rhône, red and potent
REMARKS ON INGREDIENTS: The best *osso bucco* comes from butcher
shops in Italian markets. Make sure however that you buy the
leg *osso bucco;* some butchers zero in on innocents and give
them shoulder shank instead. The leg has one large center bone
full of marrow; the shoulder can be recognized by its smaller
bones with very little marrow in only one.

*3 hind-leg shanks of veal, cut
   across into 3–4 one-inch
   pieces each*
*½ cup walnut oil or other oil
   of your choice, or lard
   (1 generous dl)*
3 large onions, sliced thick
1 large carrot, sliced thick
Bouquet garni

*½ cup dry white wine (1
   generous dl)*
*2–3 cups brown veal stock,
   enough to cover the meat
   (about 5 dl)*
Salt and pepper
4 heads of garlic
Slices of brown bread
Fresh parsley, chopped

Heat the chosen oil or fat in a large braising pot. Brown the pieces
of veal on both sides until deep golden. Remove the meat to a plate
to wait. Add the onions to the same fat in the braising pot; add also
the carrots and *bouquet garni* and toss in the hot fat until golden
brown. Tilt the pan and spoon off as much fat as you can.

Spread the vegetables evenly on the bottom of the pot; add the
pieces of meat. Add the wine; reduce completely over high heat. Add
the veal stock. Slowly bring to a boil.

While waiting for the meat to boil, detach the cloves from the
heads of garlic, crush them with the flat side of a chef's knife blade
and add them to the pot containing the veal. Add salt and pepper.
Cover the meat with a layer of foil. Turn the sides of the foil up to

form an inverted lid which will catch the steam and prevent it from diluting the sauce. Then cover with the pot lid and bake 1 hour to 1 hour and 15 minutes in a preheated 325° oven. The meat is done when it pulls away from the bones and is easily pierced by a skewer that should also come out freely.

Measure the sauce; there should not be more than 1½ cups of very thick juice left. If more is left, pour the liquid into a pan and reduce it. The sauce will need no thickening. Leave the onions and carrots in the sauce, if you desire, or purée them into the sauce, or strain the sauce clear; whatever you like best.

Toast the slices of bread lightly. Put them on a plate and pass them around with the meat dish. Gather all the mashed garlic cloves in a small dish. Serve them separately so your guests can spread them on the toasted bread.

Put the meat on a platter, pour the sauce over it and sprinkle with chopped parsley. Serve with *Truffade* (see page 84).

POURQUI FARCI DE CELEBRATION
[Holiday Stuffed Baby Pig]

SERVINGS: 12 COST: expensive EXECUTION: no problem and fun
TOTAL PREPARATION TIME: 1 hour for preparation, 3 hours for
    baking
BEST SEASON: The Christmas and holiday season
SUGGESTED WINE: Beaujolais
REMARKS ON INGREDIENTS: Suckling pigs are to be found on special
    order from butchers in Italian markets year round. At Christmas time, they are abundant. Shop two days early. For the verbena, use ½ teaspoon from a tea bag of verbena tea.

1 suckling pig, 8 lbs. maximum (*4 kg*)	*1 lb. unsalted fatback, ground* (*500 g*)
2 lbs. lean shoulder of pork, ground (*1 kg*)	*4 eggs*
	Salt and pepper

½ tsp. dried thyme

Verbena (see above)

½ bay leaf, crushed fine

2 TB butter (25 g)

1 lb. spinach, chopped very

fine (500 g)

Juice of one lemon

1 cup water, salted with 1 tsp.

salt (2¼ dl)

Soak the suckling pig in a tubful of cold water for three hours to mellow the skin. Turn often so the skin is softened evenly on both sides.

Mix together the ground pork, the ground fatback, the eggs, about 2 teaspoons salt and 1 teaspoon pepper, the thyme, verbena, and crushed bay leaf. Beat with the electric mixer to homogenize.

Heat the butter in a large frying pan and sauté the chopped spinach, without blanching it, until it has lost all its juices. Add the lemon juice, a pinch of salt and pepper and continue evaporating over high heat until the spinach is dry. Let cool and add to the prepared forcemeat.

Stuff the suckling's cavity with the mixture. Sew the opening closed and set the suckling pig on a roasting pan, the back legs stretched out. Roast 2 to 3 hours in a 325° preheated oven. During the last hour of cooking brush the skin every 10 minutes with the salted water; it makes the skin super crisp and delicious.

There will be lots of gravy. Deglaze it with a small amount of water or stock and skim the fat completely. Serve it in a bowl. For a starch, serve the *pachade* with raisins and walnuts (see page 89) and for a vegetable, baked onions (see page 85), plus a nice crisp, plain salad.

POULET AU VERJUS ET AUX RAISINS
[Sautéed Chicken with Verjus and Raisins]

SERVINGS: 6 COST: inexpensive EXECUTION: easy

TOTAL PREPARATION TIME: Overnight macerating for the raisins, 40 minutes for the cooking.

BEST SEASON: Pleasant year round

SUGGESTED WINE: A Monbazillac or Bergerac chilled properly

REMARKS ON INGREDIENTS: If you do not have Verjus, make ⅔ cup of grape juice with fresh, greenish grapes in the blender.

½ cup dark raisins (100 g)	Salt and pepper
Enough Armagnac to cover the raisins so that they are ¼ inch below the surface of the liquor	⅔ cup Verjus (1¾ dl) (see page 70)
	¼ cup brown veal stock (½ small dl)
¼ cup walnut oil (½ small dl)	¼ cup heavy cream (½ small dl)
6 chicken legs, cut into 6 drumsticks and 6 thighs	

Soak the raisins overnight in the Armagnac to plump them well.

Heat the walnut oil in a large *sauteuse* pan. Sauté the chicken thighs and drumsticks until golden brown. Salt and pepper. Discard the browning oil, add the Verjus, cover the pan, and cook 20 minutes or until tender. Add the raisins with whatever is left of the Armagnac during the last five minutes of cooking.

Remove the cooked chicken to a serving dish together with all the raisins. Add the veal stock and the cream to the sautéing pan and cook together until the sauce coats a spatula by ⅛ inch. Correct the seasoning and strain over the chicken.

Depending on the season, you can serve chestnuts or a plain dish of buttered rice as companion vegetables.

LAPIN AUX NOIX
[Rabbit Stewed with Walnut Sauce]

SERVINGS: 6 COST: moderately expensive EXECUTION: easy
TOTAL PREPARATION TIME: 1½ hours
BEST SEASON: This tastes best when fresh walnuts are still peelable by hand, September–October. Generally a cold-weather dish.
SUGGESTED WINE: A dry white Graves
REMARKS ON INGREDIENTS: You can use walnut meats bought in bags; see below how to peel them. Use a fresh young rabbit

bought in an Italian neighborhood or use frozen rabbit, but defrost it for 2 days in the refrigerator.

1 cup walnut meats (250 g) Bouquet garni
Oil bath for deep frying *2 cloves garlic, mashed fine*
3½ oz. pancetta (*see page* *2 TB chopped parsley*
  66 (115 g) *2 cups brown veal stock, or*
1 young rabbit *other stock of your choice*
Salt and pepper *(4½ dl)*
½ cup dry white wine (1 *½ lb. silverskin onions*
  generous dl) *(250 g)*

Select large walnut meats if possible; they peel more easily. Heat the oil bath. Put the walnuts in the frying basket and immerse the walnuts for 2 to 3 minutes. Empty the walnuts in a tea towel and rub well; the skin will remain attached to the tea towel. Set aside half of the walnut meats. Grind the remainder in the blender.

Dice the *pancetta* into ⅓-inch cubes. Put them in a large *sauteuse* and render them gently until the cracklings are golden and crisp. Remove the cracklings to the plate containing the reserved walnut meats.

Remove and reserve half the fat in the *sauteuse* for later use. Brown the pieces of rabbit lightly, or until golden but not deep brown, on both sides. Salt and pepper the meat. Drain off the browning fat, add the wine and let evaporate completely. Cover the meat with the *bouquet garni,* the garlic, parsley, and the ground walnuts. Pour in the stock until it just covers the meat; add salt and pepper. Cover the *sauteuse,* leaving the lid ½ inch askew. Cook simmering for 20 minutes.

Meanwhile, peel the silverskin onions. Cut a cross in their root so they do not fall apart. Brown them on all sides in the reserved *pancetta* fat. When the rabbit has been cooking 20 minutes, add the browned onions to the *sauteuse* and continue cooking together another 25 minutes.

Do not discard the browning fat, but take the reserved walnut meats and sauté them in it until they are lightly toasted. Dry them in a paper towel.

When the rabbit is done, take a good look at the sauce; it should not be too thin. If it is thinnish (it may be if you use a stock other than brown veal stock), remove the rabbit and onions to a platter. Keep them warm. Reduce the sauce until it is a demi-glaze; you should have about 1½ cups altogether. Remove the *bouquet garni*, but do not strain the sauce. Pour it over the rabbit and sprinkle the stew with the toasted walnuts.

As a second vegetable, serve *Truffade* (see page 84).

ESCALOPES D'AGNEAU A LA LIE DE VIN
[Lamb Scallops with Red-Wine Sediment Sauce]

SERVINGS: 6 COST: expensive EXECUTION: easy

TOTAL PREPARATION TIME: 1 hour; the cooking itself is only 10 minutes.

BEST SEASON: April to September, but feasible year round

SUGGESTED WINE: Of the same origin as the sediment you are using, preferably Médoc or Pauillac

REMARKS ON INGREDIENTS: The *lie* is the sediment of good, old red wine. Victoire had a barrelful of it and used it constantly. Use all the sediments from your great bottles of wine this way. What is left in a bottle after decanting is usually enough. If you have no more than ⅓ of a cup, add the same amount of good red wine from the bottle you will be drinking with dinner. The recipe can be made with ⅔ cup red wine and no sediment.

½ leg of lamb (loin end)
3 shallots, chopped fine
1 clove garlic, chopped fine
2 TB parsley, chopped fine
Walnut oil, or other oil of
*   your choice (olive oil is fine)*
Salt and pepper
½ cup brown veal stock (1
*   generous dl)*

Sediment from one bottle of
*   Grand Bordeaux*
⅓ cup of Médoc or Pauillac
*   red wine, if necessary (see*
*   above) (1 small dl)*
3 TB raw, unsalted butter,
*   very soft*

Remove the fell covering of the lamb and all the fat. The muscles of the leg of lamb will appear neatly separated. Remove each muscle from the bone. Cut each muscle *across the grain* in as many ⅓-inch scallops as you can; flatten them to a thickness of ¼ inch with a meat bat.

Have the shallots, garlic and parsley chopped fine and ready on a small plate.

Heat a film of oil in a large frying pan until it almost smokes. Brown the scallops on one side, turn them over, salt and pepper them and just as soon as the meat juices bead bright red on their surface, remove them to a plate. Keep them warm. This is done very, very, very fast.

In the same frying pan add the shallots, garlic, and parsley. Toss for one minute. Do not let the shallots burn or the dish will be bitter. Add the stock. Reduce, stirring with a spatula, to about 3 tablespoons. Add the sediment and/or wine and reduce by half. To the violently boiling sauce, add the raw butter and whisk well.

Return the scallops to the pan and toss them well in the sauce. There should be very little sauce, just enough to glaze the meat. Correct salt and pepper and serve.

SALADE DE PONOTES A LA CREME
[Lentil Salad]

SERVINGS: 6–8 COST: inexpensive to reasonable EXECUTION: easy
TOTAL PREPARATION TIME: 2 hours to cook, drain, and cool the
    lentils; 10 minutes to put the salad together
BEST SEASON: September through June, but can be used year round
REMARKS ON INGREDIENTS: The best lentils to use for this are the
    true *ponotes,* the tiny green lentils grown and bagged in Le
    Puy (France). They can be found in the best specialty shops.
    The brown lentils are also very good. After you drain the len-
    tils, keep the cooking juices. Blended with cream and chives
    they make a jolly good soup.

1 lb. lentils, cooked and
    drained (450 g)
2 shallots, chopped fine
3 TB fine cut fresh chervil or
    chopped parsley
¾ tsp. salt
Pepper

3 TB wine vinegar
¼ cup heavy cream (75 g)
½ cup walnut oil (1
    generous dl)
6 lettuce leaves (large
    Boston type)

Drain the lentils until very dry.

Prepare the dressing: squeeze the chopped shallots in the corner of a towel to extract the bothersome juices. Put the shallots in a small bowl. Add the chervil, salt, pepper to your taste, and the vinegar. Mix well; without waiting, whisk the cream and walnut oil into the vinegar mixture.

Toss the lentils into the dressing and serve on lettuce leaves. The salad is delicious either lukewarm or well chilled. Adapt the temperature to the season and the weather of the day.

SALADE DE TOMATES AU VERJUS
[Tomato Salad with Verjus or Armagnac]

SERVINGS: 6 COST: reasonable to inexpensive EXECUTION: easy
TOTAL PREPARATION TIME: 20 minutes
BEST SEASON: Exclusively August to late October, when sun-ripened
    tomatoes are available. The other so-called tomatoes are not
    worth spending the Verjus or Armagnac on.

4 large, gorgeous sun-ripened
    tomatoes (500 g)
Verjus or Armagnac (for
    Verjus, see page 70)

Salt
2 shallots, chopped fine
1 TB fresh chives, chopped

Remove the stems of the tomatoes. Immerse the tomatoes for 2 minutes in boiling water, peel them, and slice them into ⅕-inch slices. Arrange them on a platter. Sprinkle them with a maximum of 3 tablespoons Verjus or Armagnac, salt, the shallots (squeezed first in a tea towel to remove the bitter juices), and the chives. Let stand 10 minutes at room temperature to blend the flavors, and then enjoy right away. Waiting any longer brings on juicing of the tomatoes, which loose their soul in the acid Verjus or strong Armagnac.

TOMATES AU SARASSOU
[Tomatoes Filled with Cheese]

SERVINGS: 6 COST: reasonable EXECUTION: easy
TOTAL PREPARATION TIME: 1 day to drip the cheese, 10 minutes
    to put the dish together
BEST SEASON: August through October, when the tomatoes are sun
    ripened and the fresh herbs are still plentiful.

½ lb. creamed small-curd cottage cheese (250 g)	1 shallot, chopped fine
½ cup sour cream (115 g)	1½ tsp. each chopped fresh chervil, chives, tarragon, and parsley
¼ cup heavy cream (70–75 g)	3 TB boiled ham, chopped
¼ tsp. salt	Pepper from the mill
6 smallish tomatoes	6 Boston lettuce leaves

Beat the cottage cheese until the larger grains have turned into smallish ones. Beat in the sour cream. Beat the heavy cream almost stiff. Fold heavy cream into cottage cheese and sour cream. As you fold in the heavy cream, sprinkle the salt over the mixture. Place the mixture in a stainless steel colander lined with cheesecloth. Refrigerate and let drip into a bowl overnight.

The next day remove the stems of the tomatoes, immerse them in boiling water for 2 minutes, and peel them. Empty them carefully of all seeds, water, and pulp.

Squeeze the chopped shallots in the corner of a towel to remove the bothersome juices. Mix the shallots with ¾ of the herbs and the boiled ham. Fold into the dripped cheese mixture.

Fill the tomatoes with the mixture. Sprinkle the top with the remainder of the herbs and serve on lettuce leaves. If refrigerated, these tomatoes keep about 3 hours without bleeding.

PASTISSOUS
[Small Meat and Liver Pâtés]

SERVINGS: 6 COST: reasonable EXECUTION: easy
TOTAL PREPARATION TIME: 2 hours including rest for the pastry
    and baking
BEST SEASON: Serve warm in winter, cold in summer.
SUGGESTED WINE: Ordinary red Côtes du Rhône

PASTRY:
3 cups sifted flour (360–375 g)
¾ cup butter (115–125 g)
1½ tsp. salt (5 g)
3 TB sour cream (30–35 g)
3–4 TB water (5 cl)
1 egg yolk
3 TB milk
FILLING:
2 TB walnut oil, or other oil of your choice
2 onions, chopped fine (100 g)

½ lb. Italian sweet sausage without fennel seeds (250 g)
½ cup dry white wine (1.25 dl)
¼ lb. pancetta, diced into ¼-inch cubes
½ lb. pork liver, diced into ⅓-inch cubes (250 g)
¼ lb. blanched nettle or spinach leaves, chopped (125 g)
¼ tsp. ground nutmeg
½ cup corn flour (75 g)
3–4 eggs
Salt and pepper to taste

First make the pastry. Make a well in the flour. Add the cold butter cut in tablespoon chunks and the salt. Mix the flour and butter with fingertips until the butter is the size of peas. Add the sour cream and mix with the fingertips. Then add as much water as needed for the dough to hold together. *Fraiser* (see page 14) twice and refrigerate at least one hour. Mix together the egg yolk and milk to make a glaze for the pastry. Set aside.

Heat the walnut oil in a large skillet; add the onions and sauté until golden. Add the Italian sausage meat, removing it from the sausage skin. Brown well. Add the wine; let evaporate completely. Remove to a bowl. To the same frying pan add the *pancetta.* Toss it in the hot pan until it starts rendering. Add the liver cubes and toss until they just turn grayish. Remove to the same bowl as the other ingredients; cool and mix thoroughly. To all these ingredients add the blanched greens, nutmeg, corn flour and 3–4 eggs—the forcemeat should not be too liquid. Add salt and pepper to taste. Keep cool.

Cut the ball of pastry into two equal halves. Roll one out ¼ inch thick. Cut at least 6 circles, each 5 inches in diameter. Transfer to a buttered baking sheet. Brush with the pastry glaze. Put a portion of forcemeat about the size of an egg at the center of each circle of pastry. Flatten it to ½ inch thick, leaving ½ inch of pastry free all around. Roll out the second ball of pastry. Cut out as many 5½-inch circles as needed to match the circles cut from the first ball of pastry. Cut a hole in the center of each 5½-inch circle. Cover each garnished base with one of the 5½-inch circles of pastry. Seal the edges well. Brush with the remainder of the egg glaze. Let rest 30 minutes, then bake in preheated 375° oven for 35 to 40 minutes.

Serve lukewarm with a Romaine salad dressed with walnut oil.

POUNTI AUX PRUNEAUX
[Country Pâté with Prunes]

SERVINGS: 12 COST: reasonable EXECUTION: easy
TOTAL PREPARATION TIME: 2 hours
BEST SEASON: A winter or fall dish
SUGGESTED WINE: An ordinary red Côtes du Rhône or a good Beaujolais

1 dozen pitted prunes

3 TB Verjus (see page 70) or Armagnac or any brandy

½ lb. prosciutto ham, ½ lean, ½ fat (250 g)

½ lb. smoked shoulder of pork (125 g)

1 cup sifted all-purpose flour (120–125 g)

4 eggs

1 cup milk (2¼ dl)

1 large onion

2 shallots

1 clove garlic, mashed

1 cup packed chopped swiss chard leaves or spinach leaves

1 TB chopped chives

2 TB chopped parsley

Salt and pepper to taste

2 TB butter

Cut the prunes in half and soak them in the liquor while you prepare the forcemeat.

Grind the prosciutto and smoked shoulder coarse. Mix the flour, eggs, and milk as if you were preparing a crêpe batter. Mix the meats and the batter. Grate the onion and the shallots into the mixture. Add the garlic and all the greens and mix thoroughly. Salt and pepper to your taste. To test the salt level, cook a nugget of the mixture in a frying pan.

Butter a 6-cup soufflé mold with the 2 tablespoons of butter. Fill half the mold with half the forcemeat. Place the prunes on the first layer of forcemeat and push them down into it. Pack the remainder of the forcemeat on top of the prunes. Bake in a preheated 350° oven for 1½ to 2 hours. The top should be dark brown. Do not put under a weight as a terrine usually is, for the fat should be allowed to be reabsorbed into the *pounti* by the time it cools. Serve lukewarm with a Romaine salad dressed with walnut oil.

TRUFFADE DE LA VACHELLERIE
[*Mashed Potatoes with Chards and Cheese*]

SERVINGS: 6 COST: moderately expensive EXECUTION: easy
TOTAL PREPARATION TIME: 25 minutes plus 1 hour to bake the potatoes

BEST SEASON: Fall and winter
SUGGESTED WINE: Any ordinary, dry white wine

*4 large Maine potatoes
(500 g)*
¼ *lb.* pancetta (*125 g*)
*2 cups packed Swiss chard
greens, measured then
chopped*

*½ cup heavy cream (1
generous dl)*
*½ lb. Cantal cheese, grated
very coarse (250 g)*
Pepper from the mill

Wash the potatoes, prick with a needle, and bake for 1 hour in a 400° oven.

Dice the *pancetta* into ¼-inch cubes. Render it slowly in a *sauteuse* pan. When it starts coloring, add the chopped chard. Raise the heat and toss until the greens have exuded all their juices and the liquid has evaporated. Add the cream. Heat slowly and keep hot.

Extract the pulp from the baked potatoes; mash it coarsely with a fork. Add to the greens and cream mixture; stir well over medium heat to homogenize. Gradually add handfuls of cheese until the latter melts into threads. Serve immediately as a main vegetarian course with a simple salad. A slightly acid dressing would be no sin here since the potato dish is quite salty.

OIGNONS AU FOUR
[Baked Onions]

SERVINGS: 6 COST: inexpensive EXECUTION: simple
TOTAL PREPARATION TIME: 1 hour
BEST SEASON: Winter

*About 2 TB unsalted butter
(about 30 g)*
6 large yellow onions
6 small sugar cubes (⅓ inch)

Salt and pepper
*1 cup hot brown veal stock,
or any stock of your choice
(2.25 dl)*

Preheat oven to 325°.

Butter a 9-inch aluminum cake mold. Peel the onions. With a potato peeler or a corer, remove, in one piece, a core 1½ inches long from the center of each onion. Insert one sugar cube, salt, and pepper in the center of the onion. Shorten the end of the core of the onion by ⅓ inch and replace it so that the onion is closed. Put the onions in the cake pan and add the stock. Cover the onions with a buttered parchment paper and put to bake in a preheated oven for about 1 hour. While the onions bake, baste them at regular intervals with the stock at the bottom of the pan. The onions are usually done by the time the veal stock has turned to a glaze.

This is delicious with *Poulet au Verjus* (see page 75) or *Pourqui Farci de Célébration* (see page 74).

POMMES DE TERRE AUX CHAMPIGNONS SAUVAGES
[Potatoes and Wild Mushrooms]

SERVINGS: 6 COST: inexpensive with fresh mushrooms, expensive with dried morels EXECUTION: easy

TOTAL PREPARATION TIME: 30 minutes

BEST SEASON: Follow the mushrooms.

REMARKS ON INGREDIENTS: The following mushrooms are the best for this recipe: Chanterelles (*Cantharellus cibarius*) (July–August); Caesar's mushrooms (*Amanita cesarea*) July–September); Morels (*Morchella esculenta* or *Morchella deliciosa*) (early spring, April–May); Boleti (*Boletus edulis, Boletus badius, Boletus luteus*) (late July–late September, even October); Delicious Lactarius (*Lactarius deliciosus*) (July–September); Fairy Ring mushrooms (*Marasmius oreades*) (spring and fall). Dried imported morels: purchase these from gourmet shops and treat as described below.

THE MUSHROOMS:

2 TB unsalted butter (25 g)

1 lb. fresh mushrooms or 1–2
   oz. dried morels (500 g or
   30–60 g)

Salt and pepper

⅓ cup brown veal stock
   (1 small dl)

THE POTATOES:

½ cup clarified noisette
   butter or goose fat (140 g)

4 large or 6 smaller Maine
   potatoes, sliced in ⅛-inch-
   thick slices (500 g)

First prepare the mushrooms. If they are fresh, simply clean them with a towel, heat 2 tablespoons butter, and quickly sauté them. Add salt and pepper. As soon as the mushrooms have rendered their juices remove them to a plate using a slotted spoon. Add the veal stock to the juices in the pan and reduce to a glaze that will coat a spoon. Return the mushrooms to the pan and mix well. Set aside.

Heat the chosen fat in a large 9- or 10-inch skillet. Add the potatoes; sear them over high heat and then turn the heat down to cook them through to the center. When the potatoes are tender, raise the heat again to color them light golden brown. Remove the potatoes to the pan containing the mushrooms and toss together. Reheat and serve with a plain panfried piece of meat, preferably very simple veal scallops, just salted and peppered.

If you use dried morels, proceed as follows:

Cover the morels with lukewarm water and let them stand 30 minutes to one hour. Remove the morels from the water (Keep it!) and rinse, squeezing gently under running cold water to discard the grit they always contain. Sauté them in butter gently for 3 to 4 minutes. Then add the soaking juices, taking care to leave the dirt at the bottom of the bowl, to the pan together with the veal stock. Reduce the mixture to a glaze over gentle heat, rolling the morels back and forth in it until they are well coated. Proceed then as described above for the blending with the potatoes.

MESCLADE AUX POIRES
[Pear and Fresh Cheese Dessert]

SERVINGS: 6 COST: inexpensive to reasonable EXECUTION: simple
TOTAL PREPARATION TIME: 1 hour with marination of the pears
BEST SEASON: The end of August through early October when the
melting Bartlett pears are in season. But they are also good with
Comices in December and Bosc when these can be ripened perfectly, from August to January. Anjou pears are a bit too non-
commital in taste.

3 very ripe melting pears (375 g)	*½ cup sour cream (60 g)*
2½ TB Verjus or Armagnac (see page 71) (5 cl)	*Honey to taste*
½ cup creamed cottage cheese (75 g)	*¼ cup heavy cream whipped to Chantilly (60 g)*

Peel and core the pears and cut them into quarters. Then cut the
quarters crosswise into thin slices. Toss the pear slices in 2 tablespoons Verjus or Armagnac. Cover with plastic wrap and let steep
in the refrigerator for a minimum of 45 minutes. More marination
will not hurt, up to 2 hours.

Put cottage cheese and sour cream in the blender container and
blend until smooth; empty into a bowl. Sweeten with honey to your
taste but not too heavily, and refrigerate. Sweeten the heavy cream
to your taste with honey and whip to *Chantilly*. Keep refrigerated
while the pears marinate.

To put the dessert together, lightly sweeten the pears, with a bit
of honey again, and toss them well with the cottage cheese and cream
mixture. Pour into a shallow 1-quart serving dish, round or square.
Add the remaining half tablespoon of Verjus to the whipped cream;
whip to mix well. Dribble over the pear-and-cheese mixture. Serve
chilled.

PACHADE LEVEE AUX NOIX ET PETITS RAISINS
["Raised" Raisin and Walnut Pudding Cake]

SERVINGS: 6–12 COST: reasonable EXECUTION: easy
TOTAL PREPARATION TIME: Mixing, 30 minutes; rising, 5 hours;
  cooking, 20 minutes
BEST SEASON: A solid, nouishing winter dessert

½ cup Armagnac or Cognac	1½ cups milk (3½ dl)
(1 generous dl)	½ cup buckwheat flour
½ cup dark raisins (100 g)	(100 g)
1 cup chopped walnuts	½ cup sugar (125 g)
(125 g)	3 eggs
1 cup unsifted flour (125–	1 tsp. salt
150 g)	6 TB melted butter (85 g)
1 envelope yeast	50-50 mixture of heavy and
2 TB honey	sour cream (optional)

Pour the Armagnac or Cognac into a 1-quart bowl. Add the raisins.
Let them plump while the batter rises. Prepare the walnuts in a
cup; set aside.

Mix ½ cup flour, the yeast, honey, and 1 cup milk. Mix well.
Let stand 30 minutes. Then add the remainder of the milk, the
remainder of the flour mixed with the buckwheat flour, the sugar,
the eggs beaten until liquid, and the salt. Blend with a whisk
until strands of gluten clearly string from the whisk. Cover with a
cheesecloth or muslin and let stand 3 to 4 hours. The mixture will
then bubble and start to smell very yeasty and faintly sour. Fold in
4 tablespoons of the melted butter.

Heat a 10-inch iron skillet or 2-quart rectangular pyroceramic
baking dish. Brush with the remaining butter. Pour ½ cup of the
batter on the bottom of the pan or dish; turn the heat off. Let the
pancake set. Sprinkle the raisins and the walnuts over the whole
surface of the pancake. Add to the batter whatever liquor is left in
the bowl where the raisins macerated. Pour the whole amount of
batter in the dish and let stand another hour. Bake 20 to 25 minutes
in a preheated 350° oven.

Serve either sprinkled with confectioners sugar or with a dish of 50 percent heavy cream mixed with 50 percent sour cream.

L'EPASTEE AUX FRUITS
[A Different Fruit Pie]

SERVINGS: 6–8 COST: reasonable EXECUTION: easy
TOTAL PREPARATION TIME: 15 minutes for the preparation, 1 hour
    for the rising, 40–45 minutes for the baking
BEST SEASON: Strawberry season from May through July
REMARKS ON INGREDIENTS: To be prepared only in the summer
    with fragrant, juicy, ripe strawberries. They need not be gor-
    geous looking; they need to be ripe and juicy.

PASTRY:
2 cups whole wheat flour
   (275 g)
⅓ cup lukewarm water
   (1¼ dl)
1 envelope yeast
1 TB honey (20 g)
6 TB melted butter (85 g)
¾ tsp. salt
1½–2 TB white flour (15 g)

FILLING:
1 dozen prunes (pitted, soft
   California-style)
⅓ cup Armagnac or Cognac
   (1 small dl)
Juice and rind of one lemon,
   grated fine
1 quart ripe strawberries
   (500 g)
One 12 oz. jar best-quality sour
   cherry preserves (350 g)

Put the whole wheat flour in a bowl. Make a well; add the lukewarm water and the yeast. Mix well. Add the honey. Mix well again and let stand until the mixture bubbles. Add the melted butter and the salt and mix. Work the dough into a ball.

Sprinkle the white flour on the counter and coat the dough with it. Roll it out as thin as possible (it breaks easily). Then, transfer it to a 9-inch unbuttered pyroceramic pie plate and pat it evenly on the bottom and the sides of the plate no more than ⅛ inch thick. Work from the center of the pie plate out, pushing any excess pastry over the edge of the plate. Roll the excess pastry into a ball and reserve. Let the dough stand one hour. Meanwhile, chop the prunes into ⅓-inch chunks. Pour the Armagnac or Cognac over them. Add the lemon juice and rind and let macerate while the dough rises. Clean the berries.

When the dough has risen properly, it will be ¼ to ⅓ inch thick. Arrange the strawberries on the bottom of the pastry. Mix the prunes with the cherry preserves; pour over the berries.

With the remainder of the dough, make enough ⅓-inch-wide strips to build a lattice top. Bake in a 375° preheated oven, 20 minutes on the bottom shelf and 20–25 minutes on the top shelf of the oven. Let cool completely before serving.

GATEAU AUX NOIX
[Walnut and Honey Cake]

SERVINGS: 12–16 COST: reasonable EXECUTION: easy
TOTAL PREPARATION TIME: 1½ hours including the cooling of the
    cake layers
BEST SEASON: Year round, but better suited to the winter months
REMARKS ON INGREDIENTS: Use natural honey, preferably from
    mountain blossoms.

CAKE:
6 eggs, separated
½ cup honey (300 g)
1 tsp. pure vanilla extract
Pinch of salt
⅔ cup fine, light rye bread-
    crumbs (50 g)
2 cups walnuts, ground
    fine (240 g)
CREAM:
⅓ cup honey (210 g)
1 TB instant coffee dissolved
    in 1 TB water

5 egg yolks
Pinch of salt
¼ lb. plus 4 TB unsalted
    butter at room temperature
    (1¼ cup or 250 g)
DECORATION:
½ cup walnuts, ground
    fine (60 g)
⅓ cup sugar (100 g)
2 TB water
1 drop lemon juice
12 walnut halves

CAKE:

Preheat oven to 325° and butter two 9-inch cake pans. Flour the bottom very lightly.

Mix egg yolks, honey, salt and vanilla. Whip until the mixture is light, extremely foamy and forms a ribbon when lifted from the beaters.

Whip the egg whites until they can carry the weight of a raw egg in its shell without sinking more than ¼ inch. Mix one-quarter of their volume into the lightened egg yolks.

Mix together the breadcrumbs and 2 cups ground walnuts. Slide the remainder of the egg whites onto the yolks. Sprinkle the mixture of nuts and crumbs over the egg whites; fold until all three layers of ingredients are perfectly blended.

Turn half of the batter into each prepared pan and bake in the preheated oven for 35 to 40 minutes. Invert the layers on two cake racks and cool completely.

CREAM:

Bring the honey to a boil in a small pan. Add the coffee dissolved in water to the honey. Place the egg yolks in the small bowl of an electric mixer, add the salt and whip until they start to foam. Pour the honey, without bothering to let it cool, in a steady stream into the egg yolks. Continue whipping until the mixture spins a heavy ribbon and is completely cold. Reduce the speed of the mixer and gradually add the butter to obtain a smooth buttercream.

DECORATION:

Trim the edges of each cake layer if necessary for regularity of shape. Fill the layers with one-third of the cream. Spread a thin layer of cream on the sides and top of the cake and apply the remaining ground walnuts all around the cake. Use a cake comb on the top of the cake to decorate it to your taste. Put the remainder of the cream in a pastry bag fitted with a rosette nozzle. Pipe 12 rosettes around the top of the cake.

Butter a cookie sheet well. Make a small caramel by mixing the sugar, water, and lemon juice in a small pan. Cook over medium heat until it turns light brown. Keep it hot over boiling water. Dip the walnut halves in the caramel to coat them and set them to harden on the prepared cookie sheet. Top each rosette of buttercream on the cake with a walnut half.

MAOUTSA
[Rice and Raisin and Prune Pudding]

SERVINGS: 6–8 COST: inexpensive EXECUTION: easy
TOTAL PREPARATION TIME: 2 hours including baking
REMARKS ON INGREDIENTS: Be sure to use Italian arborio short-
  grained rice.

½ cup Italian arborio short-
  grained rice (150 g)
1 quart boiling water (1
  litre)
⅓ cup dark raisins (50 g)
6 soft, pitted prunes, diced
2 TB Armagnac, Cognac,
  or rum
1 quart scalded milk (9 dl)
⅔ cups breadcrumbs from
  dark, seedless rye bread
  (50 g)

½ cup sugar plus ¼ cup
  sugar (125 g plus 65 g)
Pinch of salt
3 eggs
1 drop lemon juice
2 TB cold water (½ cl)
⅓ cup sour cream (75 g)
⅔ cup heavy cream (150 g)
1 TB butter

Have a 1-quart charlotte mold ready.

Immerse the rice in the boiling water and simmer until tender. Meanwhile macerate the raisins and diced prunes in the chosen liquor.

When the rice is tender, drain the water, add 2 cups of the scalded milk to it and let simmer until the rice has absorbed all the milk but is not a solid mass of starches. Add the other two cups of milk, the breadcrumbs, ½ cup sugar, the salt, and mix well. Beat the eggs and mix into the rice base. Add the raisins and prunes.

In a small pan put the remaining sugar with the lemon juice and water. Cook to a dark caramel. Pour the caramel on the bottom of the charlotte mold, coat it well and turn it upside down until the caramel hardens. Butter the inside of the mold not coated with caramel. Pour the pudding into the mold and bake in a hot water bath placed in a 325° oven for 30–35 minutes or until a skewer inserted two-thirds of the way to the center of the pudding comes out hot and dry.

Let cool to very lukewarm in the water bath and invert onto a round platter. Serve the lukewarm pudding with both creams mixed, unsweetened, and chilled.

PRUNEAUX A L'ARMAGNAC
[Prunes in Armagnac]

SERVINGS: use one or two prunes per serving COST: expensive, a good idea for Xmas presents EXECUTION: simple
REMARKS ON INGREDIENTS: Use *unpitted* best-quality prunes. You may also use Cognac or brandy.

1 lb. best-quality large prunes   1 bottle Armagnac

Put the prunes in a fancy glass container, pour the Armagnac over them. *Do not use any sugar.* The custom is to "do" the prunes around November, when the first prunes from "this year's" crop are put on the market, and to keep them aging until Christmas "a year from now."

Henriette

———— 🌹 ———— 🌹 ————

NORMANDY

1939

W E T R A V E L E D in a Peugeot 5HP which my father considered the luxury of his life.

No *autoroutes* existed at that time in France. One reached Deauville in those days by *routes nationales* of diverse numbers. Slowly, from Evreux to Lisieux, then Lisieux to Deauville, and lastly, up the hill of narrow National 813, one inched from Deauville to Blonville, the final destination, the village where Henriette lived. Either one left Paris after work on Friday afternoon and reached 813 in a glory of sun setting into the Channel, or one got up around 4 A.M. on Saturday morning, "in the middle of the night," as it always seemed to me, and had breakfast in the small town of La Rivière Thibouville in the heart of Normandy.

At the time La Rivière Thibouville was nothing but a few houses encircled by a lazy little river in which the women were invariably doing their wash. A puny bistro was our stop. The atmosphere in there was blue with the mingled smoke of Gauloises, Gitanes, and Celtiques, and the smells of horse manure and fresh mud mingled with those of manly sweat provided an odoriferous background to large bowls of *café au lait* for Maman and me and *café* "baptized" with Calvados for Papa. The brioches—they were called *fallues*— were enormous, lovely, shiny crowns which, when broken, released a whiff of buttery, yeasty perfume. One's fingers were coated instantly with butter, and the silk paper the baker's wife had wrapped around the golden loaves had to be turned into a napkin.

Papa loved to get into conversations with the Calvados-loving farmers. Politics was often discussed with a passion so intense that Maman and I would leave to enjoy the outside. The small river may have been the Risle, or its smaller affluent the Charentonne. I cannot, some thirty-five years later, remember for sure and checking a large-scale map of Normandy would just make those warm memories all too scientific.

The village smelled of fresh grass and of freshwater fish; it was not rare to see minnows nervously jumping around the pillars of the old decaying wooden bridge. I can remember vividly the sun passing through the emerald green cathedral of a weeping willow and illuminating the sandy bottom of the riverbed with the fire of a thousand minute diamonds.

I cannot remember that my father ever came out of the bistro in anything but a state of political excitement and, knowing that sitting in the front seat of the car meant listening forever to a detailed account of why the men of La Rivière Thibouville were all too Catholic, I requested to sit in the spider, the backseat of the 5HP, where I would freeze more often than not, but from which I saw everything and did not have to listen to meaningless adult conversation.

From La Rivière Thibouville on, the countryside is nothing, even to this day, but pure unadulterated Normandy countryside which, with the variations of the seasons, offers multiple pleasures to eyes and nose. In the springtime, the apple trees are indescribably lovely with millions of blossoms giving off their delicate fragrance into the fresh air. In the summer it smells of plain grass, cows, and the warm air rising from the ground. But the great feast for the nostrils comes in the fall, when the apples are ripe and the whole countryside is thick with the scent of fresh fruit, cider, rotten apples, apple butter.

Apples, apples, apples, in the air and on the ground, puny and red-cheeked, golden-flecked, ugly to our modern eye which is by now used to standardized, technological fruit . . . but full of the promise of apple butter, jelly, cider, Calvados, and apple sugar.

We reached Lisieux very quickly and by the time we reached Pont L'Evêque, that was it, we were almost there. It was a ritual to make a stop in Canapville to pick up a couple of Pont L'Evêque cheeses for Henriette, who was waiting up there in Blonville for them almost as much as for us. The farmer's wife knew us and had yet another cup of coffee ready for us. I loved to admire the old house, built around 1650 in the old Tudor style, that bore the lovely name of Maison à Colombages. On our way back we would stop there again to bring two of Henriette's homemade Camemberts as a payment for the Pont L'Evêque.

The trip from Pont L'Evêque to Blonville was an eight-mile joyride through the busy streets of Deauville and up the hill along the Channel; a left turn onto a side street that climbed the western slope of Mount Canisi took us to the top of a plateau full of apple trees and there was Henriette's house. I have seen that small farm in all seasons, through the mists of winter, in the golden glory of fall, amid the apple blossoms in April, and yet if I were to see it again, I would wish for a Whitsunday in mid-June to smell again the thousands of roses that clung to the front wall of the old building. It was so very old even then, and it still stands—having withstood it all, the years of disrepair, the cannons of war and God knows how many passing armies from those of Viking Rollo to those of Rommel and Eisenhower.

It is a one-story, thatch-roofed building with a single-windowed attic that steadily regurgitates hay onto the ground. The roof has none of the brushed English appearance; it is bristly, with unruly grass blades sticking up rebelliously.

Henriette always appeared on the doorstep in a blue-and-white checkered apron, her hands always busy knitting or sewing. She did not look typically Normande. She had dark hair and dark eyes, and only her vividly colored cheekbones could authenticate her Viking origins. Tall, erect and as straight as a poplar, she never stopped working. Ever since she had been a widow, which was a very long time, she had raised foster children. Behind the corner of her apron, two little eyes were always peeking. Every year the child's hair color changed, for every year there was a new four-year-old to replace the sixteen-year-old who had said good-bye to Henriette in June and left to blend into society. On the day of Henriette's funeral, twenty of the adults present had been her "children."

Living with Henriette was a constantly renewed adventure. She was up at dawn and busy until late at night. It never seemed as if she was doing anything, although the cows, Rosette and Rosalie, two authentic Normande brown-and-white beauties with *lunettes* eyes, were milked every day. With their milk, Henriette produced about ten Camemberts a week that fed her constantly hungry household. If in the summer months the ladies in the barn produced more milk, the production would rise to fifteen cheeses, and there would be one or two left over for friends, or to exchange at the Trouville market for an old hen for an economical stew. It was Henriette who taught me to milk a cow and I remember fondly the spray of warm milk all over my face as I pressed on the udder, obviously missing the pail I was nervously squeezing between my knees.

Many times I looked at Henriette while she was preparing the Camembert. She heated the milk to the temperature of her wrist and dribbled rennet into it to make it curdle. After the milk had curdled, she would ladle it into molds six inches high and perforated to let the whey escape. She had those molds set on a table covered with reeds. Every fall she took the whole family to collect these reeds from a marsh down the hill between sea and land. A day or so later, Henriette would unmold the cheeses, salt them, and sprinkle them with something mysterious that she called her "favorite perfume." I did not understand until much later that only then was she really making Camembert, by sprinkling a mixture of water and mold over the perfectly white cakes.

The room where the cheeses dripped and ripened was filled with dairy smells that my young nose did not always appreciate fully. But in days of homesickness I often long for those familiar odors. It was as warm in there as in a greenhouse. The floor was covered with hay and the single window conscientiously closed against the freshness of the brisk Normandy air. The heat was naturally produced by Rosette and Rosalie living and ruminating peacefully next door. When the cheeses were dry and had shrunk to what we know as Camembert cheese, Henriette would remove them to her *haloir*. This was a sort of cellar, cool, dark, but not quite low enough into the ground to be a cellar. It smelled frankly of Camembert. It took just about six weeks to develop the Camemberts. Occasionally, when the cheeses were ready for consumption, we discovered that some of them had developed a furry appearance, were covered with what Henriette called *poil de chat*—and indeed the hair was sometimes as long and silky as the fur of a baby kitten. She carefully scraped that off before putting the cheese on the breakfast table with a huge loaf of the slightly grayish solid bread from the baker down in Blonville.

Henriette had *crème fraîche* to make all the *crème fraîche* doers, makers, and fabricators in America drool. It was light and almost liquid when she lifted it from the milk pails every morning. Within a day or so, it would thicken into an ivory-yellow mass that, spread over a slice of warm country bread, was supposed to be responsible for all the lovely pinkish complexions in Henriette's household.

In those days, the Channel was unpolluted. At low tide, Henriette would send us down to the beach with pails for cockles, the large mussels the Normandy people call *caieux* and *flions*. The continental shelf in the area is endless and one can walk on it, at low tide, for a good three-quarters of a mile. And what can be found there! For *caieux* one had to go out on the rocks on the north beach, almost at the limit of Trouville, and we were warned repeatedly to move away from there just as soon as the sea lapped the very first rock, or we would run the danger of being trapped and drowning. By then, though, the pail was full of nice, huge mussels that would soon be smothered with Henriette's luscious cream.

We came home through the Blonville beach, stopping to dig for cockles wherever the sand showed an air hole. The small, ribbed clam typical to Channel waters makes the best soup when steamed open and mixed with cream, shallots, and parsley. Most fun were the *flions*. I have seen some of those little, nearly rectangular, clams rolling onto the beach with the surf on the coast of Maine, but no one pays attention to them on this side of the ocean because they are too small. On the Blonville beach, full of the nicest shells of huge cockles and razor clams, the *flions* roll in with the oncoming tide by the millions. They are accompanied by tiny *étrilles* crabs and tiny starfish. All one has to do is bend down and pick. Was it ever a thrill; we came home with buckets full of them.

Every Sunday we went down to the Trouville market. It is still there, just as it was, still colorful, still full of ruddy Normand faces, still loud with the anguished cries of chickens held upside down by powerful hands and full of the gentler cooing of pigeons, quivering in cages.

The whole *département* of Calvados was there for sale: butter, butter, butter, creams of all colors, smells, and tastes. There were Camemberts and Pont l'Evêques, and fresh *petits Suisses* to eat on light brown bread with a pinch of salt and pepper. There were apples of all sizes, breeds, and dimensions. And way back, at the other end of the street, by the pier that overlooks the River Dives as it blends with the Channel, were the few stalls of the fish market. Any fish lying there had been swimming in the Channel around 4 A.M. that morning. This is sole country—Channel sole, not only Dover sole, as our British friends would like us to believe. There was grey sole, lemon sole, John Dory, turbot, and brill, plus the more plebeian mackerels and *daurades,* and shrimp, gray and alive and jumping if the weather was mellow but stiff and sluggish if it was cold. Only one shrimp can compare with the Channel gray shrimp and I have used it later in this chapter to duplicate Henriette's recipes. It is the small, deep-water shrimp of Maine (*Pandalus borealis*). Henriette would take a large frying pan and heat some butter in it until it turned russet; then in went the shrimp and her ivory-colored cream. What a messy, delicious, and happy feast that was for a bunch of loud kids!

If Henriette was, as she used to say, *argentée,* that is, if she had a little more money than usual, she would have a special Whitsunday dinner. She would buy a few sole and go about half a mile down the road from her farm to collect a handful of wild asparagus from a sand bed only she knew of. Out came the cream plus, to be outlandish, a piece of orange rind. This was because one day in a restaurant she had had an orange sauce on asparagus. It took me twenty years to realize that Henriette had been quite a cook. I distinctly remember a conversation around a small jar of fresh caviar that one of her sons had been given as a gift and had brought to her, puzzled as to what to do with it. Henriette had not hesitated. She dug a bottle of Champagne out of her cellar, bought a few scallops and improvised the most magnificent butter sauce, to which she added the caviar.

Henriette could improvise many dishes. After boiling her milk, as she used to put it, "to kill the bacteria," she would let it build a heavy head of cooked cream. She lifted it while still lukewarm, mixed it with "enough" flour and "enough" sugar, and a pinch of vanilla and baked for us the most delicious cookies. Or, she would make shortbread shaped like pettycoat tails, an ancient gift of the Vikings to the cooks of Normandy.

Come October, when the apple trees were bearing fruit, Henriette made cider. She always gave a barrel away to her neighbor, old Lucien, who returned it in the form of five litres of Calvados. For us children, there was apple candy rolled in coarse, crystallized sugar and made out of nothing but solidly reduced applesauce mixed with butter, Calvados, lemon rind, and a bit of cinnamon. For this Henriette only used Russet apples because they candied gloriously.

When Lucien slaughtered a pig it was Henriette who helped him dispatch the poor animal and was the creator of his renowned blood pudding. He was so well known at the Trouville market for his pudding that his supply went for a premium price within half an hour of his arrival at his stall. Henriette also cured his hams, mostly in salt mixed with a bit of lavender and thyme, but one or two of them would always be cured in hay. After salting the ham for about a week, she would scrape the salt away from the surface of the meat, wrap the ham in semi-dry hay selected carefully from her loft, and keep it wrapped until the hay had dried out completely. This took another four to five days. Then, a fragrant bath of thyme and bay leaves infused in boiling water would be prepared and Henriette would remove the hay and wash the ham carefully in the pungent water. Finally she would hang it to dry and smoke in the recesses of that great big chimney in her kitchen where it ripened peacefully for feasts to come.

Winter in Blonville dragged along with Bovarian melancholy and Henriette and her brood welcomed the weekends, when we Parisians would come to relax with big feasts in mind. The feast of the week started on Sunday at one o'clock and never ended much before seven o'clock at night; only one meal was served, which covered most of the day and after which the Parisians would leave to face again the ride to Paris through the winter night. These rides were more often than not true joyrides, full of songs and laughter.

For Henriette thought nothing of preparing her favorite *papin,* a soup of shallots and cream, or a salmon soup in the summer with a dish of mussels, unless it was oysters brought from Ouistreham or some fillets of sole positively floating in the most beautiful cream sauce. Then came the first *trou Normand;* a nice solid shot of Calvados smack in the middle of the meal, to reopen the stomach to more of that silky-tasting Normand food. . . . Not only were the stomachs reopened, but dispositions were also lifted, tongues untied and laughter released. After two or three *trous Normands,* politics lost all seriousness, the future was rosy, Munich, Hitler, and Chamberlain were altogether forgotten, and strength was unknowingly gathered for the war that was to come.

Henriette would be heard saying: "Eat, my loves, eat; let's have a lovely time, let's all have fun," and with that she went on depositing several chickens or an enormous *pirotte* (goose) on the table, the latter stuffed chock-full with apples or celery or fennel. Often there was a pork roast stuffed with pistachios. Or having sent one of us children to pick watercress at the creek down the road, she would serve juicy lamb chops coated with a cream sauce flavored with the spicy leaves of the watercress. Or, if old Lucien had just slaughtered a calf there was a blanquette of veal with leeks and tiny onions, or simple tender *escapoles à la crème.* The vegetables were plentiful: carrots with bacon, a large dish of Brussels sprouts sautéed in *graisse Normande,* that old-fashioned frying mixture of rendered kidney suet mixed with lard and butter; there may have also been apple chunks or a pie made with cauliflower and Brussels sprouts.

The meal ended up with Henriette's *pommée,* an apple tart unlike any apple tart ever. It was a shell of puff pastry filled with an apple Bavarian cream and covered with a mass of candied apples flambéed in Calvados. Sometimes the meal ended with a cherry tart, or that classic of Normandy, the *bourre-goule,* which is nothing but a variation on the favorite rice cake of classic French cuisine. But a *bourre-goule à la Henriette* was something else. It was so light and so lovely that one stuffed one's face with the greatest pleasure ever— without noticing that it was rich, rich and ever so rich.

Whenever we left for home, Henriette gave us, besides the two Camemberts for her friend in Canapville, one for our own table plus *roulettes au Camembert,* lovely concoctions filled with Camembert, or maybe a terrine of what she called her "unrefined" pâté, which she prepared with the livers of all the ducks and chickens passing through her busy kitchen. Unrefined indeed!

Those were the days, my friends, the days of fun, of love, of kindness, and of carefree laughter; the days that were never to be again, for soon the war broke out and when it ended, Henriette was no more. She had been taken away by the cruelest of sicknesses. Only her farm survives, offering, to this day, love and warmth amid the apple trees.

SOUPE DE SAUMON
[Salmon Soup]

SERVINGS: 6 COST: moderately expensive EXECUTION: easy
TOTAL PREPARATION TIME: 1 hour
BEST SEASON: Salmon season, end of May to September
SUGGESTED WINE: None
REMARKS ON INGREDIENTS: The fish stock or fumet should ideally
  be made with the heads of one or two salmons, but they are not
  easy to find. Use an ordinary fish stock made with flounder bones

and heads, whiting bones and heads or any of the sole family fishheads and bones.

1 quart fish fumet (1 litre)　　*1 TB tomato paste (5 g)*
½ cup butter (100–110 g)　　*2 TB small capers (15 g)*
⅔ cup flour (75–80 g)　　　*½ TB each: chopped chervil,*
Salt and pepper　　　　　　　*chives, tarragon, and parsley*
1 cup heavy cream (225 g or　*½ lb. raw salmon meat, free of*
*　2¼ dl)*　　　　　　　　　　*　skin and bones, cut into*
⅓ cup sour cream (80 g or　　*　⅓-inch cubes*
*　1 small dl)*　　　　　　　　*6 slices oven-dried French bread*

Bring the fumet to a boil. Melt and heat the butter and add the flour to make a roux; cook 5 minutes. Remove the pot from the heat. Whisk in the fumet and bring back to a simmer. Skim the worst of the scum from the top of the sauce for about 15 minutes. Add salt and pepper.

Mix the heavy cream, sour cream, and tomato paste. Add some of the hot sauce to the mixture, then reverse the procedure and add the mixture to the bulk of the fish sauce. Add capers and fine herbs and bring just below the boiling point. Salt and pepper the raw salmon cubes; add them to the hot soup. Reheat the soup without boiling. Correct the seasoning. Place each slice of bread in a soup plate or bowl. Ladle the soup over the bread. Serve immediately.

LE PAPIN A L'ECHALOTE
[Bread and Shallots Soup]

SERVINGS: 6 COST: inexpensive EXECUTION: easy
TOTAL PREPARATION TIME: 45 minutes
BEST SEASON: This is a winter stick-to-the-ribs concoction.
SUGGESTED WINE: None
REMARKS ON INGREDIENTS: The shallots may be replaced by scal-
　lions or leeks.

4 TB butter (50 g)

⅔ cup, or about 20 large bulbs, shallots, chopped coarse

⅔ cup whole milk (1½ dl)

6 slices of French bread, day old and crust removed, ½ inch thick

2 cups heavy veal or chicken stock (5½ dl)

Salt and pepper

⅔ cup heavy cream (115 g or 1½ dl)

⅓ cup sour cream (80 g or 1 small dl)

⅓ cup chopped fresh parsley

Heat the butter. Add the shallots and toss briefly in the hot butter without letting the vegetables color at all. Meanwhile, soak the French bread slices in the milk and let stand 10 minutes. Beat with a whisk to obtain a purée (this can also be done in the blender). Mix the bread purée with the stock. Add this mixture to the shallots and simmer together 15 to 20 minutes. Salt and pepper. Mix sour cream and heavy cream and add to the soup. Add the parsley. Reheat well. Correct the seasoning and serve very hot.

PANNEQUETS AU SAUMON
[Crêpes Filled with Salmon Mousseline]

SERVINGS: 6 COST: expensive EXECUTION: semi-difficult

TOTAL PREPARATION TIME: 2 hours. The crêpes may be prepared and filled as long as one day ahead of time and baked 20 minutes before serving.

BEST SEASON: During the salmon season, May to September

SUGGESTED WINE: Muscadet

SALMON MOUSSE FILLING:

1 lb. salmon meat, without skin or bones (450–500 g)

1 egg

1 egg white

1 tsp. salt (5 g)

½ tsp. ground white pepper (2 g)

½ cup raw unsalted butter (110 g)

2 cups heavy cream (450 g or 5 small dl)

CREPE BATTER:

¾ cup sifted flour (90 g)

3 eggs

½ tsp. salt (2.5 g)

1 cup milk (2¼ dl)
4 TB melted unsalted butter
(50 g)
2 TB chives, chopped (15 g)
SAUCE:
2 TB unsalted butter (30 g)
1 onion, chopped fine

3 shallots, chopped fine
2 TB cider vinegar
½ cup dry cider, or white wine
3 cups heavy cream
Salt and pepper
2 level TB sour cream
Clarified butter

TO MAKE THE SALMON MOUSSE:

Clean the fish meat. Make sure that it is free of skin and bones and that the brownish fatty tissues which line the skin and cover the fillets of the salmon have been removed completely. Their taste is strong and oily and damages the final taste of the mousseline. Cut the fish meat into ½-inch cubes. Beat together the egg and the egg white until liquid. Using one-third of it as liquid, purée one-third of the fish in the blender. The purée is ready when it is perfectly smooth, elastic, and shiny and falls off the sides of the blender container without sticking. Repeat this blending and puréeing operation twice more with the remaining two-thirds of the fish.

Strain the purée through a stainless steel conical strainer using a wooden spatula or through a drum sieve using either a pestle or a plastic pastry scraper. This straining may be skipped if it scares you but it definitely gives the fish a much better and finer texture. Cover the purée with a plastic wrap and refrigerate for one hour. After the hour, using the electric mixer, cream the butter with the salt and pepper; gradually add the fish purée. When the fish purée is mixed thoroughly with the butter, turn the mixer speed to low and very slowly add the two cups of heavy cream.

TO MAKE THE CREPES:

Make a well in the flour; add the eggs, lightly beaten, and the salt. With a whisk, stir the flour gradually into the liquid egg until the flour has been absorbed and the mixture shreds when falling from the whisk. Gradually beat in the milk until liquid is smooth; beat in the cooled melted butter. Strain the batter into a bowl and let stand at least fifteen minutes. Add the chives. Make one dozen crêpes using, preferably, a No. 18 crêpe pan.

TO MAKE THE SAUCE:
Heat the butter and sauté the onion and shallots very quickly. Add the vinegar and dry cider or white wine and a pinch of salt and pepper. Reduce to a tablespoon. Pour the heavy cream into another saucepan and reduce it by one-half to two-thirds, whisking at regular intervals. When the cream coats a spoon by $\frac{1}{10}$ inch, add the sour cream. Blend the vinegar reduction with the cream reduction. Correct the seasoning and keep warm. Do not strain.

TO PUT THE DISH TOGETHER:
Divide the salmon mousseline into twelve equal parts. Fill the center of each crêpe with one tablespoon of the mixture. Cut the ends of each crêpe; it will become a *pannequet* and look straight and elegant at each end. Brush one or two baking dishes with clarified butter. Line each dish with the filled *pannequets*. Brush the top of each *pannequet* with clarified butter; cover lightly with a parchment paper and bake 20 to 25 minutes in a preheated 325° oven.

To serve, spoon half the vinegar sauce on top of the *pannequets* and pass the remainder of the sauce in a gravy boat.

COQUILLES SAINT JACQUES AU CAVIAR
[Bay Scallops with Caviar Butter]

SERVINGS: 6 COST: very expensive EXECUTION: tricky; review the
    techniques of *beurre blanc*
TOTAL PREPARATION TIME: 35 minutes
BEST SEASON: This is a winter dish especially good when the bay
    scallops are in season, from January to March.
SUGGESTED WINE: The best whites of France, from Champagne to
    Montrachet
REMARKS ON INGREDIENTS: If Calvados is unavailable, do not sub-

stitute Apple Jack here but replace it with a good Fine Champagne or a well-aged Armagnac. Deep-sea scallops may also be used. Slice them in ¼-inch slices before panfrying. Use only true imported caviar. If you cannot afford it, omit it; the sauce will still be good.

1½ lbs. bay scallops (750 g)
⅔ cup fish fumet (1½ dl)
⅔ cup Champagne brut, or an
   excellent dry white wine
   (1½ dl)
3 TB shallots, chopped
Salt and pepper
½ tsp. potato starch (1 g)

¼ cup heavy cream (55 g or
   ¾ dl)
½ lb. unsalted raw butter
   (225–250 g)
1 oz. Calvados, Cognac, or
   Armagnac
1–2 oz. Beluga Malossol caviar
Lemon juice to your taste

Carefully remove the tough little ligament attached to the side of each scallop. Otherwise, it toughens while cooking and interferes with the softness of the scallop meat. Wash the scallops; pat them dry.

Place fish fumet, Champagne, chopped shallots, and a pinch of salt and pepper into a 9-inch frying pan. Slowly reduce to ¼ cup. Mix potato starch and cream and stir into the base of reduced wine until thickened. Bring to a high boil and whisk in all but 2 tablespoons of the raw butter. Strain into a clean saucepan; keep warm.

Do not clean the frying pan but leave it on the stove and add the remaining two tablespoons of butter. By the time the butter is hot, the remainder of the sauce will have turned to a light brown glaze. Add the scallops, toss them over high heat until they appear milky white; this should not require more than two minutes. Salt and pepper lightly. Heat the Calvados or other chosen spirit in a small pan, ignite and pour flaming into the pan of scallops. Shake over high heat until the flames die. Remove the scallops to a warm shallow dish. Keep warm. Reduce the juices in the pan, over high heat, to about 2 tablespoons of glaze. Strain into the butter sauce. Add the caviar to the butter sauce. Correct the seasoning by adding salt, if necessary, and pepper. Add a few drops of lemon juice. Should the caviar make the sauce a bit too salty, rebalance the taste by adding as much lemon juice as necessary. Serve on warm plates.

This dish does not wait, but is waited for by guests already sitting at the dinner table.

MAQUEREAUX AU FENOUIL
[Mackerels in Fennel Sauce]

SERVINGS: 6 COST: reasonable EXECUTION: very easy
TOTAL PREPARATION TIME: 30 minutes
BEST SEASON: All through the winter months
SUGGESTED WINE: Dry French or English cider, Muscadet
REMARKS ON INGREDIENTS: Other fish that are excellent prepared
    in this manner are: bluefish, butterfish, swordfish steaks, red
    snapper fillets, and pompano fillets.

6 medium-size mackerels
1 cup heavy cream (225 g or
  2¼ dl)
1 cup fresh breadcrumbs
  (100 g)
Salt and pepper

2 tsp. fennel seeds, uncrushed
  (5 g)
1 large onion, chopped (50 g)
1 TB butter (15 g)
½ cup dry white wine or dry
  cider (1 generous dl)
A few drops of lemon juice

Cut the head of each fish off. Cutting along the backbone, separate the fillets from the backbone on each side. Pull the backbone off and discard all the viscera. The fish will appear butterflied. Wash very carefully; pat dry. Brush a thin layer of heavy cream over each. Salt and pepper. Mix the breadcrumbs with some salt and pepper and sprinkle each butterflied fish with an equal amount of breadcrumbs.

Put ½ cup of cream in a small pot; add the uncrushed fennel seeds and reduce to ¼ cup of liquid. In another pot, sauté the onion lightly in the tablespoon of butter. Add the cider or wine, salt and pepper. Reduce by one-half. Blend the wine reduction with the cream reduction. Do not strain. Correct the seasoning and keep warm. Should the sauce have an edge of sweetness, add a few drops of lemon juice.

Dribble what is left of the cream over the mackerel fillets and broil 5 to 6 minutes. Salt and pepper after broiling. Spoon an equal amount of sauce on each mackerel and serve piping hot.

PAUPIETTES DE FILETS DE SOLES AUX ASPERGES
[Fillets of Sole and Asparagus]

SERVINGS: 6 COST: expensive EXECUTION: semi-difficult
TOTAL PREPARATION TIME: 1 hour including the making of the fish fumet, the blanching of the asparagus and the cooking of the fish
BEST SEASON: March through early June
SUGGESTED WINE: A Meursault family wine, not the best though
REMARKS ON INGREDIENTS: This recipe can be executed with any of the flatfish family (*Pleuronectidae*), the best being grey sole and West Coast sand dab. If using summer flounder fillets, cook at high temperature for a very short time. Use the asparagus stems for a salad.

3 medium-size grey sole	10 TB unsalted butter (135 g)
1½ cups dry white wine (3½ dl)	1 tsp. orange rind, grated fine (2 g)
3 cups water (7 dl)	6 egg yolks
2 onions, chopped coarse (100 g)	½ cup heavy cream (1 generous dl)
Bouquet garni, rather large	Lemon juice
18 tiny asparagus, peeled, cut 1½–2 inches long, including the spears	

Fillet the sole or have the fish merchant do it for you and give you the heads and bones of the fish. Discard the skins.

TO PREPARE THE FISH FUMET AND PAUPIETTES:
Place 1 cup wine, the water, onions, and *bouquet garni* in a small stock pot. Add the fish bones. Bring rapidly to a boil. Reduce the heat

and simmer 35 minutes. Strain. Meanwhile, peel and blanch the asparagus tips very quickly in lots of salted boiling water. You want them to remain bright green and very crisp. Drain and cool. Wash the fillets of sole carefully; pat them dry. Score the side that was originally against the skin lightly and diagonally across the fibers with a paring knife; salt and pepper the same side. Place 3 of the asparagus tips at the thick end of each fillet. Roll the tips into each fillet. Wrap the thin end of each fillet carefully around the fillet so it adheres tightly without a toothpick. Cut the asparagus ends so they are hidden in the center of each fillet.

With 1 tablespoon butter, grease a baking dish. Set the rolled fillets in the dish. Mix ½ cup wine, ½ cup of the prepared fish fumet, and the orange rind with a pinch of salt and pepper. Pour at the bottom of the baking dish. Cover the fish with a parchment paper well coated with another tablespoon of butter. Bake 12 minutes in a preheated 375°–400° oven. Remove from the oven and keep warm. The fish will finish cooking while waiting for its sauce.

TO MAKE THE SAUCE:
Pour the cooking juices of the fish into a 1-quart pot; reduce to ¼ cup. Lower the temperature under the pot to very moderate. Whisk in the egg yolks one by one. While the pot remains over low heat whisk quickly until the bulk of the yolk is thick, foamy, and very, very pale yellow. Still keeping the pot over low heat, gradually whisk in the heavy cream. While you add the cream, melt the remaining butter and also whisk it into the sauce very gradually. Correct the seasoning of the sauce; add as much lemon juice as you desire. Strain over the fillets of fish. Serve promptly.

CREVETTES A LA POELE
[Panfried Shrimp]

SERVINGS: 6 COST: reasonable EXECUTION: easy
TOTAL PREPARATION TIME: 10 minutes
BEST SEASON: February–March, when Maine shrimp is in season

SUGGESTED WINE: Muscadet, any lesser-breed Chablis, still Champagne, or Alsatian Riesling

REMARKS ON INGREDIENTS: Use the whole shrimp; head, tails and all, as sold in New England fish markets. Small San Francisco Bay shrimp will also be delicious prepared this way. Headless shrimp still in the shell will still be good although far less tasty. Peeled and cleaned shrimp as sold in supermarkets can be used, but the result will be "just another" shrimp dish.

2 lbs. Maine shrimp, unshelled and uncleaned (1 kg)	Pepper from the mill
	2/3 cup heavy cream (1 3/4 dl)
2 TB butter (30 g)	1/3 cup sour cream (1 small dl)
No salt or very little	

Sort the shrimp, one by one, to be certain you discard the baby sole or flounder, the baby starfish and the crabs that are always caught with them. *Do not wash* the shrimp. Heat a large frying pan very well. Add the butter so it sizzles. Swish it around the pan quickly so it turns *noisette* but does not burn. The taste of the *noisette* butter is the key to the final taste of the dish. Add the shrimp, put the pan on high heat and sauté very quickly until all shells turn red. Remove from the heat; cover and let steam about three minutes. Remove the shrimp to a platter; keep warm. Add a good turn of pepper from the mill to the juices in the pan. Add the cream and reduce by half. Add the sour cream. Mix well. Return the shrimp to the pan and reheat thoroughly. Add salt only if necessary and more pepper.

To eat, put the pan on the table; serve with a loaf of crisp French bread and a bar of unsalted butter. Eat each shrimp as you peel it. It will be messy but lots of fun. Remove the head; remove the first link of the tail shell. Pinch the last link of the tail shell and the shell between index finger and thumb of the left hand at the same time as you pull out the already shelled first link with the right hand. Eat the shrimp tail meat. Keep all shrimp heads to make a shrimp butter.

PATE PAS RAFFINE
[Unrefined Pâté]

SERVINGS: 6–12 COST: reasonable EXECUTION: easy

TOTAL PREPARATION TIME: ½ hour plus at least 4 hours for chilling

BEST SEASON: Year round, but is best for winter cocktail parties or as a first course at dinner

SUGGESTED WINE: Any cocktail drink

REMARKS ON INGREDIENTS: Use chicken livers for at least one-half the required amount of livers. Choose very pale fowl livers. Seal the pâté with clarified butter. In Blonville it was sealed with half beef kidney fat, half lard.

1 lb. poultry livers (duck, chicken, goose, or turkey) (500 g)
1 apple, diced into ¼-inch cubes
10 TB unsalted butter (125 g)
1½ oz. Calvados (½ dl)
1 TB onions, mashed very fine (10 g)

2 TB shallots, mashed very fine (15 g)
Salt and pepper
Pinch of allspice
½ cup heavy cream (110–120 g)
1 TB sour cream
¼ cup clarified butter (50 g)

Clean the poultry livers of all membranes. Set aside. Peel and dice the apple. Heat 2 tablespoons of butter in a frying pan and sauté the apple cubes over high heat so they color very fast. Add ½ ounce Calvados in the hot pan. Stir fast and remove to a small bowl.

Heat another 2 tablespoons of butter in the same pan until it turns *noisette*. Add the onions; sauté 2 minutes. Add the shallots and immediately add the livers and sauté over high heat until they turn uniformly gray outside but remain rare at the center. Add salt, pepper and allspice. Add the remaining Calvados and flambé. Mash all the ingredients together with a fork while still hot to obtain a semi-liquid, quite rough purée. Strain through a wire conical strainer, pushing hard with a wooden spatula.

Cool the liver purée very well. Cream the remaining butter. Gradually add the liver purée using an electric mixer if you wish, but you can obtain the same result by beating the liver into the creamed butter with a wooden spatula. Add the apple dices and their Calvados. Mix well. Mix together the heavy and sour cream. Beat until the mixture mounds slightly. Fold into the liver pâté.

Pack the pâté into a half-quart soufflé dish or earthenware terrine. Cool and pour the clarified butter over the surface of the pâté to seal it.

ROULETTES AU CAMEMBERT
[Camembert Filled Appetizers]

SERVINGS: 6 COST: moderately expensive EXECUTION: semi-difficult

TOTAL PREPARATION TIME: Pastry, 2 hours; ripening of the pastry, 4 days at refrigerator temperature; rolling, cutting, shaping, baking, 1 hour

BEST SEASON: Fall, winter, and early spring preferably, but they can be served year round

REMARKS ON INGREDIENTS: The Camembert should not be too ripe; as the Normandes say, *moitié blanc,* or half white.

PASTRY:
2½ cups all-purpose flour
    (300 g)
1 envelope yeast (10 g)
1 tsp. sugar (5 g)
¼ cup lukewarm water, or more
    if needed (½ small dl)
½ cup milk (1 generous dl)

¾ tsp. salt (3½ g)
1 cup butter (225 g)
FILLING:
1 Camembert
1 cup walnuts, coarse ground

1 egg yolk, mixed with
    3 TB milk

TO MAKE THE PASTRY:
Mix ¾ cup flour with the yeast and the sugar. Gradually add the lukewarm water and gather into a soft ball; you may need more

water. Immerse this starter in a large bowl of water at 110° F. maximum.

Meanwhile, make a well in the remaining flour. Add the milk, salt, and 2 tablespoons of melted butter. Gather into a ball.

By the time you have made the ball of dough, the starter will have come floating to the surface of the water. Stretch your right hand under the starter and lift it from the water bath, letting it drip well. Mix together the starter and the ball of prepared dough and crash on the table or counter top until it does not stick to either table or hands but it still tacky. Flatten the dough into a 7-inch square. Put it on a floured plate, cover with a plastic wrap, and refrigerate 1 hour.

After 1 hour, work the remainder of the butter into a soft, waxy-looking 5-inch square. Put the butter at the center of the dough and enclose it within the dough so the latter appears like the back of an envelope. Roll into a 7-inch by 12-inch by ⅓-inch band of dough. Fold it in three and turn the dough 90 degrees so it looks like a book ready to be opened. Roll it out again into a 7-inch by 12-inch by ⅓-inch band of dough. Fold it in three and refrigerate, after you punch 2 holes in the dough with the tip of one finger. Cover with a plastic wrap and store in the vegetable crisper of the refrigerator, not on a shelf. Let rest at least a half hour.

Then give another two turns as above and store again in the vegetable crisper. Let rest at least a half hour more and give two more turns. The dough should be given a total of six turns. Let it ripen in the refrigerator for at least 2 days before using it.

TO MAKE THE FILLING:
Scrape off the skin of the Camembert almost completely. The remaining crust should be very thin. Mash the Camembert with the walnuts and divide the mixture into 12 nut-size pieces. Keep them chilled.

TO SHAPE THE ROULETTES:
Mix the egg yolk and milk. Cut the dough into two equal pieces. Store or freeze one piece of the dough and roll the other into a circle 9 inches in diameter. Cut twelve triangles out of the circle of dough. Brush with the yolk and milk mixture. Shape each nut-size piece of

cheese and walnuts into a small cigar. Roll each cigar into a triangle of dough, starting at the base of the triangle.

Butter a large cookie sheet, rinse it with cold water, and tap it on the edge of the sink. Place the small *roulettes* on the sheet.

Preheat oven to 375°. Let the *roulettes* rise 1½ times their original volume. Brush the *roulettes* with the remaining egg yolk and milk mixture and bake 20 to 25 minutes or until a golden color.

ROTI DE PORC AUX PISTACHES
[Pork Roast with Pistachio Filling]

SERVINGS: 6 COST: reasonable EXECUTION: easy
TOTAL PREPARATION TIME: 15 minutes, plus 2½ hours for baking
BEST SEASON: This is a winter meat.
SUGGESTED BEVERAGE: Cider

One 3 lb. boneless pork roast
(1500 g)
½ lb. sweet Italian sausage
without fennel (250 g)
1 egg
¼ cup fresh breadcrumbs
(30 g)
3 dozen pistachio nuts, shelled
and blanched

Salt and pepper
Quatre épices (see page 7)
⅔ cup cider (see pages 10–11,
general information on cider)
(1¾ dl)
Lemon juice
3 TB sour cream (optional)

Preheat oven to 325°.

Put the piece of pork on a meat board, fat side down. Cut 1½ inches deep into the meat, lengthwise. Then cut another 1½ inches across the meat to the left and at the bottom of the existing cut. Now cut another 1½ inches across the meat to the right. Open the piece of meat flat on the board and smooth it with the flat side of a chef's knife blade.

Put the sausage meat, the egg, the breadcrumbs, and the shelled and blanched pistachios in a bowl. Mix until well homogenized.

Spread the forcemeat on the piece of pork; roll and sew the meat closed. Tie it at ½-inch intervals to shape it into a regular roll. Place the roast on a roasting pan. Salt and pepper it lightly and sprinkle it well with as much *quatre épices* as you would like. Be discreet; a little spice is better than too much here.

Roast the meat for 2½ hours; it is done when a skewer pushed into the center of the meat comes out freely and feels hot to the top of the hand. If you use a meat thermometer, the temperature should be between 170° and 180°.

Deglaze the roasting pan with the cider and pour the sauce into a measuring cup. Let it stand 5 minutes. Then separate the lean gravy from the fat, using a bulb baster. Reheat the gravy in a small sauce-pan. Do not thicken it. Correct the salt and pepper. If a bit too sweet, add a dash of lemon juice. Blend in the sour cream if desired and reheat without boiling.

Brussels sprouts and apples (see page 125) would be good companions to the roast.

COTELETTES D'AGNEAU AU CRESSON DE FONTAINE
[Lamb Chops in Watercress Sauce]

SERVINGS: 6 COST: expensive EXECUTION: easy
BEST SEASON: April through September
SUGGESTED WINE: Gigondas, Cairanne, a lesser Châteauneuf du Pape
REMARKS ON INGREDIENTS: There are two types of watercress, the
    stout, hardy, heavy-leafed one that can be purchased year round,
    and the more delicate type which can be purchased only in the
    spring from late April to June. The latter is better suited for
    this recipe. If only the hardy type is available, use half the
    amount indicated here.

1 cup heavy cream (2¼ dl)
12 rib lamb chops
¼ cup oil of your choice, pref-
    erably light peanut oil (½ dl)
¼ cup sour cream (60 g)

Salt and pepper
⅔ cup strong jus de veau
    (1¾ dl)
¼ cup watercress leaves,
    chopped fine (25 g)

Reduce the heavy cream by one half. Trim the chops of almost all their fat. Cut across the gristle band surrounding the meat to make sure that the meat will not buckle while cooking and will remain perfectly flat.

Add the oil to a large electric skillet, or any other skillet, and heat to 425°. The oil will start smoking. Add the chops; sear them on one side and turn them over. Salt and pepper the seared side. Sear the second side and turn down the heat to 350° or medium. The chops are done when droplets of red juices appear on the surface of the meat. Remove to a plate and keep warm.

Discard the oil completely. Add the veal stock and reduce to ¼ cup, scraping the bottom of the pan well. Add the heavy cream and blend well. Reduce to ½ cup. Add the sour cream. Reheat without boiling. Strain into a warmed sauce boat and add the chopped watercress. Correct the seasoning.

For a vegetable, consider green beans, cauliflower, and, if you can grow them, oyster plants.

ESCALOPES DE VEAU A LA CREME ET AUX MARRONS
[Creamed Veal Scallops with Chestnuts]

SERVINGS: 6 COST: expensive EXECUTION: easy but time consuming

TOTAL PREPARATION TIME: 1½ hours including the peeling of the chestnuts

BEST SEASON: October to December

SUGGESTED BEVERAGE: Cider or a nice Beaujolais

REMARKS ON INGREDIENTS: Use the nice plump chestnuts imported from Italy. But, yes, unfortunately for the dish, those canned French chestnuts can be used.

1 whole veal top weighing 2–3 lbs. (1 kg 250 g)	*Salt and pepper*
½ cup unsalted butter (110 g)	*1 lb. fresh chestnuts (450– 500 g)*
½ cup heavy cream (1 generous dl)	*3 cups extra strong jus de veau (7 dl)*

¼ cup celery rib, diced into
  ¼-inch cubes
⅓ cup sour cream (1 small dl)

1 ounce Calvados (½ dl)
Watercress

Clean the veal top of all fat and gristle. Clarify 6 tablespoons of butter while you work on the meat. Cut the veal top into as many ⅓-inch-thick scallops as you can. Be very careful to cut across the grain of the meat, in the width of the piece (not in the length, and along the grain). This will prevent the meat from being tough and buckling.

Pour the heavy cream into a saucepan and reduce by half.

Slash a cut in the fat side of each chestnut. Add a dash of salt and pepper to 1 quart of cold water. Bring to a boil. Add the chestnuts and turn the heat off. Let stand five minutes. Peel the chestnuts, taking only three or four at a time out of the water.

Place the chestnuts in a 9-inch *sauteuse* pan or skillet; add enough cold veal stock to cover them. Bring slowly to a boil. Add 2 tablespoons butter and a dash of salt and pepper. Simmer very gently until the chestnuts are done. Drain and reserve any stock not absorbed by the nuts.

Heat 2 tablespoons clarified butter in a large skillet. Add the celery and sauté until nice and soft. Add the celery to the chestnuts. Keep warm.

Salt and pepper each veal scallop very lightly. In the same skillet, panfry the veal no more than 2–3 minutes on each side, adding clarified butter as needed. The scallops will now be done; do not overcook them or they will toughen. It is recommended, as a matter of fact, to undercook them slightly for they will finish cooking while waiting to be served. Keep them warm while you prepare the sauce.

Deglaze the pan with 1 cup of stock. If you have some left over from the cooking of the chestnuts, use it, adding some new stock to make one cup. Reduce it to ¼ cup. Add the reduced heavy cream and the sour cream. Heat the Calvados in a small pan and pour, flaming, into the sauce. Correct the seasoning and strain over the meat. Surround the meat with the chestnuts.

Add bouquets of watercress and serve promptly. Plain, lightly buttered carrots will do well as a second vegetable.

QUEUE DE BOEUF AUX CINQ OIGNONS
[Oxtails with Five-Onion Sauce]

SERVINGS: 6 COST: inexpensive to reasonable EXECUTION: easy
TOTAL PREPARATION TIME: 3 hours, including the braising. It is
    better if the stew is done 24 hours ahead of time.
BEST SEASON: October through March
RECOMMENDED BEVERAGE: Dry French or English imported cider

THE STEW:
2 TB oil of your choice (not
    olive) (½ dl)
6 oxtails, cut into 2-inch chunks
1 onion, sliced thick
1 small carrot, sliced thick
1½ oz. Calvados or Apple Jack
    (7½ cl)
1 cup cider (2¼ dl)
2 cups brown veal stock
    (4½ dl)
Bouquet garni
Salt and pepper

GARNISH FOR THE SAUCE:
3 TB butter (45 g)
2 small onions, chopped fine
4 shallots, chopped fine
2 large leeks, white part only,
    chopped fine
2 cloves garlic, chopped fine
Salt and pepper
½ cup heavy cream (115 g)
1 TB sour cream (30 g)
1½ TB chopped chives
1 cup (10 oz.) cooked baby
    peas (275–300 g)

Preheat oven to 325°.
Heat the oil in a large *sauteuse*. Brown the oxtail chunks on all sides. Remove to a plate.
Sauté the onion and carrot lightly in the browning fat. Keep the vegetables in the *sauteuse* and discard the fat. Return the meat to the *sauteuse;* add the Calvados and cider. Reduce by half over high heat. Add enough stock to cover the meat; add the *bouquet garni* and salt and pepper. Cover the meat tightly with aluminum foil; turn the sides of the foil up to form a snug inverted lid. Close the pot lid and

braise 1½ to 2 hours in the preheated oven. The meat will be done when a skewer inserted at the fleshiest part of the largest oxtail chunk comes out freely.

Prepare the garnish for the sauce: Heat the butter in a large saucepan. Add the onions and toss in the hot butter. Then add the shallots, leeks, garlic, and salt and pepper and cover. Cook over slow heat until the vegetables are almost tender but still retain a bit of crunch. Add the heavy cream and sour cream. Reserve.

When the oxtail is done, remove it to a heat-proof serving dish. If necessary, reduce the cooking juices to 1 cup. Strain them into the onion mixture. No additional thickening agent should be necessary. Add the chives and peas. Pour over the oxtail and reheat without boiling. Serve with mashed potatoes or rice.

LA PIROTTE AU FENOUIL
[Fennel-Stuffed Goose]

SERVINGS: 8 COST: expensive EXECUTION: easy
TOTAL PREPARATION TIME: 3–4 hours
BEST SEASON: Late fall and the whole winter up to early March
SUGGESTED BEVERAGE: Imported French or English cider, or a light, red Côtes du Rhône
REMARKS ON INGREDIENTS: At Henriette's farm, this dish was prepared with the last wild stalks of fennel to be gathered after the first frost in October. Use cultivated fennel stalks, keeping the bulbs for a Provençal fennel soup. Keep the rendered goose fat frozen for frying potatoes.

1 large goose, about 10 lbs. (5 kg)
2 TB chopped fennel greens
Stalks of 2 fennel bulbs, sliced ¼ inch thick
4 TB butter (60 g)
Salt and pepper
6 Red Bliss potatoes, peeled and pared into olive shapes (500 g)
1 quart brown veal stock (about 1 litre)
1 cup sour cream (2¼ dl)
⅓ cup heavy cream (1 small dl)
Watercress

Preheat oven to 325°, no higher. Roasting at a higher temperature produces a very average goose rather than a tender one, burns the precious fat, and does not give a good gravy.

Empty the cavity of the goose of all fat pads. You can render them for goose fat. Salt and pepper the inside of the cavity.

Chop enough fennel greens to obtain 2 tablespoons and keep it in a small dish for later use. Chop the fennel stalks into ¼-inch-thick slices, sauté lightly in 2 tablespoons of butter; sprinkle with salt and pepper. Cover and let steam a bit. Uncover, raise the heat, and cook until dry. Cool completely.

Stuff the cavity of the goose with the fennel stalks. Place the bird on the rack of a roasting pan and roast 3 to 3½ hours. Remove the fat to a jar with a bulb baster as it renders. Gather the cooking juices into a little pan; add some stock if the amount is too small. Do not thicken. Keep warm.

Put the prepared potatoes in a *sauteuse* pan. Add enough stock to cover. Bring to a boil and simmer 12 to 14 minutes. Raise the heat and evaporate the stock into a glaze. Roll the potatoes back and forth on the bottom of the pan to coat them with the glaze. Taste for salt and pepper and correct seasoning. Add the remaining butter and the chopped fennel greens.

Mix sour cream and heavy cream; season with salt and pepper. Heat thoroughly without boiling. Serve the goose on a platter surrounded by the potatoes and watercress. Pass gravy and cream in two separate sauce boats. A tablespoon of each on a portion of goose, or on the potatoes, or on both is heavenly!

TARTE AUX DEUX CHOUX
[Cauliflower, Brussels Sprouts and Ham Cream Pie]

SERVINGS: 6–8 COST: reasonable EXECUTION: easy
TOTAL PREPARATION TIME: 45 minutes, plus 35 to 40 minutes for
     baking
BEST SEASON: This is a winter dish good up to the end of March.
SUGGESTED BEVERAGE: Imported French or English cider

PASTRY:

1 cup sifted flour (125 g)

6 TB butter (65 g)

½ tsp. salt (2½ g)

3 TB water (7 cl)

FILLING:

1 small cauliflower head (about 500 g)

1 lb. baby Brussels sprouts (500 g)

4 TB butter (50 g)

Salt and pepper

3 TB flour (30 g)

1 cup vegetable blanching water (2¼ dl)

1 cup heavy cream (225 g or 2¼ dl)

Nutmeg, grated fresh, to suit your taste

½ cup ham, diced in ⅓-inch cubes (150 g)

TO MAKE THE PASTRY:

Put the flour on the counter top; make a well. Add the butter, cut in 4 chunks, and the salt. With the fingertips, mix the flour and butter so that the butter remains in small chunks, no smaller than hazelnuts. Gradually add the water with your fingertips and without kneading. Gather into a ball. With the heel of your hand push the dough 6 to 8 inches forward, flattening into large, nut-size pieces. Reshape all the pieces into a ball and repeat the same operation. Shape the pastry into a circular 3-inch cake about 1 inch thick. Refrigerate.

TO MAKE THE FILLING:

Peel and clean the cauliflower. Cut it into small flowerets; peel the stems. Remove the outer leaf of each Brussels sprout, cut a cross in the root end with a paring knife. Blanch the two cabbages in a large amount of salted boiling water for 3 to 4 minutes. Drain well. Heat 1 tablespoon butter in a pot. Add the vegetables, salt and pepper, and cook gently, covered, for 5–6 minutes. Open the pot lid and let all the juices evaporate. Make a white roux with 3 tablespoons butter and 3 tablespoons flour. Cook 3 to 4 minutes. Use a whisk to beat in 1 cup of the vegetable blanching water mixed with half of the heavy cream. Thicken over medium heat. Salt lightly, pepper, and season with nutmeg to your taste.

Roll out the pastry ⅛ inch thick and fit it into an 8- or 9-inch pie plate. Line the mold with the cabbages; fit the ham dice between the vegetables. Pour the cream sauce over the filling. Top with the remaining heavy cream, unseasoned.

Bake in a preheated 375° oven for 35 to 40 minutes, half of the time on the bottom shelf of the oven, half of the time on the top.

CAROTTES AU LARD
[Carrots Glazed with Bacon]

SERVINGS: 6 COST: reasonable EXECUTION: easy
TOTAL PREPARATION TIME: 45 minutes
BEST SEASON: This is a year-round vegetable; omit the bacon in the
    summer.

1 lb. carrots (small midgets)
  (450–500 g)
4 quarts boiling water (4 litres)
Salt
3 oz. slab bacon, cut into ⅓-inch
  lardoons (100 g)
1 oz. Calvados or Apple Jack
  (5 cl)

1 TB butter (15 g)
1 cup warm brown veal stock
  (2¼ dl)
Chopped chives
Pepper
Sugar, a pinch if needed, or a
  dash of lemon juice

Peel the carrots. Bring the water to a boil; add 2 tablespoons salt. Add the carrots to the violently boiling water. Let them cook no more than 7 to 8 minutes. Meanwhile, cut the bacon in ⅓-inch by 1-inch lardoons; place the lardoons in a cold *sauteuse* pan over slow heat. Let the bacon render gently, then barely crisp it. Discard the fat. Add the carrots, transferring them from the water to the *sauteuse*. Add the Calvados, the butter, and the stock and bring to a good simmer. Let cook, shaking the pan back and forth over the heat until the stock is reduced to a glaze that coats the carrots. Correct the seasoning by adding salt if necessary, pepper, and the chives. If the carrots are bland, add a pinch of sugar or if they are too sweet, add a wee bit of lemon juice.

CHOUX DE BRUXELLES AUX POMMES
[Brussels Sprouts and Apples]

SERVINGS: 6 COST: inexpensive EXECUTION: easy
TOTAL PREPARATION TIME: 20 minutes
BEST SEASON: A fall and winter vegetable
REMARKS ON INGREDIENTS: You may use frozen *baby* Brussels
sprouts, the only ones that will be small enough in this country
to give the correct taste and texture. The sprouts must be overcooked and it does not matter if they are somewhat discolored.
They must be, as is said in Normandy, *prêts à fondre*, or ready
to melt. Omit glaze if unavailable.

Two 10 oz. boxes of frozen baby	*Salt and pepper*
Brussels sprouts	*A good pinch of* quatre épices
2 Russet or Granny Smith	*(page 7)*
apples	*2 TB meat glaze*
3 TB butter	

Defrost the sprouts at room temperature. Peel and core the apples;
cut them into 6 slices and then into chunks as big as the sprouts.

Heat the butter in a *sauteuse* pan or frying pan; sauté the apples
until they start browning. Add the sprouts; toss them with the apples.
Add salt, pepper, and the *quatre épices*. Cover the pan and let cook,
stirring occasionally very carefully with a spatula until the sprouts
are tender. Add the meat glaze and serve.

PETITS POIS A LA CREME
[Creamed Peas]

SERVINGS: 6 COST: reasonable to expensive EXECUTION: easy
TOTAL PREPARATION TIME: 20 minutes
BEST SEASON: Late spring and summer
REMARKS ON INGREDIENTS: Unless you cultivate your own peas,

use frozen baby peas. If they are in a butter sauce, rinse the frozen peas under warm water to discard the oversalted sauce.

3 Boston lettuce leaves, dark green	*2 TB unsalted butter (30 g)*
	Salt and pepper
1½ lbs. frozen baby peas, defrosted (700–750 g)	*½ tsp. sugar*
	2 TB sour cream

Chop the lettuce leaves very fine. Have the peas defrosted. Heat the butter gently in a 2-quart heavy saucepan. Add the chopped lettuce and toss in the hot butter. Add the peas and also toss in the butter. Add salt, pepper, and the sugar. Cover and cook no more than 10 minutes. Add the sour cream; reheat without boiling. Serve.

TOMATES A LA CREME
[Creamed Tomatoes]

SERVINGS: 6 COST: moderately expensive EXECUTION: tricky
TOTAL PREPARATION TIME: 20 to 25 minutes
BEST SEASON: August through October with sun-ripened tomatoes
REMARKS ON INGREDIENTS: Should be made with sun-ripened tomatoes only. The vine-ripened variety will taste like the chemicals from which it is grown. Use either smaller pear-shaped tomatoes cut in half lengthwise or larger tomatoes cut into ½-inch slices, no thinner. In winter, very ripe cherry tomatoes may be good.

1 cup heavy cream (225 g)	*1 small clove garlic, chopped fine*
Salt and pepper	*Flour*
2 TB butter (30 g)	*1 lb. fresh tomatoes, unpeeled*
2 TB chopped parsley	

Put the cream in a large saucepan; reduce by one-third. Add a pinch of salt and pepper. Reserve. Heat the butter in a large skillet; add parsley and garlic and toss one minute. Flour the tomato slices one by one just before you add them to the pan. Do not salt or pepper them. Cook one or two minutes on each side or until just heated through. Remove to a serving plate as soon as the tomatoes start showing signs of losing their first juices. Keep warm. Add the reduced cream to the frying pan and raise the heat; stir constantly with a wooden spatula until the cream coats the spatula. Do not overcook or the cream will separate. Pour over the tomatoes without straining.

PETIT SUISSE
[Cream Cheese Mousse]

SERVINGS: 6–8 COST: reasonable EXECUTION: easy
TOTAL PREPARATION TIME: 15 minutes plus 48 hours for dripping
    completely
BEST SEASON: Year round, but more appealing in spring and summer
REMARKS ON INGREDIENTS: Because of the unreasonable use of pre-
    servatives in many dairy products, use honest brands that adver-
    tise strictly natural products. Happy fresh cheese to those cooks
    who own a cow.

½ lb. small-curd creamed   ½ cup sour cream (4 oz.
    cottage cheese (250 g)   or 125 g)
½ cup yoghurt (4 oz.   1½ cups heavy cream (12 oz.
    or 125 g)   or 375 g)

Put the cottage cheese and yoghurt in the blender container and blend until smooth. Mix the sour cream and heavy cream and beat until stiff enough to fall from the beaters in large blocks. Mix ⅓ of the cream into the cottage cheese–yoghurt blend and then fold in the remainder.

Line a wicker basket or *coeur à la crème* mold with one layer of cheesecloth rinsed under cold water. Turn the mousse into the basket. Fold the cheesecloth over the cheese mixture. Place the basket or mold over a mixing bowl and refrigerate at least 24 hours. The mixture should lose at least ⅔ to ¾ cup of whey.

According to your mood or menu serve plain, with sugar, with salt and coarsely grated pepper, with chopped herbs, or with a purée of red berries.

LA FALLUE DE LA RIVIERE THIBOUVILLE
[Heavy Cream Brioche]

SERVINGS: up to 24 COST: inexpensive EXECUTION: easy
TOTAL PREPARATION TIME: 20 minutes for the batter, 3 hours for
    rising, 50 minutes for baking

2 TB raw, unsalted, soft butter	4 large eggs
5 cups sifted all-purpose	1 cup heavy cream (225 g)
flour (650 g)	1 tsp. salt
¼ cup lukewarm milk	1 cup cooled, melted, unsalted
5 tsps. dried yeast (1⅔	butter (225–250 g)
envelopes)	½ tsp. ground cardamom
⅓ cup sugar (90 g)	

Prepare a bundt pan by buttering it heavily with the two tablespoons of raw, unsalted butter.

Put the flour in a large mixing bowl. Make a well in the flour; add the milk and sugar. Mix well. Add the yeast and let stand until the mixture bubbles.

Beat the eggs until they are positively liquid; add the cream and salt.

Pour the cream and egg mixture into the bubbling yeast. Gather in the flour as gently as possible so as not to develop gluten. When the flour has absorbed the mixture completely, add the butter and cardamom. The batter will be almost liquid. Do not beat the butter in. As long as the batter is homogenous, it is fine. Pour the batter into the prepared mold. Let the batter rise all the way to the rim of the mold at room temperature; it will take about 2½ hours in the summer and 3½ hours in the winter. Bake on the middle rack of a 375° preheated oven for 45–50 minutes. The bread is done when a skewer inserted in the center comes out shiny with melted butter but shows no traces of batter and, when applied to the top of the hand, positively burns.

POIRES EN COCOTTE
[Baked Pears]

SERVINGS: 6–8 COST: reasonable EXECUTION: tricky, do not over-bake

TOTAL PREPARATION TIME: 1½ hours

BEST SEASON: During the Bartlett season (August through October); use slightly firm pears.

6 firm Bartlett pears, peeled and cored

1 lemon

6 slices of white bread, crusts removed

6 TB unsalted butter (65 g)

1 cup cider or more, as needed (2½ dl)

2 TB Calvados or Apple Jack

Sugar (optional)

1 cup heavy cream (optional) (2½ dl)

½ cup sour cream (optional) (1 generous dl)

Cut the pears in half; rub each half with lemon. Cut each slice of bread in half and spread thickly with 1 tablespoon of butter. Set each pear on a piece of bread.

Put the pears on their slices of bread in a large cocotte or *sauteuse* or even in a large, fireproof baking dish. Add the cider mixed with the Calvados. Bake in a 350° preheated oven. Baste the pears at regular intervals with the juices in the dish so as to build a pretty color on the fruit. Sprinkle the fruit with sugar, if you desire, during the last 15 minutes of baking. The pears are done when a needle inserted in the center of each slides in and out easily. Serve warm. If you decide to serve with cream, mix both creams together. Make sure that they are well chilled. Also serve with a small bowl of sugar.

LA POMMEE D'HENRIETTE
[Apple Cream Tart]

SERVINGS: 8–12 COST: reasonable EXECUTION: semi-difficult
TOTAL PREPARATION TIME: 1 hour for the pastry, 1 hour for the
  filling. Spread the work over two days.
REMARKS ON INGREDIENTS: Use Grannie Smith, July–September;
  Gravenstein, July–September; Greening, October–February;
  Winesap, January–May.
BEST SEASON: Follow the apples. No other pie apples resemble the
  Normandy apples enough to be used.

PASTRY:
1½ cups sifted all-purpose
  flour (175 g)
¾ cup butter (175 g)
¾ tsp. salt (7½ g)
4–5 TB water (½ dl)
1 tsp. sugar

FILLING:
1 cup heavy cream (225 g
  or 2¼ dl)
1½ cups applesauce (3½ dl)
⅛ tsp. cinnamon

½ tsp. lemon rind, grated fine
Pinch of salt
½ cup apple cider (1
  generous dl)
1 envelope gelatin
6 TB Calvados or Apple Jack
  (1 small dl)
3 TB unsalted butter (35 g)
8 peeled apples, cut into 8
  slices each
1 TB sugar (10 g)

TO MAKE THE PASTRY:
Put the flour on the counter and make a well. Cut the butter into
1½-tablespoon chunks and add. Add the salt. With the fingertips,
squeeze the butter and flour together to obtain pieces of butter no
smaller than ⅓ of a tablespoon. Sprinkle the water over the mixture
gradually and mix with the fingertips until the pastry holds together. Let rest on a plate for 30 minutes. Refrigerate. Roll out into
a strip 15 inches by 6 inches by ½ inch. Fold in three. Turn the
package of dough so it looks like a book ready to be opened. Flatten
out again into the same size strip. Fold in three. Refrigerate 15 minutes. Repeat the same operation a second time; refrigerate 15 min-

utes. Repeat the same operation a third time; refrigerate 15 more minutes. By now you will have given 6 turns altogether. Between the turns keep the dough in the vegetable crisper of the refrigerator and not on one of the shelves; the butter will be flattened and absorbed more readily this way.

Roll the pastry out into an 11-inch circle, ⅛ inch thick. Fit it into a 9-inch circular buttered cake pan. Cut away any excess pastry by rolling the pin over the edges of the cake mold. Crimp the edge of the pastry with a fork, prick its bottom, and fit a piece of aluminum foil into the unbaked pastry. Fill with dried beans or aluminum nuggets, and bake 15 minutes at 425°. Remove the beans or nuggets and foil. Sprinkle the bottom of the pie with 1 teaspoon of sugar and continue baking another five minutes. Gently unmold to cool on a cake rack.

TO MAKE THE FILLING:

Whip the heavy cream until almost mounding. Keep refrigerated. Put the applesauce into a pan with cinnamon and lemon rind; add a tiny pinch of salt and reduce to ½ cup. Put the cider in a measuring cup. Sprinkle the gelatin over it and melt it in a hot water bath. Mix with the applesauce. Liquefy the mixture in the blender. Pour into a bowl fitted over another, larger bowl containing ice and water. Add 2 tablespoons of the Calvados. Stir until the mixture starts to thicken. Fold in the heavy cream and pour into the prepared pie shell.

Heat the 3 tablespoons of butter in a 10-inch frying pan. Sauté the apple slices over high heat to color them well. Reduce the heat, sprinkle with the sugar, and let the apples soften and glaze. Flambé them with the remaining Calvados or Apple Jack. Let cool. Arrange the apples in concentric circles on top of the cream filling.

SABLES BLONVILLAIS
[Shortbread]

SERVINGS: 12 COST: expensive EXECUTION: tricky, do not work
   the flour too much into the dough
TOTAL PREPARATION TIME: 1 hour

1 cup unsalted butter (225 g)	*1 TB Calvados or Apple Jack*
plus 1 TB (15 g)	*2½ cups sifted all-purpose*
½ cup sugar (125 g)	*flour* (360 g)
¼ tsp. salt	

Cream the cup of butter with the electric mixer for 10 minutes. It
must be white with air beaten into it. Gradually add the sugar, salt,
and the Calvados. Continue beating another 10 minutes.

Sift the flour gradually over the mixture. Introduce the flour into
the sweetened butter by flattening the mixture gently on the sides of
the bowl with a flexible rubber spatula. *Do not beat* the flour in.

Butter a 9-inch round cake pan with the remaining tablespoon
of butter. Spread the dough in an even layer in the pan. Trace decorations with a fork. The usual pattern is eight triangles. Trace the portions with a knife before baking.

Bake in a 325° oven until pale gold. Cut in portions while warm.
Cool and enjoy. The shortbread should keep for months if well
tucked in a tin. I have always failed to keep any.

LE BOURRE-GOULE D'HENRIETTE
[Henriette's Rice Pudding]

SERVINGS: 8 COST: reasonable EXECUTION: tricky, do not let the
   rice set too stiffly
TOTAL PREPARATION TIME: 40 minutes plus 2–3 hours to set in
   the refrigerator
BEST SEASON: A fall, winter, and late spring dessert

1 TB corn oil, or other tasteless oil

1 cup heavy whipping cream (225 g)

2 Granny Smith apples

2 TB butter (30 g)

¾ cup sugar plus 2 TB (190 g plus 15 g)

2 oz. Calvados or Apple Jack (5 cl)

1 quart water (1 litre)

½ cup long grain rice (100 g)

4½ cups milk (1 generous litre)

8 egg yolks

Salt

1 tsp. pure vanilla extract

1 envelope gelatin

Rub a 1-quart mold with the corn oil. Turn upside down on a paper towel to let the excess drip.

Whip the cream to a very light *Chantilly*. Reserve it in the refrigerator. Peel and core the apples; dice them into ⅓-inch cubes. Heat the butter in a large skillet. Sauté the apples in it until golden. Add the 2 tablespoons of sugar and continue cooking until it caramelizes. Add half of the Calvados and stir; use a flexible spatula so as to deglaze the caramel with the Calvados but not break the apples. Reserve.

Bring the water to a boil; add the rice. Bring to a second boil and simmer 15 minutes.

Scald the milk. Pour 2 cups of it into another container; keep warm. Reserve. Add the rice to the milk remaining in the pot and add ¼ cup of sugar. Cook until the rice is pudding-like but still very soft, not dry or compact.

Mix the 8 yolks with the remaining ½ cup of sugar and a solid pinch of salt; do not make a lot of foam. Blend the reserved 2 cups of scalded milk into the yolks and stir over medium heat until all the foam recedes from the surface of the custard and the latter coats the wooden spoon. Add the vanilla.

Pour half the custard into a sauce boat. Flavor it with the remaining Calvados and refrigerate.

Melt the gelatin in 1 tablespoon of water in a double boiler. Add to the remainder of the custard. Blend with the rice pudding. Add the Calvados apples to the mixture. Let cool to room temperature.

Fold in the reserved heavy cream. Turn the mixture into the prepared mold and refrigerate until set.

To serve, unmold the rice pudding on a pretty platter and pour the sauce over it.

Mimi

—— ❦ —— ❦ ——

SAVOIE

Winter of 1940 and 1945 to 1970

Colchiques dans les prés fleurissent, fleurissent,
Colchiques dans les prés, c'est la fin de l'été.
La feuille d'automne, emportée par le vent,
En rondes monotones, tombe en tourbillonnant.

T HERE IS NO SONG more evocative of the radiant and often melancholic beauty of the Alps during the autumn months than these lovely, faintly sad verses. They tell of purple crocuses in the fields and bright leaves bristling for the last time in the October breeze before falling to the ground in slow circumvolutions and dissolving into humus.

I arrived in the Alps in the middle of October, 1939, after a long train ride toward the mountains that would protect me and many of my young compatriots from the madness of war.

And indeed, until May of 1940, life was to be nothing but warmth, beauty, love and joy, until the erratic declarations of the *Duce* just about a hundred miles away over the Franco-Italian border put us on our way back to Paris.

The happiness of those few months was to make the valleys and mountains around Annecy the paradise of my life, the elected homeland of my heart, the place where, to this day, I strive to go back for emotional replenishment, where I want to go back forever.

Traveling by train from Paris to Annecy with all the mountain valleys hidden behind Mont Veyrier and the massive tower of the Tournette, one gets a first glimpse of the Alps at Aix les Bains. There, the train jolts out of a tunnel and races along the lake that inspired Lamartine to write some of his most romantic verses. As young as I was at the time, the large band of mist lying over the lake and the toothlike mountains darting way above the clouds intrigued me. I was awed by the magnificence that was to unfold before my eyes when I reached Annecy. Annecy in those days was not yet that well known to American gastronomes, since Madame Bise's Restaurant in neighboring Talloires was still striving for its stars. It was a small, lovely, restful old town, looking very much like the favorite town of Jean Jacques Rousseau it had once been. It still had much of its 17th and 18th century charm left in the ancient stone houses bordering on canals or torrents which ran swiftly toward an enamel-blue lake.

I was to spend the year in a children's home located in the small village of La Balme de Thuy, twenty kilometers farther down on the edge of that tumultuous Fier River, the name of which in French means proud. The home had sent a gangly young girl to pick me up at the station. Her name, she said, was Mimi. She was no more than fourteen, broad shouldered with an olive complexion and the two most expressive and lovely brown eyes I have ever known. They were like those of a doe. When one looked into them, they sent back love and kindness and seemed to be able to perceive only the good things in life. I have known Mimi now for thirty-six years and she is a woman of great strength well hidden behind a façade of softness. Was she ever warm and genuinely trying to make me feel good on that day in October, 1939. First she extracted a blanket from a huge bag she was carrying, assuring me that since I had not slept well on the train and it was so chilly in the bus I would be more comfortable. She chatted all the way up to La Balme, telling me the names of mountains and villages, and explaining to me that the glorious little castle overlooking the lake had been the home of Saint Bernard, the founder of the two alpine monasteries with the huge rescue dogs.

The view from up there, at what is known as the Col de Bluffy, is beautiful at any time of the year, but on that particular day it was a glory of colors such as I have never seen anywhere else again. The jutting rock summits of the mountains, lost in a cobalt-blue sky, were sparkling with an already heavy spray of snow. On the slopes below, the forests were a mixture of dark greens with bright yellows, fiery oranges, and an occasional dab of red.

Mimi's chatter went on for the whole ride, and by the time we arrived at the turnoff to the road to La Balme de Thuy, I knew I had acquired a true friend. We left the bus at Morette, where a bridge crosses the Fier, and turned into a dirt road—now macadamed—that led to La Balme. The air was cold, crystal clear, simply beautiful. The noises were new, the smells and the colors were fresh and bright. There was a wood-cutting plant exhaling fresh pine and sap smells right by a beautiful cascade that fell some 300 feet from the top of a cliff. Millions of ice crystals and stalactites hung from the cliff; a mere trickle of water dripped from the biggest of them. Farther up the road there was a grotto with a statue of the Virgin of Lourdes. Mimi explained that the grotto had given the village its name since in Savoyard *patois* the word *balme* means grotto. I was delivered to the home but not without Mimi first telling me that if I felt like visiting her, her home was right across from mine. It was; I could see it from my dormitory window and could almost follow the rhythm of Mimi's work and life. She had finished school. Her *certificat d'études* was hanging on the wall in an old-fashioned looking oak frame her grandfather, who was an old bearded tyrant of a man, had made for her as a present. Mimi's father, whose business was in Reblochon cheeses up the valley in Thônes, appeared home only on the weekends. Her mother was one of those statuesque women with a smooth forehead and liquid blue eyes, who was always scrubbed and polished, with hair tightly knotted in the back. She was full of serenity and inner peace.

One day a week, children from the home went to visit a family in the village for a break in institutional life. And luck just had it that I was to receive my education in Savoyard life from Mimi and her family. Their chalet was in those days still old-fashioned. It was a huge, grey, stone house, with a heavily slanted roof carrying immense stones that were there to keep the snow from sliding down in heavy masses during the winter. The shutters were bright green. Inside, the first floor consisted of two rooms, a barn where ten Tarentaise cows were ruminating and producing heat for the whole house, and a huge kitchen complete with chimney and mantelpiece. It was spotless. The floor of the kitchen was of varnished, highly polished red tiles and all the furniture massive oak, somewhat darkened by the smoke emanating from the chimney.

There was a balcony-like second floor where all the beds, small and large, were separated by chintz curtains for privacy. When I asked why there was no wall I was told that the heat from the cows downstairs and from the hearth would not warm the second floor if walls existed.

Since an electric stove was still a luxury up there in 1940, Mimi's mother cooked on the hearth on wood brought in from the mountains.

Every Saturday, the dominant smell of the house was that of red wine in which either a rabbit, a hare, or a piece of pork was cooking. And every Saturday, we would be sent to the grocery store with the same inevitable regularity as we would attend Mass on Sunday. *L'Epicier,* as the grocery store was called, appeared to be a messy, disorganized place until one took a closer look. Rum was sold by the decilitre and Mimi always brought her bottle to be filled every week with one or two decilitres only, so the grandfather would not use it to make grog. The mustard, in huge barrels from Dijon, was sold by the *hecto* and one rarely purchased more than that one hundred grams. What lovely junk that fat grocer had to offer, candies of all colors, sizes, shapes, and dimensions and invariably so stuck together by the humidity that one was sold a block of eight to fifteen colored somethings all stuck to one another. The dear man would weigh all this on an authentic Roman scale, as authentic as honest, for the weight was always exact. There were other odd things in that store. Noirot extracts to make homemade liqueurs such as Vespetro which is supposed to be a godsend not only for the bladder, but also for other undistinguished parts of the human plumbing system.

And then there was that part of the store where gifts were sold, old-fashioned milk pitchers of brown earthenware naïvely decorated with edelweiss flowers, and those marvelous Opinel knives, without which no Savoyard can survive.

There were packages of dried legumes, envelopes of calcium carbonate to preserve the abundant Easter egg crop for the winter, and spices—mainly pepper and cinnamon, which exhaled the last of their tropical smell into the cool atmosphere of the Alps.

Since there was no baker in La Balme, bread was either made at home or bought from *l'épicier* who himself got it from the baker in Thônes. The bought breads came in huge wheels about 16 inches in diameter. Since they often nudged one another while baking, they had a scar on each side from being separated. While *l'épicier* was busy with another customer, Mimi and I would pull off a layer of that soft, barely baked dough and stuff our faces with it. Everyone was wise to what we were up to and good-heartedly indulged us.

Mimi already knew how to make a solid, chewy loaf of bread with cracked wheat, corn flour, and wheat flour and that nice little hunk of pungent yeast brought back from Thônes every week by her father. For Sunday morning after Mass, she often baked a dozen or so egg dough *petits pains* in which she would enclose the *grattons* or cracklings left over from making lard or rendering bacon. And all that bread would be sliced to become the support for slices of mountain ham topped with melted Reblochon cheese, or cubed to dip into a potful of Beaufort cheese melted into *berton* (fondue) with a good bottle of Roussettes wine and a few cloves of garlic.

Christmas day was to be a feast without end. Mimi's whole family had come from all over the area and from the Aravis pass way up above La Clusaz. L'Aline had brought home smoked Pormoniers, those black-skinned sausages with strong mountain herbs that, with a great prune and potato *farcement* well wrapped in bacon slices, were to be declared the favorite items of the day. Le Simon from his village of St. Jean de Sixt had brought a couple of Reblochons, as smelly and creamy as can be. There were quails which Mimi's father, a master poacher, had shot and Mimi's mother had, as she put it, "treated" with juniper berries. There were leeks bathing in cream, and yet another potato gratin fragrant with garlic and Beaufort.

A grand-uncle had insisted that Mimi make his favorite honey and walnut cream. Another old man in the company, a Reblochon maker by family tradition (the trade had passed from father to son for six generations), had declared himself in rather colorful language *prêt à crever*—ready to burst—unless he was given at once the bottle of green Chartreuse to settle his overtaxed stomach.

The winter passed in happiness. Days of snowstorms were followed by brilliant days of sun and dark blue skies, punctuated with sleigh rides with knees and feet well tucked under old blankets smelling of horse hair and cow manure. What fun!

And one day, I woke up to a strange whistling noise and one look outside told me that spring was on the way. It was the Föhn, the warm, languid and yet wild south wind that eats up snow. It was so warm that by nighttime, under a sky punctuated with brilliant stars, the snow had retreated halfway up the mountains. That Saturday, Mimi told me to put my boots on; the morels would be out in all the apple orchards. We were unsuccessful that day, but a week later we brought home a basket of large morels, one of them almost 6 inches high. It was so huge and impressive I was to have recurrent dreams about it at different times in my life. The last event of that spring took place when we took the cows up the mountain to spend the summer on the Alps. I was exhausted by the time we reached the *fruitière,* an old wooden chalet just below the summit of the Dent du Cruet in full sight of Mont Blanc. The climb on muddy trails had been trying and I failed to see how some of the cows had not gone rolling down the steep slopes. I was fascinated by the flowers. At the edge of snow patches were the blue *Soldanellae,* so daintily fringed; high up in rock crevices were bright yellow bunches of *Primulae,* the favorite of all alpine botanists and the object of multiple campaigns for preservation. On the southern slopes there were blankets of snow white crocuses. And way up above 3600 feet were these amazing forests of dwarf willows, growing tightly side by side, barely a foot high. At night before we all went to bed in lofts full of hay, there was a great feast with several *bertons* bubbling in earthenware *caquelons,* lots of singing and even more laughing. Since I was the youngest, I was given the *caquelon* to clean, but with the chore came the enjoyment of that marvelous cake of golden cheese that always sticks to the bottom of the *caquelon* and is considered the choice morsel of the evening.

It was not until 1945 that I was to come up that way again. I was almost grown up and anxious to see the beauty I had left in a great hurry to rejoin my family in Paris.

When I came back as a junior counselor in the children's home, Mimi was a woman and the mother of a blond, blue-eyed two-year-old child. She lived alone with the child in the chalet; her mother and father had been killed by soldiers for giving refuge to resistance fighters from the nearby Glières Maquis.

Mimi was the sole heir to a fortune of mountain slopes and cows, to woods, Reblochons-making *fruitières.* She signed it all over to her daughter, now thirty years old. She is still my friend and I still go to see her, stealing the time whenever I can. I barrel down the road in a rented car after spending a most expectant night on a transatlantic flight. We cook, Mimi and I. She shares with me what we call *la passion de la casserole,* the passion for pots and pans. We go gathering wild cyclamens together, or *cêpes* to make a gratin. I have never been able to catch up with the morels, but she always keeps some dried for me and never fails to bake a chicken chock-full of them for me. We go visit l'Aline in her chalet *aux* Aravis and every time we come down the mountain with a half a pound of fresh, neatly pressed butter and I rejoice, seeing the new Reblochons ripening on racks and listening happily, blissfully to the cow bells calling across the valley.

Oh! We treat ourselves to a meal at Bise and deplore the departure of Madame Bise, and come back to Mimi's new electric stove to indulge in a *civet de lapin,* well laced with Chartreuse. We laugh and think of that Christmas of old.

We still love to tease the old goats and feed them a broken cigarette or two. We go shake the walnut tree and the old Seckel pear tree with its *poires de curé* to bake some of the fruit in cream, or pick a zucchini or two to stuff, or make a delicious pie with zucchini and lemon. We still stuff our faces with bread, Reblochon and *Persillé des Aravis* and we shall forever be friends and talk and laugh around a plate of pear pancakes and glass of the sweet Génepi that she distills clandestinely in the recesses of her barn! *Ça fait mé pi pas pi Mimi, il est bon ton Génepi.*

अৎ

SOUPE A LA FARINE JAUNE
[Corn Flour Soup]

SERVINGS: 6 COST: inexpensive EXECUTION: easy
TOTAL PREPARATION TIME: 45 minutes
BEST SEASON: Fall through winter. A good skiing-weather soup
REMARKS ON INGREDIENTS: Superfine cornmeal or corn flour can
    be located in all Italian markets and neighborhoods. The soup
    may be made entirely with milk. Use Swiss Gruyère or Beau-
    fort cheese.

1 quart milk (1 litre)
½ cup corn flour (50 g)
1 cup stock of your choice, or
    water (¼ litre)
Salt and pepper
2 small zucchini or one
    large (200 g)
1 TB dried basil

⅔ cup heavy cream (150 g
    or 2 small dl)
⅓ cup sour cream (75 g
    or 1 small dl)
½ cup unsalted butter (125 g)
    (optional)
¼ lb. Swiss Gruyère or
    Beaufort cheese, grated
    (125 g)

Scald the milk. Put the corn flour in a bowl. Add the stock gradually to the corn flour, mix well and blend, stirring well, into the simmering milk. Add salt and pepper. With a hand grater, grate the zucchini directly into the pot of soup. Add the basil and stir. Simmer 40 minutes.

Mix heavy cream and sour cream and blend into the hot soup. Add the butter, if used. Reheat but do not allow to boil or you will lose the taste of the raw cream and butter. Correct the seasoning. Serve in bowls topped with grated Gruyère. Stir well before eating.

SOUPE AUX ORTIES
[Nettle Soup]

SERVINGS: 6 COST: inexpensive EXECUTION: easy
TOTAL PREPARATION TIME: 45 minutes
BEST SEASON: Summer months through the end of October
REMARKS ON INGREDIENTS: Use rubber gloves to pick the nettles
   and make sure your legs are covered. It's worth the risk!

4 TB butter unsalted (50–60 g)
4 leeks, the white part only, sliced thin
4 large potatoes (500 g)
6 cups water or light stock (1¼ litre)
Salt
Pepper from the mill

4 cups young nettle leaves
2 carrots, shredded
⅔ cup heavy cream (150 g or 2 small dl)
⅓ cup sour cream (75 g or 1 small dl)
Grated Beaufort or Gruyère cheese (optional)

Heat the butter until the foam starts receding. Add the leeks and sauté until limp and all moisture has evaporated. Add the potatoes. Cover with the cold stock and bring to a boil. Add salt, pepper and the nettles. Simmer 30 minutes. Strain through a food mill or a sieve.

Return the soup to the pot and bring back to a boil. Add the shredded carrots. Simmer until the carrots are done but still crisp. Add both creams; reheat without boiling. Correct the seasoning. Cheese is optional but does not hurt.

PAIN AU BLE ECRASE
[Cracked Wheat Bread]

SERVINGS: 12 COST: inexpensive EXECUTION: easy
TOTAL PREPARATION TIME: 45 minutes actual work plus 2 days for
    ripening the dough

1 cup cracked wheat kernels (150 g)	1 TB liquid honey
2 cups water (4½ dl)	1 cup yoghurt, or soured milk (2¼ dl)
1 packed cup corn flour (120 g)	2 TB walnut oil, or oil of your choice (¼ dl)
3 cups all-purpose, unbleached, unsifted flour (375 g)	1½ tsp. salt (7½ g)
1 envelope yeast	4 TB unsalted butter (50– 60 g)

To the cracked wheat placed in a small mixing bowl, add 1 cup of
the water and let stand 24 hours.

Mix corn flour and all-purpose flour in a large bowl. Make a well.
Add the yeast, the second cup of water, and the honey. Beat well
with a fork, incorporating about ⅓ of the flour mixture. Let stand
about 30 minutes. Add the yoghurt and the walnut oil together with
the salt. Gather into a ball. Knead 10 minutes. Cover with a towel
and let stand at room temperature until double in bulk. Punch
down and refrigerate overnight.

The next day, knead the cracked wheat into the dough. Store
again for 24 hours in the refrigerator. The dough will slowly rise
again to the top of the bowl. Punch it down and set it into 2 large
loaf pans, each generously buttered with 2 tablespoons butter. Let
the dough rise to the rim of each pan. Bake 30 minutes in a preheated 425° oven. Cool on a rack.

CROUTES AU REBLOCHON
[Reblochon Toast]

SERVINGS: 6 COST: moderately expensive EXECUTION: easy
TOTAL PREPARATION TIME: 15 minutes
BEST SEASON: July to February–March, when Reblochon can be
found in the U.S. If the Reblochon is hard, wait until it creams.
SUGGESTED WINE: A dry white Crépy, Roussette, Frangy, or Mâcon
Blanc

6 slices pain au blé écrasé
(page 144), or whole
wheat bread
6 small slices of raw butter,
unsalted, ⅙ inch thick
6 slices prosciutto ham from
the center cut

1 good creamy Reblochon
6 TB fresh breadcrumbs
3 TB fresh chopped parsley
6 TB heavy cream
Pinch of salt
Pepper from the mill

Remove the crust from the bread; toast the bread very lightly. Spread
one small slice of butter on each slice of bread. Set the bread slices
in a jelly roll pan. Top each buttered side with one slice of prosciutto
and enough ¼-inch-thick slices of Reblochon to completely cover
the ham.

Mix the breadcrumbs, the parsley, the heavy cream, a pinch of
salt, and the pepper together. Spread a thin layer of the mixture
over the Reblochon. Bake in 375° oven until heated through. Serve
before the Reblochon starts "running away" from you.

MATEFAIMS AUX CEPES ET AU JAMBON
[Ham and Mushroom Pancakes]

SERVINGS: 6 COST: inexpensive to moderately expensive EXECU-
TION: easy

TOTAL PREPARATION TIME: 30 minutes to 1 hour depending on
the mushrooms used

BEST SEASON: Late July to September with fresh *Boleti,* year round
with dried *Boleti* or ordinary cultivated mushrooms

SUGGESTED WINE: Any ordinary red wine of your choice. A light
Côtes du Rhône is pleasant.

REMARKS ON INGREDIENTS: This recipe was originally made with
fresh *Boletus badius* and *Boletus luteus.* If using the latter, peel
the skin off; it is very gelatinous. Any fresh *Boletus* can be used.
If using dried *Boleti,* use either French, Swiss, or Italian brands.

¼ lb. fresh Boleti *or commercial mushrooms (125 g)
or*
2 oz. dried Boleti *(60 g)*
*3 oz. boiled ham in one piece
(100 g)*
*1 oz. slab bacon, or fresh
fatback, or butter, or oil
(30 g)*
*1 cup sifted flour (120–
125 g)*

2 eggs, separated
Salt
Pepper from the mill
*Water, if needed (2 gen-
erous dl)*
*2 TB melted butter (25 g–
30 g)*
*¼ lb. grated Gruyère or Beau-
fort cheese (125 g)*

Clean the *Boleti;* dice them into ½-inch cubes. If you use regular
mushrooms also dice them into ½-inch cubes. If you use dried mushrooms, cover them with lukewarm water and let them stand 30 minutes. Do not discard the soaking water; use it to make the *matefaims*
later.

Dice the piece of ham into ½-inch cubes. Heat a large skillet.
Stick a piece of bacon fat or slab bacon at the end of a fork and rub
the pan until the bacon has melted enough to coat the pan well. You
may substitute the bacon or fatback with a tablespoon or more of
butter or oil. Add the ham and brown. Remove to a plate.

To the same pan, add the mushrooms and sauté. Sprinkle with a
bit of salt and cover to let the juices exude. Pour the mushroom
juices into a measuring cup. Raise the heat under the mushrooms;

toss them in the pan until they are nice and dry. Mix them with the ham and reserve.

Put the flour in a bowl. Separate the eggs. Add the yolks and a good pinch of salt to the flour. Top the mushroom juices in the measuring cup with enough water to make 1 cup. If you used dried mushrooms, use 1 cup of the soaking water of the mushrooms. Gradually add the water to the flour and egg yolks. Stir until smooth. Whip the egg whites to a good solid, but not dry, foam and fold into the flour/egg/water base.

Blend the mushrooms and ham into the batter. Heat a large frying pan quite hot. Rub with the piece of bacon or fatback. Drop large spoonfuls of batter on the hot pan to obtain 4-inch pancakes. Turn them over as soon as the batter looks dry. Top each pancake with butter and a good tablespoon of grated Gruyère. Cover until the cheese starts running.

Serve with a green salad. The escarole salad on page 165 is perfect with this dish.

TERRINE DE LAPIN AU GENEPI
[Rabbit Pâté with Hazelnuts and Génepi]

SERVINGS: 12–16 COST: moderately expensive EXECUTION: easy

TOTAL PREPARATION TIME: 3½ hours including baking; 24 hours for marination

BEST SEASON: A hearty terrine for fall and winter

SUGGESTED WINE: A dry white wine, Crépy or Roussette, Entremont, Mâcon, Châteauneuf du Pape Blanc

REMARKS ON INGREDIENTS AND IMPLEMENTS: If you hunt and can shoot a wild rabbit or a hare, use it. For the veal meat use a small shoulder. Use the trimmings and the bones to make good stock (pages 10–12) and a small veal stew. Substitutes for the French Génepi, which is not easily located in the United States, are the Italian Fior d'Alpe or Green Chartreuse. Have a 2-quart terrine or round soufflé dish.

5–6 lbs. rabbit, preferably
   wild (3 kg)
1 veal shoulder
1¼ lbs. unsalted fresh fatback
   of pork (60 g)
2 oz. Marc, Cognac, or
   brandy (½ dl)
2 oz. Génepi, Fior d'Alpe, or
   Green Chartreuse (½ dl)
1 tsp. quatre épices (see page
   7)
1½ cup dry white wine
   (3 dl)

1 onion, sliced (50 g)
2 shallots, sliced (30 g)
½ cup hazelnuts (100 g)
4 eggs
4 slices ordinary white bread,
   crust removed
½ cup milk or light cream
   (1 generous dl)
Salt
Pepper from the mill
4 TB butter, unsalted (50–
   60 g)
2 bay leaves

BONING:

Bone the rabbit entirely. Remove all skin, fat pads, and sinews. Proceed as follows to sort the meat for forcemeat or garnish.

Cut the loins, denerved and with all sinews removed, into ½-inch cubes. Put those in a bowl.

Bone the veal shoulder. From the best piece cut enough ½-inch cubes to obtain by volume as much veal cubes as you have rabbit cubes.

Cut enough ½-inch cubes from the fatback to equal by volume the rabbit cubes.

BASIC PREPARATION OF GARNISH AND FORCEMEAT

THE MARINATION:

Mix all the cubes together. Add ½ ounce of the Marc, Cognac or brandy, and the Génepi, Fior d'Alpe or Green Chartreuse. Add a good pinch of *quatre épices*. Let marinate overnight. This will be for the garnish.

Weigh the remainder of the rabbit meat. Use one-half of that weight of the veal meat. That means, if you have 1 pound (500 g) of rabbit, use ½ pound (250 g) of the veal meat. Now add the weight of the rabbit to that of the veal and use half the amount of fatback. With the example given above, you should have a total of 24 ounces (750 g) of rabbit and veal meat mixed and so you will need 12 ounces (375 g) of pork fatback. This will be for the forcemeat. Cut all these meats in large cubes. Put them in a large shallow baking dish and pour the white wine mixed with the remainder of the Marc and Génepi over them. Sprinkle the slices of onion and shallots over the meat. Add the remainder of the *quatre épices.* Cover with plastic film and leave in a cool place, but not in the refrigerator, for 24 hours. Turn the meat over once or twice during marination.

FORCEMEAT, BAKING AND COOLING:

Preheat oven to 350°. Place the hazelnuts in a 9-inch cake pan. Bake them 10 minutes. Empty them into a tea towel and rub to discard the skins. The hazelnuts should be lightly toasted. Reserve.

Beat the eggs well. Add them to the bread moistened with the milk or cream. Reserve.

Grind the meats that marinated overnight in the mixture of wine, liqueurs and vegetables twice. Also grind the onion and shallot slices.

Place the ground material in the large bowl of the electric mixer; beat in the egg/bread/cream mixture. Add 1 teaspoon salt and ¼ teaspoon pepper per pound of forcemeat. Mix in the cubed garnish. This is best done by hand. Rinse your hand in cold water and use it dripping wet.

Test the seasoning by panfrying a nugget of forcemeat in butter and cooling it fast in the freezer. Correct the seasoning of the terrine mixture. Butter the terrine (1½–2 quarts) very heavily and pack the terrine mixture into it. Top with 2 bay leaves. Bake covered with foil in a hot water bath at 350° for 1½ hours. It is done when the fat runs clear and a skewer inserted at the center of the forcemeat comes out clean and burns the top of the hand. To allow the top of the forcemeat to brown, remove the foil during the last 45 minutes of baking.

Cool in the hot water bath. Put a heavy weight on top (a large full can or the blender bottom) while cooling. Refrigerate. This needs at least 4 days of aging to develop a distinctive flavor and will keep at least 2 weeks.

TRUITE DU FIER AUX NOISETTES
[Brook Trout and Hazelnuts]

SERVINGS: 6 COST: reasonable EXECUTION: medium-difficult

TOTAL PREPARATION TIME: 1 hour with boning, 30 minutes without

BEST SEASON: June to October, but hatchery trout are available year round

SUGGESTED WINE: Crépy, Roussette, Frangy, Mâcon Blanc, or any dry white wine of your choice; no great pedigrees, however

REMARKS ON INGREDIENTS: The colder the weather and water, the firmer the meat of the trout. Bear that in mind if you purchase hatchery trout. Rainbow trout is better than golden trout. Fresh hazelnuts are to be found from September 15 until December 1.

6 trout, butterflied
Flour
1 egg
1 tsp. water
Oil of your choice, preferably walnut or olive oil
Salt and pepper
½ cup fresh breadcrumbs

from French or Italian bread (50 g)
½ cup unsalted butter (110– 120 g)
½ cup fresh peeled hazelnuts, chopped (100 g)
Lemon wedges
Parsley

Have the fish merchant butterfly the trout if you do not know how to do it. However, it is easy to do yourself. Do not open the abdominal cavity. Cut the head off. Clean the abdominal cavity. Cut along the backbone with a sharp knife. Snip the backbone free from the tail. Delicately start pulling the rib cage. The whole bone structure of the trout will come sliding out of the fillets. Open up the two fillets, wash them well, and pat dry. The trout is butterflied and ready for breading.

Flour the trout. Beat the egg, teaspoon of water, 1 teaspoon oil, and a good pinch of salt and pepper until liquid. Brush the mixture over the trout fillets and invert the fillets into the crumbs. Keep the skin side floured only. Let dry while you panfry the hazelnuts.

Heat the butter in a frying pan until the foam starts receding. Add the peeled hazelnuts chopped rather coarse and toss into the butter. Continue cooking until the hazelnuts brown visibly but lightly and the butter itself turns hazelnut-colored. Remove the hazelnuts to a small bowl. Keep warm.

Heat a large electric skillet to 375°. Add ⅛ inch of oil. Panfry the trout 3 minutes on each side. Since you can panfry only two at a time, keep those already done in a 275° oven. Do not pile one on top of the other. Salt and pepper after you take the fish out of the oven. Serve with a wedge of lemon and parsley. Spoon an equal amount of *noisette* butter over each trout.

CAILLES AU GENIEVRE
[Quails with Juniper]

SERVINGS: 6 COST: expensive, unless you can obtain *shot* birds from a hunter

EXECUTION: Worth the plucking! Otherwise, easy

TOTAL PREPARATION TIME: 45 minutes

BEST SEASON: Fall

SUGGESTED WINE: A good well-bred Châteauneuf du Pape

REMARKS ON INGREDIENTS: Quails shot by hunters are the best. Hang them and pull a feather every day. Pluck and cook on the day the feathers come out freely; plucking takes only a few minutes. If using "raised" quails already frozen, defrost in the refrigerator. Frozen quail may not always be worth the amount of money involved.

6 quails, cleaned and dressed	1 oz. gin, Marc, or grappa
24 juniper berries	1 cup brown veal stock
Salt and pepper	(2¼ dl)
3 TB butter (45 g)	A squeeze of lemon juice

Put the quails in a container with a lid. Crush the juniper berries and sprinkle them over the birds. Cover the pot tightly and keep refrigerated for 24 hours.

Bring to room temperature before cooking. Put 2 berries into the cavity of each bird; discard the other berries. Salt and pepper each bird in the cavity and truss.

Heat the butter in a cocotte-type pot. Brown the birds on all sides. Heat the gin or other liquor in a small pot and light it. Pour it flaming over each bird. Add 3 tablespoons stock, cover the pot, and cook 12–15 minutes.

Remove the birds to a deep country-type dish. Bring the butter and juices in the pot to a rapid boil, gradually adding the remainder of the stock. When the stock coats a spoon add a squeeze of lemon juice and spoon over the quails. Serve promptly with a gratin of potatoes or a pilaf of noodles.

CIVET DE LAPIN A LA CHARTREUSE
[Rabbit Civet with Chartreuse]

SERVINGS: 6 COST: moderately expensive EXECUTION: easy
TOTAL PREPARATION TIME: 2 hours plus 24 hours for marination
BEST SEASON: Late summer to early spring
SUGGESTED WINE: A good red Côtes du Rhône
REMARKS ON INGREDIENTS: In France, the binding of the sauce is
    not made with flour as it is here, but with the blood of the rab-
    bit. Instructions are given below on how to proceed.

    If you cannot obtain rabbit blood from your butcher, do not
    use any. Bind with a roux. *Do not* under any circumstances use
    pork blood. Before skinning a wild rabbit or hare, add a few
    drops of vinegar to the bowl where you will collect the blood.
    This keeps the blood from coagulating.

1 rabbit, nice size but young,
   cut into 8 pieces
4 onions, sliced thick
1 large carrot, sliced thick
2 tsp. dried basil
½ tsp. dried thyme
¼ bay leaf, crushed
12 juniper berries, crushed
6 cloves, crushed
1 bottle full-bodied red Côte
   du Rhône wine
1½ cups dry white wine
   (Crépy, Mâcon) (3½ dl)
1 lemon, sliced
Unsalted butter as needed (at
   least ½ lb.) (250 g)
½ lb. slab bacon (250 g)

½ lb. white silverskin
   onions (250 g)
Sugar
Bouquet garni
1 TB tomato paste (10 g)
Brown veal stock as needed
   (1–2 cups) (2–4 dl)
6 thin slices of French bread
1 clove garlic
½ cup heavy cream (115
   g or 1 generous dl)
3 TB flour (25–30 g)
1–2 TB green Chartreuse
⅓ cup rabbit blood (optional,
   see above)
Parsley, chopped

MARINATION:

Place the rabbit pieces in one or two glass or pyroceramic baking dishes. Put onions, carrots, basil, thyme, bay leaf, crushed juniper berries, and cloves in a pot. Add the wines. Bring to a boil. Simmer 10 minutes, then cool completely. Pour over the rabbit pieces, and add the lemon slices. Let marinate at room temperature for 24 hours.

GARNISH:

Prepare the garnish while the rabbit marinates so you can use the bacon fat later.

Cut the bacon into ⅓-inch-wide lardoons. Place them in a cold, empty pan over medium heat. Render their fat gently, pouring it off into a bowl as it melts. Cook the lardoons until they are light golden brown. Pat them dry in a paper towel. Store them in a small bowl covered with plastic wrap. Reserve most of the bacon fat; keep 2 tablespoons in the pan to brown the onions.

Cut a cross in the root end of each onion. Add the onions to the pan where the bacon rendered and brown well on all sides. Add a pinch of sugar to the pan, it will help the browning. Set aside. The onions will keep overnight in the refrigerator. Cover the bowl that contains them with a plastic wrap.

STEWING THE RABBIT:
Use a large, enameled, cast-iron pot. Remove the rabbit from the marinade. Pat it dry in paper towels. Heat some of the bacon fat in the pot. Brown the rabbit pieces on all sides. Remove them to a plate.

Discard the lemon slices. Drain all the other vegetables from the marinade and brown them lightly in the same pot and bacon fat where the rabbit browned. Pour the liquid of the marinade into a small pot and reduce it by one-third.

Build the stew as follows. Keep the vegetables at the bottom of the pot. Add the rabbit pieces. Then *strain* the marinade into the pot through a *chinois* or very fine strainer. Add the *bouquet garni,* tomato paste, and brown veal stock. They should just cover the rabbit pieces. Place foil flush against the surface of the meat. Form a tight, upside-down lid that will catch condensation while baking. Cover with the pot lid. Bring to a boil. Bake in a 325° oven for about 30 minutes.

Remove the pot from the oven. Remove the rabbit pieces to a bowl. Discard all the vegetables from the cooking juices. Return the rabbit pieces to the pot together with the small onions and bacon lardoons prepared the day before as a garnish. Cover with foil and lid again. Finish cooking on top of the stove for another 10 to 15 minutes.

BINDING THE SAUCE AND FINISHING THE STEW:
Rub the 6 slices of French bread with the clove of garlic and fry them in clarified butter or oil. Remove the well-drained pieces of rabbit, the small onions and lardoons to a serving casserole. Keep warm.

Strain the cooking juices into a measuring cup. Using a bulb baster, skim the fat completely. Reduce to 2 cups which is enough to serve 6. Reduce the heavy cream to ¼ cup.

If you bind with flour:

Mix 4 tablespoons (50 g) unsalted butter with 3 tablespoons flour (25 g). Whisk this *beurre manié* into the simmering two cups of juices. Add the reduced heavy cream and the green Chartreuse.

Correct the seasoning and strain over the rabbit in the serving casserole.

If you bind with the blood:

Put the blood in a measuring cup. Gradually add ½ cup of hot cooking gravy, whisking constantly. Remove the saucepan containing the remainder of the cooking gravy from the heat. Gradually whisk in the blood mixture. Add the heavy cream and Chartreuse. Reheat without boiling and strain over the rabbit pieces.

In either case, serve the rabbit sprinkled with chopped parsley and with the slices of bread rubbed with the garlic and fried in the clarified butter.

POULET ROTI AUX MORILLES
[Roast Chicken with Morels]

SERVINGS: 4–6 COST: inexpensive with fresh morels, expensive with
   dried morels EXECUTION: easy
TOTAL PREPARATION TIME: 30 minutes plus about 1 hour for roasting
BEST SEASON: Spring, April to June when morels are fresh, otherwise, year round with dried morels
SUGGESTED WINE: Any of the wines of the Jura, red or white
REMARKS ON INGREDIENTS: Use exclusively the pointed *Morchella
   esculenta,* which is plentiful in the forests of the northern Midwest. If using dried morels, sort them carefully. Beware of the
   helvellae often hidden "to make weight"; although they are
   not poisonous, quite a few people are sensitive to them, especially when combined with a good wine.

1 roasting chicken, 4 lbs.
   maximum (1 kg 500)
Salt and pepper
¼ cup unsalted butter (50 g)
½–1 lb. fresh morels or 1½–
   2 oz. dried morels (250 g–
   500 g or 40–60 g)

¼ cup heavy cream (½
   small dl)
1 cup excellent brown veal
   stock, pages 10–12 (2¼ dl)

Preheat the oven to 375°. Clean the chicken. Salt and pepper its cavity.

If you are using fresh morels, remove the foot, and gently squeeze the conical head under softly running water to remove the grit and gravel that the mushrooms always contain.

Heat 2 tablespoons butter in a frying pan; add the morels and salt and pepper. Sauté them gently in the butter for 5–6 minutes. Let them cool.

If you use dried morels, cover them with lukewarm water and let them stand half an hour. Remove the foot and squeeze each cone under softly running water. Sauté in butter 2 to 3 minutes. Season and cool. Do not discard the soaking water; reduce it by two-thirds.

Stuff the chicken cavity with the morels. Truss the chicken. Pour the heavy cream into the cavity.

Put the chicken on a rack fitted in a roasting pan. Rub the skin with 2 tablespoons butter. Roast 50 minutes to 1 hour, basting often with the butter in the roasting pan. The chicken is done if the juices run clear when the thickest part of the thigh is pierced with a trussing needle.

Untruss the chicken; scoop the morels out of the cavity. Add the stock to the juices in the roasting pan and the reduced morel soaking water, if applicable. Deglaze and reduce by at least one-third. Correct the seasoning. Strain the gravy into a bowl and add the morels. Serve with *Pilaf de Nouilles* (page 161) prepared without cheese.

JAMBONETTES DE VOLAILLE AU PERSILLE
[Boned Stuffed Leg of Chicken with Blue Cheese]

SERVINGS: 6   COST: reasonable   EXECUTION: medium-difficult

TOTAL PREPARATION TIME: 2 hours

BEST SEASON: This is a winter dish because it is hearty; but it can be done year round.

SUGGESTED WINE: Northern Red Côtes du Rhône, Châteauneuf du Pape or any of the Premier Crus Beaujolais

REMARKS ON INGREDIENTS: Do not use Roquefort, Gorgonzola or Danish Blue. You may use fresh *Marasmius oreades* (fairy-ring mushrooms) if you find them in the fall.

CHICKEN AND FILLING:
6 chicken legs
2 TB unsalted butter (30 g)
½ lb. fresh mushrooms,
  chopped coarse (250 g)
2 egg yolks
⅔ cup fresh breadcrumbs
  from French or Italian
  bread (60 g)
1½ TB crumbled Persillé des
  Aravis, or Bleu de Bresse,
  or Stilton cheese
Salt
Pepper from the mill
⅓ cup chopped walnuts
  (100 g)
½ cup dry white wine (1
  generous dl)
½–1¼ cups brown veal
  stock as needed (1 to
  2¼ dl)
GARNISH:
½ lb. unblanched slab bacon
24 whole shallots
Chopped parsley

Bone the chicken legs from the back, that is, from the meat side, so the outside skin remains whole and may be used as a casing. Flatten with a meat bat.

Heat the butter until the foam starts receding. Add the mushrooms, salt and pepper. Let the mushrooms loose their juices. Raise the heat very high and sauté until dry. Cool completely. Add the egg yolks, the crumbs, the cheese, a pinch of salt, three or four turns of the peppermill and the walnuts; mix well. Divide into 6 equal lumps. Stuff each chicken leg with one lump of stuffing and sew the leg closed. Do not sew tightly or the leg will burst open while cooking. Sew loosely together both long sides first, then flip the broad end over and sew closed. The legs will resemble tiny hams, hence the name *jambonettes*. Set the *jambonettes* aside.

Prepare the garnish. Cut the bacon into ⅓-inch-wide lardoons. Put them in a cold 9-inch skillet or *sauteuse* pan and render them slowly until they turn golden. Remove them to a plate. Keep the bacon fat.

Peel the shallots and sauté them in the same bacon fat until they start to color; remove them to the same plate as the bacon. Keep for later use. In the same pan where the bacon and shallots were sautéed, and in the same bacon fat, brown the chicken-*jambonettes* on both sides. Discard the bacon fat. Salt and pepper the browned chicken. Add the white wine and let evaporate almost completely. Add ½ cup of brown veal stock. Cover the pan and cook 15 minutes. Uncover the pan, add the shallots and bacon and another ½ cup of veal stock. Continue cooking another 15 minutes or until a skewer inserted at the upper part of the drumstick comes out easily. If there is from ⅔ to ¾ cup of gravy in the pan, do not add any more stock. If there is only ½ cup, add the remainder of the stock and give one or two good boils to blend the flavors. Sprinkle with chopped parsley and serve in the *sauteuse* pan. The *Pilaf de Nouilles* made without cheese is an excellent vegetable.

FRICANDEAUX AUX CHAMPIGNONS
[Veal and Ham Patties with Mushroom Garnish]

SERVINGS: 6 COST: expensive EXECUTION: easy
TOTAL PREPARATION TIME: 2 hours
BEST SEASON: July through September if one uses *Boleti,* year round
    with ordinary mushrooms
REMARKS ON INGREDIENTS: Use veal top of the round or veal "face."
    Use any *Boletus* available, the best being *edulus, badius,* or
    luteus. Peel *Boletus luteus* because of its very gelatinous skin.
    If no *Boleti* are available, ordinary mushrooms also taste very
    good.

VEAL PATTIES:
1 lb. of veal top of the round
   or "face," chopped fine
   (500 g)
¼ lb. boiled ham, chopped
   (125 g)

4 slices white bread, crust
   removed
⅓ cup milk (1 small dl)
½ cup unsalted butter (100–
   110 g) plus 2 TB (30 g)
Salt

Pepper from the mill
Flour
BREADING:
1 egg
1 tsp. oil
1 tsp. water
Salt and pepper
½ cup breadcrumbs
VEGETABLE GARNISH:
1 lb. Boleti or cultivated

mushrooms (500 g)
5 TB butter (75 g)
3 small zucchini diced into
 ⅓-inch cubes
1 tiny clove garlic, mashed
2 TB finely chopped parsley
¼ cup heavy cream (½
 small dl)
⅔ cup brown veal stock (2
 small dl)

TO PREPARE AND BREAD THE PATTIES:

Chop the veal with either a large chopping knife or a modern electric chopper such as Cuisinarts or Robot-Coupe. Also chop the ham. The meat should be so finely chopped that it mats when the knife is used to smooth its surface.

Soak the bread in the milk. Cream the butter. Gradually add the bread squeezed dry, the veal meat, and the chopped ham to the butter. Add salt, if necessary, and a good amount of pepper. Shape into twelve small, flat, oval patties. Flour the patties. Put them on waxed paper.

TO MAKE THE BREADING:

Beat the egg with the oil, water, and a pinch of salt and pepper until the mixture is liquid. Brush a thin film of it on each patty; coat with breadcrumbs.

TO COOK THE VEGETABLES AND PATTIES:

Dice the *Boleti* mushrooms. In a frying pan heat two tablespoons butter. Sauté the mushrooms until dry. Salt and pepper and remove to a plate.

Heat 1 tablespoon of butter in the pan. Sauté the zucchini until they start coloring and are semi-tender. Remove to the plate with the mushrooms.

Add the garlic and 1½ tablespoons parsley to the pan; brown

lightly. Add the cream and reduce to 2 tablespoons. Add the veal stock and reduce to ⅓ cup over high heat. Toss the mushrooms and zucchini in this reduction. Correct the seasoning. Keep warm.

Clean the frying pan and panfry the veal patties in 2 tablespoons butter until light golden on each side.

Present the patties on a dish surrounded by the mushroom and zucchini mixture.

GRATIN DE POMMES DE TERRE AUX CEPES
[Gratin of Potatoes with Boleti eduli Mushrooms]

SERVINGS: 6 COST: inexpensive if you gather the *cèpes* yourself
    EXECUTION: easy
TOTAL PREPARATION TIME: 1 hour 15 minutes
BEST SEASON: August–September
SUGGESTED WINE: A light white Crépy or Roussette de Savoie, Apremont or a light red Côtes du Rhône
REMARKS ON INGREDIENTS: The same gratin of potatoes can also be made with the following mushrooms:
    Marasmius oreades (Fairy-ring mushrooms)
    Agaricus campestris (Common mushroom or field mushroom)
    Lepiota procera (Parasol mushroom)
    Lactarius volemus (Orange milk mushroom)

3 large Maine potatoes	*Salt*
(375 g)	*Pepper from the mill*
½ lb. Boleti eduli *or other*	*1½ cups heavy cream*
mushrooms (250 g)	*1 large clove garlic*
4 TB butter (50–60 g)	

Preheat the oven to 300°.

Peel and slice the potatoes paper thin, using either a Feemster or a Mandoline. Soak them in cold water while you prepare the mushrooms. Slice the mushrooms into ⅛-inch-thick slices after cleaning them properly. Heat 1 tablespoon butter in a frying pan and add the mushroom slices, salt and pepper. Toss the mushrooms in the hot butter and cover them. Reduce the heat. They will loose their juices. Mix those juices with the heavy cream and build the gratin.

Slash the surface of the garlic clove. Rub a 1½-quart baking dish with the cut garlic. Discard all pieces of garlic; leave only the juice. When dry, rub the dish with the remaining three tablespoons of butter.

Drain the water from the potatoes. Put them in a terrycloth towel to completely dry them. Return them to the bowl and salt and pepper.

Place one layer of potatoes on the bottom of the dish. Cover with ½ the cream and mushroom juice mixture. Shake the dish to melt the salt on the potatoes. Taste the cream. If it is not seasoned enough, add more salt.

Spread the mushrooms evenly over the first layer of potatoes. Add the remainder of the potatoes, and the remaining cream and mushroom juice mixture. Taste the cream again and add salt if more is needed. The gratin should be accurately seasoned before baking, otherwise the dish will taste flat after baking.

Bake in a preheated 300° oven until the top is a golden color and the butterfat of the cream starts appearing at the edges of the baking dish.

This dish is good enough to be served as a main dinner course with a salad. To round off the meal, serve a piece of cheese and fruit.

PILAF DE NOUILLES
[Noodle Pilaf]

SERVINGS: 6 COST: reasonable EXECUTION: easy
TOTAL PREPARATION TIME: 30 to 35 minutes
BEST SEASON: Fall to spring
REMARKS ON INGREDIENTS: Can be made also with Orzo and
    angel-hair spaghetti

6 TB butter (65 g)
2 large onions, chopped
  (100 g)
2 cups Tubettini soup macaroni
  (1 lb. or 500 g)
Salt and pepper

2 ½ cups hot chicken or
  beef broth (5 dl)
¼–½ lb. grated Beaufort or
  Gruyère cheese (125–
  250 g)

Heat the butter well in a cocotte-type pot. Add the chopped onions and sauté until golden. Add the noodles and toss in the hot fat until very hot to the top of the finger.

Add the hot stock; bring to a boil. Turn down to a simmer. Stretch several thicknesses of paper towels over the opening of the pot and put the pot lid on. Cook 14 to 15 minutes.

To serve, alternate in a dish layers of noodles with layers of cheese. Use as much or as little of the cheese as you wish.

FARCEMENT DE THONES
[Potato, Bacon and Prune Pudding]

SERVINGS: 6 COST: inexpensive EXECUTION: easy
TOTAL PREPARATION TIME: 2 ½ hours including 2 hours for baking
BEST SEASON: Fall through late spring
SUGGESTED WINE: A nice dry white or red wine without too much
  pedigree
REMARKS ON INGREDIENTS: If corn flour is not available, prepare
  the recipe without it. Do not substitute regular or whole wheat
  flour; the pudding will not set properly.

3 large or 4 medium potatoes,
  preferably Maine (500 g)
2 eggs
2 egg yolks
⅓ cup corn flour or fine
  cornmeal (40 g)
Salt and pepper

½ cup unsalted butter
  (100–110 g)
8 dried, pitted, soft prunes
  ready to eat
1 dried pear
½ lb. slab bacon or ½ lb.
  thick, sliced bacon (250 g)

Place the potatoes in a pot and cover them with cold water. Bring to a boil, reduce to a simmer and cook covered for 20 minutes.

As soon as the potatoes are cooked, peel and purée them using a strainer or a sieve placed over a large mixing bowl. Add the eggs and egg yolks, the corn flour, salt and pepper to suit your taste, and the butter. Set aside.

Cut the prunes in half and the pear into ½-inch dice. Cut the bacon into ⅛–⅙-inch-thick slices. Line a 1–1½-quart charlotte or soufflé mold with the bacon slices. Pack half of the potato mixture at the bottom of the mold. Add the prunes and pears, alternating the fruit pieces. Cover with the remainder of the potatoes. Cover the top of the pudding with lightly buttered foil. Bake in a hot water bath in a 325° oven for 1½–2 hours. The pudding is done when a needle inserted at the center of the potatoes comes out clean and is hot to touch.

This is customarily served with the rabbit civet on page 152, but as a good, cheap main course served with a green salad, it is delicious.

POLENTA DE MIMI
[Mimi's Polenta]

SERVINGS: 6 COST: inexpensive EXECUTION: easy
TOTAL PREPARATION TIME: 1 hour
BEST SEASON: Fall through early spring, but can be made year round
SUGGESTED WINE: A nice red or white wine, dry, without pedigree

TOMATO SAUCE:
2 TB bacon fat, oil or
   butter
1 onion, chopped fine
1 clove garlic, mashed
1 TB chopped parsley
1½ lb. fresh plum
   tomatoes, peeled, chopped
   and seeded, or 1 can Italian

plum tomatoes with
half of their liquid
POLENTA:
¼ lb. slab bacon cut into
   ⅓-inch dice (125 g)
¼ lb. boiled ham cut into
   ⅓-inch dice (125 g)
2 TB chopped Italian flat-
   leafed parsley

(CONTINUED ON NEXT PAGE)

1 large or 2 small cloves garlic, mashed	*Salt*
	Pepper from the mill
1 cup yellow cornmeal (150 g)	*1 TB butter (15 g)*
	¼ lb. grated Beaufort or Gruyère cheese (125 g)
1 cup cold chicken broth (2¼ dl)	*1 TB butter (15 g)*
3 cups boiling chicken broth (7 dl)	

TOMATO SAUCE:

Heat the bacon fat, oil or butter in a frying pan and in it sauté the onion until golden. Add the garlic and parsley; sauté a few more minutes. Add the tomatoes; reduce the heat. Cook until most of the moisture has evaporated. Correct salt and pepper. Set aside for later use.

POLENTA:

Cut the bacon into ⅓-inch cubes; render them slowly in a frying pan and cook until golden. Remove all but one tablespoon of bacon fat from the pan. Add the ham and sauté for a few minutes. Add the garlic and parsley and mix well. Allow the garlic to color slightly. Set aside. Mix the yellow cornmeal with the cold chicken broth. Gradually whisk in the boiling chicken broth. Transfer to a pot and bring the mixture to a boil. Let simmer about 5 to 6 minutes. Meanwhile, butter a 1-quart round baking dish with 1 tablespoon butter. Pour half the polenta into the dish. Sprinkle with the mixture of ham, bacon, garlic and parsley. Top with the remainder of the polenta. Spread the tomato sauce on top of the polenta; sprinkle with the grated cheese and dot with small pieces of butter. Bake in a 325° oven until bubbly.

Serve either as a starchy vegetable or as a main course with a green salad.

GRATIN DE POIREAUX
[Leek Gratin]

SERVINGS: 6 COST: reasonable EXECUTION: easy
TOTAL PREPARATION TIME: 2 hours including baking
BEST SEASON: Fall through early spring

12 leeks	*1 cup heavy cream (2¼ dl*
1 TB butter (15 g)	*or 225 g)*
Salt and pepper	*¼ lb. grated Beaufort or*
1½ cups brown veal stock	*Gruyère cheese (125 g)*
or other stock of your	
choice (3½ dl)	

Remove the roots of the leeks and all but about ½ inch of the green part. Cut through the center of the leeks lengthwise 1½ inches from the root. Wash the leeks thoroughly, running the tap water liberally through the leaves to discard the sand. Butter a 2-quart oblong pyroceramic baking dish. Put the leeks in the dish. Salt and pepper them. Add the stock. Bake in a 325° oven for 45 minutes. Add the heavy cream. Turn the leeks so their exposed side is now bathing in the mixture of stock and cream. Place parchment paper loosely on the surface of the vegetables. Continue baking another 30 minutes. Finally, sprinkle the leeks with the cheese; return to the oven uncovered until the cheese is melted and golden.

SALADE DE SCAROLE
[Escarole Salad]

SERVINGS: 6 COST: inexpensive EXECUTION: easy
TOTAL PREPARATION TIME: 15 minutes
BEST SEASON: Winter through end of April

1 large escarole, white at the heart	*Pepper from the mill*
1 TB vinegar	*3 TB walnut oil, or other oil of your choice*
2 tsp. Dijon mustard	*1 clove garlic*
1 shallot, chopped fine	*Chopped parsley, or chives and walnuts*
2 TB heavy cream	
Salt	

Wash and clean the head of escarole. Tear the leaves into bite-size pieces. Blot dry very fast in tea towels to prevent bitterness.

Put vinegar, mustard, shallot, and heavy cream in a bowl and mix well. Add salt and pepper. Whisk in the oil. Correct the seasoning.

Slash the clove of garlic and rub it briskly against the salad bowl to press the juices out against the side of the bowl. Let dry. Add the dressing and toss well. Sprinkle with chopped parsley, or chives and walnuts. Toss and serve immediately.

POIRES DE CURE AU FOUR
[Baked Seckel Pears]

SERVINGS: 6 COST: inexpensive EXECUTION: easy

TOTAL PREPARATION TIME: 2 hours

BEST SEASON: Seckel pear season is from mid-September to late October.

REMARKS ON INGREDIENTS: Only use ripe Seckel pears. All other types fall apart if ripe or are tasteless if not quite ripe and still slightly hard. Ripen Seckel pears in a brown bag.

2 TB unsalted butter (30 g)	*½ cup light cream (1 generous dl)*
3 lbs. ripe Seckel pears (1 kg 500)	*½ cup heavy cream (1 generous dl) (optional)*
6 TB sugar (90 g)	*½ cup sour cream (1 generous dl) (optional)*
Pinch of salt	
2 TB water	
¼ cup chopped walnuts (40 g)	

Butter an 8-inch round pyroceramic baking dish with the 2 table-spoons of unsalted butter. Peel the pears; do not core them. Put ¼ cup (70 g) sugar at the bottom of the dish. Add the water and sit the pears in the dish. Bake in a preheated 350° oven for 30 minutes. Sprinkle the remainder of the sugar over the pears.

Transfer the dish to a burner on the top of the stove. Turn the heat high. Add the walnuts and let the caramel color until deep golden. Pour the light cream between the pears. As soon as this is done, place the dish under the broiler and let the pears color until deep golden. Serve lukewarm with a dish of the heavy cream well mixed with the sour cream. Although this is optional, it was always done at Mimi's to offset the sweetness of the pear sauce.

MATEFAIMS AUX POIRES
[Country Pear Pancakes]

SERVINGS: 6 COST: inexpensive EXECUTION: easy
TOTAL PREPARATION TIME: 30 minutes
BEST SEASON: Bartlett pear season is from September to November.

¾ cup all-purpose flour (90 g)	2 TB sugar (20 g)
6 eggs	2 TB Marc or grappa
⅓–½ cup milk (1 small dl)	3 TB butter, more if needed (45 g or more)
Pinch of salt	Confectioners sugar
3 Bartlett pears, preferably the red type	

Put the flour in a bowl. Break the eggs into the same bowl. Mix with a whisk until the mixture is smooth and shows gluten strands. Add the milk and salt; stir until smooth. Let stand while you peel the pears.

Peel and core the pears. Cut them into quarters and then into eighths. Slice each eighth of a pear across into ⅛-inch slices. Sprinkle with sugar and add the Marc or grappa. Mix well.

Mix the pancake batter with the pears and stir until all sugar has dissolved.

Heat 1⅓ tablespoons butter in a large electric skillet preheated to 375°. Drop six spoonfuls of batter to make 6 *matefaims*. Let cook 3 to 4 minutes on one side, turn over and cook another 4 minutes on the second side. Transfer to a heat-proof plate and keep hot in a 350° oven. Repeat with the remainder of the batter to make 6 more pancakes. Serve piping hot sprinkled with confectioners sugar.

LA CREME DU GRAND-PERE DELEAN
[Walnut and Honey Custard]

SERVINGS: 6–8 COST: reasonable EXECUTION: easy
TOTAL PREPARATION TIME: 2 hours plus 4 hours for chilling. Prepare 24 hours ahead of time.
BEST SEASON: Good year round

2½ cups boiling milk	1 TB butter (15 g)
(½ litre)	⅓ cup liquid honey
1 cup chopped walnuts	(1 small dl)
(120 g)	3 eggs
¼ cup granulated sugar	3 egg yolks
(35 g)	Pinch of salt
2 TB water	

Scald the milk. Put the walnuts into the blender container. Pour the scalded milk over the walnuts; blend until smooth. Let steep one hour.

Mix the sugar and water in a small pan. Cook to the deep caramel stage, but *do not burn or let smoke at all!* Pour the caramel into a 6-cup soufflé or charlotte mold; twist the mold so the caramel covers the bottom evenly. Place upside down on a cookie sheet or wooden board. Let cool. When the pan is cool, rub with soft butter every bit of the inside surface of the mold not covered with caramel. Preheat oven to 300°.

Beat together the honey, eggs, and egg yolks with a pinch of salt. Gradually add the walnut milk. Strain the custard into the prepared mold and bake in a hot water bath, covering both with a large lid, for 45 to 50 minutes. It is done when a skewer inserted ⅔ of the way into the center of the custard comes out clean. Cool in the water bath and chill, preferably overnight.

Unmold on a plate and serve well chilled.

TARTE AUX COURGETTES ET AU CITRON
[Zucchini and Lemon Pie]

SERVINGS: 8 COST: inexpensive EXECUTION: easy
TOTAL PREPARATION TIME: 1½ hours
BEST SEASON: Spring and summer when zucchini are small, but
   feasible year round

PASTRY:
1 cup flour (115–120 g)
6 TB butter (60 g)
½ tsp. salt
3½ TB yoghurt (natural,
   unflavored)
FILLING:
3 zucchini, as small as possible,
   sliced ⅛-inch thick
1 TB unsalted butter,
   melted (15 g)
2 TB sugar (30 g)
Pinch of salt
⅓ tsp. caraway seeds
Juice of half a lemon

½ tsp. grated lemon rind
LEMON CUSTARD:
6 TB unsalted butter,
   creamed (60–70 g)
⅔ cup granulated sugar
   (170 g)
Juice of two lemons
2 eggs
2 egg yolks
Pinch of salt
2 TB white or dark rum
2 TB flour (15–20 g)
Grated rind of one lemon

1 TB superfine sugar (15 g)

TO MAKE THE PASTRY:
Make a well in the flour. Cut the butter into large chunks, 1 tablespoon each, and add. Add the salt. With the fingertips, flatten the but-

ter in the flour until the mixture is mealy and the butter is in pieces
the size of large peas. Add the yogurt. Mix with the fingertips but
don't knead. *Fraiser* twice (see page 14). Flatten into a round ½-
inch by 4-inch cake. Refrigerate.

TO MAKE THE FILLING:
Use the smallest zucchini you can possibly find. Slice into ⅙-inch-
thick slices. Heat the butter in a skillet. Add the zucchini and stir.
Sprinkle with sugar and a pinch of salt. Add the caraway seeds, the
lemon juice and rind and let cook until the zucchini loses its green
color and the juices in the pan look somewhat thickened. The pectin
of vegetables, when combined with sugar and butter, forms a thick
syrup. Cool completely.

TO PREPARE THE CUSTARD:
Cream the butter well. Beat in the sugar, the juice of two lemons,
2 eggs, 2 egg yolks, a pinch of salt and the rum. Mix well. Fold in
the flour and the grated lemon rind.

TO BAKE THE PIE:
Preheat the oven to 375°. Roll out the pastry to fit a 9-inch quiche
pan, preferably of fireproof white porcelain. Line the bottom of the
pie with the slices of zucchini and their juices. Bake 20 minutes on the
bottom rack of the oven.

Pour the custard over the zucchini and raise the pie to the top rack
of the oven. Bake another 20 to 25 minutes or until the custard is set.
Sprinkle the top of the custard with the superfine sugar and broil one
minute. Serve lukewarm or cold.

CREME GLACEE AUX MYRTILLES
[Frozen Blueberry Cream]

SERVINGS: 6–8 COST: inexpensive EXECUTION: easy
TOTAL PREPARATION TIME: 30 minutes plus 4 hours for freezing
BEST SEASON: Summer

REMARKS ON INGREDIENTS: Use only wild blueberries. If you cannot find them fresh, use frozen Maine blueberries.

1 lb. wild blueberries (500 g)
24 oz. wild blueberry jam
*   (or cultivated blueberry*
*   jam)*
Juice of one lemon

2 cups heavy cream, whipped
*   to the soft Chantilly*
*   stage (5 dl)*
Grated rind of one lemon

Place blueberries and jam in a pan and heat until the mixture is entirely liquefied. Add the lemon juice. Transfer to the blender container and blend until smooth. Strain through a sieve into a large bowl. Freeze until the mixture is semi-solid. Stir at regular intervals to prevent the formation of lumps.

Whip the cream to the light, still fluid *Chantilly* stage; add the lemon rind. Fold the cream into the semi-solid sherbet until homogenized. Pour into a shallow cake pan. Freeze until solid. Let mellow 5 minutes at room temperature before dishing out with an ice cream scoop.

Claire

—— ⊘ —— ⊘ ——

TOURAINE

1940–1955

CLAIRE WAS THE PROFESSIONAL among us; the mistress of a small country inn, the Hôtel des Voyageurs in Château-la-Vallière, at the heart of that lovely, so deeply and explicitly French province of Touraine. Château, as the Chabrolesque little town was called for short in our family midst, had two poles of activity. The mayor and the schoolmaster were the secular authorities. They reigned over the town hall, an ugly affair of a building, planted squarely in the center of town and boasting the three favorite claims of our Republic: Liberty, Equality, Fraternity. Of liberty there was plenty, for this little town was full of a typical bourgeoisie exercising its "discreet charms." Finding traces of equality and fraternity was more difficult. The bourgeoisie practiced money exchanging with name changing and fortunes were consolidated with wedding rings. After ten years of exemplary marriage and two heirs, a citizen could, with the indulgence of the whole town, start taking liberties.

That part of town was bustling with activity especially on cattle market days. Claire's hotel faced the town hall and the great distraction was to sit on the terrace and watch the people go by. The older generation, who had already passed from the age of liberties to that of wisdom, kept a running commentary on the foibles of the younger ones and the stories one heard were more often than not hilarious. Old Jean the bachelor, who came every morning for his glass of *blanc* at eleven-thirty, could give you an earful of the emotional state of the town. He would deposit his straw hat on the *zinc,* start with "I could tell you . . ." and that was it; here came the hottest news. I did my best to be busy around him, but was always chased away to work in the kitchen. Who cared; I would catch up with the news when Claire's daughter dutifully reported it to her mother half an hour later.

The spiritual end of town was most respectable and peaceful. The church, the "castle"—every little town in Touraine has its castle— and the old-folks home were situated on a lovely hill overlooking a lake. When I was a child, the lake seemed huge. It is indeed sweet and lovely, but so tiny to my adult eyes.

The society on church hill was without liberties. An antique curate said Mass every day and had a very long line at his confessional on Saturdays. At the castle, a 75-year-old baron lived his last days in the glorious shadow of his noble ancestors who dated back to the 1300s. At the old-folks home, the sisters took care of their patients and made a little money exhibiting a faded portrait of Louise de Lavallière, the most sensitive of Louis XIV's three wives. She had ended her life there. Rumor has it in our family that we are descended from her son the Duc du Maine. If, indeed, that tiny droplet of Bourbon blood remains in my veins, it may account for my deepseated dislike of the new rich and their snobbery.

I first visited Château-la-Vallière in June of 1940 when we took refuge there after the invasion of Paris. I remember a long walk; it is a good two miles from the station to Claire's hotel. We arrived in the middle of the dinner service. The house had that smell of generous, voluptuous food so typical of good French restaurants; it was the rush hour. Things looked rather interesting to my young eyes, but I was sentenced to bed. It was not until the next morning that I could start investigating the house. Dining room and lounge were hushed, sacred places. I was to learn that one should never dare show one's face there unless it had been scrubbed and unless one's dress was absolutely spotless. As a child, I did not wear a kitchen apron; they were ten times too large for me. I vividly remember painstakingly rearranging the pleats of my cotton smock to make sure that the annoying little stains one gathers in a kitchen were well tucked under.

The staircase leading to the hotel rooms had a beautiful bannister, each of its massive posts a handcarved bull or dog head. I loved the good smell of fresh bee's wax and was soon to learn how to make the highly polished snouts shine even shinier.

Upstairs, everything looked peculiar; the rooms were ordinary country inn rooms, but since the building had once been the chapel of a monastery, the outside wall of each of them was curved like the nave of a church with the tip of the ogive lost in the attic above more recently built ceilings. All rooms looked out on a gravel courtyard shaded by a single beautiful linden tree which, during the summer nights, would weep tiny tears of sweet and sticky sap. There was a long rambling shed along one whole side of the courtyard; it was old, built of greenish wood and happily festooned with the huge blue-eyed clematis so common in Touraine. Blue and pink hydrangeas stood in large bright clay pots. Deep in the darkness of that shed things happened; wood was split and stacked, the family caldron boiled away loads of laundry or puffed while jars and jars for fruit or pâtés were sterilizing. It was under that shed that I was to hold the feet of the hundreds of chickens, rabbits, and ducks that Claire sacrificed and turned into her famous concoctions. I still recoil at remembering how the poor things wriggled in my hands. I fondly recall Claire's voice saying in her beautiful French, "Tiens bon, ma mignonne." Calling me *ma mignonne* was her way of letting me know that she knew how I hated being her helper right at that moment.

The usual comment on learning that I was Claire's niece was: "Madame Robert . . . oh, she is a Cordon Bleu." Her cooking was the pride of the town, the talk of the province. Famous three-star chef Barrier in those days was a young boy. Many people took the trip from Tours—even from Orleans, Angers or Saumur—to enjoy

Claire's specialties, and it was not rare for food writers to travel from Paris. I saw Madeleine Decure there, although I met her officially only years later. The Docteur de Pomiane was a respected customer, and that lovely, witty but so human Curnonsky was a friend of the house. He often came during the hunting season with friends and left with a basketful of *rillettes* and pâtés.

Claire's kitchen, a Michelin-starred kitchen, would have been considered a hole in the wall by most Americans. Big it was not, nor modern, nor full of gadgets. It consisted of a huge sandstone sink, a huge stove on which she cooked with coal and wood, a huge table at which workers sat, and a collection of old, shiny coppers that positively covered one solid wall. On the opposite wall hung sieves of all sizes and gauges, *chinois, araignées,* pestles, all the real tools of the trade. Electric implements had not yet made an appearance in France, so whisks were plentiful and wooden spatulas and knives. Many she had had since she was a child apprenticing in the kitchen of a neighboring castle. She must have known how I so wanted my own knife, for on my twelfth birthday I received from her my first Sabatier and a sweet little kit of pastry nozzles; both have graced my cooking classes. I have noticed, not without emotion, that every year there is a student chef who starts a love affair with that knife. I have been tempted to give it away but who would want to give away such an *amulette,* and the only tangible possession that I have left from Claire.

What else she gave me was intangible. She gave me the profession that was to become the joy of my active life, and she never knew that the essence of her work and wisdom would be communicated to so many eager young persons in America.

She was not much of a woman as size went, but her personality made up for it. She was small, slightly built, and said to have a famous temper. I never noticed it, for I loved and admired her with my whole soul. I loved to watch her hands wield the knife or work on pastry. They flew; she kneaded *fouaces* the texture of which put all the bakers' *fouaces* to shame. Above all, she looked beautiful. Not that her face was that well shaped, but it reflected a soul full of peace, integrity, and love of work well done. She dressed in a white smock which was always immaculate. Even in the middle of the dinner service her apron remained spotless, a feat that I know by now I shall never achieve.

She introduced me to the great cooking of the women of France in the most natural manner. On the day after I arrived in Château— I still remember that it was June 10, 1940—she let me look the house over; then at 9 A.M. she gave me ten pounds of green beans and nicely asked me to peel them. I promptly started to do so by snapping the ends and pulling the strings. Claire stopped me quickly; she wanted those beans Frenched and the strings removed with a paring knife. *Au couteau, ma mignonne, au couteau,* so I started. My hand soon developed a severe cramp and I blessed my mother for coming to the rescue and helping me finish on time.

While I was growing up Claire gave me odd jobs like vegetable peeling or salt grinding. As I grew more experienced and capable of understanding, I was entrusted with many more serious things, such as the omelettes at lunch time or the salad dressing. One day in the middle of the noon meal rush, she wanted a mayonnaise. With trepidation I made it, scared to death, drop by drop of that oil, building that emulsion she had told me about. And it worked! Then the time came for soups and sauces and finally during the last years of her life, when she was slowly giving in to the devastation of a painful illness, I was introduced to fish pâtés, terrines, mousselines, and quenelles and roast venison and game.

Her food was the lovely food of the Touraine. She was an artist at making the white pudding of Christmas, that *boudin blanc* flavored with *duxelles* and a huge fresh truffle. She faithfully followed the seasons, using in the summer the pike that my father fished out of the lake or the carp and tench, which she would turn into *matelotes.* As soon as the salmon was running in the Loire, she had some shipped to the restaurant and sent Papa to catch an eel to promptly make both into one lovely pâté. She was so honest that she even gave credit to my grandmother for bringing her that recipe for *Carpe à la Saint Léonard* from L'Ile-Bouchard. The Gault and Millau guide of the French provinces to this day mentions a fillet of beef as a specialty of Château-la-Vallière; it was one of her specialties.

She loved to use the mushrooms that grew in the forest during the summer months to make the most extravagant and delicious skillet dishes. For years I was her chief provider. She was a great *charcutière* and I had to admire her skill when she and her sisters sat twisting tripe to make *andouillettes*. She made pâté after pâté during the late summer and fall when the hunting season was open and Monsieur le Baron and his friends brought her numerous hares and pheasants. She canned them and stored them in the dark, cool cellar where the Vouvray and Chinon wines made by diverse members of the family were resting. When she died in 1955, her cellar still contained a few bottles of those marvelous Vouvray of 1921 and 1928.

Every year in October, Monsieur le Baron would send me an invitation on vellum for a true *chasse à courre le cerf,* a real deer hunt in the old royal French style. Monsieur le Baron had taught me to ride at the same time he had taught two of his granddaughters. Each year one of the young women would lend me an outfit so I could follow the hunt in style. What strange feelings those autumnal forests brought when the air echoed with sad horn calls and a beautiful deer fell prey to the rage of a pack of English dogs. On one side I loved the stimulating horse ride and exercise; on the other I kept praying that the shot that meant the end of a beautiful animal's anguish would echo fast, very fast, through the cathedral of the trees.

Once a year, Claire had her daughter replace her at the stove. Claire put on her best black dress, had her hair done professionally and then proceeded to the castle to join the officials of the town in a celebration of Saint Hubert, where not only venison and game were served in large quantities, but veal, beef, and cheeses of all sizes and dimensions. Everyone brought a masterpiece in one of those categories and, accompanied by the best wines in France, the rejoicing went on very lovingly and very discreetly for hours on end. As Claire would put it the next day, "Monsieur le Baron should understand such a *Balthazar* is not for people our age anymore." It did not look to me, however, as if anyone was suffering at all. My regrets not to be included were often severe.

Only once did my cousins and I get the brunt of Claire's famous temper. That was when we took the liberty of interfering with the peace of a coop full of chickens. It was when the last white *brugnons* —a crossbreed of white peach and green gage plum—had been gathered from the small trees spread here and there at the edge of the vineyards. Claire told us that cousin Alexandre needed hands for the vintage in Chinon. So to Chinon we went and picked while my father and Alex made the new wine. We loved to drink that new-born wine from Cabernet franc that we called *guilleret,* but it made us quite silly and somewhat overhappy. Once we had such a good time sampling the new wine that we stole some of the must and fed it to the chickens. Not only did the hens go into some kind of a frenzy, making a din of unending cackling all through the night, but they stopped laying eggs for two days. The funniest sight was that great big grotesque old rooster that waddled forward for a few yards and finally collapsed onto its belly, its eyes closed and its head hopelessly tilted. We were all too old to be spanked, but we got, as the French expression goes, our heads shampooed and were restricted to quarters. I was to learn though, through the family grapevine, that everyone had had a good laugh over our prank.

There was no way to develop a big head around Claire. She was down to earth and could not tolerate pompous people. She once taught me quite a lesson. On learning that sixty unexpected guests would arrive for lunch the next day, she entrusted me with candied chestnut purée and cream and the order to produce something nice for dessert. I made some kind of a Bavarian cream and proudly boasted of having created a new dessert. The answer was fast and most effective: "Why sure, *ma mignonne,* you just reinvented Nessel-rode pudding." A great deflation of my ego, but a great lesson also. The best compliment Claire could give was: "This is nice and very presentable." "Presentable" meant you could serve it; it had passed the test for the dining room. It would not give the house the reputation French people fear the most, that of *laissez-aller,* the lackadaisical sloppiness that is the antithesis of the class they talk so much about. How many times was I reminded while I was working to picture my work finished, to picture it beautiful and classy, always to do it so I would be proud of it.

What a woman you were, Claire, to look straight into the eyes of that French police officer who came to investigate two Jewish guests hiding at the inn in 1943 and say: "The Bernheims are my guests, Monsieur, and nothing will happen to them." Something did happen, however. Germaine Bernheim survived and stayed on to help in the restaurant for years but Léon, who was completely deaf, was arrested while taking a stroll on a solitary forest path. The traitor had been so close to all of us.

The Hôtel de Voyageurs still exists in Château-la-Vallière. It is nothing now but one of those many tourist restaurants where the tables are squeezed like sardines in a can and covered with garish tablecloths and where one is served, of course, the eternal *coq au vin*. All that would not matter so much, after all life must go on, but why was that beautiful linden tree that weeped its tears through the summer nights cut down and replaced by a grey concrete wall?

CREME TOURANGELLE
[*Cream of Vegetable Soup*]

SERVINGS: 6 COST: reasonable EXECUTION: easy, reheats well
TOTAL PREPARATION TIME: 1 hour
BEST SEASON: Early to late fall when vegetables are abundant

1 quart water (1 litre)
3 medium potatoes, peeled and cut into 1-inch chunks (375 g)
½ lb. green beans, peeled and cut into 1-inch chunks (250 g)
6 leeks, white and light green parts only, sliced thin (500 g)
Salt and pepper

1 TB chopped parsley
1 tiny clove garlic, chopped
4 TB unsalted butter (50 g)
½ cup sour cream (125 g or 1 generous dl)
¼ cup heavy cream (60 g or ¾ dl)
¼ lb. wax beans, peeled and cut into ½-inch chunks (125 g)

Bring the water to a boil. Prepare all the vegetables on a tray; peel them, cut them, and wash them. To the boiling water, add the potatoes, green beans, leeks; bring back to a boil. Add salt and pepper to your taste and simmer 45 minutes.

Strain the soup through a sieve or a food mill. Bring back to a violent boil. Add the parsley, garlic, and butter, cut into small pieces, to the center of the boil. Turn the heat off, cover the soup and let steep for 10 minutes. Mix both the creams in a bowl. Blanch the wax beans in 2 cups of rapidly boiling water; drain. Add the beans and the mixture of creams to the soup. Reheat without boiling. Correct the seasoning and serve piping hot.

LA SOUPE AUX PETITS POIS FRAIS
[Lettuce and Sweet Pea Soup]

SERVINGS: 6 COST: reasonable EXECUTION: easy, may be reheated
TOTAL PREPARATION TIME: 1 hour
BEST SEASON: June to the end of September
REMARKS ON INGREDIENTS: If sweet, tiny fresh peas are not to be
    located, use frozen petits pois.

4 TB unsalted butter (50 g)
1 onion, minced fine
2 leeks, minced fine
    (white part only)
1 very large head or 2 small
    heads of Boston lettuce,
    green and yellow leaves,
    cut in thin chiffonade *strips*
1 tsp. granulated sugar
Salt and pepper

1 quart brown veal stock
    (1 litre)
1 cup freshly shelled petits
    pois (300 g)
½ cup sour cream (125 g or
    1 generous dl)
¼ cup heavy cream (60 g or
    ¾ dl)
6 TB butter-fried croutons

Heat the butter until the foam starts receding. Add the onion and leeks and sauté until translucent. Add the *chiffonade* of lettuce, which is obtained by rolling the leaves into tight cigars and cutting them across into ⅙-inch-wide *chiffonade* strips. Toss the lettuce until wilted. Add the sugar, salt and pepper to your taste, and the veal stock. Bring to a boil and simmer 30–35 minutes.

Strain the soup through a sieve or a food mill. Return to the cooking pot; bring back to a boil. Add the peas and simmer 10 more minutes. Mix sour cream and heavy cream; blend into the soup. Reheat without boiling. Correct the seasoning. Serve piping hot with the butter-fried croutons as a garnish.

OMELETTE AUX CHANTERELLES
[Chanterelle Omelette]

SERVINGS: 2 COST: inexpensive if you gather the mushrooms your-
self EXECUTION: easy; use a No. 22 omelette pan
TOTAL PREPARATION TIME: 30 minutes
BEST SEASON: July and August
REMARKS ON INGREDIENTS: If the true chanterelle (*Cantharellus cibarius*) is not available, use brown mushrooms from Cali-
fornia. They are better than the overpriced, soggy, metallic-
tasting European canned chanterelles.
SUGGESTED WINE: Vouvray Moëlleux, Chinon, or Bourgueil

6 TB butter (75 g)	⅓ cup heavy cream (1
½ lb. sliced chanterelles or	small dl)
brown California mush-	1 TB chopped chives
rooms (250 g)	1 TB sour cream
Salt and pepper	4 jumbo or large eggs

Heat 3 tablespoons butter in an 8-inch skillet. Add the mushrooms; toss them in the butter. Add salt and pepper and cook over a moder-ate high flame until the mushrooms release their juices. Add the heavy cream and let cook gently until the cream has reduced and coats the mushrooms well. Add chives and sour cream and mix well. Keep warm.

Melt the other 3 tablespoons of butter in the omelette pan. Mix the eggs with salt and pepper. Beat until just homogenous. Pour into the hot pan. Count to 4, then continue beating as if the eggs were still in the bowl. As soon as the egg is 90 percent solidified, slide the omelette back and forth on the bottom of the pan to build its bottom. Spoon the mushroom mixture in the center of the omelette, fold and invert onto a plate. Enjoy *immediately*.

CARPE A LA SAINT LEONARD
[*Carp Stuffed with Pike Mousseline*]

SERVINGS: 6 COST: expensive EXECUTION: requires care and understanding

TOTAL PREPARATION TIME: 2 hours

BEST SEASON: Carp and pike are available year round in fish markets but are easier to find during the Jewish High Holidays.

REMARKS ON INGREDIENTS: If carp and pike are not to be located, a striped bass and fillets of grey sole will also be an excellent combination.

SUGGESTED WINE: Vouvray Sec

FORCEMEAT AND FUMET:
One 2-lb. pike to obtain ½ lb. pike meat without skin or bones (1 kg. to obtain 250 g of meat)
1 whole egg
3 TB unsalted butter (45 g)
Salt
White pepper from the mill
1–1¼ cups heavy cream (3 dl)
½ cup Vouvray Sec (1 generous dl)

1 large onion, sliced
Bouquet garni
2 cups water (½ litre)
CARP AND SAUCE:
One 3-lb. whole carp, uncleaned (1 kg 250)
1 lb. very white mushrooms, sliced thin (500 g)
½ cup Vouvray Sec (1 generous dl)
⅔ cup reduced fish fumet (2 small dl)
Salt and pepper
2 shallots, minced fine

½ *lb. very fresh unsalted* *Lemon juice, if needed*
butter plus 2 TB at room *Parsley bunches*
temperature (250 g plus *Lemon slices*
30 g)

TO PREPARE THE FORCEMEAT AND FUMET:

Lift the fillets of pike, weigh them; there should be ½ pound of meat without bones or skin. Separate the meat into two ¼-pound portions. Beat the egg until liquid. Measure 2 tablespoons of egg into the blender container; add half of the pike meat. Blend on high speed until the meat is reduced to a smooth, shiny purée that pulls away by itself from the sides of the container. Repeat with the remainder of the egg and fish meat. Mix both portions of purée well. Strain through a sieve. With an electric mixer cream the butter. Add about ¾ teaspoon salt and ⅓ teaspoon of pepper; mix well. Set the mixer on medium speed; gradually add the fish meat. Refrigerate one hour. Place the bowl containing the mixture into another bowl filled with ice cubes and water. Set the electric mixer on low speed and slowly blend in the heavy cream. Correct the seasoning. Keep refrigerated until ready to use.

While the fish mousseline is chilling, prepare a fish fumet or stock by putting the pike head and bones, ½ cup of Vouvray, 2 cups of water, sliced onion, and the *bouquet garni* into a saucepan. Bring to a boil. Reduce the heat and simmer 35 minutes. Strain and reduce to ⅔ cup. Set aside for later use.

TO PREPARE THE CARP AND SAUCE:

Remove the fins of the carp with scissors. Cut the back of the fish open with a very sharp knife. Do not clean the fish through the gills or by opening the abdomen. With your knife, loosen the meat from the backbone until the latter is completely exposed on both sides. Cut the backbone just below the head and just above the tail. Pull the backbone gently from head to tail, so it comes out in one piece. Remove all the by now well-exposed insides. Rinse the cavity well, pat it dry with paper towels, and salt and pepper it.

Place the fish on its tummy and fill the cavity with the forcemeat. Sew the fish closed with a needle and white thread.

Butter a large fireproof dish with 2 tablespoons butter. Sprinkle the mushrooms on the bottom. Lay the fish over the mushrooms. Add ½ cup of Vouvray Sec and ⅔ cup reduced fish fumet, salt, and pepper. Cover the fish with aluminum foil and bake in a 350° oven for one hour. The cooking time varies with each fish. Test for doneness at the center of the mousseline with a skewer.

Remove the cooked fish to a platter. Surround it by the well-drained mushrooms and keep warm. Strain the cooking juices into a *sauteuse* or a frying pan, add the shallots and reduce to a scant ¼ cup. While the reduction is violently boiling, whisk in ½ pound of butter. Correct the seasoning very carefully, adding a drop or two of lemon juice if necessary. Remove the top skin of the fish. Strain the sauce over it. Serve promptly, decorated simply with bunches of parsley and a few lemon slices or wedges.

L'ALOSE DE LA COUSINE CHARLOTTE
[Fillets of Shad with Sorrel Butter]

SERVINGS: 6   COST: moderately expensive   EXECUTION: easy
TOTAL PREPARATION TIME: 30 minutes
BEST SEASON: March and April
SUGGESTED WINE: Muscadet sur lie

3 lbs. fillet of shad (1 kg 500)	2 shallots, chopped fine
½ cup fresh breadcrumbs (50 g)	½ cup Muscadet white wine (1 dl)
½ cup clarified butter (100 g)	¼ cup raw sorrel, chopped very fine (50 g)
Salt and pepper	½ cup unsalted butter at room
1 cup fish fumet (2¼ dl)	temperature (125 g)

Brush the fillets of shad with the clarified butter and sprinkle with the breadcrumbs. Lightly salt and pepper. Put the fish fumet and shallots at the bottom of a fireproof baking dish. Set the fillets in the dish and broil 4 inches from the flame for 7 to 8 minutes.

Remove the fillets to a serving platter. Add the Muscadet to the juices in the baking dish and strain into a heavy saucepan. Add a good pinch of salt and pepper. Reduce to a glaze of 3 tablespoons. Add the chopped sorrel; it will immediately loose its juices. Raise the heat under the glaze and sorrel mixture. When it boils, whisk in the soft butter. Correct the seasoning very carefully, spoon over the shad fillets, and serve promptly.

ESCALOPES DE SAUMON AUX CONCOMBRES FONDANTS
[Salmon Scallops with Cucumbers]

SERVINGS: 6 COST: expensive EXECUTION: easy
TOTAL PREPARATION TIME: 45 minutes
BEST SEASON: Salmon high season, from the end of May to the beginning of September
SUGGESTED WINE: Muscadet sur lie

3 cucumbers, peeled, seeded, and cut into olive-size chunks	1 TB shallots, chopped very fine
Boiling water, salted	1 TB lemon juice
9 TB raw unsalted butter (125 g)	3 TB each: heavy and sour cream (½ dl each)
Salt and pepper	3 lbs. salmon fillets
⅔ cup fish fumet (2 small dl)	Flour
	Clarified butter
	1 TB fresh tarragon, chopped

Blanch the cucumbers in the boiling salted water for two minutes. Drain. Heat one tablespoon butter in a 1½-quart saucepan. Add the cucumbers and salt and pepper. Cover and cook gently for 5–6 minutes. The cucumbers should be soft and ready to melt in the mouth. Set aside on a plate for later use.

Place the fish fumet, shallots, lemon juice, and a good pinch of salt in the same saucepan. Reduce to 1 tablespoon.

Remove the saucepan from the heat and whisk in the remaining 8 tablespoons of raw, unsalted butter. Add both creams and the cucumbers. Reheat very slowly; do not boil. Correct the seasoning.

Cut the salmon fillets into twelve ¼-inch-thick scallops, holding your knife at a 45° angle while cutting. Flour the scallops lightly. Heat enough clarified butter in a large frying pan to cover the bottom with ⅛ of an inch liquid butterfat. Cook the scallops very quickly, four at a time. Count slowly from 1 to 3, turn the scallops over; count from 4 to 6 and remove the fish to a platter. Repeat with the remaining scallops. Season the scallops. Add the tarragon to the sauce. Serve two scallops per person and spoon the sauce over the fish. Serve promptly.

PATE D'ANGUILLE
[Eel Pâté]

SERVINGS: 12 COST: moderately expensive EXECUTION: medium-difficult

TOTAL PREPARATION TIME: 2 hours

BEST SEASON: In France, made in the spring with eel and salmon. In the United States, may be better at Christmas time when the Italian neighborhood fish markets have fresh live eels.

SUGGESTED WINE: Muscadet sur lie, Vouvray Sec

REMARKS ON INGREDIENTS: If eel is not available, replace it with fillet of striped bass cut into 1-inch-wide strips. For the forcemeat use salmon in spring and summer and sole in winter.

PASTRY:
3 cups flour, sifted (300 g)
½ cup butter (125 g)
1½ tsp. salt (7 g)
1 egg, beaten

½ cup water or less
   (1¼ dl)
FISH AND FORCEMEAT:
1 large eel, skinned and boned
1 egg white, beaten lightly

1 cup chopped Italian parsley
12 ounces raw sole or salmon
   meat, very fresh (375 g)
2 whole eggs
2 tsp. salt (10 g)
1 tsp. ground white pepper
   (3 g)
Pinch cayenne
1 cup breadcrumbs from

French or Italian bread
   (about 100 g)
¾ cup milk plus 2 TB (2 dl)
½ cup unsalted butter
   (160 g)
1 egg yolk
Light lemony mayonnaise
⅓ cup chopped watercress

TO PREPARE THE PASTRY:

Make a well in the flour; add the butter cut in large chunks, the salt and the beaten egg. Mix well. Add as much water as will be necessary to obtain a smooth ball of pastry. *Fraiser* the pastry twice. Shape it into a rectangle 9 inches by 2 inches and cut into 2 pieces, one 5½ inches long, the other 3½ inches long. Refrigerate while you prepare the forcemeat.

TO PREPARE THE FORCEMEAT:

Lift the fillets of the eel from the center bone. Cut them into 3-inch-long pieces. Beat the egg white lightly. Dip the pieces of eel into the egg. Roll each of them in the chopped parsley. Set aside on a plate. Separate the sole or salmon meat into four 3-ounce portions. Beat the eggs. Blend each portion of fish in the blender with two tablespoons of the beaten egg.

Put the salt, pepper, and cayenne in a bowl and beat in the smooth purée of fish. Refrigerate while you prepare the *panade*, as follows: Measure the weight of breadcrumbs. Bring ¾ cup milk to a boil, add the crumbs and stir over medium-high heat until the mixture is very thick and heavy. Remove the mixture to a buttered plate. Lightly rub the surface of the *panade* with a piece of butter and cool completely.

With the electric mixer, cream the butter in a large bowl. Gradually beat in the cooled *panade*, then the chilled salmon purée. Keep refrigerated while you fit the pastry into the pâté mold.

TO "BUILD" THE PATE:

Butter an oblong 1½–2-quart pâté mold. Roll out the larger portion of pastry ¼ inch thick and fit it into the mold, letting the excess dough hang loosely over the edges of the mold. Line the bottom and sides of the pastry with ¼ inch of forcemeat. Then spread ½ of the remaining forcemeat on the bottom of the mold. Salt and pepper the parsleyed eel strips; press them on top of the layer of forcemeat. Cover the eel strips with the remainder of the forcemeat. Pack well.

Cut the hanging pastry evenly to measure 1 inch all around the mold; close it over the forcemeat. Mix the egg yolk with the remaining milk to make a *dorure*. Brush it over the pastry. Now roll out the second portion of pastry ¼ inch thick. Cut two vent holes, evenly spaced. Transfer the pastry over the pâté, seal well, and cut off the excess pastry with the back of a knife. The lid of the pâté should be flush with the edge of the mold. Crimp the edges of the pâté with a fork or pastry crimper. Cut any design of leaves and/or flowers you may like out of the remaining pastry and decorate the top with them. Brush with the remainder of the *dorure* and bake 1 hour in a 375° oven. Cool completely. Chill overnight. Serve with watercress mixed with mayonnaise.

BOUDIN BLANC DE NOEL
[*White Christmas Sausage*]

SERVINGS: 6 COST: moderately expensive EXECUTION: easy

TOTAL PREPARATION TIME: 1½ hours for the making of the sausage and its poaching, 8 to 10 minutes to panfry the *boudin* before serving

BEST SEASON: Customarily served at Christmas dinner, but can be served year round

SUGGESTED WINE: Vouvray Moëlleux

REMARKS ON INGREDIENTS: Sausage skins can be located in butcher shops in Italian neighborhoods. The truffle makes a great deal of difference in the taste and price.

1 ½ lbs. raw white meat of chicken, without skin or bone (750 g)
6 whole eggs
2 ¼ tsp. salt
1 tsp. pepper
½ lb. unsalted butter

4 mushrooms, chopped fine
1 large black truffle, chopped fine (optional)
2 cups heavy cream
Sausage skins
Clarified butter

Cut the meat into 1-inch chunks and divide it into 6 equal portions. Beat the eggs. Blend each portion of meat to a purée using 2 tablespoons of egg as a liquid. Empty the chicken purée into a bowl; add salt and pepper. Mix well and refrigerate one hour.

Heat one tablespoon of butter in a small frying pan and add the chopped mushrooms and salt and pepper. Cover the pan to extract all the moisture out of the mushrooms; uncover the pan and stir over high heat until the moisture has completely evaporated. Add the chopped truffle and mix well. Remove from the heat and let cool completely.

Cream the remainder of the butter. Gradually beat in the chicken purée and then the mushroom-truffle hash. Place the bowl containing this mixture into another bowl containing ice cubes and water. Very slowly, beat in the heavy cream. Rinse the sausage skins several times, letting the water run through their center. Tie a knot at one end of each. Using a large funnel known as a sausage stuffer (which can be bought cheaply in all Italian neighborhoods) stuff the mixture into the sausage skins. Twist to make twelve 3-inch sausage links. Tie in between the links. Poach in simmering salted water for 20 minutes. Rinse and cool. Keep refrigerated.

To serve, prick with a very fine needle and then fry slowly in clarified butter over low heat.

RILLETTES
[Touraine Pork Hash]

SERVINGS: 6 cups of hash COST: inexpensive if made with uncooked
leftovers from roasts, chops, and so forth EXECUTION: easy
TOTAL PREPARATION TIME: 7 to 8 hours, depending on volume
BEST SEASON: Year round
SUGGESTED WINE: Chinon or Bourgueil
REMARKS ON INGREDIENTS: In Touraine, no special meat is ever
bought to prepare this dish. When a large joint such as loin
is bought to make a pork roast or chops or *noisettes*, whatever
is left of the meat is cut coarsely and put to cook as follows
for a good 12 hours. If the meat is bought for the purpose of
making *rillettes*, the best cuts to use are the upper shoulder
and the neck. Accumulate leftovers in the freezer until you
have enough to make a good batch.

6 lbs. pork meat, ⅔ lean, ⅓
fat (essential) *(3 kg)*
2 lbs. meaty pork bones from
chops, ham hocks, etc.
(essential) *(1 kg)*
½ lb. fatback (250 g)

Salt and pepper
1 tsp. dried thyme
1 large bay leaf
1½ tsp. quatre épices *(page*
7)

Put the meat, fat, and bones in a large kettle and cover with water.
Bring to a boil slowly; skim well. Add salt and pepper in moderate
amounts, the thyme, bay leaf, and *quatre épices.* Let simmer, covered
with a lid left opened a crack, for 4 to 5 hours. Uncover the pot;
let the liquid reduce until there is no more than one inch at the
bottom of the kettle. This will take another 2 to 3 hours. Let cool
overnight in the refrigerator.

Remove all the meat from the bones. Mash about ½ cup each
of meat, fat, and meat jelly together with the tip of a large chopping
knife until smooth and creamy. Blend the whole mixture very well.
Correct the seasoning. If the *rillettes* are not salted enough, bring

2 tablespoons water to a boil; add 2 tablespoons salt; cool, stirring to dissolve the salt. Gradually blend teaspoons of this brine into the *rillettes* until they have acquired the taste you like. Pepper can be added from the mill.

Pack into small, 1-cup crocks. Seal the top of the jars with ¼ inch of melted, clarified butter or lard.

The mixture, sterilized by the long cooking, will keep at least three weeks in the refrigerator. It freezes very well. Serve at room temperature with crisp French bread.

FAISAN AUX RAISINS
[Pheasant and Grapes]

SERVINGS: 4 COST: reasonable if the pheasant is shot, not bought
    EXECUTION: semi-difficult
TOTAL PREPARATION TIME: Marination, 24 hours; cooking, 40 minutes maximum
BEST SEASON: September 15 to December 15
SUGGESTED WINE: Chinon or Bourgueil
REMARKS ON INGREDIENTS: Do not, under any circumstances, use either Concord or Thompson seedless grapes. You need a *vinifera* type, a nice dark grape that will retain a lot of dark red pigmentation on the surface of the berry even after being peeled. It does not matter whether the grapes have seeds or not. The tannin on the surface of the berry and around the pits tempers the sweetness of the juice and is useful in the making of the final sauce.

    A pheasant born in the spring of the year is better than any other bird; it will be recognized by the softness of both the beak and the breastbone. Let the pheasant hang for at least five days. It is ready to cook when the feathers pull away easily from the body. Pluck the pheasant and flambé it with Cognac to remove the small feathers. Clean the inside very carefully, taking care not to break the gall bladder.

1 pheasant, preferably born in
the spring, cleaned and
feathered as explained
above
1 bottle Chinon
2 onions, chopped fine
2 dozen crushed juniper
berries
1 tsp. dried basil

10 TB butter (125 g)
3 cups excellent jus de
veau (7½ dl)
2 dozen grapes (dark red),
peeled
2 dozen shallots
4 white bread croutons
1½ tsp. potato starch
Chopped parsley

Cut the pheasant into two legs and two cutlets with only the little wing drumstick attached. Be careful, the aged white meat is extremely fragile and tears easily. Make sure while you are boning that your knife blade scrapes along the breastbone. Place in a 13- by 9-inch baking dish.

Heat the Chinon in a pot. Add the chopped onions, 12 crushed juniper berries, and the dried basil. Simmer 20 minutes. Cool completely. Pour the cold marinade over the pheasant. Let marinate for 24 hours in the refrigerator. Turn the meat over once while marinating.

Crush all the pheasant bones, including all the wingtips and neck bones. Brown well in 1 tablespoon butter. Add the *jus de veau* and reduce slowly to 1½ cups to obtain an essence of pheasant.

Blanch the grapes in boiling water; peel them. Do not pit; the incision in each berry would liberate too many sweet juices and would flood the sauce. Peel the shallots and sauté them whole in 1 tablespoon butter until they are semi-cooked. Reserve both grapes and shallots in a saucepan.

To cook the pheasant, heat 2 tablespoons butter in a *sauteuse*. Dry all the pieces of meat. Brown them on each side over slow heat. Remove the breast cutlets to a plate. Salt and pepper the legs, add some of the marinade to the *sauteuse* and cover. The legs will be done in about 20 minutes. Add more marinade every five minutes. During the last five minutes of cooking, return the breast cutlets to the *sauteuse* to finish cooking them. They will be done very quickly; do not overcook or they will be stringy. While the pheasant cooks, fry the croutons in 2 tablespoons butter. When the pheasant is cooked, remove it to a plate; keep warm. Mix the lukewarm essence of pheasant with the potato starch. Pour into the *sauteuse;* mix well. Bring to a boil to thicken lightly.

Drain any grape juice that may have accumulated in the saucepan containing the grapes and the shallots; strain the sauce over them. Add the other 12 juniper berries and simmer about 10 minutes. Remove the juniper berries. Bring the sauce to a rapid boil, add the remaining butter, and shake the pot back and forth over the heat.

Place the pheasant in a small country-style casserole. Pour the sauce over it and sprinkle with parsley. Decorate with the fried croutons. For a vegetable consider white rice pilaf or a *paillasson* of potatoes.

NOISETTES DE PORC AUX PRUNEAUX
[Pork Noisettes with Prunes]

SERVINGS: 6 COST: moderately expensive EXECUTION: easy
TOTAL PREPARATION TIME: 1 hour plus 24 hours to macerate the
    prunes
BEST SEASON: Winter
SUGGESTED WINE: Bourgueil or Chinon
REMARKS ON INGREDIENTS: The original Touraine recipe is usually
    made with white wine. If you want to execute it with a white
    wine use the same proportions of a Vouvray Sec.

One 5-lb. loin of pork	stock (*jus de veau*)
(2 kg 500)	(4½–5 dl)
Quatre épices (*page 7*)	1 cup heavy cream (225 g
2 dozen large, soft prunes,	or 2¼ dl)
unpitted (250 g)	Salt and pepper
1 bottle Bourgueil or Chinon	Unsalted butter
2 cups excellent brown veal	Lemon juice, if needed

Bone the loin of pork, removing all the fat, to obtain a solid piece of lean meat. Cut as many *noisettes* ¾ inch thick as the piece will yield. If this confuses you, buy large rib or loin chops and trim around the center *noisette* of meat to free it of all fat and bone. The result will be the same. With all the trimmings, you can make a small jar of *rillettes* (see page 190).

Sprinkle the *noisettes* very sparingly with *quatre épices*. Put them on a plate, cover them loosely with plastic wrap and let stand overnight in the refrigerator.

Put the prunes in a small bowl and pour the bottle of wine over them. Add a pinch of *quatre épices;* mix well. Let macerate 24 hours.

The next day remove the pork to room temperature for 2 hours before cooking. Transfer the prunes and wine mixture to a small saucepan, bring to a boil, and simmer no more than 5 minutes. Remove the prunes to a bowl. Add the stock to the wine in the saucepan and reduce to 1½ cups. Panfry the *noisettes* in butter in a large frying pan. Do not overcook them; they are done as soon as the tip of a skewer goes in and comes out freely. Salt and pepper each of them. Remove to a platter and keep warm.

Add the cream to the frying pan and deglaze it with a spatula, scraping to dissolve the caramelized juices of the meat. Cook over high heat until the cream coats the spatula by ¼ inch. Add the wine and stock mixture. Cook together until the spatula is coated, this time by only ⅙–⅛ inch. Turn the heat off. Roll the *noisettes* and prunes in the sauce to blend the flavors. Correct the seasoning with salt, pepper and a dash of lemon juice, if necessary. Serve piping hot with plain buttered Swiss chard sprinkled with parsley as a vegetable.

FILET DE BOEUF DE CHATEAU-LA-VALLIERE
[Fillet of Beef as prepared by Claire Robert]

SERVINGS: 6–8 COST: expensive EXECUTION: medium-difficult
TOTAL PREPARATION TIME: 3 hours. Operation may be split into
several steps. See recipe.
BEST SEASON: A winter meat, served for Christmas mostly
SUGGESTED WINE: A great Burgundy

4 lbs. tenderloin of beef (1
    kg 750–2 kg)
Walnut or olive oil
1 lb. sweetbreads or one pair
    (about 500 g)
1 lb. mushrooms (500 g)
4 TB unsalted butter (50
    to 60 g)
Salt and pepper
1 carrot, sliced thick

1 onion, sliced thick
Small bouquet garni
5 cups excellent brown veal
    stock (jus de veau) (1 ¼
    litres)
1 cup heavy cream (225 g
    or 2 ¼ dl)
2 TB sour cream (25–30 g)
1 large black truffle (40 g)
Madeira (optional)

Peel and trim the tenderloin of all fat and conjunctive tissue to have only the edible meat left. Rub it with a thin layer of oil and keep at room temperature for four hours before roasting.

Soak the sweetbreads under slowly running cold water until they show no more traces of blood. Drain them. Put the sweetbreads in a pot and barely cover with cold water. Bring slowly to a simmer; let blanch 5 to 6 minutes. Drain, rinse under cold water, and remove all the heavy conjunctive tissues and blood vessels. Do not remove the thin, outside conjunctive membrane or the sweetbreads will lose shape and fall apart.

Cut the mushrooms into ⅓-inch cubes. Heat 2 tablespoons butter in a 9-inch frying pan. Add the mushrooms, sauté them with salt and pepper. Cover until the mushrooms have released all their moisture. Remove from the heat.

In a heavy *sauteuse* pan sauté the carrot and onion in the remaining butter. Spread the vegetables in the bottom of the *sauteuse*. Add the sweetbreads; strain the mushroom juices over them. Salt and pepper. Add 1 cup brown veal stock, a small *bouquet garni,* and bring to a boil. Cover the meat with foil placed flush over it; turn up the sides to form a deep inverted lid; this will catch the condensation. Cover with the pot lid. Braise 40 to 45 minutes in a 325° oven. Remove the sweetbreads to a plate when done.

Raise the heat under the *sauteuse* very high and reduce the cooking juices to a heavy, very tasty glaze. Add one cup of stock; reduce again to a glaze. Repeat the same operation twice with two more cups of stock.

While you are preparing the glaze, reduce the heavy cream to ½ cup. Blend that cream with the glaze. Place the sour cream in a clean saucepan. Gradually strain the mixture of glaze and cream into the sour cream, whisking continually to blend both without lumps.

Dice the sweetbreads and the black truffle; mix them into the mushrooms and add that mixture to the prepared sauce. Reheat together. Keep warm.

Roast the meat on a rack in the middle of a 400° preheated oven for 45 to 60 minutes. Salt and pepper about 15 minutes before the end of the cooking.

As soon as the meat is done, add the remaining cup of stock to the roasting pan, deglaze it and reduce to ¾ cup. Add to the prepared sweetbread sauce.

Reheat the sauce. Add Madeira to suit your taste, but no more than two tablespoons. Correct the salt and pepper. Serve over the slices of roast beef.

Use plain buttered green beans as a vegetable.

FOIE DE VEAU AU CITRON
[Steamed Calf's Liver with Lemon Sauce]

SERVINGS: 6 COST: reasonable EXECUTION: tricky
TOTAL PREPARATION TIME: 1 hour
BEST SEASON: Can be enjoyed year round
SUGGESTED WINE: Chinon
REMARKS ON INGREDIENTS: The best small, whole calf's livers can
    be located in all Italian neighborhoods. Although they are
    usually plentiful, order ahead of time just to be sure.

1 calf's liver or 1½ to 2 lbs.
   (about 750 g to 1 kg)
Melted butter or oil
1 quart brown veal stock
   (1 litre)

1 lemon
Unsalted butter, as much as
   you wish
2 TB chopped parsley
Salt and pepper

Remove the membrane that covers the liver or it will not cook properly. Cut the liver in ⅓-inch-thick slices, brush the slices with a thin layer of melted butter or oil. Place the liver slices on a rack. Place in a large baking dish. At the bottom of the dish, place the quart of veal stock. Cover and bring to a boil; reduce to a simmer and let the liver cook until a fine needle inserted in the center moves in and out freely. The liver should remain uniformly pink inside.

While the liver steams, make a fine julienne with the rind of the lemon and blanch it. When the liver is ⅔ done, do not remove it from the steamer, but remove about 2 cups of the stock to a very shallow frying pan or *sauteuse*. Reduce the stock to ⅔ cup. Add the lemon rind and a good dash of lemon juice. While the reduction is boiling, add as much butter as you wish to the center of the boil. The author of this recipe used a whole stick (4 ounces or 100 grams). Add the parsley, more lemon juice if you desire, and salt and pepper.

ASPERGES EN CASSEROLE
[Asparagus and Ham Casserole]

SERVINGS: 6 COST: expensive EXECUTION: medium-difficult
TOTAL PREPARATION TIME: 1 hour
BEST SEASON: April and May
SUGGESTED WINE: Vouvray Moëlleux
REMARKS ON INGREDIENTS: Use jumbo California asparagus and
    Danish ham. *Careful:* Extremely delicious, but extremely rich.

2 lbs. asparagus (1 kg)	*Salt and pepper from the mill*
½ lb. boiled ham in one	*Freshly grated nutmeg*
piece (250 g)	*1 TB lemon juice*
3½ cups heavy cream (7½ dl)	*3 egg yolks*
½ cup sour cream (1	*½ lb. unsalted butter*
generous dl)	*(250 g) plus 1 TB (15 g)*

Bend the asparagus head to foot; it will break where the fibers stop being edible. Discard the foot. Peel the asparagus and cut into ¾-inch chunks. Separate the tips from the pieces of stem. Blanch the stems in a lot of boiling salted water for about 5 minutes. Then blanch the tips for 2 minutes. Drain well. Keep ½ cup (a generous dl) of the cooking water. Dice the ham into ¾-inch cubes. Pat the asparagus dry; mix them with the ham.

Reduce 3 cups of heavy cream to 1½ cups. Mix reduced heavy cream and sour cream; add the mixture of ham and asparagus and blend well. Correct the seasoning. Add nutmeg to your taste and keep hot.

Place the reserved cooking water of the asparagus, the lemon juice, salt and pepper in a small 1-quart pot. Reduce gently to ¼ cup. Meanwhile, separate the eggs. Melt the ½ pound butter until it darkens and turns to *noisette* butter.

When the reduction is ready, add the egg yolks. Using a whisk, fluff the mixture over low heat until it is foamy, heavy, and until the bottom of the pot remains visible for a split second at a time.

Remove the pot from the heat and gradually whisk in the *noisette* butter. *Do not* add the brown solids to the sauce. Whip the remaining heavy cream lightly; add it to the hollandaise. Correct the seasoning.

Butter a 1-quart baking dish with the remaining 1 tablespoon of butter. Add the hot *ragoût* of asparagus and ham. Strain the hollandaise over it. Put under the broiler for 2 to 3 minutes.

Serve with a plain salad and *Bijane* without cream for dessert (page 207).

DARREE
[*A Brussels Sprout Casserole*]

SERVINGS: 6 COST: inexpensive EXECUTION: do not overcook or undercook; otherwise, easy
TOTAL PREPARATION TIME: 45 minutes
BEST SEASON: A fall and winter vegetable
REMARKS ON INGREDIENTS: If you have baby Brussels sprouts, there

is no need to blanch them. If they are large and mature, blanch them in lots of salted water for 5 minutes before braising them.

1 lb. Brussels sprouts, preferably small and young (500 g) *2 TB walnut oil* *Salt and pepper*	*1½–2 cups brown veal stock (jus de veau) (about 4 dl)* *2 TB excellent wine vinegar* *4 TB butter cooked to the noisette stage (50 g)* *1 TB chopped parsley*

Preheat the oven to 325°.

Wash and trim the sprouts. Cut a tiny cross in the root end to prevent them from falling apart while cooking. Heat the walnut oil in a fireproof cocotte or cast-iron enameled skillet. Toss the sprouts in the hot oil, salt and pepper them. Add enough veal stock to just cover them. Bring to a boil. Butter a parchment paper and lay it flat over the vegetables. Cover the pot and bake until a skewer moves in and out of the sprouts freely. Remove the sprouts to a serving dish. Keep warm.

Put the vinegar and a dash of salt and pepper in a small pot. Reduce to 1 tablespoon. Strain the cooking juices of the sprouts over it; mix well. If there are no juices left in the cooking pot, add about ¼ cup veal stock. Reduce to a good glaze, or about 2 tablespoons. Blend the glaze and *noisette* butter over high heat and pour over the sprouts. Sprinkle with chopped parsley.

BLETTES AUX FINES HERBES
[Swiss Chard and Fines Herbes]

SERVINGS: 6 COST: inexpensive EXECUTION: easy
TOTAL PREPARATION TIME: 1 hour
BEST SEASON: Late summer and fall
REMARKS ON INGREDIENTS: Do not discard the greens. They are a good addition to mashed potatoes, make a good soufflé of

greens, and add zest to a vegetable soup. You may keep the blanching water of the chard to start the soup.

The ribs of two bundles of *¼ cup heavy cream or 4 TB*
    Swiss chard (750 g)   *butter (60 g cream or*
3 quarts water   *50 g butter)*
Large bouquet garni   *1 tsp. each: chopped fresh*
Salt and pepper   *parsley, chives, chervil,*
3 TB lemon juice   *and tarragon*

Peel the ribs of the chard; that is, cut a 1-inch piece, almost cutting all the way through the rib but not quite, and pull downward. All the "strings" of the vegetables will come off. Repeat all along the rib, changing sides after cutting a piece so that the vegetable will be entirely free of strings.

Bring the water to a boil. Add the *bouquet garni,* salt, pepper, and lemon juice and boil rapidly for 15 minutes. Add the *blettes* and bring back to a boil; simmer 15 minutes. Remove the *blettes* to a colander and rinse under cold water. The vegetable may then be refrigerated until needed. If it is used immediately, do not rinse it. Put it in a large frying pan over high heat and let all the steam evaporate, tossing the vegetable to prevent it from sticking to the pan. When the vegetable is hot, add either heavy cream or butter (I use both). Reduce the heat almost completely; shake the pan back and forth and sauté until the vegetables are nicely coated. Add salt, pepper, and fines herbes.

HARICOTS VERTS TOURANGELLE
[Green Beans the "Touraine" Way]

SERVINGS: 6 COST: moderately expensive EXECUTION: easy, but
    a bit time consuming
TOTAL PREPARATION TIME: 1 hour
BEST SEASON: In the summer months when the beans are abundant,
    crisp, and fresh, but can be prepared year round

REMARKS ON INGREDIENTS: Green beans prepared in this manner look very elegant. To save money, use the pulp removed from each side of the beans to make the *Crème Tourangelle* soup on page 179. To obtain one pound of beans ready to cook, buy one and one half pounds of beans as sold in groceries. Farm stands offer better beans than supermarkets.

1½ lbs. green beans	*1½ cups heavy cream (3½*
(750 g)	*dl or 350 g)*
3 quarts water	*Lemon juice*
1½ TB salt	*Freshly grated nutmeg*
	Salt and pepper from the mill

Snap the ends of each bean. With a parer, a potato peeler, or whatever gadget works for you, remove the "strings" side of each bean taking at least ¹⁄₁₆ inch of pulp away. Wash the beans. Boil the water in a wide-mouth pot. Add salt.

Add ⅓ of the beans to the water. Bring back to a boil; keep at a rolling boil, pot uncovered, for 7 to 8 minutes. The cooking time will vary with each type of bean. Keep the vegetable very green and slightly crisp, but do not undercook it so it still tastes grassy. That grassy taste is quite un-French.

Remove the beans to a large container of cold water to stop their cooking, then to a terry towel to absorb the excess moisture. Remove from the towel and store in a bowl or flat dish in the refrigerator until ready to use.

Repeat with the remainder of the beans. To serve the beans, reduce the heavy cream by ½ or until it coats a spoon by ⅛ of an inch. Toss the beans in the cream to heat them well. Add nutmeg, lemon juice, salt and pepper to suit your taste. Serve with any meat.

CELERI-RAVE A LA GLACE DE VIANDE
[Celeriac with Meat Glaze and Herbs]

SERVINGS: 6 COST: moderate EXECUTION: easy
TOTAL PREPARATION TIME: 35 minutes
BEST SEASON: October through January
REMARKS ON INGREDIENTS: If meat glaze is not available, use the
natural gravy of any meat; chicken is especially good.

1½ lbs. celeriac
  (750 g)
3 quarts water
1½ TB salt
3 TB unsalted butter (35 g)

Meat glaze or meat juices, as
  much as you like
Salt and pepper
1 TB chopped chives

Peel the celeriac. Cut them into olive-shaped chunks and trim. Bring
the water to a boil; add the salt and the celeriac. Bring back to a
boil and continue boiling until the vegetables are tender but still
quite crunchy. Drain all but 2 tablespoons of the water.

Transfer the celeriac to a small skillet; add the reserved cooking
water, the butter, the meat glaze or meat juices, salt and pepper and
chives. Roll the vegetables in the mixture. Shake the pan back and
forth over high heat until the juices in the pan are reduced to a glaze
that coats the vegetables. Good with all meats.

POELEE DE CHAMPIGNONS SAUVAGES
[Sautéed and Creamed Wild Mushrooms]

SERVINGS: 6 COST: minimal if you collect the mushrooms EXECU-
TION: easy
TOTAL PREPARATION TIME: Varies with the type of mushrooms
used, averages 30 minutes
BEST SEASON: May through September
REMARKS ON MUSHROOMS: Use them only if you know them well
or if an expert can positively identify them for you. The follow-

ing mushrooms found in Europe and in the U.S. are edible. Not all mushrooms are. Use alone or in any combination.

Agaricus campestris (Meadow mushroom or *Rosé des prés*)

Tricholoma georgii (True *mousseron*)

Marasmius oreades (Fairy ring mushroom or *faux mousseron*)

Lactarius deliciosus (*Lactaire délicieux*)

Polypilus frondosus (Hen of the woods or *poule des bois*)

Boletus edulis (Steinpilz or *bolet de bordeaux*)

Boletus luteus (*Nonette voilée*)

Craterellus cornucopioides (Trumpet of death, or *trompette de la mort*)

Cantharellus cibarius (Chanterelle)

Amanita cesarea (Caesars' amanita or *Champignon des Césars*)

Amanitopsis vaginata (*Grisette*)

In all cases, clean the mushrooms as you gather them. Remove the sticky top skins of *Boletus luteus,* discard the stems of *Marasmius oreades,* which are pure string, and cut off all traces of earth or dead leaves at the foot. Rinse the mushrooms under cold water only if very dirty and roll them in a terrycloth towel to absorb all excess moisture. Slice or dice as you prefer, then cook using the following proportions and ingredients:

1½ lbs. mushrooms, cleaned, sliced or diced (750 g)
2 TB butter (30 g)
1 onion, sliced thin or chopped fine (50 g)
1 tiny clove garlic

2 TB chopped parsley
Salt and pepper
1 cup heavy cream
3 TB sour cream
Tartlet shells or toast points, butter-fried or toasted

Have the mushrooms ready to cook. Heat the butter in a large 10-inch skillet, add the onion and sauté until it turns golden. Add the garlic and parsley; toss in the butter for two minutes, stirring constantly. Add the mushrooms; stir well. Add salt and pepper. Reduce the heat and let the mushrooms lose all their moisture. Remove the mushrooms to a plate. Add the heavy cream to the mushroom juices in the pan and reduce by one-half. Return the mushrooms to the pan and continue cooking until the cream becomes so thick the butter starts breaking. Stir the sour cream until it is smooth and liquid and blend it into the mushrooms. Reheat for a minute or so and correct the seasoning.

Serve in tartlet shells or on toast points.

SALADE JARDINIERE DE CLAIRE
[Claire's Garden Salad]

SERVINGS: 6 COST: moderately expensive, unless you grow most of your vegetables EXECUTION: easy

TOTAL PREPARATION TIME: 1½ hours with the cooking of the flageolets

BEST SEASON: Summer and fall

½ lb. green beans, frenched properly (see page 200, Haricots Verts Tourangelle)

½ cup flageolets or white beans, cooked

1 large carrot, cut into 2-inch by ¼-inch sticks

1 large white (white only) turnip, cut into 2-inch by ¼-inch sticks

½ cup baby peas, cooked

The white of one leek, cut into paper-thin slices, unblanched

2 tomatoes peeled, seeded, and cut into ¼-inch-thick strips

1 small zucchini, cut into ¼-inch-thick strips

1 Boston or Batavia lettuce

FOR THE DRESSING:

1½ TB wine vinegar

1½ TB sour cream

Salt

Pepper from the mill

1½ tsp. each: chives, chervil, tarragon, chopped

1 TB chopped parsley

½ cup walnut oil

"French" the beans; blanch them in a large pot of boiling salted water for 7 minutes. Drain and cool under cold water. Pat dry. Mix with the cooked white beans or flageolets.

Blanch together the carrot and turnip sticks for 4 minutes. Rinse under cold water; pat dry. Mix with the beans; add the peas. Slice the leek; mix into the salad.

Remove the stems of the tomatoes. Immerse the tomatoes in boiling water for one minute; peel them. Cut them into quarters, remove the seeds and water, and cut the pulp into strips. Mix with the other vegetables.

Cut the zucchini into strips and salt them lightly. Let stand while you make the dressing.

Mix vinegar, sour cream, salt and pepper. Add 1½ teaspoons each: chives, chervil, tarragon, and chopped parsley. Gradually whisk in the walnut oil until well homogenized.

Clean the lettuce leaves. Reserve six large leaves to present the salad and store the remainder in a plastic bag for later use.

Drain any water exuded by the zucchini, rinse, and pat dry. Add the zucchini strips to the other vegetables. Add the dressing and toss well. Correct salt and pepper again. Spoon an equal amount of salad over each lettuce leaf, sprinkle with a pinch of the remaining parsley and serve promptly.

LA FOUACE RABELAIS
[Easter Brioche]

SERVINGS: 6 COST: moderately expensive EXECUTION: easy

TOTAL PREPARATION TIME: 10 minutes to prepare the dough; 6
   hours for it to rise, ferment and cool overnight in the refrigerator; 1½ hours to prove and bake

BEST SEASON: Customarily made at Easter, but can be made year
   round

REMARKS ON INGREDIENTS: If you have no orange flower water,
   please do not replace it with orange rind. Instead, omit the
   saffron and use a pinch of lemon rind and cinnamon, or ½
   teaspoon ground cardamon.

3 cups sifted flour (375 g)	1 tsp. orange flower water
1 envelope dried yeast	1/8 tsp. pure saffron, powdered
2 TB sugar	4 eggs
Lukewarm water	1/2 lb. unsalted butter at room
1 tsp. salt	temperature plus 1 TB
6 TB lukewarm milk	1 egg yolk

Place 1 cup sifted flour in a bowl. Add the yeast mixed with the sugar and enough lukewarm water to make a small, soft ball of dough. Cut a cross on the top of this starter and immerse it into a bowl of water no warmer than 110°.

Place the remaining flour on the counter top. Make a well; add the salt, dissolved in 3 tablespoons milk, the orange flower water, the saffron and the eggs, lightly beaten. Gradually gather the flour from the edges of the well into the eggs to make a soft batter.

By the time the eggs and flour are mixed, the ball of starter will have come floating to the surface of its water bath. Lift it out with your hand, fingers outstretched to let all the water drip down into the bowl. Mix the batter and starter together.

Now place 4 tablespoons of butter north, south, east, and west of the dough. Gradually work each portion of butter into the dough by twisting the butter into the dough with your fingertips and at the same time pulling the dough from the counter top. Give about 10 good pulls to the whole bulk of the dough to homogenize it. Put it to rise in a large mixing bowl. Let the dough rise at least 6 hours, punching it down whenever it reaches the top of the mixing bowl. Cover with a clear plastic wrap and refrigerate overnight.

Butter an unbendable cookie sheet. Roll the brioche dough in your hands quickly to make a 12" x 14" x 2" roll. Close the roll into a circle. Cut small incisions about 3/4 inch deep into the top of the bread, at regular intervals. Let rise again until 1 1/2 times its original volume. Mix the egg yolk with the remaining milk and brush all over the bread. Bake in a preheated 425° oven for about 20 minutes.

BIJANE AUX FRAISES
[Strawberries Steeped in Wine]

SERVINGS: 6–8 COST: expensive EXECUTION: simple
TOTAL PREPARATION TIME: 20 minutes
BEST SEASON: May, June, and the beginning of July
REMARKS ON INGREDIENTS: Any good red wine of any origin can
    replace Chinon.

1 quart strawberries, very ripe	*1 bottle of Chinon wine*
3 dime-size pieces of lemon	*1 cup of heavy cream,*
rind	*whipped to* Chantilly *(2 ¼ dl)*
A squeeze of lemon juice	*(optional)*
3–4 TB honey, or to your taste	*1 ounce Cointreau (optional)*

Clean the strawberries; wash them carefully. Put them into a bowl
with the lemon rind, the lemon juice and the honey. Toss well to
dissolve the honey. Let stand 10 minutes. Add the wine and let
steep another ten minutes. Add more honey if you desire. Serve in
champagne cups. This dish is *never refrigerated* since the cold
deadens the fragrance of the berry-wine mixture. If you wish to use
the cream, add the Cointreau to it, a little honey, if you wish, and
beat until semi-stiff. You can either top each cup of berries with some
cream, or, better, pass a dish containing the cream and let your guests
help themselves.

CHICOLLE AUX PECHES
[Peaches Steeped in Sweet Vouvray Wine]

SERVINGS: 6 COST: medium-expensive to expensive EXECUTION:
    simple
TOTAL PREPARATION TIME: 2 hours
BEST SEASON: When the white peaches are in season. It will vary
    with the area; in the United States it's from the end of June to
    early September.

REMARKS ON INGREDIENTS: The peaches may also be yellow peaches. Whether white or yellow, they must be very ripe and drip with sugary juices. If sweet Vouvray wine is not available, you may use sweet Barsac or Sauternes or even a German Spätlese wine.

6 sun-ripened peaches   *1 bottle sweet Vouvray wine*
Sugar to your taste, but little

Bring a pot of water to a boil; immerse the peaches in the boiling water for one minute and peel them. Slice them into a bowl. Sprinkle each fruit layer with a little sugar. Pour just enough sweet Vouvray over the peaches to cover them. Cover the dish with a plate and refrigerate at least 1 hour. Serve chilled, but not deep chilled, in chilled champagne cups.

This is a potent dessert; enjoy yourselves!

GROS DAMAS AU VOUVRAY
[Prunes Steeped in Vouvray Wine]

SERVINGS: 6 COST: moderately expensive EXECUTION: simple
TOTAL PREPARATION TIME: 30 minutes plus 3 days to steep the prunes
BEST SEASON: This is a generous and rich winter dessert.
REMARKS ON INGREDIENTS: The only prunes resembling the *Gros Damas de Tours* prunes are the soft, pitted prunes of California. Preferably choose some which have not been treated with sulfur dioxide.

1 lb. soft, pitted California   *10 cloves*
  prunes (500 g)   *Large pinch of cinnamon*
No sugar   *(3-finger pinch)*
1 bottle sweet Vouvray wine   *Tiny pinch of salt (2-finger*
1 large strip of lemon rind   *pinch, very small)*
1 dime-size piece of orange   *1 cup heavy cream (2¼ dl)*
  rind   *1½ oz. Cointreau*

Put the prunes in a large mixing bowl. Empty the wine into a large saucepan; bring to a boil. Add lemon and orange rind, cloves, cinnamon, and the tiny pinch of salt. Simmer 10 minutes. Pour the hot wine with all the spices on top of the prunes. Cover and refrigerate for three days. Serve with unsweetened cream whipped and flavored with Cointreau.

PECHES A LA ROYALE
[Peaches with Cream and Raspberry Purée]

SERVINGS: 6 COST: expensive EXECUTION: semi-difficult
TOTAL PREPARATION TIME: 1 hour
BEST SEASON: July to September 15
REMARKS ON INGREDIENTS: White peaches are far better than
   yellow peaches for this particular dish.

1 quart boiling water
   (1 litre)
6 white or yellow peaches,
   juicy and ripe (750 g
   to 1 kg)
½ cup sugar (125 g)
1 cup water (2¼ dl)
Pinch of salt

½ cup sweet Vouvray wine
   (1 generous dl)
3 egg yolks
½ pint fresh raspberries or
   1 package frozen rasp-
   berries (200 g)
½ cup heavy cream, whipped
   to a soft Chantilly
   (1 generous dl)

Bring one quart of water to a boil, immerse the peaches in the water for one to two minutes and peel them. Cut each peach in half.

Prepare a syrup with ½ cup of sugar and 1 cup of water. Bring to a simmer. Immerse two peach halves at a time in the syrup and poach 3 to 4 minutes. Remove the cooked peaches to 6 champagne cups. Chill.

Reduce the syrup until it reaches the hard crack stage. Let it cool; add the Vouvray and stir over medium heat until the sugar has dissolved. Beat the egg yolks until they foam heavily; gradually whisk in the hot wine and put to cook over medium heat until the custard is thick. *Do not boil.* Cool completely. If the custard has been well cooked, it will not separate, but will stay thick and foamy.

When the custard is cool, whip the cream and fold it into the custard. Press the raspberries through a sieve to obtain a seed-free purée. If you use frozen berries use just enough syrup to loosen the texture of the purée.

To serve, first spoon some of the custard over the peaches, then some of the purée of raspberries. Pass the remainder of each in separate sauce boats.

QUATRE GLACES A LA PUREE DE FRAISES
[*Four Fruit Ices with Strawberry Purée*]

SERVINGS: up to 15 COST: reasonable EXECUTION: easy
TOTAL PREPARATION TIME: 15 minutes for each batch of ice, 15
    minutes for the purée
BEST SEASON: Summer desserts

RASPBERRY ICE:
1 lb. fresh raspberries (500 g)
1 lb. 8 oz. raspberry jam
  (750 g)
Juice of 1 lemon or more
  to taste

PINEAPPLE ICE:
1 lb. very ripe pineapple
  pulp (500 g)
1 lb. 8 oz. pineapple jam
  (750 g)
Juice of 1 lemon or more
  to taste

BLACK CURRANT ICE:
1 lb. wild Maine blueberries
  (500 g) (or in Canada,
  black currants) (750 g)

1 lb. 8 oz. black currant jam
Juice of 1 lemon or more,
  to taste

APRICOT ICE:
1 lb. apricot halves (500 g)
1 lb. 8 oz. apricot jam
  (750 g)
Juice of 1 lemon or more,
  to taste

STRAWBERRY PUREE:
2 quarts juicy and ripe
  strawberries
Lemon juice, to taste
Sugar, to taste
1/4 cup Kirschwasser

TO PREPARE THE ICES:

Proceed exactly the same way for each ice. Put the fruit, pulp or berries in the blender and blend. Strain into a bowl. Heat the jam until liquid. Strain into the fruit pulp. Add lemon juice and stir until completely blended. Pour each ice into a 9-inch cake pan and freeze. The texture will be smooth. There is no real need to stir or mix during freezing to avoid crystals but if you do not mind a few minutes of additional work the texture will be even finer.

TO PREPARE THE STRAWBERRY PUREE:

Put the berries in the blender with the lemon juice; blend until liquid. Strain through a fine strainer to discard as many seeds as possible. Add the Kirsch and sugar. Stir thoroughly to dissolve the sugar. Keep chilled.

Serve any of the four ices alone or in combinations in champagne cups. Top with the strawberry purée.

TARTE AUX BRUGNONS
[Nectarine Tart]

SERVINGS: 6–8 COST: moderately expensive EXECUTION: medium-difficult

TOTAL PREPARATION TIME: 1 hour

BEST SEASON: A light summer pie

REMARKS ON INGREDIENTS: *Brugnons* are the nectarines growing in the vineyards of the Touraine. Their pulp is white with the texture and juiciness of a nectarine.

PASTRY:

1 cup sifted flour (125 g)
¼ cup ground blanched almonds (25 g)
½ tsp. salt
1 tsp. sugar
6 TB butter (75–80 g)

3 TB water

FILLING:

8–10 nectarines
½ cup sugar (125 g)
½ cup water (1⅛ dl)
1 cup heavy cream (2¼ dl)

　　　2 TB confectioners sugar　　　pistachios (50–60 g)
　　　2 TB each Cointreau and　　　½ cup strained apricot jam
　　　　　Kirsch　　　　　　　　　　(⅔ of a 12 oz. jar)
　　　½ cup chopped, blanched

TO MAKE THE PASTRY:

See details, page 13. Mix the flour and the almonds. Make a well.
Add the salt, sugar, and butter; mix until the butter is the size of
peas. Gradually add the water without kneading. *Fraiser* twice and refrigerate 30 minutes. Roll out and fit into a 9-inch flan ring or china
quiche pan. Bake blind for 10 minutes at 425°.

TO MAKE THE FILLING:

Bring a pot of water to a boil; immerse the nectarines for 2 minutes; peel them. Cut them in half.

　　Make a syrup with ½ cup of water and the sugar and poach the
nectarine halves in it, two at a time. Cool on a rack.

　　Whip the cream, gradually adding half the pistachios, the confectioners sugar and 1 tablespoon each of the Cointreau and Kirsch.
When the cream is stiff, fill the pastry shell with it.

　　Arrange the nectarine halves on the cream. Glaze with the apricot
jam, melted and cooled but not cold, and flavored with the remaining
Cointreau and Kirsch. Sprinkle with the remaining pistachios. Since
the pie will not keep more than 3–4 hours, you may want to finish
all its elements and put it together as late as possible.

GATEAU CASTEL VALLERIEN AUX NOISETTES
[Hazelnut Cake as Made in Château-la-Vallière]

SERVINGS: minimum 12 COST: expensive EXECUTION: semi-diffi-
　　cult
TOTAL PREPARATION TIME: 2 hours plus 2 days to ripen in the
　　refrigerator
BEST SEASON: A rich, winter-holiday cake
REMARKS ON INGREDIENTS: Be sure that the hazelnuts are fresh and

do not have a rancid taste. Use Swiss bittersweet chocolate for the *ganache,* it is worth the difference in price. Use Dutch cocoa.

CAKE LAYERS:
1 cup plus 1 TB sugar
  (250 g plus 15 g)
3 cups ground hazelnuts
  (300 g)
1 TB cocoa (3 g)
9 egg whites
Pinch of salt

BUTTERCREAM:
1 cup sugar (250 g)
½ cup water (1¼ dl)
3 drops lemon juice
1 lb. unsalted butter (500 g)

9 egg yolks
Pinch of salt
Rum to suit your taste,
  dark or light

GANACHE CREAM:
7 oz. Swiss bittersweet
  chocolate (200 g)
3 TB unsalted butter (45 g)
⅓ cup scalded heavy cream
  (75 g or 1 small dl)

DECORATION:
½ cup hazelnuts, toasted
  and chopped coarse (60 g)

TO PREPARE THE LAYERS:
Preheat oven to 325°. Butter 2 unbendable cookie sheets, flour them lightly. Using a 9-inch cake pan as a pattern, trace circles with the tip of a knife. Two circles fit on a large 17-inch baking sheet that fits in a home oven. Mix 1 cup sugar, the hazelnuts, and cocoa on wax paper. Beat the egg whites with a pinch of salt, and a tablespoon of sugar to start with. When they are stiff enough to carry the weight of a raw egg in its shell without it sinking more than ¼ inch into the foam, sprinkle the mixture of dry ingredients over the whites and fold until homogenous. Divide into 4 equal parts, spread evenly on the traced circles and bake 25 minutes or until the edges are a blond color.

Let cool one minute. Gently loosen from the cookie sheet and with the help of a spatula transfer to cool on cake racks. If your oven is too small to do more than one layer on a sheet at a given time, keep the batter refrigerated. It keeps very well.

TO MAKE THE RUM BUTTERCREAM:
Mix sugar, water, lemon juice and make a syrup. Cook it to the thread stage. Meanwhile, cream the butter; set it aside. Clean your

mixer whisk, beat the egg yolks until foamy. By the time you have done that, your syrup will be spinning a thread. With the mixer on high speed, pour the hot syrup in one steady slow stream over the yolks and continue whipping until the mixture is cold. Add a pinch of salt. Reduce the mixture to creaming speed, add the butter and add rum to suit your taste. It should be in the vicinity of ⅓ cup.

TO MAKE THE GANACHE:

Melt chocolate and butter in a double boiler. Pour the scalded cream into the chocolate, whisking constantly. Keep ready to use.

TO PUT THE CAKE TOGETHER:

Trim each layer with a paring knife to discard uneven edges; once more use the 9-inch cake pan as a pattern.

Set one layer on a cake plate; spread it with ⅓-inch-thick rum buttercream. Top with a second layer. Spread the second layer with the *ganache*. Top with the third layer, spread with buttercream. Top with the last layer. Spread ⅙-inch buttercream on the sides and top of the cake. Apply the toasted hazelnuts all around the sides of the cake. Using a cake comb, weave a decoration on the top.

Refrigerate and let ripen at least 24 hours, 48 hours would be better. You will have buttercream left over. Freeze it for another cake or for waffles. To use frozen buttercream, let defrost and mellow completely; then whip to rehomogenize.

Eugénie

———— ❀ ———— ❀ ————

ALSACE

1880s *and* 1950s

E VERY FAMILY has a legend; Eugénie, my mother's mother, was ours. We all knew that she had been an outstanding woman, only we did not know why. She was Alsatian, said her sisters-in-law, a superlative cook, a beauty, a lovely, lively person; but neither Maman nor I had known her, for she had died quite young.

For one reason or another—families are always full of reasons—Maman had lost contact with her grandfather in Alsace, and with her Aunt Alwine. She did not even know whether there were any other relatives in Alsace, alive or dead. All we knew was that the family was from the village of Woerth and if anyone was left, he or she must be very very old.

Since everyone in my family had always learned German on principle, I did of course learn German, and ended up spending a summer in Saarland with a delightful family who wholeheartedly adopted me.

I was there in 1948 and spoke at length of the Alsatian part of my family and that was enough for everyone to get excited and launch an investigating party southward. On a lovely Sunday morning we loaded up with sandwiches of *Grauwurst* and *Hausbrot* and drove down to Woerth to start our detective work. There are two places in Alsace where one can always find information: the cemetery and the village inn. We went first to the cemetery and found the grave of Josef Velter, who had died in 1895; he had been my great-grandfather. We had the right village! From the cemetery we went to the inn. That was something else! It was in the late morning just before Mass broke and everyone was getting ready for the Sunday Sauerkraut; it smelled high and mighty all over the house. No one was interested in our problem until one of us decided that an old pair of cronies who were talking about their crop of hops in rapid Alsatian dialect might be what we were looking for. We bought them a *dezi* of Edelzwicker and proceeded to ask our question: Did they know of an Alwine Velter? There was no Alwine Velter, there was no one by that name in the village. One of the cronies struck his forehead. Do you mean Alwine and Franzle? Her name isn't Velter and there followed a long biography with names, first names, numerous children, some our age, some older. It looked pretty much like I had found my great-aunt Alwine. It had been almost too easy. When I ventured to say that she might be very old, one of the cronies ventured to say that in Alsace they called people her age young and she sure was young. I had to wait and see until I met her.

It took another few hours to get to her. It was Sunday dinner time and so as not to intrude we sat down to a juicy *Schweinskarree mit Kräutern* accompanied by stewed hops shoots and a marvelous sauerkraut flanked with smoked bacon, sausage and potatoes baked in their jackets. On the table came the fine, ritual jar of strong mustard and a large white piece of the best butter. What delight, especially those strong juniper berries that left such a strange and strong taste in the mouth and sent you quickly scurrying for your glass of Riesling.

After lunch and after having looked with great interest at the "Klapperstorks" in their nest high up on the tip of the church steeple, we proceeded to my great-aunt Alwine's house. It appeared to me a paradise, an old, handsome timbered house with bright green shutters and a garden full of leeks and flowers.

There was no need to knock at the door; it stood open. As I walked in, all the eyes around the table focused on me. The women wore Alsatian black silk dresses. Several black coifs were hanging on the backs of chairs. There were children, so many children.

An ancient woman wearing a coif helped herself up with a cane, came straight to me, stared at me for a few seconds and asked point-blank, almost brusquely, "Are you Eugénie's granddaughter?" With a rather shaken "yes," I reentered the fold of my Alsatian family.

How did she know? It turned out that I look quite a bit like Eugénie; resemblances in Alsace seem to skip a generation.

I was seated at the table and given cakes, three or four pieces, with quetsches; mirabelle; apples; a piece of *Kugelhopf* full of raisins; *Plätzle* cookies full of spices and cinnamon; and coffee, coffee, coffee full of whipped cream; and Kirsch and quetsch brandy. It was fun and it was so nice and so warm and I felt as if I had always been there. Suddenly old Alwine's face became serious and she said to one of my distant cousins, *"Hole mal den Franzle."*

Who was that? Franzle?

"He was a good friend of your grandmother and he will want to see you. He is an old bachelor."

When Franzle came in, I saw a very old gentleman with a white beard wearing the black yarmulke of the Alsatian Jews. Tall, white, and as straight as they come, the old man looked at me as if I had come from another world; I had the awkward feeling that his eyes were filling with tears. But he regained his composure and started to talk. He told me that when he was growing up he had lived in the house next door. He and Eugénie had always played together and had gone to school together. He had watched her catch crawfish with a mutton head locked in a trap, or catch frogs in years when the Klapperstorks left some to catch. He said he had hated to touch these himself. He had been the one who caught the trout, using a bottle cut open at one end and a piece of bread hidden in the neck of the other end as a trap.

Franzle had always been part of the family. During the last war he had to cut his hair, stop wearing his yarmulke, and hide in one of Alwine's attic rooms for four long years. He only went out at night to poach silently for rabbit or quail.

I was adopted by Alwine and Franzle and invited to come back again and again. Having me around, they said, was like being young again. And I went as often as I could. I went in April when the asparagus were in season and served drenched in butter, lemon, or coriander, or in the delicious gravy of tiny squab chickens that roasted slowly on the spit.

I went in October and helped pickle the sauerkraut, packing the patiently shredded white Quintal cabbage between layers of salt and putting heavy stones on the barrel to extract the juices.

The last time, before Alwine and Franzle both left for a better world two weeks apart from each other, I spent the last Christmas of their life with them and the crowd of children and adults that were our family. What a lovely ritual. Near the big chimney was a huge Christmas tree full of little wooden hand-cut objects and real candles burning fiercely. At eight o'clock Alwine's son Hansi read the story of the Nativity and we all sang Christmas carols in German. Everyone gave presents and mine was precious. It was a package containing Eugénie's diary and her cook book, both in her own hand written in German.

A big surprise was awaiting me. Old Alwine and my cousins had cooked the whole meal from Eugénie's recipes. It was a fabulous feast with a fresh ham and sauerkraut, quenelles of pheasant, a truffled chicken with *Pflütten* covered with *foie gras,* and another chicken with quenelles and Riesling sauce. Franzle had brought a goose. There were noodles and cakes—the Christmas *Stollen* and the *Birewecke* spicy and full of dried nuts—and there was fruit served on brightly flowered Strasbourg china. The feast lasted a long time, well moistened with the best Gerwürztraminer served in graceful glasses with long green stems.

I went to bed exhilarated with love for two very old people and scared that I would, considering their age, lose them too soon after finding them. I propped myself against my pillow and tried to decipher Eugénie's diary. The inside cover ws inscribed: "In case of my death, I wish this book to be sent to my sister Alwine Oberlin, rue de Strasbourg, Molsheim."

It took me a while to get used to the very vertical and elongated German script with the funny double *s* that looks more like an *f*, but after a while I was able to read quite fast. Fascinated, almost hypnotized, I discovered Eugénie's secret life from her own handwriting:

December 27, 1888. . . . Since I asked to visit Stoffels, my sister Alwine and old aunt Marie Becker for the end of the year, Papa took me to Haguenau in the coach. Mr Stoffel was waiting for us in front of the church. I had to change my shoes which were soaked with slush before climbing aboard the always immaculate Stoffel coach. Mr Stoffel chatted and chatted about their Christmas and how Marie was so anticipating my arrival. . . . I barely listened to him. I answered automatically and felt worse and more and more lonesome as we approached Truchterheim. I had only one huge thought: Franzle, Franzle, Franzle. And then, another thought came to me like a knife thrust: Papa . . . I had kissed him good-bye and would never see him again. . . . He would be hurt, upset. He would even cry, but he would never cry as much as I had, nor feel as guilty as I feel about thinking this way. He deserves to be hurt for listening so much to priests and rabbis.

Marie was happy to see me and we talked after dinner while Mr Stoffel opened several bottles of Edelzwicker to celebrate her birthday in style. Young Mr Biedermeyer was there; Marie loves him and there are no priests and rabbis fighting there. . . .

December 29, 1888. . . . I have stopped crying and now I feel empty. Madame Stoffel seems to have noticed that something is out of the ordinary with me and finds me very pale. She keeps repeating it and it bothers me. Marie by now is suspicious and while we were cutting noodles together she tried to make me tell her what bothers me so much. Yesterday was Sunday, and so as not to go to Mass, I pretended to be sick. While everyone was in church I took a walk up the hill on the Molsheim road. It was discouragingly cold and snowflakes kept

falling and turning to water on my cape. I wonder whether it
will be that cold on the other side of the mountains. . . .

December 30, 1888. . . . I left Truchterheim early this
morning by public coach to go and visit Alwine in Molsheim.
The children were all dressed up to welcome me and there was
a great big pot of sour turnips with Bratwurst and apple cake.
By now, Alwine knows. I have told her. She understood although she is scared for me and promised to have Hansi take
me to Schirmeck to Marie Becker's house. She was not really
surprised, knowing what had happened these last two years
to the peace of our parents' house. It feels good to have someone understand.

There was a great New Year *Messti* at the Molsheim Metzig
tonight and we danced until late. Hansi sang a few old songs
and told the same Alsatian jokes he had told at every gathering
since I have known him. Franzle used to laugh so hard at him.
Franzle, oh Franzle. What were you doing while I forced myself to dance here to send the pain down to my feet? . . .
Were you studying as usual, since that is all they will ever let
you do, Franzle, study. . . .

December 31, 1888. . . . Schirmeck at old Aunt Marie
Becker's. Tonight, after the *Vin Gris* at midnight, everyone will
go to bed and I will stay awake. Dear old Marie is cooking a
nice dinner to celebrate the New Year, some of the same old
beans with bacon that she cooks so well and her François will
give us some good schnaps. They looked both so happy that I
came to be with them and I feel guilty and selfish, for they are
too old to discover that I have disappeared leaving all my
possessions in their house. Now, I am really afraid. . . .

The diary did not start again until more than a week later and told
the end of Eugénie's story:

January 8, 1889. . . . I am in France and the name of the
village is Cirey. It sounded familiar but I was so tired that it
took me a while to connect it to Voltaire. . . . And suddenly

reality became reality, I was on the other side. I was answered in French when I spoke Alsatian and I am in France forever. Franzle can study his Talmud and I will not have to look at him anymore through the window, cry, and feel desperate. By now they all know that I have gone and will never come back and all I have to do is work and make a new life for myself.

And she did. The trip over the Vosges forests in the depth of winter had been dangerous. She had plodded through deep snows, her diary says, doggedly following the young Sarre river that flows down the Donon mountain toward French Lorraine. She had been lucky enough never to meet a patrol of Uhlans or police dogs. She had not even been aware of crossing the border. For a year she worked as a cook in Lunéville. She saved for the train fare to Paris and there she met and married my grandfather, who hammered for her the copper pots that now hang on the wall of my cooking school.

Alwine gave me her sister's old red silk Alsatian coif, neatly folded in a box, worn out and cut at the creases. It has become for me a symbol of courage, self-reliance and freedom.

MORCHEL SUPPE
[Morel Soup]

SERVINGS: 6 COST: see below EXECUTION: easy

TOTAL PREPARATION TIME: 45 minutes plus 35 minutes soaking
   for dried morels

BEST SEASON: With fresh morels, April–May; with dried morels,
   September through May. A bit too heavy for the summer months

REMARKS ON INGREDIENTS: The soup will be inexpensive with fresh
   morels and expensive with dried morels. You may use the following species fresh: *Morchella anguticeps, Morchella esculenta,
   Morchella crassipes.* The dried species imported from Europe
   are mostly *Morchella conica.*

1 lb. fresh morels (500 g) or 3–4 oz. dried morels (100–125 g)
10 TB unsalted butter (130–140 g)
Salt
Pepper from the mill
½ cup flour (60–65 g)

5–6 cups veal stock or chicken stock, positively homemade
4 egg yolks
1 cup heavy cream (2¼ dl)
Lemon juice
1 cup tiny croutons

If you use fresh morels, wash them thoroughly under cold running water. Let the water run into the gills and dislodge insects and sand or soil.

Cut off the end of the stems, or even the whole stem, if it is too stringy. Chop fine. Reserve.

If you use dried morels, put them in a small bowl. Cover them with lukewarm water and let stand about 35 minutes. Then rinse the cones under running water, cut the ends of the stems and chop fine. Reserve the soaking water.

Heat 2 tablespoons butter in a heavy saucepan. Add the morels, salt, and pepper; cover and let steam for about ten minutes. Meanwhile, heat the remainder of the butter in another saucepan and add the flour; cook over low heat 8 to 10 minutes. Whisk in 6 cups of stock if you use fresh morels and 5 cups of stock plus 1 cup morel soaking water if you use dried morels. In the latter case, pour slowly, making sure that you do not include any of the sand at the bottom of the dish. Add the chopped stems.

Bring to a boil and simmer, skimming well for about 20 minutes. Strain into a clean pot. At this point add the morels to the sauce and simmer very slowly for another 15 minutes.

Mix the egg yolks with the heavy cream in a 2-cup measuring cup or bowl. Slowly add about 1 cup of the hot soup. Then, reverse the process and pour the mixture back into the bulk of the soup, stirring well. Bring back to a slow simmer very slowly and make sure that the soup has shown two or three definite boils. Correct the seasoning with salt, pepper, and maybe a drop or two of lemon juice. Serve piping hot over the croutons.

LINSENSUPPE MIT BRATWURSTSTERNEN
[Lentil Soup with Bratwurst]

SERVINGS: 6–8 COST: inexpensive EXECUTION: easy

TOTAL PREPARATION TIME: 2 hours plus overnight soaking

BEST SEASON: Late fall through early spring

REMARKS ON INGREDIENTS: Use the true German white veal and
   pork bratwurst, not frankfurters, as garnish. Keep the cooked
   slab bacon for a good Alsatian sandwich made with mustard
   and leftover sauerkraut.

½ lb. lentils (large brown
   type) (250 g)
3 quarts cold water (3 litres)
1 large onion
2 cloves
Bouquet garni
3 oz. smoked slab bacon
   (100 g)
Salt and pepper

2 veal bratwurst (not frankfurters)
2 leeks
1 carrot
½ cup unsalted butter
   (about 100 g)
½ cup sour cream (1 gen-
   erous dl)

Soak the lentils overnight in cold water. Sort them carefully to
eliminate small stones; put them in a pot. Add the three quarts cold
water and bring to a boil. Stick the cloves in the onion. Add the
onion and the *bouquet garni,* the bacon, salt, and pepper. Turn down
to a simmer and cook until the lentils are tender. Remove the bacon
and keep for another use. Strain the soup through a sieve and test its
consistency. It should be that of heavy cream. If it is not, reduce until
this consistency is reached. If it is too thick, add enough light broth
to bring to the correct consistency.

   Cut the bratwursts into ¼-inch slices and with a star-shaped aspic
cutter, cut one small star out of each slice. Cut the carrot and the
white part of the two leeks into fine ⅛-inch-wide julienne or paysanne. Heat the butter in a small pan. Add the vegetable julienne,
salt and pepper and cover. Cook until tender. When the vegetables
are almost done, toss the bratwurst stars into them. Keep the pot
uncovered and cook together for a few minutes.

Add this garnish to the lentil soup and lightly simmer together for a few minutes. Mix one good ladle of soup with the sour cream and pour back into the bulk of the soup. Reheat without boiling and serve piping hot.

SAUERKRAUT SUPPE
[Sauerkraut Soup]

SERVINGS: 6 COST: moderately expensive EXECUTION: easy
TOTAL PREPARATION TIME: 1½ to 2 hours
BEST SEASON: The winter months. If served with bread and butter, a meal in itself.
REMARKS ON INGREDIENTS: Use *fresh* sauerkraut processed *without sugar;* the canned variety has lost its body and soul.

3 oz. smoked slab bacon (100 g)
1 lb. fresh sauerkraut (500 g)
2 medium onions, diced fine
1½–2 cups Riesling or Sylvaner wine (3–4½ dl)
2 quarts brown veal stock or other stock of your choice (2 litres)
Salt and pepper
2 potatoes (preferably Maine) diced into ¼-inch cubes
½ cup butter (110–115 g)

Dice the bacon into ¼-inch cubes. Put into a deep heavy pot and let it render slowly and brown evenly to a light golden. Remove the cracklings to a plate and reserve.

While the bacon renders, wash the sauerkraut twice and squeeze it dry. Keep ready to use. Brown the onions lightly in the rendered bacon fat. Add the sauerkraut and mix well. Add the wine, bring to a boil, cover with a buttered paper and the pot lid, and cook gently for 45 minutes. Uncover the pot, add the stock, salt and pepper and cook until about 7 cups of liquid and solids are left. Add the diced potatoes and cook, uncovered, another 15 minutes. Bring to a violent boil. Add the butter to the center of the boil. Correct the seasoning and serve very hot with bread and butter.

FLAMMKUCHE
[Onion and Bacon Pie]

SERVINGS: 6 COST: inexpensive EXECUTION: easy
TOTAL PREPARATION TIME: 2 hours plus 1 hour for the dough to
    prove, and 25 minutes to bake
BEST SEASON: Eaten year round in Alsace. Best when it is very cold.
    A meal in itself.
SUGGESTED WINE: Sylvaner

DOUGH:	FILLING:
2 cups unsifted all-purpose flour (250 g)	6 oz. smoked slab bacon (175–180 g)
½ envelope yeast	3 lbs. white onions (1 kg 500)
¾ cup water, warm (small 2 dl)	4 TB butter
2 TB melted lard	Salt
1½ tsp. salt	Pepper, ground coarse
1 TB oil	2 oz. Kirschwasser
	1 cup heavy cream (2¼ dl)

Cut the slab bacon into ¼-inch-thick slices, then into 1-inch-wide
pieces. Cook gently over slow heat until the bacon has rendered most
of its fat, but not yet taken on any color. Remove the bacon to a
bowl and proceed to make the dough. Do not discard the bacon fat
or wash the pan.

Make a well in the flour. Add the yeast and half of the water. Mix
well with a fork. Let stand until the yeast bubbles. Then mix the
remainder of the warm water with the salt and melted lard. Add to
the well. Gather the flour to make a ball of dough. Knead 10 minutes
until smooth and elastic. Put to rise in a bowl brushed with the oil.
Roll the dough around the bowl to coat with the oil. Let rise in a
warm place until double in bulk.

Peel and slice the onions into ¼-inch slices. Add the butter to the
bacon fat in the pan, sauté the onions until translucent and add salt
and pepper. Cool. Add 2 ounces Kirschwasser and the cream.

Punch the dough down and roll it out ¼ inch thick. Fit it into a 12-inch pizza pan. Spread the onions on the bread dough. Dot with the bacon flakes. Let stand 45 minutes. Bake in a 375° preheated oven for 30 to 35 minutes.

Serve when lightly cooled.

KUMMELWEIHE
[Cheese and Cumin Quiche]

SERVINGS: 6 COST: medium expensive EXECUTION: easy
TOTAL PREPARATION TIME: 1½ hours, including making of the pastry
BEST SEASON: A perfect dinner first course, or supper or luncheon main course, in the cold months
SUGGESTED WINE: Sylvaner or Riesling

1 recipe ordinary short pastry, page 13	*2 cups heavy cream (4½ dl)*
	1 oz. Kirsch
½ lb. Swiss Gruyère (250 g)	*1 TB cumin seeds*
2 eggs	*Salt*
3 TB flour (20–25 g)	*Black pepper, ground coarse*

Prepare the pastry on page 13. Roll it out ⅛ inch thick and fit it into a 9-inch porcelain quiche pan. Let rest 15 minutes. Fit the pastry with a foil, fill with dried beans and bake 15 minutes in a 400° preheated oven. Remove the beans and foil.

While the pastry bakes, grate the cheese fine. Beat the eggs, sprinkle the flour over them and beat together until smooth. Beat in the heavy cream and Kirsch. All that beating should be done with a hand whisk, not an electric mixer, which would produce too much foam.

Sprinkle the cheese on the bottom of the pastry shell. Add the cumin seeds, sprinkling them evenly into the cheese. Pour the custard over the cheese slowly and gradually. Turn the oven down to 375°, bake on the top rack of the oven for 10 minutes. Grate the pepper coarse over the top of the custard and continue baking until the custard is set. Let cool to warm before serving.

FASANEN-TERRINE
[Terrine of Pheasant with Morels and Foie Gras]

SERVINGS: 12–24 COST: very expensive EXECUTION: difficult

TOTAL PREPARATION TIME: 48 hours marination, 3 hours preparation and baking, 12 hours minimum cooling

BEST SEASON: September through the end of November with wild pheasant, September through April with domesticated pheasant. A bit too rich for spring and summer.

REMARKS ON INGREDIENTS: A good way to utilize old pheasants with a hard breastbone or commercial pheasants with a deficient game taste.

Use a baby bloc of Strasbourg foie gras.

THE TERRINE:
2 pheasants
½ lb. lean veal meat (250 g)
½ lb. pork meat (Boston butt) (250 g)
1 lb. unsalted fatback (500 g)
1 bottle Riesling
4 oz. Cognac
1 carrot
2 onions
1½ oz. dried morels
½ tsp. quatre épices
1 juniper berry, crushed
5 eggs
Salt
Pepper from the mill

1 egg white
1 small can Strasbourg foie gras, about 4 oz.
2–3 TB unsalted butter

THE JELLIED ESSENCE:
Pheasant bones
½ lb. gelatinous veal bones
1 carrot
1 onion
1 leek, white part only
Bouquet garni
1 quart brown veal stock or 1 quart chicken stock (homemade)
1 envelope gelatin (if needed)

DAY ONE: TO MAKE THE TERRINE:

Bone the pheasants, starting through the back. Take great care not to damage the skins. Keep the skins rolled in wax paper in the refrigerator. Keep the bones also.

Remove the two largest supremes (white meat from both sides of the breast) and dice them into ⅓-inch cubes. Put this in a dish and reserve.

Put the other two supremes and all the brown meat of the pheasants in a large baking dish. Take care to remove all the nerves, fat, and sinews from all the meat, and cut it into 1½-inch cubes. Do the same with the veal meat, the pork meat and ½ pound of the fresh fatback.

Mix 2 ounces Cognac with the Riesling; pour over the meat. Add the carrot, sliced thick, and the onion, sliced thick. Mix into the wine and meat. Cover with a plastic wrap and marinate in a cool place (cellar, pantry), but not in the refrigerator, for 48 hours. At the same time, marinate the supremes in 1 ounce Cognac; keep covered with plastic wrap.

DAY TWO: TO MAKE THE JELLIED ESSENCE:

Brown the pheasant bones and veal bones in a 400° oven. Deglaze this pan with some water. Keep the deglazing.

Put the bones in a 4-quart pot. Add the veal stock and strain the deglazing water into the pot. Bring to a boil. Add the vegetables and *bouquet garni* and simmer until reduced to 2 cups. Strain and keep refrigerated until the next day. If the stock is not solid enough, melt it and add some gelatin. You will have to judge how much according to the solidity of the stock.

DAY THREE:

Soak the morels in enough barely lukewarm water to cover them. Let them stand 30–35 minutes. Rinse under cold running water and chop fine. Reserve the soaking water.

Meanwhile, grind the marinated meats and fat twice. Put them in the large bowl of an electric mixer. Add ½ teaspoon *quatre épices*, the juniper berry crushed to powder, the chopped morels, the five eggs well beaten, 2½ teaspoons salt, 10 turns of the mill of fresh pepper and ⅓ of whatever is left of the liquid of the marinade. Mix well until perfectly homogenous. Fry a little patty of forcemeat in a small frying pan and cool in the freezer to check the level of salt. Add more salt and pepper if necessary. Cut ¼ pound fatback into ⅓-inch cubes, season with salt, pepper and a bit of *quatre épices.* Rinse your hand under cold running water and then mix into the forcemeat.

Cut the foie gras in half lengthwise. Cut the remaining fatback into thin sheets and use as many of them as needed to wrap the foie gras completely.

Now butter a 1½-quart terrine; put half of the forcemeat on the bottom. Lightly beat the egg white; roll the foie gras wrapped in the fatback in it and bury the foie gras pieces, placed end on end, in the forcemeat. Pack the remainder of the forcemeat over the foie gras. Cover with the pheasant skin or skins (as much as will be needed). Melt the remainder of the butter and brush the pheasant skin with it. Bake in a hot water bath for 1½ hours at 350° or until the fat runs clear.

While the terrine bakes, reheat the pheasant essence. Add the soaking water of the morels, reduce to 2 cups and add 1 ounce of Cognac to correct the seasoning.

As soon as the terrine is baked, pour off the liquid fat. Immediately prick it in 12 different places with a skewer and pour the essence into the terrine through the holes made in its top and all around the terrine. Let the essence cover the terrine by at least ½ inch. Cool at room temperature. Refrigerate for a minimum of 12 hours.

Serve chilled with Riesling, and toast or French bread.

PATE DE TRUITES DE SAINTE-MARIE-AUX-MINES
[*Trout Pâté*]

SERVINGS: 8 COST: affordable EXECUTION: difficult
TOTAL PREPARATION TIME: 4 hours with baking plus time for cooling

BEST SEASON: Serve cold in the spring.

SUGGESTED WINE: Riesling

REMARKS ON INGREDIENTS: The best place to locate excellent pike and lake salmon trout is in a fish store located in a predominantly Jewish neighborhood. The fish there is sold whole or filleted; purchase the pike already filleted. However, purchase the trout whole so you can use the heads for the stock used in the sauce.

PATE:

½ recipe semi-puff pastry, page 17

½ lb. pike meat without bones or skin (250 g)

½ lb. lake salmon trout meat without bones or skin (250 g)

2 whole eggs

¾ cup milk (2 small dl)

7 slices of ordinary white bread, crust removed (140–150 g)

1 cup unsalted butter (225 g)

1¾ tsp. salt

½ tsp. white pepper

3 fresh trout (brook, rainbow or golden)

8 strips of lemon peel, 2 inches long, without pith

1 egg white, lightly beaten

Chopped parsley

1 beaten egg for brushing on the pastry

SAUCE:

Heads of the trout

1 cup water (2¼ dl)

1 cup dry white wine (2¼ dl)

1 onion, sliced coarse

½ small carrot, sliced coarse

Bouquet garni

1 onion, chopped fine

2 TB vinegar

Salt

Pepper from the mill

1 TB Dijon mustard

1 egg yolk

1 cup corn oil

Chopped parsley

Chopped chives

Lemon juice

TO MAKE THE PATE:

First have the pastry ready. The pastry can be made ahead of time and kept refrigerated.

Cut both fish meats into ½-inch cubes. Mix both meats together and divide into 2 equal parts. Beat each egg separately.

Using either a mortar, the blender, or a modern food processor, pound half of the meat and one egg together to obtain a fine purée. Repeat with the other half of the fish and the second egg. Strain the mixture through a sieve to discard all the connective tissues. Cool in the refrigerator for one hour.

Bring the milk to a boil. Crumble the bread and add; stir to obtain a *panade.* Dry thoroughly by stirring over a medium heat; remove to a buttered plate. Let cool until almost cold but do not let get hard. Using the electric mixer, cream the butter, add the salt and pepper, and slowly add the bread mixture so that butter and *panade* are homogenous. Then add the fish meat and beat until the mixture is smooth and even. Season. Refrigerate while you bone the trout.

Cut along the backbone of each trout, sliding the blade along the backbone on both sides. When the bone is visible, cut it just under the head and just before the tail and pull gently. The whole bone structure will come out easily. Cut the head off, discard the insides, and cut the tail off. To skin the fillets, put them on a board, skin down. Now, cut ¼ inch above the tail end into the fillet and slide your blade at a 45 degree angle upward, under the skin. Proceed in large strokes, holding the skin in your left hand and slicing forward with the right one. Discard the skin, rinse the fillets in cold water, pat them dry, salt and pepper them. Scan the fillets for tiny bones, which are plentiful.

Blanch the lemon peels in boiling water for a full five minutes. Drain and cool.

TO BUILD THE PATE:

Cut the pastry into two halves. Butter a 9-inch porcelain quiche dish. Roll out half of the pastry ⅛ inch thick. Fit into the quiche dish. Let the pastry hang about ½ inch over the edge of the plate; trim a neat, regular edge all the way around the dish with a knife.

Spread one-half of the forcemeat on the pie bottom. Roll the trout fillets in the lightly beaten egg white. Cover the forcemeat with the trout fillets; you should not hesitate to cut the fillets to suit the shape of the dish and obtain a solid sheet of trout fillet. Put the blanched lemon rind strips on top of the fillets, sprinkle with a solid blanket of chopped parsley. Then, cover with the remainder of the forcemeat.

Pack well. Fold the pastry hanging over the edge of the dish over the forcemeat. Brush the pastry with beaten egg.

Roll out the second sheet of pastry ⅛ inch thick and place it over the dish. Pass the rolling pin over the edges of the dish to cut the excess pastry off. Push the edges of the pastry down into the dish to seal well. Brush with the egg, trace a crisscross pattern to decorate. With the tip of scissors, cut a few little openings to form steam vents.

Let rest at least 30 minutes before baking.

Bake in a 350° preheated oven for 1 hour or until the pâté is brown and a skewer inserted in its center comes out hot and clean. Cool completely.

TO MAKE THE SAUCE:

Place the trout heads, water, wine, sliced onion, carrot and *bouquet garni* in a pot. Bring to a boil and simmer about 35 minutes. Strain. Place the chopped onion, the vinegar, salt and pepper in a small pot and add ½ cup of the stock. Cook until 1½ tablespoons liquids and solids are left. Transfer to a bowl; add the mustard, salt and pepper, the egg yolk and mix well. Gradually add the oil to make a mayonnaise. Lighten the mayonnaise as you go along with a bit of the remaining fish stock, and finish with fresh parsley, chives and lemon juice if you desire. Correct the seasoning.

Serve the pâté in wedges with the mayonnaise and asparagus.

QUENELLES DE CUISSES DE GRENOUILLES AUX HERBES
[Quenelles of Frogs Legs with Herb Sauce]

SERVINGS: 6 COST: expensive EXECUTION: difficult, spread the work over two days

TOTAL PREPARATION TIME: 3 hours

BEST SEASON: Whenever you can find good-quality frogs legs. Enjoyable year round.

SUGGESTED WINE: Riesling

REMARKS ON INGREDIENTS: Buy the smallest possible frogs legs from a reputable fish market.

FORCEMEAT:

2 lbs. small frogs legs (1 kg)

1 whole egg

⅓ cup milk (1 small dl)

1 slice French bread
   (4″ x 2½″ x ⅓″),
   crusts removed

1½ TB unsalted butter (20 g)

¾–1 tsp. salt

¼ tsp. white pepper

¾ cup heavy cream
   (1¾–2 small dl)

SAUCE AND POACHING OF THE QUENELLES:

1 lb. unsalted butter (500 g)

Flour

Salt and pepper

½ tiny clove garlic, mashed

2 quarts excellent fish fumet
   (page 12) (2 litres)

2 large shallots, mashed fine

1 tsp. each dried chervil and
   tarragon

3 TB freshly chopped parsley

3 egg yolks

Lemon juice

1 TB chopped chives

TO PREPARE THE QUENELLES:

Separate the thighs from the drumsticks. Bone the thighs completely and remove the very apparent blood vessel. Keep the bones.

Put the meat and the egg in the blender or in a mortar or modern food processor and purée until perfectly smooth. Strain through a tamis or conical strainer. Keep chilled.

Put the milk in a small pot, add the crumbled bread and heat until a paste forms. Dry well, as you would a cream puff dough. Remove to a lightly buttered plate and cool the *panade* completely.

Cream the butter. Gradually add the cold *panade,* salt and pepper, and finally the frog purée. Beat until very smooth. Place the bowl containing the mixture over ice and refrigerate one hour. Slowly beat in ¾ cup heavy cream, preferably by hand, using a wooden spatula. Keep chilled overnight.

TO PREPARE THE SAUCE:

Heat about 2 tablespoons butter in a frying pan. Lightly flour the frog drumsticks and sauté them gently in the butter until just done. Season with salt, pepper and the bit of garlic. Add about ¼ cup of fish fumet to the pan; mix well. Remove the drumsticks to a plate and bone them.

Keep the meat covered with plastic wrap.

Return the bones to the frying pan; add the raw bones from the thighs, 2 cups fish fumet, the shallots, the chervil and tarragon, 2 tablespoons freshly chopped parsley, a bit of salt, and three turns of the pepper mill. Reduce to ½ cup of liquid; strain into a 2-quart saucepan. Add the egg yolks and poach them. Whisk them over low heat until the mixture is very foamy and light in color. Whisk ¾ pound melted unsalted butter into the egg pan, making absolutely sure the butter is warm, not hot. Lighten the sauce with lemon juice to suit your taste. Correct the seasoning. Add the last tablespoon of parsley, the chives, and the drumstick meat and keep warm over warm water.

TO POACH AND PRESENT THE QUENELLES:
If you do not have enough fish fumet to poach in, use salted water.

Heat the remainder of the fish fumet in a shallow frying pan; keep it at a low simmer.

With two teaspoons, shape 18 small quenelles and poach them for about 12 minutes. Cover with a buttered paper while poaching to prevent the top from drying. Turn the quenelles over once while poaching. Remove the cooked quenelles to the sauce.

To serve, either place the quenelles in a pastry shell or on a small bed of rice; decorate the plate with parsley and slices of lemon.

GRENOUILLES SAUCE ROSE ET VERTE
[Frogs Legs in Green and Pink Sauce]

SERVINGS: 6 COST: expensive EXECUTION: medium-difficult; do not overcook the frogs legs
TOTAL PREPARATION TIME: 45 minutes

BEST SEASON: Whenever you can locate good frogs legs. Enjoyable
   year round as a first course.
SUGGESTED WINE: Pinot Rouge d'Alsace or Riesling
REMARKS ON INGREDIENTS: See page 233.

3 shallots, chopped fine	*¾ cup butter (170–175 g)*
1 cup Pinot Rouge d'Alsace	*1½ TB chopped chives*
(2¼ dl)	*½ cup heavy cream (1 gen-*
2 TB red wine vinegar	*erous dl)*
Salt	*2 dozen frogs legs*
Pepper from the mill	*Flour*

Place the shallots, Pinot Rouge d'Alsace, red wine vinegar, a good
pinch of salt and pepper in a small pot and reduce to ¼ cup. Bring
to a rapid boil and fluff in 10 tablespoons of butter with a whisk.
Heat the cream mixed with the chives in a small pan. Keep both the
butter sauce and the cream ready to use.

   Salt and pepper the frogs legs lightly and flour them. Pat well to
discard any excess flour.

   Heat the remaining butter in a large electric frying pan preheated
to 375°. Let the butter turn brown and smell like hazelnuts. Turn
the heat down to 325° and cook the frogs legs until just tender.
It requires only a few minutes. Turn the heat off. Season the legs
well; otherwise they are very bland.

   Add the butter sauce and the chives and cream mixture to the pan.
Blend together. Correct the seasoning and serve immediately.

SAUMON DE L'AUBERGE DU BATEAU
A ILLHAEUSERN
[*Salmon as Served at the Old Auberge du Bateau in Illhaeusern*]

SERVINGS: 6 COST: moderately expensive EXECUTION: easy
TOTAL PREPARATION TIME: 1 hour
BEST SEASON: April through September
SUGGESTED WINE: Pinot Rouge d'Alsace or Riesling

6 *salmon steaks, 1 inch thick*
2 *cups Pinot Rouge d'Alsace*
 (two-thirds of a bottle)
2 *white onions, chopped fine*
Bouquet garni
1 *tsp. dried tarragon*
Salt

Pepper from the mill
2 *leeks (white and light green*
 parts), cut into ¼-inch
 paysanne
½ *lb. unsalted butter (250 g)*
½ *cup heavy cream (1 gen-*
 erous dl)

Remove the skin of the salmon steaks with a sharp knife and discard it. Pour the wine into a 2-quart pot. Bone the salmon steaks. Each will separate into two pieces, called *darnes*. Add all the bones to the wine and simmer down to 1 cup.

While the wine reduces, reshape the steaks into medallions. Arrange the *darnes* so that the thick parts of each pair are facing each other; that is, put the sides that were in contact with the bone before boning against each other, but with the belly flaps placed one toward the right, the other toward the left. Wrap the belly flaps around the thick part of the salmon either clockwise or counterclockwise and press well together. You have obtained a salmon medallion. Secure with four toothpicks. Keep ready to use.

Strain the reduced wine into a 1-quart pot. Add the chopped onions, the *bouquet garni,* the tarragon, a pinch of salt and pepper. Reduce to 2–3 tablespoons of solids and liquids.

Heat 2 tablespoons butter in a small pan, sauté the paysanne of leeks, salt and pepper them. Cover and *étuvé* for 5 minutes. Add the heavy cream and simmer about 5 minutes, uncovered. Keep warm.

Butter the rack of a fish poacher with a tablespoon of butter. Set the salmon medallions on it. Fill the poacher with hot water. Bring to a boil and add plenty of salt. Immerse the salmon into the rapidly boiling water; bring back to a violent boil, cover, and remove from the heat. Let stand 8 to 10 minutes.

Meanwhile, finish the sauce. Whisk the remaining butter into the reduction of wine and shallots either over high heat or over a very low heat. Strain the sauce into the leek and cream mixture. Mix well; correct the seasoning carefully.

Spoon the sauce over the salmon medallions decorated with parsley and lemon slices and serve.

SCHINKEN MIT SAUERKRAUT
[Fresh Ham and Sauerkraut]

SERVINGS: 12 COST: affordable EXECUTION: easy

TOTAL PREPARATION TIME: Two days of dry marination for the ham plus three hours for baking. Four hours preparation and cooking for the sauerkraut

BEST SEASON: The depth of winter. A great New Year's Eve dinner.

SUGGESTED WINE: Let the Riesling flow.

REMARKS ON INGREDIENTS: The best slab bacon is to be found in Italian neighborhood markets. Split the baking of the sauerkraut and the ham over two days, unless you have two ovens and can use both at once.

HAM:
1 fresh ham
2 tsp. quatre épices (see page 7)
1 TB ground coriander
1 tsp. salt
½ tsp. pepper
1 bottle Riesling
12 medium Maine potatoes in their jackets
Potato starch

SAUERKRAUT:
6 lbs. sauerkraut
Rind of the ham
½ cup goose fat or lard
6 onions, chopped fine
24 juniper berries
½ tsp. thyme
2 bay leaves
1 bottle Riesling
Brown veal stock or other stock of your choice
1 lb. smoked slab bacon
½ lb. unsalted butter

DAY ONE:

Remove the rind of the ham. Scrape every bit of fat from the surface of the rind. Keep it for later use.

Smooth the surface of the ham with a sharp knife. Make sure that there is ⅓ inch of fat left covering the meat. Mix the *quatre épices,* the coriander, the salt and pepper and sprinkle all over the meat. Let marinate two days in a cold place or even on the lowest shelf of the refrigerator.

DAY TWO:
Prepare the sauerkraut. Blanch the ham rind. Keep ready to use.

Wash the sauerkraut in cold water three times and squeeze very dry between your hands.

Heat the goose fat or lard in a pot and brown the onions in it; push them to the side of the pot. Place the ham rind, fat side down, on the bottom of the pot. Spoon the onions over it. Sprinkle half of the sauerkraut over the onions; add the juniper berries without crushing them. Sprinkle the remainder of the sauerkraut over the berries and add the thyme and bay leaves. Add the bottle of Riesling and enough stock just to cover the sauerkraut. Cover with a parchment paper and the pot lid; bring to a boil, then braise 1 hour in a 325° preheated oven.

After one hour, uncover the pot, toss the sauerkraut with a large fork and add salt and pepper. Place the piece of smoked bacon in the center of the kraut, recover with the paper and lid, and continue braising another 1½ hours.

There should be about 1 cup of liquid left at the bottom of the braising pot. Collect it into a small bowl and cool the sauerkraut.

All you will have to do the next day is reheat the sauerkraut on top of the stove about 40 minutes before the ham is done. Before doing so, cut the cold butter into 32 small cubes and put on the surface of the sauerkraut. Before serving, correct the seasoning with salt and pepper.

DAY THREE:
Put the ham on a rack fitted over a roasting pan. *Do not scrape off* the marinade. Preheat the oven to 325° and roast about 3 to 3½ hours or until a meat thermometer shows the temperature at the bone to be 175°. During the last hour of cooking, remove the lard to a bowl with a baster. Keep adding a little Riesling to the roasting pan

at regular intervals; it will build a good gravy. Put the potatoes to bake on the oven rack around the ham. When the ham is done, remove it to a platter.

Pour all the cooking juices in a measuring cup and with a baster, remove the fat-free gravy to a saucepan after noting how much gravy you have. Strain the reserved sauerkraut cooking juices into the gravy. Add one cup of wine and simmer fifteen minutes. Thicken with 1 ¼ teaspoons of potato starch per cup of gravy. Dissolve the potato starch in a few tablespoons of cold water and whisk the mixture into the simmering gravy.

TO PRESENT THE DISH:
On a large heated turkey platter, make a bed of sauerkraut and set the ham in the center. Surround with the potatoes. Serve with the bacon sliced into 12 slices, mustard, the gravy, and butter for the potatoes. *Guten Appetit!*

FRANZLE'S JUDISCH GANS
[Goose Jewish Style]

SERVINGS: 6 COST: medium expensive EXECUTION: easy
TOTAL PREPARATION TIME: 2½ hours
BEST SEASON: November through January
SUGGESTED WINE: Sylvaner or Riesling
REMARKS ON INGREDIENTS: Use the potato parings to make a small
   Grumbeerkuechle (see page 252).

One 10-lb. goose	*Chicken stock*
6 onions, cut into ¼-inch slices	Bouquet garni
3 cloves garlic, mashed	*1 tsp. coriander seeds*
2½ TB flour	*3 Maine potatoes*
1 bottle Sylvaner or Riesling	*Chopped parsley*

Remove the fat pads of the goose. Put them in a pot containing 2 cups of water. Heat slowly and let cook until the water has evaporated, the fat has melted, and only the cracklings are left floating in the liquid fat. Remove the cracklings and reserve them.

Cut the goose into 12 pieces. Heat some goose fat in a large cocotte and brown the onions and garlic well, but do not let them burn or fall apart. Remove them to a plate.

In the same fat, brown the pieces of goose on all sides until the skin is nice and crisp. Sprinkle with the flour and turn often to brown the flour as evenly as possible. Add the wine and enough chicken stock to cover the pieces of meat, then add a *bouquet garni* and the coriander seeds. Place a piece of foil flush against the surface of the meat and form an inverted lid to catch the condensation. Cover with the pot lid and bake in a preheated 325° oven for 1½ hours.

Peel the potatoes, cut them into ¾-inch-wide strips. Pare the strips to obtain elongated olive-shaped chunks with no sharp angles. Uncover the pot, add the potatoes, cover the pot again and continue baking another ½ to ¾ hour. When both meats and potatoes are done, remove them to a heated casserole and defatten the gravy by separating the lean gravy from the fat with a baster. Spoon or pour the defattened gravy over the meat and potatoes. Correct the seasoning. Brown the parsley in ½ tablespoon of goose fat, mix in the reserved cracklings and sprinkle over the meat. Serve very hot on hot plates.

For an accompanying vegetable, prepare the *Brésy* (see page 255) with goose fat instead of bacon fat.

COQ AU RIESLING
[Sautéed Chicken with Riesling Sauce]

SERVINGS: 6 COST: medium expensive EXECUTION: medium-
    difficult
TOTAL PREPARATION TIME: 2 hours spread over 2 days
BEST SEASON: Good year round
SUGGESTED WINE: Riesling

Two 3½-lb. chickens (1 kg
 250 each)
2 onions, sliced
1 carrot, sliced
1 TB chopped parsley stems
¼ tsp. dried thyme
½ of a Turkish bay leaf,
 crumbled
2 bottles Alsatian Riesling
1 egg
2¼ cups heavy cream (about
 5 dl)
Salt and pepper
Dash of nutmeg
1 TB fresh or 1½ tsp. dried
 fines herbes

1 quart chicken stock (to
 poach the quenelles)
½ lb. mushrooms, sliced thin
 (250 g)
¼ lb. slab bacon, cut into
 ⅓-inch cubes (125 g)
Butter, unsalted
1½ quarts brown veal stock, or
 best available homemade
 broth (1¼–1½ litres)
1 TB cornstarch
2 egg yolks
Lemon juice
Chopped parsley leaves

DAY ONE:

Cut the chickens up into 4 drumsticks, 4 thighs, and 4 pieces of breast meat. Keep the breast meat from one chicken only.

Bone and reserve the breast meat, both cutlets, of the second chicken to make the quenelles.

Put the other chicken pieces in a large baking dish, sprinkle them with the sliced onions, the carrot, parsley stems, thyme and the crushed bay leaf. Pour the Riesling over the meat and marinate overnight. Turn the chicken over once while marinating.

While the chicken marinates, prepare the quenelle forcemeat. Place the egg in the blender, dice the chicken cutlets very small and blend together until very smooth and until the meat is shiny and forms a paste. Remove from the blender and strain through a tamis or sieve, if desired. The texture is more even when strained. Place the blended meat in a bowl and refrigerate overnight.

DAY TWO:

Finish the quenelle forcemeat first. Using an electric mixer on low speed, whip 1–1¼ cups heavy cream into the meat paste. When half of the cream is added, add the salt and pepper and nutmeg. When it is all added, fold in the fines herbes. Keep chilled 30 minutes. Then, shape one dozen small quenelles with two teaspoons and poach in barely simmering chicken stock. Keep warm in the chicken stock while you cook the chicken. The quenelles keep very well if not allowed to boil or simmer after they are finished; their keeping temperature should be between 150° and 165°. Use your thermostat burner if you have one.

Now sauté the chicken as follows: render the diced bacon until crisp. Remove to a plate. In the bacon fat sauté the mushrooms with salt and pepper until they are dry, nice and brown. Reserve them with the bacon. In the same pan, add 2 tablespoons butter and sauté the vegetables of the marinade so that the fat mixture acquires the taste of the vegetables. Discard the vegetables. In the same fat mixture, brown the pieces of chicken until they are very crisp and brown on all sides. Remove the breast meat to a plate. Add the bacon and mushrooms to the *sauteuse*. Add ½ of the marinade, salt and pepper and let cook for 15 minutes. Add the remainder of the marinade and put the white meat on top of the pieces of dark meat; continue cooking another 8 to 10 minutes. The chicken should now be done. Remove it and the mushrooms and bacon to a casserole and keep warm. Add 2 cups of stock to the *sauteuse* and reduce again to 1 cup. Mix ½ cup of heavy cream with 1 tablespoon of cornstarch. Whisk the mixture into the simmering cooking juices. Now blend the egg yolks and the remaining ½ cup of cream, add some of the simmering sauce to that liaison and then pour it all back into the sauce. Give the whole mixture one or two boils, stirring well. Remove from the heat, correct the seasoning, and add a dash of lemon juice, if needed.

Add the quenelles to the chicken casserole and strain the sauce over all the meat. Sprinkle with chopped parsley. Serve hot with *Wasserstrivela* (see page 253) and asparagus during the season (see page 257).

WEINACHTS HUHN
[Christmas Chicken]

SERVINGS: 6 COST: very expensive EXECUTION: easy
TOTAL PREPARATION TIME: 2 hours spread over 2 days
BEST SEASON: December through February
SUGGESTED WINE: Gewürztraminer (a very personal taste; some
   may prefer a full-bodied red wine)
REMARKS ON INGREDIENTS: Use Strasbourg foie gras; at least two
   reputable brands are sold in fine food stores in the U.S. Semolina
   is available in all Italian neighborhood grocery stores.

CHICKEN:
Two 3½-lb. roasting chickens
   (1 kg 500 each)
3 truffles, as good as you can
   afford (75 g)
1 cup brown veal stock (see
   page 10) (2¼ dl)
2 TB heavy cream (⅓ dl)
2 TB butter (30 g)
Lemon juice

PFLUTTEN:
1½ lbs. potatoes, preferably
   Maine, in their jackets
   (750 g)

3 cups milk (¾ litre)
½ cup semolina (150 g)
¼ cup raw butter (50–55 g)
Salt
Pepper from the mill
Nutmeg
3 eggs
1 tsp. water
1 tsp. oil
Flour
Dry breadcrumbs
Clarified butter
1 small can Strasbourg foie gras,
   about 4 ounces

DAY ONE:
Remove the fat pads from the cavity of each chicken. Salt and pepper
the chickens in their respective cavities. Cut two of the truffles into
paper-thin slices with a potato peeler. Gently loosen the skin of the
chickens and slide the slices of truffle under the skin to cover the legs
and breasts. Truss the chickens, wrap them in wax paper, and refrigerate for one full day and night.

While the chickens rest in the refrigerator, bake the potatoes in their skins for one hour in a 400° preheated oven. During the last 30 minutes of their baking, bring the milk to a boil. Gradually add the semolina and stir over medium heat until the mixture is thick and the wooden spoon you are using stands in the cereal mush without falling over. By then the potatoes will be done. Peel them and strain them into the semolina. Add butter, salt, pepper from the mill, 2 eggs beaten well and freshly grated nutmeg. Stir until smooth. Grease a jelly roll pan with a bit of butter and pour the mixture into it, spreading it as much as it will spread to a thickness of ⅓ inch. Cover with a buttered paper and let cool completely. Refrigerate overnight.

DAY TWO:

Remove the chickens from the refrigerator four hours before cooking and leave them at room temperature.

Prepare the *pflütten* as follows:

Dip a 2-inch cutter into cold water. Cut as many circles of dough as you possibly can from the potato batter. You can obtain 8 to 12 circles, called *pflütten*. Flour them. Mix the last egg with the teaspoons of water and oil. Beat until liquid. Brush the *pflütten* with the mixture and coat with breadcrumbs. Let dry on a cake rack.

Roast the chicken for one hour in a preheated 375° oven. During the last ten minutes of cooking, panfry the *pflütten* on both sides in clarified butter. Top each *pflütten* with a thin slice of foie gras. Keep warm.

As soon as the chickens are done, deglaze the roasting pan with the stock.

Strain the gravy into a measuring cup and use a baster to defatten it completely. Bring the gravy to a boil. Add the heavy cream and butter, correct the salt and pepper, and add a dash of lemon juice. Dice the last truffle and add it to the gravy. Simmer together 3 to 4 minutes. Serve the chicken with the thin truffle gravy and the *pflütten*. The gravy is spooned over the *pflütten* and is delicious.

As a second vegetable try plain buttered kohlrabi.

QUENELLES DE FAISANS AUX MORILLES
[Quenelles of Pheasant with Morel Sauce]

SERVINGS: 6 COST: expensive EXECUTION: difficult

TOTAL PREPARATION TIME: 3 hours spread over 2 days

BEST SEASON: All through the late fall and winter using dried morels. If you want fresh morels, you may have to use frozen pheasant, since their seasons do not coincide.

SUGGESTED WINE: A great Burgundy or a Châteauneuf du Pape in a great year

REMARKS ON INGREDIENTS: Try to obtain a fresh pheasant. This recipe is particularly useful if you have an old bird that would be stringy if roasted. Pheasants are always available frozen either ready to cook, or better, in plumage. Those in plumage are always bigger and have a lot more flavor. Go to a meat purveyor, not to a butcher shop.

1 pheasant, preferably large and older

1 large onion, chopped coarse

½ carrot, chopped coarse

1 leek, chopped coarse

1½ quarts brown veal stock (1¼–1½ litres)

Large bouquet garni

2 cloves

2 egg whites

1 egg yolk

2¼ cups heavy cream (3 dl)

½ lb. raw, unsalted butter (250 g)

Salt

Fresh pepper, ground fine

Nutmeg

3 oz. dried morels or 1 lb. fresh morels (90 g or 450 g)

2 oz. Cognac

Lemon juice

1 prebaked pastry shell from ordinary pastry (see page 13)

DAY ONE: TO PLUCK, BONE THE PHEASANT AND PREPARE THE ESSENCE:

Hang the pheasant whether it is fresh or frozen in a cold cellar. Let it hang until a feather or two pulled from the breast comes out easily. If it does, then clean and pluck the bird right then and there, not in your kitchen. It is better to pluck dry. If you are sensitive to feathers, put a wet cloth around your nose.

Plucking a ripe pheasant even if you are a novice takes no more than 10 minutes. It is easier to grab the bird between your knees and pluck very close to the skin with short, rapid movements of your hand. Some of the big feathers have to be yanked. Clean and eviscerate the pheasant.

Bone the pheasant entirely. Remove as much clean meat as you possibly can. Weigh the meat; you will have between 12 and 16 sources. Separate the bones and remaining meat (sinews, stringy parts) into two piles. Chop up the first, which should contain the back, neck, and wings, to make the essence. Brown this together with the onions, carrots, and leeks in a large *sauteuse.* Add the brown veal stock, *bouquet garni* and 2 cloves. Cook until 3½ cups of excellent stock remains. Strain. The second pile of scraps of meat, gristle and nerve, plus the drumstick and thigh bones, should be set aside.

TO MAKE THE QUENELLES:

Gear yourself to work like a professional. You need per pound of meat, 2 egg whites, 1 egg yolk, 4 tablespoons raw butter, 2¼ cups heavy cream, 1½ teaspoons salt, ½ teaspoon grated nutmeg, and ½ teaspoon fine ground pepper. *Weigh* your pure meat and calculate the proportions of all the above ingredients you need to combine with your weight of meat. To measure the eggs, beat the 2 whites and yolk together; that should give you 7 tablespoons. Do this calculation twice to be sure.

Now put the eggs and meat either by halves in the blender or the whole amount at once in a vertical cutter and blend until smooth. The meat should be elastic and shiny and pull by itself from the sides of the blender or cutter.

Strain the meat into a bowl. Cover with a plastic wrap and refrigerate overnight.

DAY TWO: TO FINISH AND POACH THE QUENELLES:

To the cold puréed meat, add salt, pepper and nutmeg. Mix. Cream the butter with an electric mixer set on medium in the large mixer bowl. Gradually add the meat. When the meat is completely incorporated into the butter, turn the mixer down to low and slowly pour in the heavy cream in one steady stream. If the quenelle looks stiff and heavy, do not hesitate to add a little more cream than the recipe requires. Refrigerate 30 minutes.

Shape the quenelles with two spoons. Butter a large *sauteuse*. Drop the quenelles gently on the bottom of the pan and pour in salted boiling water, or better, any good homemade chicken or veal stock you have. Leave the poached quenelles in the warm water or stock after they are done.

TO FINISH THE SAUCE:

Brown the drumsticks and thigh bones and all the meat scraps kept the day before in butter. Soak the morels in enough lukewarm water to cover them.

Once the morels are rehydrated, wash them under cold running water to remove all sand.

Flambé the bones and scraps of meat with 1 ounce Cognac, then add the strained morel soaking water and reduce to 2 tablespoons. Then add one cup of the prepared pheasant essence and reduce to 3 tablespoons. Add a second cup of essence and reduce to ¼ cup. Finally, add the last cup of essence. By now you have a sauce that is naturally sticky and super-gelatinous. Keep ready to use.

In a small pot, heat a tablespoon of butter and sauté the morels very gently until they are heated through. Strain the sauce over the morels and simmer 10 minutes. Then bring the sauce to a high boil and emulsify ½ cup of soft butter into it. Correct the seasoning with pepper and lemon juice. Heat 1 ounce Cognac in a small pan and light it. Pour it flaming into the sauce and stir.

TO PRESENT THE DISH:

Keep both quenelles and sauce warm. Roll out the pastry. Fit it into a 9-inch pastry ring, cover it with foil and fill with dried beans, and bake at 425° until golden. Cool the pastry to warm.

Spoon 2 tablespoons of sauce on the bottom of the pastry. Line the quenelles in the shell and spoon most of the morels over them. Serve the sauce in a warmed boat.

FOIES DE VOLAILLES AUX RAISINS SECS
[Fat Goose or Duck Liver with Raisins]

SERVINGS: 6 COST: inexpensive EXECUTION: Watch the cooking of the livers.

TOTAL PREPARATION TIME: 1 hour plus 24 hours to macerate the raisins

SUGGESTED WINE: Gerwürztraminer

REMARKS ON INGREDIENTS: This recipe is feasible in the United States with pale-colored livers of goose, duck, or fowl. Fowl livers, very fat, almost milky, can be purchased from wholesale butchers. Please order ahead of time. Large geese and ducks will always have very blond livers.

2 cups brown veal stock (4½–5 dl)	1 lb. blond livers, cleaned (500 g)
1½ oz. blanched, slivered almonds (45–50 g)	Dash of ground cloves
	Salt
2 TB each, dark and light raisins	Pepper from the mill
1 bottle Gewürztraminer	1 cup heavy cream (2¼ dl)
1½ oz. Kirschwasser	2 TB sour cream
¼ cup clarified butter	6 toast points

Reduce the stock to ⅓ cup. Pour into a bowl. Cover with a plastic wrap and keep ready to use.

Toast the almonds in a 350° oven for 8 to 10 minutes or until an even golden color. Reserve.

Mix the raisins. Add enough Gewürztraminer to cover them. Add ½ ounce of the Kirschwasser. Mix well. Cover with a plastic wrap and let macerate overnight.

When you are ready to cook the livers, heat the clarified butter in a large frying pan. Add the livers and cook them gently over medium heat, turning them often. Add the dash of cloves, salt and pepper after they are well seared. Do not use high heat; it would coagulate the outside and result in a tough outside crust with a semi-raw center. With medium heat and a covered pan the result will be a soft liver, cooked evenly to the center. *Do not overcook.*

While the livers are cooking, pour the heavy cream into a large frying pan and reduce by half. Add salt, pepper, the macerated raisins, and the meat glaze; mix well. Pour the mixture over the livers; mix well.

Dissolve the sour cream in a few tablespoons of the sauce and add to the pan. Mix well. Heat the remaining ounce of Kirschwasser and pour it flaming into the pan. Correct the seasoning and serve promptly on toast points.

NOISETTES DE CHEVREUIL EUGENIE
[Noisettes of Deer as Prepared by Eugénie]

SERVINGS: 6 COST: medium expensive with shot venison, expensive with purchased venison EXECUTION: difficult

TOTAL PREPARATION TIME: 3 hours

BEST SEASON: November through December with fresh deer; up to early March with frozen deer

SUGGESTED WINE: An excellent red Burgundy or an old Châteauneuf du Pape

REMARKS ON INGREDIENTS: If you can obtain fresh venison, be sure that it is well hung since aging is crucial for palatability and flavor in venison. Frozen, good-quality venison is imported into the United States from New Zealand. Go to a wholesale butcher way ahead of time and order it since the shipments are irregular. The saddle or a whole back (loin rack and rib rack) are difficult to obtain but legs are found more easily.

The same recipe can be used for *escalopes* of deer cut across the grain of the top, bottom and true eye of the round. Any leftovers from a leg can be made into a Bourguignon-type stew.

MEAT AND MARINADE:

1 saddle or whole rib rack of
   venison
¼ cup oil (any kind but olive
   or safflower) (1 small dl)
2 onions, chopped
½ small carrot, chopped fine
1 TB chopped parsley stems
2 cloves garlic, chopped coarse
1 bottle Alsatian Riesling
½ tsp. dried savory
½ tsp. coriander seeds
½ tsp. dried thyme
12 crushed juniper berries
1 bay leaf, crushed
1 oz. Cognac or Armagnac

SAUCE:

Oil (see above)
Meat trimmings
1 quart brown veal stock
   (1 litre)
1 tsp. orange rind, cut into
   ⅒-inch julienne strips
Cognac or Armagnac
¾ cup unsalted butter (160 g)
1½ tsp. cracked black pepper
2 TB hazelnuts, chopped coarse
Salt
1½ TB heavy cream
1½ TB sour cream
Lemon juice, if needed

Bone the saddle completely to obtain 4 pieces of meat without fat or gristle: 2 sirloin strips from which you will obtain 5 portions, and 2 tenderloins from which you will obtain one portion. Reserve all the leftover meat trimmings.

TO PREPARE THE MARINADE:

Heat the oil in a large frying pan. Sauté the onions, carrots, and parsley stems until the onions turn a golden color. Add the garlic. Toss one more minute over medium heat, then pour in the Riesling and bring to a boil. Add savory, coriander, thyme, crushed juniper berries, and the bay leaf. Turn down and simmer 15 minutes. Remove from the heat and cool completely. Add the Cognac or Armagnac.

Place the meat in a glass baking dish and pour the marinade over it. Marinate 4 hours, turn the meat over and marinate another 4 hours. Marination should last no more than 8 hours at room temperature.

TO PREPARE THE SAUCE:

Heat about 2 tablespoons oil in a frying pan and brown all the meat trimmings well. Discard the oil. Add 1½ cups of veal stock and reduce slowly to a glaze. Add another 1½ cups of veal stock and reduce to a second glaze. Add the remaining cup of stock and reduce to a total of ⅓ cup of glaze. Reserve.

Lift two strips of the rind of an orange with a potato peeler so they are free of white pith. Cut them into ⅒-inch julienne strips and blanch for five full minutes in boiling water. Drain, pat dry, and reserve.

When the meat has finished marinating, empty the marinade into a large saucepan and reduce it slowly to a one cup total of liquids and solids. Empty into the frying pan containing the meat glaze. Heat well and strain through a *chinois*-type strainer.

Cut the meat into as many ¾-inch-thick *noisettes* as possible and flatten the *noisettes* with a meat bat. Panfry the *noisettes* in hot oil so they remain rare. Season well on both sides. Remove to a plate and keep warm.

Deglaze the pan with the Cognac; add the strained marinade–meat glaze mixture and bring to a high boil. Whisk in the butter. Add the pepper, hazelnuts and orange rind; continue boiling one minute.

Put both creams into a small bowl, whisk in the hot sauce and return to the pan. Add the *noisettes*. Toss the *noisettes* one or two minutes in the hot sauce to reheat thoroughly; do not boil. Correct the seasoning very carefully with salt and lemon juice, if needed. Serve promptly.

As vegetables, consider *Spaetzele* or fresh homemade noodles and *Brésy* (see page 255).

WEISS- UND ROTKOHL SALAT
[*White and Red Cabbage Salad*]

SERVINGS: 6 COST: inexpensive EXECUTION: easy
TOTAL PREPARATION TIME: 1 hour
BEST SEASON: A cold weather salad

1 very small white cabbage	*1 cup vinegar*
1 very small red cabbage	*Salt*

Pepper from the mill

3 oz. slab bacon, cut into ⅓-inch
  cubes (175–180 g)

½ tsp. coriander seeds

6 juniper berries, whole

¼ tsp. rubbed sage

Oil of your choice (neither
  safflower nor olive)

Chopped parsley

Cut each cabbage into four wedges. Cut the core off so as to discard the rough part that is too fibrous. Cut each wedge across into ⅙-inch strips. Keep cabbages separated.

Bring a 4-quart pot of water to a boil. Add a good tablespoon of salt and the white cabbage. Bring back to a rolling boil. Boil 1 full minute. Remove from the hot water bath and rinse under cold running water. Drain and pat dry in a tea towel. Remove to a bowl.

Bring the hot water bath back to a boil. Add ½ cup of vinegar and the red cabbage. Bring to a full boil for 1 minute. Drain, rinse, and pat dry as you did for the white cabbage. Keep cabbages separated. Render the diced bacon slowly in a frying pan until golden. Remove the bacon to a bowl; discard the rendered bacon fat. To the frying pan add ½ cup vinegar, the coriander seeds, juniper berries, the rubbed sage and a teaspoon of salt. Cook together until ⅓ cup reduced vinegar is left. Add 1 to 1⅓ cups oil and mix with a whisk to obtain a good emulsion. Correct the salt and pepper and add more of each herb if you desire.

Toss each cabbage separately with half the dressing and present in a glass bowl, alternating colors. Sprinkle with the reserved bacon and chopped parsley.

GRUMBEERKUECHLE
[Potato Pancake]

SERVINGS: 6 COST: inexpensive EXECUTION: medium-difficult
TOTAL PREPARATION TIME: 45 minutes
BEST SEASON: Good year round
REMARKS ON INGREDIENTS: You may use the pieces left over from
  panfried potatoes (see page 239).

3–4 cups potatoes, grated coarse
2 eggs
¼ cup chopped parsley
1 clove garlic, mashed fine

Salt and pepper
Clarified butter, or better,
goose fat

You have two options: either wash the potatoes in three successive waters and pat them very dry, or soak them in an egg or two well beaten, which is the real Alsatian way.

If you are using the leftovers, chop the potatoes lightly to equalize their size; otherwise, coarsely grate enough potatoes to obtain 3 to 4 cups. Pat very dry in a towel.

Beat the eggs until they are extremely light and foamy. Add the parsley, garlic, salt, and pepper and mix into the potatoes.

Heat ⅛ inch of clarified butter or goose fat in a large frying pan. Add the potatoes and pack well. Fry until golden. Slide onto a plate. Add more fat to the pan and invert the cake back into the hot fat. Brown the second side. Once both sides are sealed, turn the heat down and let cook gently until the center is done. Salt and pepper and serve piping hot.

ASPERGES DE WOERTH
[Asparagus in Lemon Butter]

SERVINGS: 6 COST: expensive EXECUTION: easy
TOTAL PREPARATION TIME: 1 hour
BEST SEASON: April through June when the succulent, large aspara-
gus of California are available
REMARKS ON INGREDIENTS: The Woerth asparagus are white with a little green tip and are in every way as succulent as our green asparagus. A soup for two persons can be made with the stems.

18 jumbo asparagus
Water
4 TB butter
One 1-inch piece of lemon rind

Salt and pepper
½ tsp. ground coriander
Lemon juice

Cut the asparagus stalks into pieces 2 to 2½ inches long. Peel the skin off below the tip. Blanch 5 minutes in rapidly boiling water. Drain.

While the asparagus blanch, melt the butter. Squeeze the lemon rind backward to release the oil of lemon into the butter. Drop the piece of rind into the pan and cook gently over very low heat so the butter acquires the taste of the oil of lemon. Remove the rind. Let the butter turn brown. Add the asparagus, coriander, salt, and pepper. Continue cooking gently for another five minutes. *Do not overcook.* Add a dash of lemon juice and toss well before serving. Good with *Coq au Riesling* (see page 240), and *Foies de Volailles aux Raisins Secs* (see page 248).

KOHLRABI A L'ANETH
[Kohlrabi in Cream and Dill Sauce]

SERVINGS: 6 COST: inexpensive EXECUTION: easy
TOTAL PREPARATION TIME: 45 minutes
BEST SEASON: May through September

8 heads of kohlrabi	½ cup heavy cream (1 generous dl)
1 quart water	
Salt	Pepper
2 TB butter	1 TB chopped dill
	Lemon juice

Peel the kohlrabi. Slice them into ¼-inch-thick slices and then into julienne matchsticks also ¼ inch wide. Bring the water to a boil. Add salt and the kohlrabi and blanch 2 to 3 minutes. Drain.

Heat the butter; add the kohlrabi and toss well. Add the cream, salt and pepper and let cook until the cream coats the vegetables. Add the dill and lemon juice, if needed, and serve.

Good with ham (see page 237).

GURKEN RAGOUT
[Pickling Cucumber with Vinegar Sauce]

SERVINGS: 6 COST: inexpensive EXECUTION: easy
TOTAL PREPARATION TIME: 35 minutes
BEST SEASON: Fall
REMARKS ON INGREDIENTS: If the small, rough-skinned pickling
  cucumber is not available, use sliced, young cucumbers.

1½ lbs. small pickling cucumbers, cut into ¼-inch slices (450 g)	*Salt and pepper*
	1 tsp. dill seeds
	2 TB white wine vinegar
2 TB unsalted butter	*1 cup heavy cream (2¼ dl)*

Cut the pickles into ¼-inch slices, cutting the slices on the bias and
very elongated. Discard the ends. Heat the butter in a *sauteuse* pan.
Add the pickles; toss well in the butter and salt and pepper. Then add
the vinegar. Mix well again. Cover and cook until tender. Meanwhile,
reduce the cream to ½ cup. Uncover the pot, raise the heat to high
and evaporate all but two tablespoons of the cooking juices. Add the
cream and the dill seeds and toss together. Correct the seasoning. Excellent with *Jambon au Riesling* (see page 237).

BRESY
[Braised Cabbage]

SERVINGS: 6 COST: inexpensive EXECUTION: easy
TOTAL PREPARATION TIME: 1 to 1½ hours
BEST SEASON: Winter
REMARKS ON INGREDIENTS: Use small cabbages; remove completely
  the green leaves.

2 small heads of cabbage	*½ cup butter (110 g)*
3 oz. slab bacon (100 g)	*Salt and pepper*

Cut the cabbages into quarters. Bring a large pot of water to a boil and blanch them two or three minutes, no more. Drain well. Cut into ¼-inch-wide slivers; discard the core.

Cut the bacon into ¼-inch cubes. Put it into a cocotte and render over medium-low heat. Cook until the cracklings are golden. Add the butter and the slivered cabbage and toss together. Salt and pepper and let cook until the vegetable is very tender and appears well coated by the butter. Serve with all meats.

SENFNUDELN
[Noodles Alsatian Style with Mustard Butter]

SERVINGS: 6 COST: inexpensive EXECUTION: easy
TOTAL PREPARATION TIME: 2 hours
BEST SEASON: Good year round, but excellent in the winter with
    game birds, venison, or ham

NOODLE DOUGH:	BUTTER:
4 cups flour (500 g)	*1 cup butter*
5–6 eggs	*⅓ cup strong Dijon mustard*
4 egg yolks	*¼ cup chopped parsley*
1½ tsp. salt	*2 TB chopped chives*
	2 cloves of garlic, mashed

TO MAKE THE NOODLES:
Make a well in the flour. Add four eggs and the egg yolks as well as the salt. Beat with a fork until liquid. Using your right hand only, gradually incorporate the flour into the egg. When the dough cannot absorb any more flour, add an additional whole beaten egg a tablespoon at a time until all the flour has been incorporated. Knead without interruption until the dough is smooth, elastic and soft, and when cut through the center, the bubbles imprisoned in the batter are tiny. Cut into eight pieces of equal volume. Let stand under a bowl for one half hour.

Roll out into 1-millimeter (¹⁄₂₀-inch)-thick sheets and cut into noodles either with a machine or by hand. To cut by hand, flour the sheet evenly; roll into cigars and cut across into ¼-inch bands. Unroll and set the noodles to dry for about 30 minutes.

Meanwhile, bring a large pot of water to a boil. Salt the water only when you are ready to cook the noodles.

TO PREPARE THE BUTTER:
Cream the butter. Add the mustard, chopped parsley and chives, and the garlic. Mix thoroughly.

Cook the noodles al dente. Put one-third of the butter in a *sauteuse* and add half the noodles; then add another third of butter and the remaining noodles; then the remainder of the butter and toss together. Serve piping hot.

WASSERSTRIVELA
[Alsatian Spaetzele]

SERVINGS: 6 COST: inexpensive EXECUTION: easy
TOTAL PREPARATION TIME: 25 minutes

2 cups flour (250 g)	*Butter*
6 eggs	*Fresh chives*
⅔ cup milk (2 small dl)	*Pepper from the mill*
1 tsp. salt	

Make a well in the flour. Add the eggs, stirring to break them. Gradually stir in about half the flour. Add the milk and continue stirring, incorporating the flour as you go along. Add the salt and mix until the batter is smooth and shows a certain body without being too stringy.

Bring a large pot of water to a boil. Add salt. Pour about ⅓ cup batter on the bottom of a 9-inch cake pan. Hold the pan at a 45-degree angle over the water and shave ¼-inch-wide strips of batter one at a time into the water. As soon as the *Strivela* come floating to the surface of the water, remove them to a pan containing a lot of hot, melted butter. Toss well. When all the *Strivela* are done, correct the seasoning. Keep hot and add chopped fresh chives and pepper.

BIREWECKE
[Dried Fruit Bread]

SERVINGS: 12 COST: inexpensive EXECUTION: easy
TOTAL PREPARATION TIME: 3 hours plus steeping of the fruit in
    Kirsch overnight
BEST SEASON: A great energy bread for winter
REMARKS ON INGREDIENTS: Please use dried fruit prepared *without*
    sulfur dioxide. Use Greek or Turkish imported figs.

FILLING:
1 lb. dried pears (500 g)
¼ lb. dried prunes (125 g)
¼ lb. dried figs (125 g)
2 oz. dark raisins (50–60 g)
2 oz. light raisins (50–60 g)
½ cup lukewarm water
1 oz. Kirsch
1 oz. rum
Grated rind of one lemon
½ tsp. cinnamon
Good dash of grated nutmeg
Good dash of ground cloves

1 oz. chopped hazelnuts
  (25–30 g)
1 oz. chopped walnuts
  (25–30 g)
1 oz. chopped unblanched
  almonds (25–30 g)
DOUGH:
3 cups sifted flour (350 g)
1 envelope yeast
Lukewarm water
2 eggs
1½ tsp. salt
Oil

TO SOAK THE FRUIT:
Cut all the fruit into ¼-inch-thick slivers. Remove all pits, stems and cores in the process. Mix with the two types of raisins. Mix ½ cup lukewarm water with the Kirsch and rum. To these liquids add the lemon rind, cinnamon, nutmeg and cloves. Pour over the dried fruit and let soak until the latter has completely absorbed the moisture. Keep at room temperature while soaking.

TO MAKE THE DOUGH:

Mix 1 cup flour with the yeast. Add enough lukewarm water to make a ball of dough. Cut a cross in the obtained starter and immerse in a bowl of lukewarm water until the starter comes floating to the surface of the water.

Mix the remainder of the flour with one egg, salt and about ⅔ cup of water and work into a ball of dough. As soon as the starter floats, mix it into the egg dough and knead together for 10 minutes, or until smooth and silky. Place in a lightly oiled bowl. Oil the surface of the dough and let rise until double in bulk.

TO SHAPE THE BREAD:

Punch the dough down and mix the fruit and nuts into it. Let rise again until double in bulk. Then shape into one or two oval loaves. Place the shaped loaf or loaves on a buttered baking sheet and once again let rise until double in bulk. Brush with the second, well-beaten egg. Bake in a 375° oven for 30 to 35 minutes or until a skewer inserted in the center comes out hot and dry. Cool. Keeps well wrapped in aluminum foil.

ALWINE'S KUGELHOPF
[Kugelhopf as Prepared by Alwine]

SERVINGS: 12 COST: affordable EXECUTION: easy
TOTAL PREPARATION TIME: 3 hours plus overnight soaking for the
    raisins

½ cup raisins (100 g)
¼ cup rum, preferably dark
  (½ small dl)
⅔ cup milk (1½ dl)
2 TB sugar (30 g)
1½ envelopes dried yeast
1 cup unsalted butter plus 2 TB
  (250 g)

½ tsp. salt
6 eggs
2⅔ cups sifted flour (350 g)
½ cup whole blanched almonds
  (100 g)
Confectioners sugar

Soak the raisins overnight in the rum. Scald the milk, add the sugar, stir well, and cool to lukewarm. Sprinkle the yeast over the milk. Let stand 15 minutes until the yeast bubbles.

Meanwhile, cream 1 cup butter with a whisk or wooden spoon until very soft; add the ½ teaspoon salt at this time. Add the eggs and the bubbling yeast to the flour. Mix well, pulling the dough with your hands to develop a good gluten structure and to aerate the dough. Still with your hand, blend the creamed butter into the batter until well homogenized. Add the raisins with whatever rum is left, if any. Let rise in a large bowl until 1½ times its original volume. Punch down.

Butter a Bundt pan with the remaining butter, sprinkle with the almonds, and fill with the batter. Let the batter rise to within ⅓ inch of the rim of the cake mold and bake 25 to 30 minutes in a preheated 375° oven. Unmold immediately on a rack and cool. Sprinkle with confectioners sugar.

MANDELBAEBBE-TAERTEL
[Cream and Almond Tart]

SERVINGS: 8 COST: affordable EXECUTION: easy
TOTAL PREPARATION TIME: 1½ hours with baking
BEST SEASON: Year round
REMARKS ON INGREDIENTS: The pie is better when made with blanched sliced almonds, but slivered can be used.

1 recipe for ordinary short pastry, page 13	½ cup sugar (125 g)
	Large pinch of salt
1 TB butter (15 g)	2 cups heavy cream (4½ dl or
12 oz. sliced almonds (340– 350 g)	450 g)
	2½ TB Kirsch
2 TB flour (15 g)	½ tsp. almond extract

Prepare the pastry. Chill it half an hour. Butter a 9-inch porcelain quiche pan with the butter. Roll the pastry out ⅛ inch thick and fit into the plate. Add the almonds.

Put the flour, sugar, and salt in a large bowl. Gradually add the heavy cream. Add the Kirsch and almond extract. Pour over the almonds, letting the cream seep well between them.

Bake on the bottom rack of a 375° preheated oven for 30 minutes. Turn the heat down to 300° and raise the pie to the top rack of the oven. Continue baking another 25 to 30 minutes or until the top of the pie is a golden color. Serve cold.

KIRSCHAUFLAUF MIT KIRSCHENSAUCE
[Kirsch Soufflé with Cherry Sauce]

SERVINGS: 6 COST: moderately expensive EXECUTION: easy
TOTAL PREPARATION TIME: 1 hour for the cherry sauce, 30 minutes
    for the soufflé
BEST SEASON: When the cherries are fresh, late June to middle July
REMARKS ON INGREDIENTS: Homemade lady fingers or a butterless
    Génoise are best for the center of the soufflé. Investigate the
    method of freezing an uncooked soufflé batter if you do not
    intend to use it immediately.

CHERRY SAUCE:
1 lb. Bing cherries (500 g)
2 crumbled lady fingers
Dash cinnamon
½ tsp. grated lemon rind
¾ cup granulated sugar (190 g)
1½ cups red wine (3 dl)
1½ cups water (3 dl)
Kirschwasser

SOUFFLE:
1 TB unsalted butter (15 g)
⅓ cup sugar (75 g)
¼ tsp. salt
2 TB flour (15 g)
½ cup cold milk (1 generous dl)
4 egg yolks
Kirschwasser
5 egg whites
5 lady fingers

TO MAKE THE CHERRY SAUCE:
Pit the cherries over the saucepan where they will be cooked, so as not to lose any of their juices. Drop the pitted juices into the sauce-

pan. Add the crumbled lady fingers, the cinnamon, grated lemon rind, sugar, wine, and water. Cook uncovered until the cherries are soft and completely falling apart. Strain the sauce to discard the cherry skins and make sure that the texture is that of heavy cream. If it is not, reduce the sauce. Finally, add Kirschwasser to your taste. Keep warm.

TO MAKE THE SOUFFLE:
Butter a 6-cup soufflé dish with the butter. Sprinkle with 1 tablespoon of the sugar. Set aside.

Mix the remainder of the sugar, the salt, and flour in a 2-quart saucepan. Gradually add the milk and thicken over medium heat. Off the heat, add the egg yolks, one by one, whisking well. Add 2 to 3 tablespoons Kirschwasser. Beat the egg whites until they can carry the weight of a raw egg without the latter sinking into the mass of the whites by more than ¼ inch. Mix ¼ of the whites into the soufflé base and fold in the remainder. Spoon ½ of the batter into the dish.

Pour about ¼ cup Kirschwasser onto a plate and dip the lady fingers into it. Set the lady fingers onto the first layer of soufflé batter. Leave about ½ inch of free soufflé batter around the edges of the dish so it will fuse easily with the second half of the soufflé batter that you will now spoon over the lady fingers.

Cut three or four indentations into the top of the soufflé with scissors and bake in a preheated 400° oven for 14 to 16 minutes. The center should still be soft. Serve with the cherry sauce.

BIREKUCHE, ZWETSCHKEKUCHE
[Pear or Prune Plum Cake]

SERVINGS: 8   COST: affordable EXECUTION: easy
TOTAL PREPARATION TIME: 3 hours plus overnight chilling of the
    dough
BEST SEASON: For prune plums, middle July through September;
    for pears, August through March

DOUGH:

2 ¼ *cups unsifted all-purpose*
flour (300 g)
1 *envelope dried yeast*
¼ *cup sugar (60 g)*
⅓ *cup milk (1 small dl)*
½ *tsp. salt (2.5 g)*
½ *tsp. cinnamon*
Grated rind of ½ lemon

2 *eggs*
½ *cup unsalted butter, melted*
and cooled (110 g)

FRUIT:

8 *ripe but firm pears (750–*
800 g) or
2 *lbs. prune plums (1 kg)*
Granulated sugar

TO MAKE THE DOUGH:

Place the flour on a table or counter top. Make a large well in it. Add the yeast, sugar and milk. Mix well and let stand 20 minutes or until the yeast starts to bubble. Then add the salt, cinnamon, and grated lemon rind. Break the eggs into the well, mix until the eggs are liquefied. Add 7 tablespoons of melted and cooled butter. Mix again. Gradually gather the flour from the edges of the dough and gather into a ball. Knead about five minutes and set in a large bowl to rise. Let the dough rise until 1½ times its original size. Punch down and refrigerate overnight.

TO MAKE THE CAKE:

Peel the pears or pit the prunes. Butter a 9- or 10-inch quiche pan with the remaining tablespoon of butter. Roll the dough out ⅛ to ¼ inch thick and fit it into the mold, forming a slightly thicker border around the rim of the pie plate. Arrange pears or prunes on top of the dough and let stand 1 hour at room temperature. Bake 1 hour in a preheated 375° oven.

Remove from the oven and while still hot, sprinkle liberally with sugar. Let cool before eating.

DAMPFNUDELN MIT WEINSAUCE
[Steamed Cooked Dumplings with Wine Custard]

SERVINGS: 6 COST: medium expensive EXECUTION: cooking the noodles is tricky

TOTAL PREPARATION TIME: 3 hours plus chilling of the dough overnight
BEST SEASON: A sturdy winter dessert

DAMPFNUDELN:	CUSTARD:
1 recipe for sweet yeast dough on page 263	*½ cup sugar*
Butter	*Pinch of salt*
	1 dozen egg yolks
	2 cups Gewürztraminer or Traminer

Make the dough as described on page 263. Chill it overnight. After
the first rising, roll it out into one sheet ⅓ inch thick. Cut as many
circles of dough 2 inches in diameter as you can. Place on a floured
baking sheet and let prove until 1½ times the original volume.

Butter heavily a 4-quart cast-iron enameled cocotte. Transfer as
many dumplings as you can to the bottom of the cocotte. Add enough
water to cover the base of the *Dampfnüdeln* by ¼ inch. Bring to a
boil, cover with a terry towel and the pot lid and keep over medium-
low heat until you hear the butter "sing" in the cocotte. Let cook
another 3 to 4 minutes. Uncover the pan and serve warm with the
custard. Failure to wait until you hear the butter sizzle will result in
deflated, undercooked *Dampfnüdeln* that are irretrievably lost.

To make the custard, mix egg yolks, sugar, and salt. Dilute with
the wine and thicken over medium heat until the custard coats
a wooden spoon. Strain into a sauce boat and serve with the
Dampfnüdeln.

GATEAU AU KIRSCH DU MARIAGE D'ALWINE
[Alwine's Kirsch Wedding Cake]

SERVINGS: 16 COST: affordable EXECUTION: will seem long but
   quite easy
TOTAL PREPARATION TIME: 2 hours

THE CAKE:
1 TB butter (15 g)
4 eggs
¾ cup sugar (180 g)
¼ tsp. salt
*⅔ cup Kirschwasser plus 2 TB
  (2 small dl)*
1 cup sifted flour (120–125 g)
*One 24-oz. jar raspberry jam,
  strained and warm (about
  700 g)*
⅔ cup water (2 small dl)

**THE FILLING AND
DECORATIONS:**
1½ quarts strawberries
¾ cup granulated sugar (180 g)
Juice of 1½ lemons
Pinch of salt
5 TB Kirschwasser
2½ envelopes gelatin (5 g)
*3 cups heavy cream
  (6¾ to 7 dl)*
Confectioners sugar
1 pint fresh raspberries

Grease lightly a 17-inch by 13-inch jelly roll pan. Line the bottom and sides with parchment paper.

Place the eggs in the large mixer bowl. Add ½ cup sugar and the salt and whip at very high speed until the mixture foams heavily and falls from the beaters in one heavy ribbon. Add 2 tablespoons Kirschwasser. Beat another moment; then fold in the flour. Spread into the jelly roll pan and bake in a preheated 325° oven until done or about 14 to 15 minutes.

Immediately remove from the pan. Cut the edges of the cake, brush with the warm raspberry jam and roll as tightly as you can. Cool completely on a rack.

Cut the cake into ⅓-inch-thick slices. Mix the water with ⅔ cup Kirsch and ¼ cup sugar and stir until the sugar has melted. Dip one side only of each cake slice into the syrup. Line a 10-inch cake pan with the slices of cake so as to leave no spaces between the pieces of cake and to form a casing. Drizzle what is left of the syrup inside the cake and pack well with the back of your hand. Cover with a plastic wrap and refrigerate while you make the filling.

TO MAKE THE FILLING:
Clean the berries; purée them. Add the sugar and cook until the mixture is reduced to 1¾ cups. Add the lemon juice, salt and 3 table-

spoons Kirsch. Melt the gelatin in a double boiler and add it to the warm purée, stirring well. Whip 2 cups of cream with 2 tablespoons of Kirsch and 2 tablespoons confectioners sugar to a light Chantilly or until it barely mounds. Keep refrigerated. Place the strawberry purée over ice and stir until the purée starts to thicken. Immediately fold in the prepared cream and turn into the cake casing.

Cover again with a plastic wrap and refrigerate.

When ready to serve or about 1 hour before, unmold onto a round cake platter. Whip the last cup of heavy cream, lightly sugared with 2 tablespoons confectioners sugar, to the stiff stage. Pipe tiny rosettes of cream all around the base and the top of the cake and crown each rosette with a raspberry. Keep chilled until ready to use.

Loetitia

BRITTANY

1935–1939 *and* 1970s

LOETITIA IS A GREAT STORYTELLER who lived most of her active life in Paris. Now in her seventies, she has gone back to the Bigouden country of her birth at the extreme south-western point of the French Cornouailles. She peacefully lives her retirement years in one of those low one-storey bungalows so numerous on the coast of Brittany. She is a quiet woman, still beautiful with the slanted eyes and prominent cheekbones of the Bigouden people, who, says the legend, are descended from the Sun. She now wears only the black clothes of widows. To go to Mass on Sundays she arranges on her head the simple, tall, organdy headdress that she embroidered after the death of her husband. Sunday afternoons she sits in her tiny garden full of roses and remembers her youth in the company of Corentine and Thumette, her lifelong friends. They talk about Brittany, about life when they were growing up, about the food which is not the same any more, about all those beautiful trees that were cut down so unmercifully, about the Breton moors once full of purple heather and yellow flowers now replaced with field after field of vegetables. Not much is left, they lament, not much; only the sea, the inexorable sea that pounds so hard on the rocks at Pen'March that one can hear it some fifteen miles away in the quiet of the night.

Loetitia had been a special child; she had been born on that happiest night of all, that of the sacred fire of Saint Jean. One of her brothers had heated a branch of laurel in the fire so her mother could apply the lukewarm leaves to the baby's eyes and save her from a blindness still dreaded in those days. Loetitia still loves to evoke her father, a true Bigouden with his typical black-ribboned round hat and the old but beautiful clothes he wore even to work in the fields. These were embroidered with thousands upon thousands of silk stitches, so tight and close to one another that the black material below almost disappeared completely. Her father had been a farmer not too far from Plomeur. He had raised his family by selling the very best produce from the farm every Sunday at the Plomeur market. Loetitia loves to tell how one day, while digging those beautiful Holland potatoes with the firm yellow pulp that he was so proud of growing, he had found fragments of human bones and pottery not too far from an old fallen menhir. All the teachers in the area had congregated around his find, which was finally sent to the museum in Brest for identification. Everyone had been impressed and moved at the same time, for the remains had been those of an ancestor of times past.

Loetitia spoke and still speaks Breton with her friends, slipping often into French. *Tad* and *mamm,* the Breton words for father and mother, recur again and again in her speech. The memories of parents long lost comfort this old woman in her lonely days. Loetitia's Mamm had been another beautiful woman. Every Sunday she had combed and brushed and brushed and combed her long hair upward to tie it on top of her head so it would disappear inside her handwoven lace headdress. Her magnificent black Sunday dress, all embroidered with red and yellow flowers, still hangs in Loetitia's closet, a bit old, a bit passé, but evocative of all the religious *pardons* of summers gone by. The dress recalls memories of those Sunday celebrations when Mamm would put on the table a large, decorated block of fresh, salty butter, black and white bread; *krampoch,* now

called crêpes or *galettes,* cider wine, brandy, and a nice, large piece
of pork brisket with fork and knife planted straight into it. Mamm
had kept the most beautiful farmhouse, full of rare old Breton
furniture that Loetitia still owns. It gives her bungalow one of the
most remarkable Breton interiors existing in Brittany today. Loetitia
has had two walls torn down so that she could reproduce the very
same atmosphere as in her native farm. At one end is her kitchen,
where she cooks and eats; it is separated from the *joli-bout* (the
pretty part of the house), where she lives and receives her friends, by
her old cupboard-bed, with the two white silk curtains hand embroidered with red stylized flowers. There are two huge *armoires*
made of heart of chestnut wood, highly polished and adorned with
hundreds of shiny copper nails. The doors are full of hand-cut
birds and flowers, and there is a tall grandfather clock decorated
with a large heart crowned with the Holy Cross and encasing the
religious initials J.H.S. Many times antique dealers had appeared at
the farm in the hope of acquiring those beautiful pieces, but her
Tad had resisted all offers, and here they were. The anxiety over
the beautiful furniture remains though, for Loetitia has never had
any children. She wonders where all of it will end up—probably and
hopefully in a Breton museum on Breton soil.

To this day, age has not yet taken its toll and Loetitia remains one
of the finest Breton cooks I have ever met. She started cooking
early in Pont l'Abbé, where one of her aunts, with the lovely first
name of Tudyna, had a *crêperie.* Thursday was a busy market day for
Tudyna, and a no-school day for Loetitia, so she helped in the
crêperie making huge buckwheat crêpes on a large *bilig* held over
the open hearth flame. It had apparently taken her no time to learn
to grease the *bilig* with a piece of pork fatback stuck on the tynes
of a fork, to spread the batter really thin with the *rouable,* and then
to pass the crêpe upside down to another *bilig* to cook the second
side. She learned everything from making *galettes aux pommes* to
krampoch à la canelle, those lovely raised crêpes of the Bigouden
country, all fragrant with butter, fresh yeast, and sometimes cinnamon or orange flower water. As she grew older, she became known
as such a fine cook that everyone wanted her to prepare all those

special meals for first Holy Communions and weddings. Pretty soon her dishes of tripe, cooked for four long hours, were the talk of the Bigouden country. There was no one like her to season a lobster from Pont l'Abbé or the delicious langoustines from Le Guilvinec. While she was going to school in Quimper, she lived with another aunt who owned a bakery. Loetitia rescued me from my search for the techniques of the true Breton butter cake, the old *Kouign Amann,* which nowadays one finds only with difficulty in a very small number of bakeries of Cornouailles. She knew the technique and she gave me a true, learned and detailed lecture on how to make the dough from bread leaven or from scratch. I shall always remember never to include an egg because it is not the true way and makes the cake too tough. If the cake looks that yellow in Brittany, she assured me, it is because the butter there is so superior.

I have shared hundreds of meals cooked by Loetitia at Loetitia's table. What feasts she could prepare! Nowadays, she walks almost every day to the boats that bring in the fish and for a few francs she chooses the best sardines of the catch, nice and huge, or tinker mackerels that not too many young families want, for larger fish are far better to feed hungry children. She can make a fish soup out of the heads fishermen discard, a few mussels and clams and all those greens that grow so fast in her garden.

She knows of my fondness for shellfish and often she greets me on one of my visits with a beautiful dish of *Coquilles Saint Jacques,* coated with a sauce made with those incomparable Breton onions and butter. Her fondness for the Belon oysters that come from Locmariaquer is so great that I took her there one Sunday in September to see the parks and eat oysters. We were both disappointed for there was little to see at that time, the big activity taking place in the spring when the tiles are painstakingly laid for the oyster larvae to find a home.

She makes the best *Cochonnaille,* blood pudding and sausages. Going with her to enjoy a dish of tripe in one of the bistros of Pen'March after Sunday mass is quite an experience for the soul and the stomach. After such a repast, there is no need to think about any more nourishment for the rest of the day, especially if the tripe came with buckwheat *krampoch* and bowl after bowl of cider—unless Loetitia has, in some recess of her brand-new refrigerator, a dozen *Caillettes* that she has "just made" while talking to Corentine that same day. Then the feasting starts all over again and Loetitia starts talking again.

"Do you remember, Thumette, when Mamm had the last *boudinnerie* . . ." and out comes more on the old customs of Lower Brittany. After a pig had been slaughtered, one held a huge party. If one served blood pudding it was called a *boudinnerie;* if one chose to offer cracklings it was given the name of *gratonnerie*. The whole feast was positively drenched with cider and *eau de vie*. It was always such a great occasion for exchanging good things, for the guests would bring some good *andouille* or other marvelous *cochonnailles*. Everyone was so happy and both young and old would end up the day with a little song which kept the assembly happy for months to come. The jokes were not always the most refined, but they made you laugh so hard.

And those vegetables . . . only in Provence are they as pretty, as fresh, as tempting, but with all due respect to the Provençaux, they just cannot grow artichokes like the Bretons can. Why, their artichokes are positively as big as cauliflowers, and delicious.

I have had the very rare experience of finding in the fields behind Loetitia's house many a good mushroom. In spite of the fact that buckwheat fields are disappearing, it looks like the huge parasol mushrooms that used to grow there are still to be found. Dear readers, if you find a buckwheat field, look for *lepiota procera,* it is sure to be there. It is a handsome morsel when broiled and drenched in garlic and parsley butter.

And then there is the porridge. Porridge in France is made only by the Bretons, and that has to come from their affiliation with the people of Cornwall. Once raised on porridge, says Loetitia, always a prisoner of porridge because there will always be a yearning for it on cold mornings.

To make a good *youd kerc'h* you need three days, says Loetitia. Two days to soak the oats and one hour to cook the *peux,* as the porridge is called. It is not ready to eat unless you let it *vesser* (boil and positively explode) nine times! Then and only then can you consider eating it with butter and sour milk. The eating will take no more than five minutes but the rest of the day is spent, says Loetitia, assimilating it. It is so nutritious. The Parisian in me recoils as I recall the porridge I was given for breakfast on Loetitia's recommendation that it would fatten me up. I guess only a Breton soul can have an affinity for the *farz*. As a child, when I first saw Loetitia make a *farz sac'h* with buckwheat and prunes, pour it into a *chausse* and hang the bag to cook in the soup pot with the pork brisket and cabbage, I thought, ah, these Bretons, they can enjoy funny things. But I soon found myself looking forward to those funny things all drippy with salty butter and blending so well with the tender pork flavored by the soup vegetables. Still, I much preferred her dessert *farz*, those made with apples that had fallen early from the trees, or blackberries gathered from all the bushes that border on the country lanes that crisscross the Brittany countryside.

If you are in Pen'March ever, look for Loetitia's house; it is right under the shadow of the big Eckmühl lighthouse that sends its powerful beams seventy miles into the darkness over the Atlantic Ocean. Loetitia will be there, making *kunpods* for Corentine or Thumette and talking, talking, half in Breton, half in French, about Brittany, and her long gone beautiful trees. All the while her busy hands flash a needle, and weave a stream of cool white lace that inches slowly down the pleats of her black dress.

SOUP DE POISSONS AU VERT
[Fish Soup with a Garnish of Greens]

SERVINGS: 6 COST: affordable EXECUTION: easy
TOTAL PREPARATION TIME: 2½ hours including the fish fumet
BEST SEASON: Best in the winter months. Can be made year round
     with bottled clam juice.
SUGGESTED WINE: If used, consider a Muscadet.

REMARKS ON INGREDIENTS: Use the tiniest possible clams available in your area. If no fresh shellfish is available, bottled clam juice, though not ideal, is still usable in this preparation. If no sorrel is available, use twice the amount of spinach and plenty of lemon juice.

2 dozen black mussels

2 dozen clams, as small as possible

½ cup dry white wine (1 generous dl)

Bottled clam juice, only if necessary

5 cups fish fumet (1 ⅛ litre)

1 cup salted butter (best-quality AA 93 score) (250 g)

2 onions, chopped fine

2 leeks, white part only, chopped fine

¼ cup flour (30–35 g)

2 cloves garlic, chopped fine

¼ lb. sorrel leaves, chopped

¼ lb. spinach leaves, chopped

6 outside dark green leaves of Boston lettuce, chopped

4 outside dark green leaves of escarole, chopped

2 potatoes, diced into ⅓-inch cubes

2 TB dried chervil or ¼ cup fresh chopped chervil

3 egg yolks

1 cup heavy cream (225 g or 2 ¼ dl)

Lemon juice, if needed and to follow your taste

Place the mussels and clams in a kettle. Add the wine and steam open. You should have 2 cups of liquid. Should there be less, add enough commercial clam juice to make 2 cups. Strain through several layers of cheesecloth. Mix with the fish fumet and keep simmering. Reserve the shellfish.

Heat ¾ cup butter in a soup kettle. Add the onions and leeks and sauté until both are translucent. Add the flour and cook 5 to 6 minutes, stirring occasionally. Off the heat, bind this roux with the mixture of shellfish liquid and fumet and bring to a boil. Reduce to a simmer. Add the chopped garlic.

Sauté the sorrel, spinach, lettuce, and escarole, all chopped fine, in the remainder of the butter. Add to the soup and simmer 20 to 25 minutes. Add the potatoes and the chervil and simmer another 15 minutes.

Mix the egg yolks and the cream in a 2-cup measuring cup. Add about 1 cup of the hot soup and mix well. Then pour the liaison back into the bulk of the soup, stirring constantly. Do not hesitate to reboil the soup since it contains flour. The egg will curdle only if you heat it too fast. Add the mussels and clams, correct the seasoning with salt, pepper, and lemon juice, if needed. Serve piping hot with crisp bread and salted butter to spread on it.

CREME DE SARRASIN AUX LEGUMES
[Buckwheat Cream Soup]

SERVINGS: 6 COST: inexpensive EXECUTION: easy
TOTAL PREPARATION TIME: 1 hour 15 minutes
BEST SEASON: Late fall through early spring
REMARKS ON INGREDIENTS: Dark buckwheat flour is used here, but
   any buckwheat flour, light or whole grain, can be used.

3½ oz. smoked slab bacon
   (100 g)
1 large carrot, peeled and diced
   into ¼-inch cubes
3 leeks (white and light green
   parts), diced into ¼-inch
   cubes
1 onion, diced into ¼-inch
   cubes
2 TB parsley, chopped coarse

2 cloves garlic, chopped fine
6 cups boiling chicken broth or
   broth of your choice (1½
   litre)
Salt and pepper
¼ cup buckwheat flour (50 g)
1 cup heavy cream or milk
   (2¼ dl or 225 g)
½ cup salted butter (or less to
   taste) (110–115 g)

Dice the bacon, rind and all, into ⅛-inch cubes. Put it in a cold soup kettle and cook it very slowly until it is a light golden color and has rendered most of its fat.

Add all the vegetables; toss them in the bacon fat until the onions and leeks turn translucent and add 5 cups chicken broth. Bring back to a boil. Add salt and pepper and simmer 30 minutes, uncovered, to reduce the broth to about 4 cups.

Mix the buckwheat with the cold heavy cream and the remaining cup of broth to make a slurry and pour, stirring, into the vegetable soup. Simmer another 20 minutes. Bring the soup to a heavy boil and add the butter to the center of the boil. Correct the seasoning and serve very hot.

GROSSE COCHONNAILLE
[Coarse Country Pâté]

SERVINGS: 12 COST: moderately expensive EXECUTION: easy
TOTAL PREPARATION TIME: 3½ hours with the baking
BEST SEASON: Winter. This is good but very hearty and highly
    seasoned.
SUGGESTED WINE: Muscadet
REMARKS ON INGREDIENTS: In this type of totally unrefined terrine,
    use even the hearts of pigs or calves or chicken if you can find
    them. They are cheap and make a good forcemeat.

1 lb. calves or pork liver | *4 slices ordinary white bread,*
* (500 g)* | * crust removed (80 g)*
2 lbs. Boston butt of pork | *½ cup milk (1 generous dl)*
* (1 kg)* | *6 eggs*
1 lb. unsalted fatback (500 g) | *4½ tsp. salt*
4 cloves garlic | *1 tsp. quatre épices (page 7)*
2 onions | *Pepper from the mill*
4 shallots | *A good pinch of cayenne*
½ cup parsley, chopped coarse

Remove the membranes from the liver. Cut into 1-inch cubes. Cut the butt and the fatback also into 1-inch cubes. Have the garlic, onions, shallots and parsley ready on a plate. Soak the bread in the milk for 5 minutes, then break the eggs into the same bowl and beat well with the salt, the teaspoon of *quatre épices*, 6 turns of the mill of pepper and the cayenne. Grind the liver, pork, fatback, garlic, shallots, onions, and parsley only once. Mix the ground forcemeat with the mixture of egg and spices. Cook a little patty of meat in a small frying pan, cool it in the freezer and taste it for seasoning. Add more salt, pepper, and spices if needed. Pour the forcemeat into a large flat baking dish (Bourgogne earthenware is customarily used in France), and bake in a 350° oven until nice and brown and a skewer inserted at the center of the pâté comes out clean and burns the top of the hand. Cool without putting a weight on top. Serve chilled with lots of pickles.

SALADE MERVEILLEUSE
[Seafood Salad]

SERVINGS: 6 COST: moderately expensive EXECUTION: easy
TOTAL PREPARATION TIME: 2 hours
BEST SEASON: September through October for fresh tomatoes; but
    exclude the asparagus then. March through the end of April
    for all other fresh ingredients.
SUGGESTED WINE: Muscadet

THE SALAD:
2 dozen black mussels
½ lb. medium shrimp (250 g)
½ lb. deep sea scallops
   (250 g)
Olive oil
Salt
Pepper from the mill
2 tomatoes
1 red pepper
1 green pepper
6 mushrooms
1 head Boston lettuce
12 small asparagus
Fresh chopped parsley

1 lemon, scalloped and cut into
   slices
Parsley bouquets
THE SAUCE:
1 egg yolk
1 TB mustard
Salt
Pepper from the mill
1⅓ cup olive oil or peanut oil
   (3¼ dl)
2 TB tomato purée
Lemon juice
1 TB dry Madeira or Fino sherry
2 TB chopped fresh chives
Cooking juices of the mussels

Place the mussels in a small pot with about ¼ cup water. Cover and steam open. Cook until the mussels are completely done but not shriveled. Shell the mussels. Discard the shells. Keep the mussels and their juices in a bowl.

Make sure the shrimp are peeled raw. In France, they are never deveined. They look better that way. Heat 2 tablespoons oil in a frying pan. Toss the shrimp in the hot oil for a few minutes until they curl up. They are done when the curl is three-quarters closed; if the curl is tightly closed they will be overdone. Remove to a plate, leaving most of the oil in the pan.

Remove the tough tendon on the side of the scallops; cut them into ¼-inch slices. Heat the oil in which the shrimp cooked, adding a bit more if needed and toss the scallops in the hot oil until they turn opaque. This happens within minutes; do not overcook. Remove to the same plate as the shrimp and reserve. Keep both shellfish covered with a plastic wrap. Prepare the vegetables. Peel and seed the tomatoes and both peppers. Cut them all into ¼-inch julienne strips. Cut the mushrooms into ¼-inch slices, then across into ¼-inch-wide sticks. Clean the Boston lettuce, remove the ribs from the leaves. Peel the asparagus and blanch it in boiling salt water. Make sure that it remains very green and quite crunchy. Drain; cool under cold water. If the asparagus is very thin, cut it in half crosswise. If it is as much as ⅓ inch thick, cut it in halves crosswise and lengthwise.

Keep all the elements of the salad separated until you are ready to season it.

TO MAKE THE SAUCE:
Mix egg yolk and mustard with a pinch of salt and three turns of the mill of pepper. Gradually whisk in the oil, lightening the sauce at regular intervals first with the tomato purée, then with lemon juice, added very sparingly at this point. Add the Madeira and chives. Let stand 15 minutes. Taste the sauce; now lighten it a bit more with 2 tablespoons of the mussel juice and then correct the salt and pepper. The sauce should not be stiff at this point. It should be fluid enough to coat the elements of the salad without sticking to them

too much. Mix all the ingredients of the salad in a large bowl. Toss with as much dressing as needed. Line a round platter with the lettuce leaves. Pile the salad at the center. Sprinkle with chopped parsley and surround with slices of scalloped lemon and parsley bouquets. Served chilled.

COQUILLES SAINT JACQUES A LA BRETONNE
[Scallops Brittany Style]

SERVINGS: 6 COST: expensive EXECUTION: medium-difficult

TOTAL PREPARATION TIME: 2½ hours including the fish fumet

BEST SEASON: September through April for deep sea scallops, January through early March for bay or cape scallops

SUGGESTED WINE: Alsatian Riesling, Graves Blanc, Moëlleux, Vouvray Moëlleux. A Muscadet would not show to best advantage, because of the sweetness of the shellfish.

REMARKS ON INGREDIENTS: In all cases, remove the tough tendons from the side of the scallops and reserve them. Cut sea scallops and cape scallops from New England into ¼-inch slices. Tiny ⅔-inch by ⅓-inch bay scallops can be left whole. A paysanne is an ⅛-inch-wide julienne.

1½ lbs. scallops of your choice (750 g)	Salt and pepper from the mill
½ cup clam or mussel juice (1 generous dl)	¾ lb. unsalted butter at room temperature (375 g)
1½ cups dry white wine (3½ dl)	4 onions (1½–2 inches in diameter), cut in paysanne
1½ cups fish fumet (see page 12) (3½ dl)	½ cup heavy cream (1 generous dl)
2 TB cider vinegar	¼ tsp. cornstarch
1 onion, chopped very fine	1 TB sour cream
4 shallots, chopped very fine	2 TB chopped fresh parsley
	Lemon juice, if needed

Remove the tendons of the scallops.

Put the tendons of the scallops, the mussel or clam juice, the wine, fish fumet, vinegar, chopped onion, and shallots in a heavy saucepan. Bring to a boil. Lower to a simmer and cook until the mixture is reduced to 1½ cups. Add about ¼ teaspoon salt and three turns of the mill of pepper and continue cooking until ½ cup of ingredients (solids and liquids) is left in the pan.

While the sauce reduces, prepare the paysanne of onions. Heat 1½ tablespoons butter in a small, heavy pot. Add the onions and roll them into the butter. Salt and pepper lightly. Cover the pot and *étuvé* them for about 10 minutes. Keep the onions slightly crunchy. Set aside when ready.

The onions and the reduction should be ready at the same time. Make sure that they are both ready before you start cooking the scallops.

Heat 3 tablespoons butter in a 9- or 10-inch frying pan until the foam starts receding. Add the scallops and stirfry them very fast over high heat until they are almost cooked. In the process, add a pinch of salt and pepper and make sure that you stop the cooking as soon as the shellfish starts to lose its natural juices. Remove the scallops to a colander placed over a bowl.

Reduce whatever shellfish juices are in the pan to a glaze. Add ⅓ cup heavy cream and reduce until it is thick and the butter nearly separates. Add whatever juices (there will be some) that have escaped from the shellfish to the pan and reduce again to a thick consistency. Add the paysanne of onions to that glaze; mix well. Turn the heat off.

Finally, prepare the sauce. Cook one half pound of butter to the *noisette* stage; it should be as brown as possible without the whey and milk solids burning. Strain and separate the brown solids very carefully.

Bring the first reduction to a simmer, add the remainder of the heavy cream, mixed with the cornstarch into a slurry, and thicken. Bring to a high boil and whisk in the *noisette* butter in a steady stream.

Put the sour cream into a small bowl. Strain the butter sauce over it very gradually and whisk both until smooth. Blend with the onions. Add the scallops; mix thoroughly. Reheat gently without boiling, shaking the pan back and forth over the burner. Add the parsley.

Finally correct the seasoning, adding lemon juice, salt, and pepper as needed. Serve with braised or boiled rice.

ANIAUX AU BEURRE NOIR
[Tinker Mackerels in Black Butter]

SERVINGS: 6 COST: inexpensive EXECUTION: easy
TOTAL PREPARATION TIME: 45 minutes
BEST SEASON: Any time you are lucky enough to find tinkers
SUGGESTED WINE: Muscadet
REMARKS ON INGREDIENTS: If no tinker mackerels are available, use ordinary mackerel, not too big. Also, the smaller the capers, the better.

1 dozen tinker mackerels	*½ cup salted butter (AA 93*
Flour	*score) (110 g)*
Salt and pepper	*1 small jar tiny capers in vinegar*
Peanut oil	

Cut the heads off the tinkers. Open them through the back so as to keep the fillets attached by the tummy skin. Remove the backbone and insides. Wash carefully and pat dry. Flour and lightly salt and pepper the fillets.

Heat about ¼ inch of oil in a large skillet and fry the fish on both sides until golden. It takes 3 to 4 minutes. Set the fish on a tray in a 200° oven to keep warm.

When all the fish is cooked, discard the cooking oil. Add the butter to the pan and cook until it turns dark brown, but does not burn. Empty the capers and their canning vinegar into the hot butter. Add salt and pepper and spoon over the tinkers.

Serve with plain, well-buttered mashed potatoes.

PAIN DE SOLES AUX ARTICHAUTS
[Fish Loaf with Artichoke and Shrimp Sauce]

SERVINGS: 6 COST: affordable EXECUTION: medium-difficult
TOTAL PREPARATION TIME: 3 hours
BEST SEASON: During the artichoke season, September through April
REMARKS ON INGREDIENTS: If sole is too expensive, winter flounder,
 whiting, hake or haddock will do very well. Make a soup with
 the artichoke meat in the leaves. The work can be split over
 2 days. First day: prepare the artichokes, bone the fish, and make
 the fumet. Second day: make the sauce and the loaf.

6 largest possible California
 artichokes
½ lb. unsalted butter (250 g)
1 TB each fresh chopped tarragon and chives or 1 tsp. dried
Salt
Pepper from the mill
1 large grey sole or sand dab
 to obtain 1 lb. pure fillets
 (450–500 g)
2 onions, sliced
Large bouquet garni
1 cup dry white wine (2¼ dl)

2 cups water (4½ dl)
Lemon juice
Flour
1 cup scalded milk (2¼ dl)
Pinch of cayenne
1 cup heavy cream
2 eggs
3 egg yolks
½ lb. small cooked shrimp,
 shelled (250 g)
Scalloped lemon slices
Parsley bouquets

In a large kettle bring 6 quarts of water to a boil. Salt with 1½ teaspoons salt per quart. Trim the stems and top of the leaves of the
artichokes. Immerse the artichokes in the rapidly boiling water and
cook until an outside leaf just pulls away from the artichoke bottom.
Remove the artichokes to a large sinkful of cold water and immediately pull off the leaves. Remove the choke and slice the artichoke
bottoms, which should be still crunchy, into ¼-inch-thick slivers.
Place in a bowl and mix with 1 tablespoon melted butter, the tarragon, chives and a pinch of salt and pepper. Cover the bowl.
 Bone the fish, or have the fish store bone it for you and give you

the heads and bones. Place these in a 4-quart pot with the onions, *bouquet garni,* white wine, and water. Bring to a boil and then simmer 35 minutes. While the mixture cooks, break down the fish bones. Strain into a clean bowl. You should have two cups of finished fish fumet.

Clean the fish meat in cold water acidulated with lemon juice. Dry it and cut into one-inch pieces. Keep ready to use. With 3 tablespoons butter, 3 tablespoons flour and the cup of scalded milk prepare a thick white sauce. Season it with 1½ teaspoons salt and ½ teaspoon pepper from the mill; add a pinch of cayenne. Let the sauce cool a little and then blend in ⅓ cup of heavy cream. Keep covered with a buttered paper and cool completely.

Beat 2 eggs and one egg yolk together well. Place half of the mixture in the blender container and add half of the fish. Blend on high speed until the mixture is smooth, elastic and shiny, and is separating readily from the sides of the blender. Empty into a bowl. Repeat with the remainder of the egg and fish.

Using a mixer on slow speed, blend the fish purée with the cold prepared cream sauce.

Butter a one-quart Charlotte mold generously and pile the fish mixture into it. Cover with a buttered parchment. Preheat the oven to 325° and bake the loaf in a hot water bath 30 to 35 minutes or until a skewer inserted almost to the center of the loaf comes out clean.

While the loaf bakes, prepare the sauce. Make a white roux with 3 tablespoons butter and 3 tablespoons flour; bind with the hot fish fumet. Simmer 20 to 25 minutes and skim. Season properly. The sauce should reduce to 1⅓ cups.

While the sauce cooks, heat 1 tablespoon butter in a small pan. Add the artichokes and *étuvé* them for about 5 minutes. Add them to the finished velouté and simmer another five minutes. Add the shrimp; reheat without boiling.

Prepare a "liaison" with the remaining cream and 2 egg yolks. Add some of the hot sauce to the "liaison," then blend it into the bulk of the sauce and reheat until a couple of boils appear in the center of the pot.

Add a solid squeeze of lemon juice, more salt and pepper to suit your taste, and blend in 2 tablespoons butter.

Unmold the fish loaf onto a dish, spoon the artichoke sauce over it and surround with scalloped lemon slices and parsley bouquets.

As a vegetable you will need rice.

HUITRES KERNEVEN AU FENOUIL BRETON
[Oysters with Muscadet Fennel Butter]

SERVINGS: 6 COST: medium-expensive EXECUTION: difficult
TOTAL PREPARATION TIME: 1 hour
BEST SEASON: September through April
SUGGESTED WINE: Muscadet
REMARKS ON INGREDIENTS: Oysters must be purchased *alive* in their shell and opened at home. Purchase an oyster knife for this. Check that they are not dead in the shell by touching the beard with the tip of a knife. If it retracts, the shellfish is alive. The best oysters to use for this preparation are: Chincoteagues and Wellfleet on the East Coast, and Olympia on the West Coast. If you do not have a meat glaze, leave it out; the recipe will still be good.

3 dozen large or extra-large oysters
1 cup Muscadet, or other dry white wine (2¼ dl)
2 shallots, chopped fine
1 white onion, 1 inch in diameter, chopped fine
1 dozen (no more) fennel seeds, crushed

1½ TB homemade meat glaze (see page 12). No meat extract, please!
1 cup unsalted butter at room temperature (250 g)
1 oz. Marc, Calvados, Cognac, Armagnac, or whisky

To shuck the oysters open, hold each oyster in a tea towel in your left hand. Insert the tip of your knife at the pointed end of the shell where the top and bottom shells meet. Your knife will insert between the shells by almost ¼ inch without difficulty. Turn the knife either left or right by ¼ inch; you will hear a definite snap as the two shells separate. Now slide the blade of the knife flat against the side of the top shell all the way to the front of the shell to cut the muscle valve that controls the opening of the shell when the oyster is immersed in sea water. Lift the top lid and set it aside.

Empty each oyster, juice and all, delicately into a small pan. Bring to a light simmer for a few minutes until the oysters have plumped up and look noticeably shorter and swollen. Remove the beard and transfer the oysters to a small bowl.

Leave the juices in the pan and add the Muscadet, shallots, onion, crushed fennel seeds, and meat glaze. Also add any oyster meat left attached to the top shell of each oyster when you opened them. Reduce the mixture slowly to 2½ tablespoons of liquids and solids.

While the oyster essence is reducing, rinse the oyster shells in hot water and dry them. Place them in two large jelly roll pans containing some kosher salt so they will not wobble and keep warm.

When the oyster essence is reduced, turn the heat down and whisk in the butter, tablespoon by tablespoon. After using ¾ cup butter, sample to make sure that the taste of the sauce is not getting too weak. If not, continue adding the remainder of the butter.

Heat the chosen spirit in a small pan and light it. Whisk it flaming into the sauce. Strain into a lukewarm bowl. Preheat the broiler of your oven. Return each oyster to its shell and spoon an equal amount of the sauce over each oyster. Broil two minutes and serve piping hot.

HOMARD DE LA JARDINIERE BRETONNE
[Lobster with Garden Vegetables]

SERVINGS: 6 COST: expensive EXECUTION: easy
TOTAL PREPARATION TIME: 1 hour 15 minutes
BEST SEASON: Year round
SUGGESTED WINE: Muscadet, Sancerre, Pouilly-Fuissé, or Vouvray
    Moëlleux
REMARKS ON INGREDIENTS: Any type of lobster may be used here.

Female lobsters are easily recognized by the size of the feelers situated directly below the head. They are very flexible and barely ⅛ inch wide; while in the male they are ¼ inch wide and much stiffer.

1 large kettle of boiling, salted water (1½ tsp. per quart)
6 lobsters, 3 male and 3 female, 1¼ lb. each
Seaweed
4½ cups fish fumet (see page 12) (1 litre)
1 cup unsalted butter plus 2 TB
3 TB flour
1 shallot, chopped fine
1 small zucchini
1 small yellow squash
1 very small purple-top white turnip, peeled
1 medium carrot, peeled
2 leeks (white and light green part), cut into ⅛-inch fine julienne strips
1¼ cup heavy cream (2¾ dl)
¼ cup sour cream (½ small dl)
Salt
Pepper from the mill
1½ oz. Cognac, Armagnac, Marc, or whisky
Lemon juice

Add the lobsters to the kettle of boiling water. Also add the seaweed. Bring back to a boil, turn the heat down, and barely simmer for 8 minutes. Drain the lobsters into a colander. Cool the lobsters just enough to handle them; remove the claws and the tail. Empty the tomalley and coral into a small bowl. Discard the upper part of the shell and chop the body and small legs.

Bring the fish fumet to a boil. With 3 tablespoons butter and the flour, make a white roux; cook it for 5 minutes. Bind the roux with 3½ cups of the fish fumet. Bring to a boil; turn down to a simmer. Add the chopped lobster bodies and legs and continue simmering for 25 minutes while you add the remaining cup of fumet gradually, ¼ cup at a time every 5 minutes. In the meantime, skim all the scum coming to the top of the sauce. There should be 3 cups of sauce when the cooking is finished. Strain the sauce into a bowl; press the pieces of lobster to extract the juices. Reserve.

Completely shell the claws and larger legs of the lobsters as well as the tails. Slice the latter into ⅓-inch-thick slices. Remove the center vein. Keep ready to use in a small bowl.

Score the surface of the vegetables with a lemon zester so as to obtain a scalloped design. Cut the vegetables into paper-thin slices. Cut the leeks into ⅛-inch fine julienne or paysanne. First, mix and blanch the carrots and turnips and remove to a bowl or plate; then blanch the leek julienne.

With the tomalley and coral and ¾ cup of butter, make a compound butter by creaming both together with an electric mixer. Strain the butter through a conical strainer or a sieve.

To finish the dish, heat the last two tablespoons of butter in a 4-quart heavy pot. Add the shallots and toss one minute in the butter. Add the sliced zucchini and yellow squash. Toss in the butter until well coated. Add the carrots, turnips, and leeks and toss together. Add salt, pepper and then the prepared velouté. Bring to a simmer; add the lobster meat and reheat.

Mix both creams together and add to the pot; reheat. Finally blend in the strained lobster butter and reheat without boiling.

Heat the spirit and light it. Pour it flaming into the sauce. Correct the seasoning with salt, pepper, and lemon juice, if needed, and serve immediately.

Serve in soup plates with a side dish of rice. Offer a fork and spoon; this is a souplike stew.

SELLE D'AGNEAU AU LARD
[Saddle of Lamb Roasted with Bacon]

SERVINGS: 6 COST: expensive EXECUTION: watch the roasting carefully

TOTAL PREPARATION TIME: 1½ hours

BEST SEASON: April to September

SUGGESTED WINE: Any good red Bordeaux, Châteauneuf du Pape, a good red Burgundy, a Beaujolais Premier Cru, or an Hermitage or Côte Rôtie

REMARKS ON INGREDIENTS: Purchase a whole saddle of lamb, called pic by professional meat people. Have the butcher prepare it English style; see below for description. Slab brisket of pork can be found in Italian and German neighborhood butcher shops. Do not use salted or smoked bacon slices.

1 whole saddle of lamb (pic)	*1 quart brown veal stock*
½ lb. fresh, unsalted and un-	*(page 10) (1 litre)*
smoked brisket of pork	*2 small onions, sliced fine in*
(250 g)	*paysanne (see page 278)*
Fresh or dried savory leaves	*2 shallots, sliced fine in paysanne*
Salt	*1 small carrot, sliced fine in*
Fresh pepper, grated coarse	*paysanne*
4 TB unsalted butter (55–60 g)	*2 TB chopped parsley*

A saddle of lamb prepared English style looks this way. The fell on the top has been removed, the fat scored in a crisscross pattern, and the ribs removed. The brisket normally covering the ribs is rolled under so as not to cover the tenderloins and prevent them from roasting. The saddle or pic comes tied across to prevent the rolled flaps from unrolling. Have the butcher give you the piece of flanken attached on both sides of the pic.

TO PREPARE THE SADDLE:
First, slice the brisket of pork into ⅛-inch slices and remove the pork rind. Cut an incision on either side of the backbone and on the full length of the lamb saddle. With a sharp paring or boning knife, lift the fat and gristle covering completely, exposing the bare muscle on both sides. Cut the flap obtained on each side but do not remove the flap rolled under by the butcher or the saddle will not stand properly on the roasting rack. Replace the natural fat covering of the lamb with the slices of brisket, applied crosswise on the whole width of the cut. The slices should overlap one another slightly. Tie in 4 places if you desire, but this is not absolutely necessary. Sprinkle the brisket with savory (very little). Place on a roasting pan fitted with a rack

and roast to an internal temperature (taken in the sirloin strip with a meat thermometer) of 135°. Let rest 10 minutes before carving. While the meat cooks, prepare the sauce.

TO PREPARE THE SAUCE:

Take the flanken, remove as much lean meat as you can and discard the fat and bones. You should obtain about 1 to 1½ cups of meat. Cut it in ½-inch cubes and brown it in 1 tablespoon butter. Add 1 cup stock; slowly reduce to a good glaze. Repeat again with two more cups of stock so as to obtain about ¼ cup of a good, syrupy glaze. Add the last cup of stock; mix well.

While the stock reduces, sauté the onions, shallots, and carrots in the remaining butter. Add salt, pepper, and another pinch of savory and strain the obtained sauce over the vegetables. Simmer five minutes. Finally, add the parsley.

Discard all the fat in the roasting pan and deglaze it with a few tablespoons of the sauce. Strain the deglazing into the bulk of the sauce and stir well. Correct the seasoning with salt and pepper.

TO CARVE THE SADDLE:

Remove the brisket of pork. Lift first the sirloin strips and cut them into ⅟₁₆-inch-thick slivers, lengthwise. Repeat with the tenderloins. This is best served as quickly as possible. If, however, you wish to present the dish, straddle the meat slivers across the backbone, alternating them with the brisket slices.

As a vegetable, serve *Haricots Verts à la Bretonne* (see page 301).

"BIFSTECKS" AUX CHAMPIGNONS
[*Mushroom-Stuffed Ground Patties with Tomato Fondue*]

SERVINGS: 6 COST: affordable EXECUTION: simple
TOTAL PREPARATION TIME: 1½ hours
BEST SEASON: September and October when the tomatoes are fresh. Good year round if the sauce is made with a No. 303 can Italian-style plum tomatoes.

SUGGESTED WINE: Any red wine of your choice without too much
    pedigree

½ lb. fresh, preferably golden,
    natural mushrooms (250 g)
Unsalted butter
Salt and pepper
2 slices white bread, crust
    removed
3 TB milk
3 onions, chopped fine
1 tiny clove garlic, chopped fine
1 lb. extra-lean ground beef
    (500 g)

2 eggs
Flour
Peanut or corn oil
1 tsp. water
½ cup dry breadcrumbs
2 lbs. fresh, sun-ripened tomatoes,
    peeled, seeded, and chopped
Thyme
Savory

Clean the mushrooms, pare them, and chop into ¼-inch hash. Heat
1 tablespoon butter in a skillet; add the mushrooms and sauté them
with salt and pepper until nice and brown. Cool completely.

Soak the white bread in the milk and let stand. In the same pan
where the mushrooms cooked, heat another tablespoon of butter and
sauté one chopped onion until soft and translucent. Add the garlic
and mix well. Continue cooking one more minute; mix into the
softened bread.

Put the ground beef in a bowl; add the mixture of bread, onion,
and garlic and one egg, lightly beaten with a good pinch of salt and
pepper. Mix thoroughly. Shape six balls of meat. Make a hole in the
center of each and fill with ⅙ of the mushrooms. Close the meat
over the mushrooms and flatten into a ½-inch thick beef patty. Flour
the patties.

Beat the second egg with a teaspoon each of water and oil and a
good pinch of salt and pepper. Beat until liquefied. Brush over each
patty and coat each patty with the dry crumbs. Let dry on a cake rack
while you prepare the tomato fondue.

Heat 2 more tablespoons of butter in a large saucepan, add the last
two chopped onions and sauté until translucent. Add the tomatoes,
thyme, and savory to your taste and cook until the tomatoes have
fallen apart and lost most of their moisture.

Heat about 3 tablespoons oil in a large skillet and brown the meat patties on both sides. They are rare when the crust is a light golden color and medium-rare when it is a dark golden color. Remove the patties to a platter and top with the tomato sauce.

CAILLETTES DE PORC DE KERNEVEN
[Pork Sausages with Pickle Sauce]

SERVINGS: 6 COST: inexpensive EXECUTION: easy
TOTAL PREPARATION TIME: 2 hours
BEST SEASON: A hearty winter dish
SUGGESTED WINE: Muscadet
REMARKS ON INGREDIENTS: Fresh pork brisket (unsalted bacon), dried mushrooms (*Porcini* or *Boleti* or *Mousserons*), and pigs cauls are all available in Italian neighborhood markets. If you cannot locate the cauls, cut ½ lb. fresh fatback into ⅛-inch-thick slices, then into ⅛-inch-wide strips and wrap the patties with those, crisscrossed at ⅓-inch intervals.

THE FORCEMEAT:
1 oz. dried Mousserons or
  Boleti (30 g)
1½ lb. Boston butt, boneless, or
  country-style pork ribs, boned
  (net pure meat weight)
  (750 g)
2 chicken livers
¾ lb. fresh pork brisket
  (375 g)
Salt
Pepper from the mill
3 TB lard or butter
2 small onions, chopped fine
1 shallot, chopped fine
1 large clove garlic, mashed

2 small eggs
Pigs cauls or fresh fatback
  (see above)
THE SAUCE:
3 TB lard or butter
1 large onion, chopped fine
1 clove garlic, mashed
2 TB chopped parsley
2 cups dry white wine
  (Muscadet) (4½ dl)
½ cup tomato purée
  (1 generous dl)
Salt
Pepper from the mill
3 sour pickles, sliced thin

Soak the dried mushrooms in just enough lukewarm water to cover them. Let stand while you prepare the forcemeat. If you use *Mousserons,* remove the stems *before* soaking.

Grind the pork meat, liver, and pork brisket only once. Add salt and pepper. Mix well and set aside.

Heat the lard or butter in a small frying pan, add the onions, and sauté lightly. Add the shallots, and garlic; cover. Cook for two minutes. Drain the mushrooms; reserve their soaking water for the sauce. Chop the mushrooms coarse and add them to the pan. Keep the pan uncovered and cook the mushrooms. Let all the juices in the pan evaporate. Cool completely and add to the forcemeat.

Add the eggs, lightly beaten. Mix well. Test the seasoning by cooking a nugget of the forcemeat in a small pan.

Rinse the cauls in lukewarm water and pat dry. Wrap small oval patties of forcemeat 3 to 4 inches long and ½ inch thick in small pieces of caul. Set aside.

Now prepare the base for the sauce. Sauté the onions in 2 tablespoons lard or butter until translucent. Add the garlic and continue sautéing until the onion begins to turn a light golden color. Add the parsley, wine, tomato purée, the mushroom soaking water and salt and pepper. Reduce to 1½ cups and add the pickles.

Heat a last tablespoon of lard in a large skillet and panfry the *caillettes* until they are a golden color on both sides. Once the *caillettes* are done, remove them to a platter. Discard the fat in the pan and add the prepared sauce to the frying pan, scraping well to dissolve the glaze from the *caillettes.* Spoon the sauce over the *caillettes.*

Serve either with well-buttered spinach, mashed potatoes, or a purée of navy beans.

ROTI DE PORC EN SANGLIER
[*Roast Pork Boar Style*]

SERVINGS: 6 COST: affordable EXECUTION: easy
TOTAL PREPARATION TIME: 3 days for the marination, 3 hours for
    the preparation and cooking

BEST SEASON: November through January
SUGGESTED WINE: Châteauneuf du Pape Rouge or Côtes du Rhône
REMARKS ON INGREDIENTS: Use a boneless pork roast cut half from
the rib and half from the shoulder. One end of the roast will
show a cut in the meat indicating that the shoulder blade has
been removed.

One 3-lb. boneless pork roast	Salt
3 cups dry red wine (preferably	Pepper from the mill
Côtes du Rhône) (6¾ to	3 firm ripe pears
7 dl)	Unsalted butter
1 cup dry white wine (2¼ dl)	Flour
2 onions, chopped coarse	Dry Madeira
4 shallots, chopped coarse	Sugar
1 small carrot, chopped coarse	1 recipe for kunpods (see page
One 2-inch piece of celery rib	294)
20 juniper berries, crushed	Flour
¼ tsp. quatre épices (see page	2 TB raisins
7)	3 TB chopped parsley
4 cloves	Meat extract
6 crushed black peppercorns	Lemon juice

Remove all but ¼ inch of the fat covering of the pork roast. Let
stand at room temperature while you prepare the marinade.

Mix the red and white wines in a large saucepan. Bring to a boil,
add the onions, shallots, carrots, celery, crushed juniper berries, cloves
(crush their buds into the wine), peppercorns, and the *quatre épices*.
Bring back to a boil. Reduce to a simmer and cook 20 minutes. Cool
the marinade completely.

Put the roast into a large loaf pan and pour the marinade over it.
Marinate 3 days, at room temperature and in a cool room. Turn the
meat over every twelve hours.

Pat the meat very dry with paper towels. Put it in a roasting pan
in a preheated 325° oven and roast it slowly for about 2½ hours.

Meanwhile, empty the marinade into a saucepan and reduce it by
two-thirds. While the marinade reduces, peel the pears and dice them
into ½-inch cubes. Heat 2 tablespoons butter in a frying pan and

sauté the pears for two or three minutes. Add ¼ cup dry Madeira and evaporate completely. Add a dash of salt and the smallest pinch of sugar. Set aside.

To make the *kunpods,* follow the directions given on page 295, replacing the bacon fat with butter and adding 2 tablespoons raisins. Poach the *kunpods* in simmering salted water. Keep them waiting in the same water, off the heat.

As soon as the marinade has reduced, strain it into a bowl through a fine strainer to discard all the vegetables and other matter floating in the liquid.

When the pork roast is three-quarters done, salt and pepper the outside. When it is done, defatten the juices in the roasting pan and add the reduced marinade and parsley. Scrape well to dissolve all the meat juices attached to the bottom of the pan. Measure the pan gravy obtained. Thicken it with 1 tablespoon butter mixed with 1 tablespoon flour per cup of gravy. Whisk the mixture into the simmering gravy.

Strain the gravy over the pears and add the *kunpods* to the sauce. Correct the seasoning with salt, pepper and if needed to strengthen the taste of the sauce, a bit of meat extract and a dash of lemon juice.

Serve the roast sliced and topped with the pear cubes and surrounded by the *kunpods.*

POULARDE AUX KUNPODS ET AUX CEPES
[Poached Chicken with Bacon Dumplings and Wild Mushrooms]

SERVINGS: 6 COST: affordable EXECUTION: easy
TOTAL PREPARATION TIME: 1½ hours
BEST SEASON: Can be made year round
SUGGESTED WINE: A Vouvray Moëlleux
REMARKS ON INGREDIENTS: The best chickens for poaching can be found in kosher butcher shops. Have the butcher give you the feet; blanch them in boiling water and add them to the pot. Dried mushrooms (*Boleti eduli, Steinpilze, Porcini*) can be found in all Italian neighborhood grocery stores.

THE CHICKEN:

3 quarts brown veal stock or the
   best possible stock (3 litres)
Two 4-lb. roasting chickens
   (1 kg 500–1 kg 750 each)
Salt and pepper
6 TB lightly salted butter (AA
   93 score) (80–90 g)
½ lb. fresh Boleti eduli, or other
   cèpes (250 g) or 2 oz. dried
   mushrooms as mentioned
   above (60 g–75 g)
1 large clove garlic
2 TB finely chopped parsley
¼ cup flour (30 g)

¾ cup heavy cream (1⅓ dl)
2 TB sour cream

THE KUNPODS:

4 oz. slab bacon (125 g)
Butter, lightly salted (AA
   93 score)
½ cup brown veal stock, or
   other stock of your choice
   (1 generous dl)
½ cup milk (1 generous dl)
¼ tsp. salt
1 cup flour (120 g)
3 eggs
Parsley bouquets

TO POACH THE CHICKENS AND MAKE THE SAUCE:

Bring the stock to a boil. While it heats, salt and pepper the chickens in the cavity; truss them. Tie a band of parchment paper around the breast. Immerse the chickens in the simmering stock, bring back to a simmer, and cook covered for 40 minutes.

If you are using dried mushrooms, soak them while the chicken cook, for about 30 minutes. Then, proceed as follows for both fresh and dried mushrooms:

Heat 2 tablespoons butter in a frying pan. Add the mushrooms and sauté them with a pinch of salt and pepper over high heat. Add the garlic and parsley and allow them both to brown with the mushrooms. Set aside.

As soon as the chickens have been in the stock for 40 minutes, remove 3 cups of stock for the sauce. Turn off the heat but keep the chickens covered in the hot stock; they will finish cooking all by themselves. To make the sauce, heat 4 tablespoons butter in a 1-quart pot. Add the flour and cook 4 to 5 minutes, stirring occasionally. Whisk in 2½ cups of stock, bring to a boil and skim, adding the last ½ cup of stock gradually until the sauce is reduced to 2 cups and is as clean as possible.

Bring the sauce to a rapid boil and gradually add the heavy cream, stirring constantly with a wooden spoon until the sauce coats the spoon by about $\frac{1}{6}$ inch. Add the mushrooms to the sauce. Simmer together 5 minutes. Off the heat pour a little of the sauce into the sour cream and mix until homogenous. Then pour back into the bulk of the sauce and mix well. Correct the seasoning. Reheat without boiling.

TO MAKE THE KUNPODS:
These can be done easily at the same time as you cook and skim the sauce, after it has come to a boil and simmers.

Dice the bacon into $\frac{1}{4}$-inch cubes. Put those into a frying pan and render them slowly until they are crisp and a golden color. Measure the bacon fat in a measuring cup; add enough melted butter to make $\frac{1}{3}$ cup.

Mix $\frac{1}{2}$ cup stock with the milk. Add the melted fat, the salt, and bring to a boil. Add the flour off the heat and stir to make a ball. Return the pot to the heat and dry for a few minutes, flattening the paste on the bottom of the pot to let as much water as possible evaporate.

Take the pot off the heat and beat in the lightly beaten eggs with a wooden spoon one at a time. Then add the bacon cubes.

Remove another $1\frac{1}{2}$ to 2 quarts of stock from the chicken pot. Bring to a simmer in a shallow pan. Shape 12 *kunpods* with two spoons so they resemble eggs and drop them into the simmering stock. Let them float to the surface of the stock and almost double in bulk.

TO SERVE THE CHICKENS:
Present them on a platter surrounded by the dumplings. Spoon a bit of the sauce over them and decorate with parsley bouquets. Serve the remainder of the sauce in a warmed boat or small pot.

CANARD AUX FIGUES ET AU CITRON
[Duck Stuffed with Figs and Lemon Sauce]

SERVINGS: 6 COST: moderately expensive EXECUTION: easy
TOTAL PREPARATION TIME: 3½ hours
BEST SEASON: September through early November
SUGGESTED WINE: A German Moselle wine has proved best with
 this almost-sweet bird.
REMARKS ON INGREDIENTS: Fresh figs in season are available in all
 Italian neighborhood produce markets and stands.

Two 4½-lbs. ducks (2 kg each)
1 TB oil
1 gelatinous veal bone
½ cup butter (110 g)
1 carrot, chopped coarse
1 onion, chopped coarse
4 TB flour (30 g)
1 quart warm chicken or veal
 stock (1 litre)
½ cup dry white wine (1 gen-
 erous dl)
1 TB tomato paste
Bouquet garni

One dozen ripe but firm figs
 (preferably a small pale
 variety)
½ lemon, cut in half and
 blanched in boiling water
Salt
Pepper from the mill
1 strip lemon rind, 2 inches
 long
Rum, preferably dark
Lemon juice, if needed
Pinch of sugar, if needed
Parsley or watercress bouquets

Remove the giblets from the ducks' cavities. Keep the livers to use in a terrine (see index). Lightly oil a small ovenproof dish and put the veal bone, the giblets, and the wingtips of the ducks in it. Brown in a preheated 400° oven.

Meanwhile, heat 5 tablespoons butter in a 3-quart saucepan. Add the chopped carrot and onion and brown lightly. Add the flour and continue browning until the onion is dark brown. By this time the flour will have browned just enough to give a good color to the sauce. Off the heat, add the warm stock and bring to a boil. Add the browned bones and giblets to the sauce. Discard the fat in the roasting pan and deglaze the pan with the white wine, scraping well to loosen all the caramelized meat juices. Add to the sauce. Also add the tomato paste and *bouquet garni.* Simmer 1½ hours, skimming as much as possible to discard the flour proteins and fat.

While the sauce cooks, cut the stems from the figs and cut a tiny cross in their root end. Wash the figs. Salt and pepper the cavity of each duck and blanch the lemon quarters. Stuff the cavity of each bird with one lemon quarter placed way up in the thorax and then with 6 figs. Do not truss the ducks, but stretch their legs forward as much as possible. Place on a roasting pan and roast 2½ hours in a preheated 325° oven. Prick the skin of the ducks after they have been baking for a full hour; remove most of the fat in the roasting pan as it melts. After one hour of baking, start tilting the birds forward to let the cavity juices escape into the roasting pan and build a good gravy. Be careful not to spill the fruit out.

While the ducks cook, finish the basic sauce. By the time the sauce has been cooking for 1½ hours it will be reduced to about 2 cups. Strain into a one-quart pot; add the lemon rind and continue cooking and skimming until the sauce is clean, measures 1¼ cups and has a definite oil of lemon taste.

To finish the dish, remove the cooked ducks from the oven. Remove the figs to a small plate and keep warm. Empty the pan gravy fat and all into a fireproof measuring cup; let stand so the lean juices can separate from the fat. Siphon the lean juices with a bulb baster and add them to the basic lemon sauce.

Simmer together five minutes. Brush a small amount of the sauce on each duck and broil until brown and crisp.

Heat 1 ounce of rum and pour it flaming into the sauce. Finish the sauce with salt, pepper, 4 tablespoons butter and, depending on what is needed, a dash of lemon juice or a pinch of sugar (depending on the sweetness of the figs).

Serve the ducks on a platter, surrounded with the figs and parsley or watercress bouquets.

For vegetables, consider *kunpods* (see page 295), replacing the bacon fat with butter and using raisins instead of bacon, and a crisp, very refreshing, classic green French salad.

PIGEONS AU FARZ BREZED
[*Pigeons on Butter and Prune Pudding*]

SERVINGS: 6 COST: moderately expensive EXECUTION: medium-
difficult
TOTAL PREPARATION TIME: Marination of the prunes, 2 days; cook-
ing, 1 hour 20 minutes
BEST SEASON: Winter. Good, but robust food.
SUGGESTED BEVERAGE: French or English imported cider

12 prunes (soft, pitted Cali-
fornia)
1 bottle cider (7½ dl)
2 cups sifted flour
Dash of ground cloves
3 TB sugar (45–50 g)
2 cups milk (4½ dl)
3 eggs

¾ cup lightly salted butter
(AA 93 score) (170 g)
Salt and pepper
6 squabs
1 cup brown veal stock (page
10) (2¼ dl)
⅓ cup sour cream (1 small dl)
Lemon juice
Watercress

Soak the prunes two full days in the cider. Drain and cut into quarters. Reserve whatever cider is left in the bowl.

Put the flour in a bowl. Add the clove, sugar, and gradually add
the milk. Beat the eggs until the foam is almost stiff; fold into the
flour and milk mixture. Melt ½ cup butter, cool it, and fold it into
the batter. Taste and add a dash of salt, if needed.

Butter a 10-inch cake pan with 1–2 tablespoons butter. Line it
with the cut prunes; pour the batter over them. Bake in a 375°
oven for about 1 hour or until the *farz* is cooked and a skewer inserted in its center comes out clean and hot to the top of the hand.

While the *farz* bakes, salt and pepper the cavities of the squabs,
truss them, and brown them well in 2 tablespoons butter. Cover the
pot and cook for 45 to 60 minutes, gradually adding whatever cider
was left from the prunes. When the squabs are done, remove them
from the pot and keep them hot. Add the brown veal stock to the
cooking juices and reduce to about ½ cup. Whisk this sauce into the

sour cream, then reheat thoroughly without boiling. Correct the seasoning with salt, pepper, and lemon juice if needed.

Present as follows: unmold the *farz* on a round platter, set the squabs on it, and surround with fresh watercress. Spoon a little of the sauce on top of the birds and serve the remainder in a sauce boat.

PETITS ARTICHAUTS A LA COCOTTE
[Fricassée of Artichokes]

SERVINGS: 6 COST: expensive EXECUTION: easy
TOTAL PREPARATION TIME: 2 hours
BEST SEASON: For baby artichokes, September through April

3 dozen baby artichokes
Lemon juice
Water
2 TB butter
1 tsp. flour
1 cup brown veal stock (page

10), or other stock of your
choice
Salt and pepper
2 TB each: sour and heavy cream
1 TB chopped fresh parsley or
tarragon

Using gloves, peel the leaves off the artichokes until one inch of the vegetable is left. Using a sharp, preferably stainless steel, parer, cut the stem and round off the bottoms so they are even. Cut ⅓ inch of the tip off the leaves. Soak the artichokes in water acidulated with lemon juice. As soon as the artichokes are all peeled, bring 2 quarts of water to a high boil; add lemon juice. Blanch the artichokes for 3 to 4 minutes. Drain. Heat the butter in a heavy pot or casserole, toss the artichokes in the butter, sprinkle with the flour, toss another minute, and add the stock. Add salt and pepper. Cover and cook over very low heat until the stock just coats the vegetables. At that point the vegetables should be done. Test them with a skewer; it should come out of the vegetable without difficulty. Mix both creams together and stir into the artichokes. Add the parsley or tarragon. Correct the seasoning and serve.

JARDINIERE DE LEGUMES SAUCE CITRON
[Spring Vegetable Medley with Lemon Sauce]

SERVINGS: 6 COST: affordable EXECUTION: easy

TOTAL PREPARATION TIME: 1 hour

BEST SEASON: All through summer when vegetables are fresh, but
feasible all year round

REMARKS ON INGREDIENTS: Unless you grow your own peas, use
frozen.

½ lb. fresh baby carrots
  (250 g)
½ lb. fresh purple-top turnips
  (250 g)
Salt
Pepper
½ lb. shelled baby peas, fresh
  or frozen (250 g)

½ lb. green beans, cut into
  ¾-inch pieces (250 g)
2 small baby zucchini (200 g)
2 TB chopped fresh parsley
1 cup heavy cream (2¼ dl)
3 egg yolks
Lemon juice to suit your taste

Peel the carrots and turnips and cut them into olive-shaped chunks.
Do not peel the zucchini; cut them into olive-shaped chunks. Round
off all angles to prevent mushing up.

Bring a large pot of water to a boil. Salt well. Add the carrots and
bring back to a boil. Add the turnips, bring back to a boil; add the
peas and beans, bring back to a boil; add the zucchini, bring back to
a boil, and drain. All the vegetables will be done, nice and crunchy.

Put the vegetables in a large frying pan; salt and pepper them.
Add the chopped parsley and toss over the heat until the surrounding
water has evaporated. Mix egg yolks and cream; pour over the vegetables. Shake the pan back and forth over the heat until the custard
sauce thickens lightly. Add lemon juice to taste. Correct the seasoning.
Serve promptly. There will be just enough sauce to coat the vegetables.

EPINARDS AU LARD ET POMMES DE TERRE
[Spinach with Brisket of Pork]

SERVINGS: 6 COST: inexpensive EXECUTION: easy
TOTAL PREPARATION TIME: 1 hour

1 lb. potatoes (500 g)	1 onion, chopped fine
2 lbs. leaf spinach (1 kg)	Salt and pepper
¼ lb. fresh brisket of pork or	½ cup scalded milk or cream
slab bacon, to your taste	(1 generous dl)
(125 g)	Butter to your taste

Boil the potatoes in their jackets.

Stem the spinach. Wash it carefully and chop it very fine, as fine as parsley.

Cut the pork brisket into ¼-inch cubes and render it slowly. Cook until the bits of meat and fat turn a golden color. Add the onion and sauté until translucent. Add the spinach and toss into the mixture. Salt and pepper and cover. Let cook about 5 to 6 minutes; then uncover and let the moisture completely evaporate.

By the time this is done, the potatoes will be cooked. Peel them and strain them into the spinach; mix well. Add the scalded milk or cream and as much butter as you like (four tablespoons give a delicious purée). Correct the seasoning and serve.

HARICOTS VERTS A LA BRETONNE
[Green Beans Brittany Style]

SERVINGS: 6 COST: inexpensive EXECUTION: easy
TOTAL PREPARATION TIME: 45 minutes if you just string the beans,
1½ hours if you French them correctly

1 lb. (1½ if you French) green	4 TB lightly salted butter (AA
beans (500 g and 750 g)	93 score) (50–55 g)
Salt	1 clove garlic, mashed
2 large onions	2 TB chopped parsley
	Pepper

To French the green beans, remove the string on each side with a paring knife. Bring a large pot of water to a boil and add 1½ teaspoons salt per quart. Add the beans and cook at a rolling boil for 6 to 8 minutes, depending on the size. Drain, refresh under running cold water, and pat dry in a towel.

Slice the onions into ⅛-inch thin paysanne or julienne. Heat 1 tablespoon butter in a large skillet and add the onions. Sauté them over medium heat until soft and translucent. Add the beans; toss them with the onions. While they heat slowly, mix well 3 tablespoons butter with the garlic and parsley and spread bits of this compound butter all over the beans. Mix thoroughly without breaking the beans. Correct the seasoning and serve.

KRAMPOUEZ KRASS
[Buckwheat Crêpes or Pancakes]

YIELD: 3 dozen No. 20 crêpes COST: inexpensive EXECUTION: simple

TOTAL PREPARATION TIME: 30 minutes for the batter, 2 minutes *per galette* (crêpe) for cooking

BEST SEASON: Made year round in Brittany

REMARKS ON USES: See text on Loetitia, page 269. Crêpes made without sugar replace bread and are wrapped around sausages. Use the *caillettes* on page 290 without sauce for this use. Crêpes made with sugar are used for dinner with jam, honey, and melted butter, or for dessert.

1 cup sifted all-purpose flour (120 g)	*¾ tsp. salt*
	1 cup milk (2¼ dl)
½ cup buckwheat flour (100 g)	*2 cups water (4½ dl)*
	1 tsp. orange flower water
½ cup sugar (if used for dessert) (125 g)	*(if used for dessert)*
	¼ cup melted, lightly salted
4 eggs	*butter (AA 93 score) (50 g)*

Mix the all-purpose flour with the buckwheat flour and the sugar, if you are using it. Add the eggs and the salt and mix well to obtain a rough batter. Add the milk and gradually the water. Stir until smooth and add the orange flower water if applicable. Then stir in the melted butter. Let stand 20 minutes. Stir before making each crêpe.

Heat a No. 20 crêpe pan and pour one serving spoon of batter into the lip of the pan. Let the batter cover the bottom of the pan. Cook one minute, then turn over. Enjoy while nice and hot.

KRAMPOCH DE FROMENT BIGOUDEN
[Wheat-Flour Crêpes from Bigouden Country]

YIELDS: 2 dozen No. 20 crêpes COST: inexpensive EXECUTION: simple

TOTAL PREPARATION TIME: 1 hour for the batter to rise, 2 minutes cooking per crêpe

BEST SEASON: Made year round in Brittany

> 1¼ cups milk (2½ dl)
> ½ cake fresh yeast (5 g)
> 1 cup sifted all-purpose flour (120 g)
> 2 eggs
>
> ¼ cup sugar (60–65 g)
> 1 tsp. orange flower water
> 4 TB melted, lightly salted butter (AA 93 score)

Heat the milk to barely lukewarm and crumble the yeast into it. Let stand 10 minutes.

Make a well in the flour, add the eggs and sugar and mix well. Dilute with the mixture of milk and yeast. Add the orange flower water and the melted butter. Strain into a clean bowl and let double in bulk. With the batter, make crêpes the usual way and serve with melted butter, jam, or honey.

FARZ AUX POMMES ET AUX MURES
[Apple and Blackberry Pudding]

SERVINGS: 6–8 COST: inexpensive EXECUTION: easy

TOTAL PREPARATION TIME: 2 hours

BEST SEASON: Follow the apples; see dessert recipes in the chapter on Henriette.

10 TB lightly salted butter (AA 93 score) (140 g)	2 cups sifted flour (240–250 g)
6 TB sugar (90 g)	3 eggs
4 baking apples, preferably Granny Smith	2 cups milk (4½ dl)
1 cup blackberries	1 tsp. orange flower water

Grease a 10-inch cake pan very heavily with 2 tablespoons butter; sprinkle the mold with 3 tablespoons sugar.

Peel the apples and cut them in quarters. Cut the quarters across the width into ⅛-inch slivers; if sliced very thin, the slivers will not separate. Flatten the quartered, slivered apples rounded side down on the bottom of the pan. Bake 30 minutes in a preheated 350° oven. Sprinkle with the blackberries. Raise the oven to 375°.

Melt the remainder of the butter; let cool. Make a well in the flour, add the eggs, and, gradually, the milk. Add the melted butter and orange flower water, mix all ingredients together and strain over the fruit. Finish baking in the oven until the top of the cake is golden. Unmold onto a cake plate while still hot. Let cool to lukewarm before eating.

GATEAU BRETON AUX PRUNEAUX
[Brittany Cake Filled with Prune Paste]

SERVINGS: 8 COST: inexpensive EXECUTION: easy
TOTAL PREPARATION TIME: 2 hours
BEST SEASON: Eaten year round in Brittany

1 dozen soft, pitted California prunes	½ cup sugar (125 g)
1 cup cider (2¼ dl)	1 tsp. orange flower water
1 cup lightly salted butter (AA 93 score) (225 g)	1⅔ cup sifted flour (180 g)
1 egg	2 TB sifted cornstarch (5 g)
3 egg yolks	1 TB butter to butter the cake pan

Put the prunes into a one-quart saucepan. Add the cider and cook the prunes until they fall apart. Reduce to a stiff paste by stirring well over medium heat. Cool completely.

Cream the butter in a bowl until positively white. Add the whole egg, 2 egg yolks, sugar and orange flower water. Beat without stopping for 10 minutes on medium speed. Mix the flour and the cornstarch. Add to the butter and egg mixture without beating; just mix in the flour, flattening the batter against the edges of the bowl.

Butter a 9-inch baking pan with one full tablespoon of butter. Spread half of the cake batter on the bottom of the pan. Spread the prune purée on that first layer of batter. Leave about ¾ inch all around the cake free of paste.

Finish the cake by topping the prune layer with the remainder of the cake batter. Smooth the top of the cake. Brush with the last egg yolk and trace a crisscross pattern on the cake with a fork. Bake in a 350° oven for 30 to 35 minutes. Unmold only when cold.

KOUIGN AMANN
[Traditional Butter Cake of Brittany]

SERVINGS: 6–8 COST: expensive EXECUTION: difficult
TOTAL PREPARATION TIME: 3 hours with rising

1½ cups unsifted flour, less	½ cup lukewarm water
1 TB (180–190 g)	(1 generous dl)
1 TB cornstarch (3–4 g)	10 TB lightly salted butter
½ tsp. orange flower water	(AA 93 score) (125 g)
A pinch of salt	½ cup granulated sugar
½ envelope (1½ tsp.)	(125 g)
dried yeast	1 egg yolk

Put the flour and cornstarch in a bowl; add the orange flower water, the salt, yeast, and lukewarm water. Work into a soft dough and flatten into a round, ½ inch thick by 6 inches in diameter, cake. Set on a lightly buttered plate. Cover with a plastic wrap and let rise until double in bulk.

Knead the butter with your thumb or fingers to make sure that it is soft and pliable. Have the sugar ready.

Flatten the cake of dough into a small 6-inch square. Put the butter in the center, shaped as a square 4 inches by ½ inch thick. Enclose the butter in the dough. Let stand 5 minutes. Roll the dough into a 12-inch-long flat band, keeping it 4 inches wide. Sprinkle with ⅓ of the sugar. Pass the rolling pin over the sugar to impress it into the soft dough. Fold the bottom of the dough toward the center, then the top to cover the bottom. Turn the dough by 90 degrees so that it will now look like a book ready to be opened. Cover with plastic wrap and store in the crisper of the refrigerator for at least 20 minutes.

Take the dough out of the crisper and give it a second turn. Before closing the dough, sprinkle with the second ⅓ of the sugar. Fold and give a third turn. Before the third folding, sprinkle the last third of the sugar on the dough, less 1 teaspoon. Refrigerate another half hour. Give a last turn and with the rolling pin tease the dough into a round cake as close as possible to an 8- or 9-inch cake pan. Transfer the dough to the cake pan. Dock (slash) the top of the cake into a crisscross pattern, cutting at least ¼ inch deep into the dough.

Keep the cake at room temperature and let the dough rise within ¼ inch of the edge of the cake pan. Brush the top with the egg yolk, sprinkle with the last teaspoon of sugar, and bake in a preheated 375° oven for 25 minutes. The top of the cake should be nice and brown and on its bottom, a lovely buttered caramel layer will build.

Enjoy the cake on the day you bake it. It is a good seller with children.

TARTE AUX FIGUES FRAICHES
[Fig Tart]

SERVINGS: 6 COST: expensive EXECUTION: easy
TOTAL PREPARATION TIME: 2 hours
BEST SEASON: August through October

24 fresh figs, of a light-   1 recipe for ordinary short
  skinned variety   pastry (page 13)
1 TB butter (15 g)   1 cup heavy cream (2¼ dl)
1 cup cider (2¼ dl)   2 TB dark rum
1 TB honey   1 TB granulated sugar
                      (15 g)

Remove the stems of the figs and cut a tiny cross in their root end.
Grease a fireproof baking dish with the tablespoon of butter. Put
the figs in the baking dish. Mix the cider and honey and pour into the
dish. Bake in a 375° preheated oven until the fruit is soft (it will
vary with the breed). Baste with the cooking juices once or twice
while baking. Cool.

Roll out the pastry into a sheet ⅛ inch thick. Fit into a pastry
ring 8–9 inches in diameter. Cut and shape the edge properly, fit
with a foil, and fill with dried beans. Prebake 12 to 15 minutes in a
preheated 425° oven. Remove the beans, turn the oven off, and let
the pastry dry. Remove from the oven after 5 minutes and cool on
a rack.

Whip the cream with the dark rum and the tablespoon of sugar
(you may use more sugar if you please) until stiff. Fill the pastry
shell with the cream.

Arrange the figs on the cream and brush over them with any
glaze left in the baking dish. Serve at room temperature.

CREME FOUETTEE AUX FRAISES ET FRAMBOISES
[Strawberry Mousse Garnished with Raspberries]

SERVINGS: 6–8 COST: moderately expensive EXECUTION: easy
TOTAL PREPARATION TIME: 2½ hours, chilling of the strawberry
    purée included
BEST SEASON: May through July

1½ quarts very ripe, fresh strawberries	1 pint fresh raspberries
½ cup sugar (125 g)	1 cup heavy cream (2¼ dl)
Pinch of salt	2 TB Kirschwasser or Framboise
Juice of half a lemon	

Purée 1 quart of strawberries in the blender. Add ⅓ cup of sugar and pour into a saucepan; reduce to 1 cup.

Strain into a bowl and add the salt and lemon juice; deep chill.

Purée the remaining pint of strawberries. Sweeten it with the tablespoon or so of remaining sugar. You may use more sugar if you wish. Mix this strawberry sauce with the raspberries just before serving. Whip the heavy cream to the Chantilly stage (not too stiff, just until the cream almost mounds), whip in the Kirschwasser. Fold the cream into the chilled, reduced strawberry purée.

Present as follows: Pour the mousse into a one-quart crystal dish. Spoon on top the strawberry purée containing the raspberries. Serve nice and cold.

Magaly

—— ❧ —— ❧ ——

PROVENCE

1970s

E VERY YEAR since I first saw Les Grandes Garrigues, I have been back to admire it, enjoy its smell again and listen. Les Grandes Garrigues, the choice vineyard of the Domaine de Mont-Redon in Châteauneuf du Pape, is a huge field of large, smooth round pebbles planted with row after row of vines crouching close to the ground. All the leaves and tendrils bend gracefully toward the stones and hug them for warmth. From May to October, the sky above Les Grandes Garrigues is more often than not deep blue and stretches over the horizon, across plain and rivers all the way up to the Alps. There looms the peaceful cone of the Ventoux with its great slope of white chalk shining like snow in the sun and often trembling lightly behind a curtain of barely purple heat waves. The silence is almost total, and is broken only by the quick buzzing of a fly or the rustling of the breeze in what is left of the natural growth of thyme, lavender and yellow-flowered Scotch brush at the edges of the vineyard. It smells good, of stones heated by the sun, of wild herbs drying in the heat, of flowers exhaling their heady perfume.

In October, the whole atmosphere can change from one hour to the next and the paradise disappears under the wild influence of the mistral. With terrible strength the wind rages over the plateau, tearing the last leaves off the vines, chilling the ground, the atmosphere, the people. That's when Magaly's kingdom at Mont-Redon appears as a refuge and becomes a lovely warm place to be and to enjoy life.

A few years back I was intrigued by a course offered by Richard Olney in Avignon. I decided to join him on a culinary investigation of Provence. Richard's "frenchization" proved to be about as successful as my americanization, but I shall be forever grateful to him for introducing me to the lovely woman who was to become my friend and open to me her home and heart, Magaly Fabre.

Magaly showed me the real Provence, that of the people who live and work there, and not the commercial Provence wrapped in soleiado cloth aprons made for tourists that offers washed-out fish soup with second-rate Italian cheese. That had been my lot in my many trips south of Montélimar.

Magaly is my exact contemporary, we speak the same emotional language. Our education has been identical in many ways, so we have the same background and understand each other so well that often we do not have to talk, we can just look at each other and enjoy whatever we are doing together.

Daughter, wife and mother of vintners, Magaly's life is totally dedicated to the preservation and the development of Mont-Redon. All her activities focus on her side of the operation, which is not so much the making of wine as the social life of a great French wine house. This does not mean that she would not be able to cope with any aspect of the vineyard operation. She would. She knows how to gather grapes and process them to make wine. She knows every nook and cranny of the economy of her vineyards, the yield, the quality of the wine produced by each plot, how to blend grapes from different plots to obtain the very best Mont-Redon in a given year, and would be able to take over without hesitation should all the men, young or old, who tend to the making of the wine disappear at once.

A typical French woman, always aware of what is happening in the business and wine world, she gave a group of my students the best and most literate lecture I had ever heard on Châteaneuf du Pape wines. On that day all the gentlemen in the family were promoting the vineyard's name in the four corners of the earth and she was left alone to introduce us to her domain. She welcomed us, wined and dined us, and entertained us with her wit, wisdom, and extreme kindness. Every one of us returned to our Avignon tourist world a little better, a little warmer, and much happier for having seen this woman in action.

Magaly's house, Les Tilleuls, is a massive mansion situated on one of those beautiful sycamore-lined avenues of Provence. The windows open onto sycamore leaves on one side and a beautiful long garden full of exotic camellias and mimosa on the other. The garden is also full of fresh, healthy vegetables that appear year round on the family table, carefully and lovingly cooked by Magaly and Rose, the faithful Rose who has been helping her for thirty-five years. On one side of the garden are chicken and rabbit coops which, the last time I visited them, harbored two baby wild boars found starving in one of the deep recesses of the Camargue by the hunters in the family.

Magaly's family lives in the vineyards or in the offices, and the laugh-loving clan gathers in the warm old *salle de séjour* for the happiest meals one can imagine. The room is huge and high-ceilinged and the big fireplace is used in the cold months to roast venison, game birds, and the beautiful *broutard* lamb that grazes on the slopes of the Ventoux.

There are deep red coppers hanging on walls or sitting on top of massive oak furniture. The smells drift over from the kitchen, where Rose continues wielding her pots and pans while Magaly offers her guests aperitifs that she has made herself. There is *suze,* made with the bitter root of yellow gentian, the traditional *pastis,* and a walnut wine for which she owes the recipe to the "vieux Monsieur Hiély" in Avignon. I too would like to make the walnut wine but am never able to, for walnut trees are always too far from me on St. John's day. It is important for the success of the wine to have soft, milky walnuts picked fresh on that particular day in June, and to marinate them in red wine and sugar for long months so the flavors and colors blend. It is strong and, according to Magaly, a great tonic too.

Then to the table we go for the most delicious meal ever. Everything on that table is fresh and natural; the bread and Roquefort come from the Aveyron, where Magaly's husband was born and where they travel often to fish trout or bring back a beautiful country ham that can rival any Serano or prosciutto.

The mushrooms have been picked in the early morning under the pines in the *garrigue* at the edge of the domain. The snails with their definite fennel taste were picked off the fennel stalks growing in front of the Château in the village of Châteauneuf and prepared in a *court-bouillon* and sauce reminiscent of Africa.

One winter day, my husband and I were treated to the most enormous, shiny and glorious *brouillade aux truffes* I had ever laid eyes upon. That was a special treat, especially for us. There was as much truffle as there was egg. Some of the truffles had even been found by a poacher on the grounds of Mont-Redon and quickly claimed by the master of the place. Magaly buys fresh truffles in the late winter when they are best and less expensive and cans them herself with a good dose of Fine de Châteauneuf du Pape, of which there are several barrels in the deep cellars of the domain.

The *gratin d'aubergines* with its odoriferous sauce full of the herbs gathered in the *garrigue* is, as far as I am concerned, the star of Magaly's prolific kitchen; unless it is the *Pistou* soup or that delicious *fricassée* of lamb laced with a basil and garlic paste in the summer months.

Magaly knows of my love for her *garrigues*. She takes me on walks across the domain to thickets and recesses where no tourist ever goes. I come back happy with my provision of fresh rosemary and thyme for the year plus a good dose of savory, which she calls *poivre d'âne.*

There are always mushrooms in large quantities. It was on one of my walks with Magaly at a stage of my life when I certainly would not be expected to behave with childish excitement that I discovered an old favorite. I started a near-dervish dance in my enthusiasm at stumbling upon a growth of true Caesar's Amanita, that *oronge* of the French, the most delicious of all wild mushrooms. Magaly did the mushrooms justice with a nice *persillade* well browned in olive oil.

The fruit at Mont-Redon grows in abundance. Peaches, apricots, and cherries come from the domain, as do the honey figs that one can pick right off the tree and that release a burst of sugar and perfume into the mouth. Nothing is ever done to those figs; they are served as plain as when they were born, for they are perfect and need no adornments.

As the summer passes by, Magaly builds a great big vat of *Confiture de Vieux Garçon*. Her "Bachelor's Jam" in no way resembles that well-disciplined and totally civilized jar of brandied fruit available in sleek New York stores under a fancy expensive label. It is the real thing; cherries sneakily get mixed with black currants, then Reine Claude plums mix with red quetch plums and small Seckel pears, and if there is a second growth of late raspberries, they join the crowd with a few of the late-September figs. A few months later, this fruity world is nicely blended and drunk with its own essences to the great pleasure and enjoyment of Magaly's guests. And jams, real jams for breakfast, she makes out of everything from plums to cantaloupe, green tomatoes, and lemons.

Not only does Magaly take me on tours of the domain, she also takes me on tours of Provence. One of our favorite trips takes us into the delta of the Rhône to what is left of that beautiful Camargue.

When I was growing up it was really huge and wild. Now, it remains wild only at the very end of the Rhône delta. Most of the birds have disappeared but not the red flamingoes that fly, a dramatic sight, in elongated formation over the bright waters of the Mediterranean.

Come September, when the weather is still good, the Parisians are back at work, and Magaly is gathering strength for the vintage to come, we go gather tellins, those lovely almost-rectangular little clams that roll in toward the shore on the waves of the Mediterranean. We cook a nice big cauldron of them on the beach and add a few of the little green crabs called *étrilles* that pinch one's toes when one walks too slowly into a *laune*. The *launes* are water channels that carry the water of inland salt marshes to the sea. The water is warmish and teeming with crabs.

More often than not we come back from these expeditions happily exhausted, our fingers sticky with the salt of the sea and our noses full of the pungent smell of the *persillade* that accompanied the shellfish.

There is a great lesson to be learned from Magaly: never appear rushed however rushed you may feel. Magaly's guest room is never empty and every morning she is up to prepare her delicious coffee and to present a new guest with her delicious jams for breakfast. Every day she appears happy, cheerful, and rested even though her life is one of unending work.

The last time I visited her, she was preparing the quarters and dormitories for the students who were due the following week for the vintage. I observed her the whole day, a bundle of incessant energy hidden behind a façade of serenity and kindness. For years I have wanted to be there for the vintage and help her cook the tons of food needed to preserve the energies of an army of pickers. Every year so far something has interfered. Someday I will be there, working with Magaly to help make some of the best wine in France. Why is it that one always reads about the men who make wines and so rarely about the women who, with unflagging energy, keep alive the reputation of domains and are the souls of the big wine houses of France?

SOUPE DE POISSON
[Provençal Fish Soup]

SERVINGS: 6 COST: inexpensive EXECUTION: medium difficult
TOTAL PREPARATION TIME: 1½ hours
BEST SEASON: Best in winter since hardy, but enjoyable year round. Fennel stalks are available only from November through February.
REMARKS ON INGREDIENTS: It is absolutely impossible in the U.S. to make a 100 percent true Mediterranean fish soup, due to the absence of the small *poissons de roche* among which the *rascasse* has an especially fine flavor. The fish indicated here will give

as close an approximation as can be obtained. Please do not interchange them. All herbs and spices are needed for an explosion of taste.

FISH SOUP BASE:
¼ cup olive oil (½ dl)
4 large onions, chopped
  (1 lb.)
4 stalks of fresh fennel with
  all the greens, chopped
½ of a celery rib, chopped
  (25–30 g)
Large bunch of parsley stems,
  chopped (50 g)
3 large shallots, chopped
  (40 g)
The cloves of 2 heads of
  garlic, crushed in the
  skin (125 g)
½ small carrot, chopped
  (50 g)
2 cups dry white wine
  (4½–5 dl)
2 cups clam juice or mussel
  juice (4½–5 dl)
2½ quarts water (2 litres)
2½ lbs. whiting or sole
  heads (1 kg)
2½–3 lbs. red ocean perch,
  heads and frame (1½ kg)
1 tsp. fennel seeds, crushed
  (3 g)

1 TB dried basil
1 tsp. dried thyme
2 small bay leaves
One 2-inch strip of orange
  rind
1½ cups tomato purée (2 dl)
2 small packets of twig
  saffron
Salt and pepper
6 toasted slices of French
  bread, cut small
Parmigiano-Reggiano cheese,
  grated

FAUSSE-ROUILLE:
4–6 large cloves garlic
Salt
2 egg yolks
1 tsp. Dijon mustard
½–1 tsp. cayenne, to your
  taste
2 TB sweet paprika
2½ cups olive oil
Cold salted water to lighten
  the sauce
2 TB boiling salted water
  or broth

TO MAKE THE SOUP:
Heat the olive oil in a large pot; add the onions, chopped fennel stalks, celery, parsley, shallots, garlic and carrot. Toss in the hot oil

until the onions start turning a golden color. Add the white wine and reduce by half. Then add the clam juice and water, the fish heads and frames, and bring slowly to a boil. When the water boils, add the fennel seeds, the basil, thyme, bay leaves, orange rind, and tomato purée and bring back to a boil. Reduce the heat and simmer 35 minutes, uncovered. Stir often to break down the fish bones as much as possible and release all their flavor. After 35 minutes, crumble the saffron in the palm of your hand and add it to the soup. Let simmer another 15 minutes. Strain the soup into a clean pot and add salt and pepper. If not strong enough, reduce a little. While the soup cooks, prepare the *fausse-rouille*.

TO MAKE THE FAUSSE-ROUILLE:
Mash the garlic cloves in a mortar until they are reduced to a fine paste. Add about ⅛ teaspoon salt, the yolks, mustard, cayenne, and paprika. Gradually add the oil bit by bit until the mixture starts to thicken. Add more, whisking constantly until all the oil has been absorbed. Lighten the sauce every so often with a teaspoon of cold salted water. Finally add the boiling salted water or broth and strain into a clean bowl.

TO SERVE THE SOUP:
Put a crouton or two in a soup bowl or plate and ladle the soup over the bread. Serve the *fausse-rouille* in a bowl and let your guests help themselves. Serve a bowl of Parmigiano-Reggiano to sprinkle over the soup.

SOUPE DE MOULES AU SAFRAN
[*Saffron Flavored Mussel Soup*]

SERVINGS: 6 COST: moderately expensive EXECUTION: easy
TOTAL PREPARATION TIME: 2 hours with mussel cleaning
BEST SEASON: September through April
SUGGESTED WINE: Châteauneuf du Pape Blanc
REMARKS ON INGREDIENTS: Use the thread saffron rather than the
    powder.

5 lbs. mussels (4–5 litres)

2 large onions, chopped
(150 g)

4 shallots, chopped (50 g)

2 cloves garlic, crushed

⅓ cup chopped parsley stems
(30 g)

2 tsp. dried basil or a few
chopped basil stems and
leaves

1½ cups dry white wine
(3 dl)

Fish fumet, or water and clam
juice

Butter

Flour

2 pinches of saffron
threads, or ¼ tsp. powdered
saffron

3 TB basil leaves, scissored
very fine

½ cup heavy cream

1 cup sour cream

Freshly grated black pepper

Immerse the mussels in plenty of heavily salted water for 30 minutes to let them release their sand. Scrub them, pull out the beard, and put them in a large steam kettle or stock pot. Add the onions, shallots, garlic, parsley stems, and basil. Add the wine; cover tightly and toss.

Put the kettle over medium high heat and steam the mussels open five to six minutes, tossing them at regular intervals. As soon as the mussels are open (they should open but not overcook and shrink) shell them, put the mussels in a bowl, and discard the shells. Pour enough of the mussel juice to cover the mussels and stir for a few minutes to extract the sand left in the mussels. Transfer the mussels, one by one, to yet another bowl. Strain through several layers of cheesecloth all the mussel juice left in the first bowl and in the kettle into a large measuring cup. Make sure that there is no sand present in the mussel juice.

Mix the mussel juice with twice its own volume of fish fumet. Take note of the total volume of liquid and measure 1 tablespoon butter and 4 teaspoons flour per cup of liquid. If you have no fish fumet, you may cut the mussel juice with water and ⅓ clam juice, but the taste of the soup will not be as fine.

Make a roux with the butter and flour. Add the mixture of shellfish juice and fish fumet. Bring to a boil, stirring constantly. Simmer

20 minutes. Add the saffron and the basil and simmer no more than 10 minutes.

Mix the heavy and sour creams in a bowl. Add two ladles full of soup to the cream and mix well. Pour the mixture back into the soup pot and add the mussels. Reheat thoroughly without boiling. Season with black pepper and serve piping hot with toasted French bread.

SOUPE AU FENOUIL
[Fennel Soup]

SERVINGS: 6 COST: moderately expensive EXECUTION: easy
TOTAL PREPARATION TIME: 1 hour
BEST SEASON: November to February

4 bulbs of fennel with stalks
    and greens
1/4 cup olive oil (1 small dl)
6 cups stock of your choice,
    lukewarm (1 1/2 litres)
Salt and pepper
1 cup heavy cream (2 1/4 dl)

1/2 cup fennel greens,
    chopped fine
3 TB butter or olive oil
    (45 g)
1 clove garlic, sliced
1/2 cup French bread, cut
    into 1/3-inch cubes

Cut the fennel bulbs in half, then slice the halves across into 1/4-inch strips. Heat the olive oil. Toss the fennel in the hot oil and cover with the stock; bring to a boil. Add salt and pepper. Let simmer until the fennel is overcooked and nearly falls apart. Purée the soup either through a sieve or in the blender. Add the heavy cream and the chopped fennel greens and reheat well without boiling. Correct the seasoning. Keep hot.

Heat the butter or olive oil in a small pan, sauté the slices of garlic until they start coloring; discard them. Add the croutons and sauté them in the butter or oil until a golden color.

Pour the soup into a heated tureen and float the croutons on its surface.

SALADE AU SAFRAN ET BASILIC POUR L'ETE
[Salad with Saffron and Basil Dressing]

SERVINGS: 6 COST: moderately expensive EXECUTION: easy

TOTAL PREPARATION TIME: 45 minutes

BEST SEASON: Summer months

REMARKS ON INGREDIENTS: Arugula is not easy to find, but scan the vegetable stands in Italian and Spanish neighborhoods. Nothing can replace its fresh pungent taste. Young, fresh spinach, although not an adequate substitute, will taste very pleasant.

GREENS:

1 young zucchini

1 red pepper

1 green pepper

Olive oil to oil a pastry sheet

2 sun-ripened tomatoes

¼ lb. arugula

*1 small head of Boston
    lettuce*

1 small red onion, sliced thin

1 clove garlic

DRESSING:

2 TB lemon juice

2 TB orange juice

*⅛ tsp. orange rind, grated
    fine*

Salt and pepper

*2 TB basil leaves, scissored
    fine*

1 TB chopped chives

½–⅔ cup virgin olive oil

1 large pinch powdered saffron

2 TB chopped parsley

Wash the zucchini, slice it thin, salt it lightly, and let it stand for 20 minutes. Meanwhile, cut the red and green peppers in four wedges each, discarding the stems and all the seeds.

Place the pepper wedges on a lightly oiled pastry sheet. Broil 4 inches away from the broiler element until the pepper skins look blistered and the juice starts oozing out of the vegetables. Roll the pepper wedges in paper towels and peel as soon as possible. Cool completely. Cut into ¼-inch julienne strips. Remove the stem ends of the tomatoes, blanch the tomatoes, and peel them. Cut in wedges. Remove the seeds and cut the pulp into ¼-inch julienne strips. Mix with the pepper julienne. Keep chilled.

Clean the arugula and the lettuce. Tear them both into bite-size pieces and roll them in a terry towel. Keep them refrigerated.

Peel and slice the onion into thin slices. Separate the slices into rings. Rub a glass or china salad bowl with a crushed clove of garlic. Discard the pieces of garlic sticking to the bowl and make the dressing. Add to the bowl the lemon juice, orange juice, orange rind, salt, pepper from the mill, basil, and chives. Add one-half the oil, the saffron and then whisk in the remainder of the oil. More may be needed. Correct the seasoning.

Add the salad elements in the bowl in the following order: cross the salad fork and spoon over the dressing. Add half the arugula and Boston lettuce, then half the pepper and tomato julienne. Rinse the zucchini, pat them dry, and add them all. Then use the remainder of the greens and the mixed julienne. Sprinkle generously with the chopped parsley. Take hold of the salad fork and spoon; toss and serve immediately.

CHAMPIGNONS MARINES
[Marinated Wild Mushrooms]

SERVINGS: 6 COST: inexpensive EXECUTION: easy
TOTAL PREPARATION TIME: 45 minutes
BEST SEASON: July through September
REMARKS ON INGREDIENTS: The mushrooms used in Provence are
    Amanita caesarea or *Boleti* such as *Boletus badius* or *Boletus edulis,* but you may use any mushrooms, either commercial or wild.

3 lbs. mushrooms (1 kg 500)	*¾ cup wine vinegar*
½ cup olive oil (1	*(2 small dl)*
generous dl)	*1 heaping tps.*
Salt and pepper	*Provençal herbs*
1½ cups dry white wine	*2 TB chopped parsley*
(about 3 dl)	*2 small cloves garlic,*
	mashed

If possible, clean the mushrooms well without using water. If the mushrooms are too gritty, rinse them well and dry immediately. Heat about 3 tablespoons olive oil in a large skillet. Add the mushrooms and sauté quickly in the hot oil. Add salt and pepper and cover until all the water has oozed out of the vegetables.

Add the wine, wine vinegar, remainder of the olive oil, the Provençal herbs, parsley and garlic. Continue cooking over high heat until only about ⅔ cup of well-emulsified liquid is left. Chill and serve with crackers.

SALADE DE CALMARS ET DE POULPE
[Salad of Squid and Octopus]

SERVINGS: 6–8 COST: expensive EXECUTION: easy, but time consuming

TOTAL PREPARATION TIME: 3 hours

BEST SEASON: Year round, since both squid and octopus are always available

SUGGESTED WINE: Cassis, Châteauneuf du Pape Blanc; if neither is available, Mâcon Blanc, Graves Blanc, or Entre-Deux-Mers

REMARKS ON INGREDIENTS: To find squid, octopus, mussels, small clams, and shrimp all in one store, take a trip to your nearest Italian neighborhood fish market. Although you can expect the squid and cured octopus to be frozen, they are always of good quality if prepared properly. Do not use the tomatoes in winter.

1 octopus (*medium size*)	2 dozen large shrimp
2 onions, sliced thick	Lettuce leaves
Large bouquet garni	3 hard-boiled eggs
2 cups dry white wine	3 sun-ripened tomatoes
2–3 cups water	Lemon juice
2 dozen large mussels	½ tsp. crushed fennel seeds
2 dozen small clams	Pinch of oregano
Olive oil	2 cloves garlic, chopped fine
1 dozen small squid	⅓ cup chopped parsley
Salt	Oil-cured olives
Pepper from the mill	

Place the octopus in a 4- to 5-quart pot. Add the onions, *bouquet garni,* the wine, and water. Bring to a boil. Reduce to a regular simmer and simmer until tender. This will require from two to three hours, depending on the size of the fish.

Scrub the mussels and clams and steam them open together. Add their juices to the *court bouillon* in which the octopus is cooking. Shell the mussels and clams and toss them in a tablespoon or so of olive oil. Keep them refrigerated.

Cut the heads of the squid, discard all of the head but the crown of tentacles which is delicious. Open the body of each squid. Scrape all the inside into the trash can. Remove the ink-dotted skin, which pulls off easily when tugged with the fingers. Slice each squid into ⅓-inch-wide strips. Heat 2 tablespoons oil in a large frying pan. Add the squid, salt and pepper, and toss over high heat for just a few minutes until the squid turn opaque. Remove from the heat before the fish hardens. Should you cook it too long by mistake, cover the pan and cook over slow heat until the fish has softened again through overcooking. It will not taste quite as good, but will still be usable. Cool and refrigerate in a bowl. Add the juices to the octopus *court bouillon.*

Shell the shrimp raw. To be 100 percent French, do not devein them; the French never do. In the same pan where you cooked the squid, heat another tablespoon or so of oil and toss the shrimp in it for a few minutes until they just start to curl up in a semicircle. Remove to the same bowl as the squid. Add any cooking juices to the octopus *court bouillon.*

As soon as the octopus is tender, remove it from the *court bouillon* and let it cool. Slip the skin from the body and the tentacles and discard it. Cut the octopus into slices ⅓ inch thick; cut at an angle.

Mix the mussels and clams, squid and shrimp, and the octopus in a large mixing bowl. Clean the lettuce leaves. Hard-boil the eggs; cool and peel them. Blanch the tomatoes; peel and slice them into ¼-inch slices. Pit as many olives as you wish.

Now, prepare a salad dressing as follows. Reduce one cup of the octopus *court bouillon* to ¼ cup. Add ⅓ cup of lemon juice and emulsify a cup and a quarter of olive oil into the mixture. Add the crushed fennel seeds, the oregano, garlic, and parsley. Mix well; let steep while you prepare the platter. First make a border of lettuce leaves on a large round or oval platter. Make a second border of alternating slices of tomato and hard-boiled egg. Correct the seasoning of the dressing carefully. Toss the shellfish with the dressing and pile in the center of the prepared platter. Dot the shellfish with the pitted black olives and serve well chilled.

ESCARGOTS CANAILLE
[Snails in Provençal Sauce]

SERVINGS: 6 COST: expensive EXECUTION: easy but time consuming,

TOTAL PREPARATION TIME: 3 hours

BEST SEASON: Preferably in September, October when the tomatoes are ripe

SUGGESTED WINE: Châteauneuf du Pape Blanc or Cassis

REMARKS ON INGREDIENTS: Use canned imported French snails.

6 dozen canned French snails
¼ cup olive oil (½ dl)
2 large onions, chopped fine
3 shallots, chopped fine
3 ounces fresh pork brisket (fresh uncured bacon), diced fine (100 g)
3 TB flour (25–30 g)
1 lb. fresh sun-ripened tomatoes, seeded and chopped (500 g)
1 ripe dark red pepper, seeded and chopped (125 g)

¼ tsp. fennel seeds, crushed fine
Small bouquet garni
The canning juices of the snails (about 4½ dl)
3 cups dry white wine for canned snails (6½ dl)
Pinch of cayenne pepper
Salt
2 cloves garlic, mashed
A good pinch each: cumin, cinnamon, and ground coriander
2 TB parsley, chopped fine

Drain the canned snails into a colander placed over bowl to collect the canning juices.

Heat the olive oil in a large saucepan. Add the onions and brown them until a golden color. Add the shallots and pork brisket at once and let melt slowly; allow the meat to take on barely any color. Add the flour and cook until the flour turns a nice hazelnut brown.

Add the tomatoes, red pepper, fennel seed, *bouquet garni,* snail canning juices, white wine, cayenne, a good pinch of salt, and bring to a boil. Reduce the heat and simmer for a couple of hours. At this point the sauce should be reduced to about 3 cups (6–7 dl).

Strain the sauce into a large saucepan. Add the garlic, cumin, cinnamon, coriander and chopped parsley. Simmer together 30 minutes or so. Add the snails and reheat very well. Correct the seasoning. Serve piping hot with a good loaf of French bread to soak up the sauce.

If the snails were fresh and still in their shells, you could suck them right out of the shell. This procedure is called *à la suçarelle* from the French *sucer,* which means to suck, and this recipe is a variation of a regional Provençal recipe called *Escargots à la Suçarelle.*

BAR AU SAFRAN
[Fish Baked with Saffron Sauce]

SERVINGS: 6 COST: expensive EXECUTION: medium-difficult
TOTAL PREPARATION TIME: 1½ hours
BEST SEASON: Fall and winter
SUGGESTED WINE: Châteauneuf du Pape Blanc, Cassis
REMARKS ON INGREDIENTS: The best fish to use for this preparation
   is red snapper or striped bass.

¾ lb. unsalted butter (350–375 g)
2 onions, sliced thin
Salt and pepper
1 clove garlic, mashed
One 4–5-lb. striped bass or red snapper, cleaned and scaled (2–2½ kg)
1½ lbs. golden or white mushrooms, sliced thin

12 *chopped basil leaves or*
   1 *tsp. dried basil*
1 *tomato, sliced thin*
1 *lemon peeled to the blood,*
   sliced thin
One 2-inch piece of orange
   rind
1 *quart fish fumet* (*see page*

12) (1 *litre*)
1½ *cups dry white wine*
   (3 *dl*)
¼ *tsp. powdered saffron*
Bouquet garni
Lemon juice
2 *TB chopped parsley*

Preheat the oven to 375°.

Heat two tablespoons of butter in a frying pan. Add the sliced onions, salt and pepper, sprinkle with the garlic and mix well. Cover the onions; let them steam and mellow and cool completely. When the mixture is cold, stuff it into the cavity of the fish. Do not sew the latter closed; let the onion and fish juices escape into the baking dish.

Butter a long, oval baking dish with 2 tablespoons of butter. In a skillet heat another 2 tablespoons of butter, sauté the mushrooms with a good pinch of salt and pepper until they render their juices. Empty the mushrooms over the bottom of the prepared baking dish. Sprinkle with the basil. Let cool. Set the fish on the bed of mushrooms. Slice the tomato and the lemon into six ⅙-inch slices. Set the tomato slices on top of the fish and top each tomato slice with a slice of lemon. Salt and pepper the top of the fish lightly.

Mix the orange rind, fish fumet, white wine, saffron, and *bouquet garni*. Pour the mixture around the fish. Bake in a preheated oven for 35 to 40 minutes, basting the fish every 10 minutes with the juices from the baking dish. In between bastings, keep the fish covered with buttered paper. When the fish is done, do not remove it from the dish, but spoon all the cooking juices of the fish with the mushrooms into a large flat-bottomed *sauteuse*. Reduce the cooking juices to ⅓ cup. Remove the orange rind and *bouquet garni*. In the violently boiling reduction, whisk in the remainder of the butter. Add lemon juice to your taste and the chopped parsley.

Remove the slices of tomato and lemon from the top of the fish and delicately remove the top skin. Replace the slices of tomato and lemon on the top fillet, spoon the sauce over the fish, and serve promptly. Rice is the best accompaniment to this dish.

CIGALE DE MER AU PASTIS
[Lobster Flambéed with Pastis or Pernod]

SERVINGS: 6 COST: expensive EXECUTION: easy

TOTAL PREPARATION TIME: 1 hour

BEST SEASON: November through February, when fennel bulbs are
  in season

SUGGESTED WINE: Cassis, Châteauneuf du Pape Blanc

REMARKS ON INGREDIENTS: Any type of lobster will be good in
  this dish. *Do not* overcook it, please. To limit expenses, you
  can buy culls or odd-sized lobsters. For Pastis, use Ricard, but
  if you cannot locate any, Pernod 51 will be fine.

*4 gallons boiling water
  (15 litres)
Salt
Six 1¼–1½-lb. lobsters,
  or about 8–9 lbs. total
  (4 kg)
1 quart heavy cream
  (1 litre)*

*Pepper from the mill
2 fennel bulbs, preferably not
  too large, sliced into
  ⅓-inch strips
⅓ cup olive oil (1 small dl)
1½ oz. Pastis or Pernod
Lemon juice
2 TB chopped fennel greens*

Bring the water to a violent boil. Add ½ cup of salt (4 ounces or 120 g). Add the lobsters to the violently boiling water; bring back to a boil. Reduce heat and simmer no more than 6 to 7 minutes. Drain head down into a colander and cool. Shell as soon as the lobsters can be handled comfortably. Cut the lobster tails into ⅓-inch-thick slices. Keep lobster meat ready on a plate.

While the lobsters cook, empty the cream into a large, 2-quart saucepan. Bring to a boil, reduce to a simmer, and whisk at regular intervals. Reduce to 2–2¼ cups. Salt and pepper. Set aside.

Cut the stalks and greens from the fennel bulbs. Remove the root end and slice each bulb in half lengthwise, then into ⅓-inch strips crosswise. Wash well and pat dry in a paper towel. Chop enough greens to obtain 2 tablespoons. Set them aside.

Heat 3 tablespoons olive oil until it almost starts smoking. Add the fennel strips, salt and pepper and sauté in the olive oil until the fennel barely softens and starts loosing its juices. Add the fennel to the saucepan containing the reduced heavy cream. Mix well; keep warm.

Heat the remaining olive oil in the same frying pan where the fennel cooked. Add the lobster meat, two or three turns of the mill of pepper and toss until the meat turns bright red and starts loosing its pigmentation in the oil, which will turn orange. Add the Pastis, light it, and shake the pan. Add the cream and fennel mixture to the lobster and mix together well. Correct the seasoning. Add a squeeze or two of lemon juice if the sauce seems a trifle too sweet. Serve from the frying pan with plain buttered rice, or if you want to be fancy, in patty shells (see puff pastry, page 14). Sprinkle with fennel greens.

LANGOUSTE OU HOMARD AU GRAND MARNIER
[Lobster Grand Marnier]

SERVINGS: 6 COST: expensive EXECUTION: medium difficult
TOTAL PREPARATION TIME: 1½ hours
BEST SEASON: September through April
SUGGESTED WINE: Meursault, Viognier de Condrieu
REMARKS ON INGREDIENTS: If fresh, sun-ripened tomatoes are out of season, use canned plum tomatoes imported from Italy, Greece, or Spain.

Olive oil
Four 1½-lb. live lobsters, preferably from Maine but any type of live lobster is acceptable (a total of 6–7 lbs. or 3 kg)

3 oz. Grand Marnier (1 small dl)
5 sun-ripened tomatoes, peeled, seeded, and chopped (600–650 g)
3 cloves garlic, mashed

5 shallots, chopped fine
2 onions, chopped fine
2 TB parsley stems, chopped fine
2 TB fresh chopped tarragon,
    or 2 tsp. dried
2 TB fresh chopped chervil, or
    2 tsp. dried
2 TB fresh chopped chives, or
    2 tsp. dried
2 TB freshly scissored basil
    leaves, or 2 tsp. dried
1 cup fish fumet (2¼ dl)
1 cup clam juice (2¼ dl)

2 cups dry white wine (4½ dl)
One 2-inch strip of orange rind
1 dime-size piece of lemon rind
11 TB butter (150–160 g)
3 TB flour (25–30 g)
1 cup scalded milk (2¼ dl)
1½ cups heavy cream
½ tsp. powdered saffron
Salt and pepper
Chopped parsley
Rice pilaf for six, recipe of
    your choice

Warning: This recipe is a derivative of the famous *homard à l'Américaine.* Before you start working, make sure that all your ingredients are ready on trays and can be used in the following order without interruption. This will be half as tense and twice as much fun if on your first try you work with another kitchen enthusiast.

TO MAKE THE LOBSTER STEW:
Heat about an ⅛ inch of olive oil in a large *sauteuse* pan. While the oil heats, rub the head of each lobster with the flat of your thumb to put the shellfish to sleep. At the base of the head you will find a small horizontal line; spear the tip of a large chef's knife through this line 1 inch deep. The lobster is now dead and you can cut it as follows: first cut the claws off; crack them with the back of your knife. As soon as a piece of lobster is cut off, throw it in the pan. After the claws are removed, sever the tail from the head. Cut the tail into 3 to 4 pieces; add them to the pan. Cut the head in half lengthwise. Remove the stomach sac behind the eyes and discard it. Collect the green livers and dark green eggs in a 1-quart bowl. Add the head to the pan. Toss all the lobster pieces in the oil over high heat until they turn bright red. Heat 2 ounces of Grand Marnier in a small pan and pour flaming over the lobsters. Shake the pan until the flames die out.

If you do not own a pan large enough to contain all four lobsters, do not hesitate to separate the ingredients in half and stew in two different pans. You can later consolidate both sauce bases into one pan.

To stew, add tomatoes, garlic, shallots, onions, all the herbs, the fumet, clam juice, white wine, and rinds of citrus to the pan or pans. After the mixture has come to a boil, cover and simmer barely 8 minutes.

TO MAKE THE SAUCE:

While the lobsters are stewing, make a white roux with 3 tablespoons butter and the flour. Bind with the scalded milk to obtain a heavy, almost pasty sauce base. Keep warm.

As soon as the lobster is done, remove the pieces to a bowl. Leave the cooking juices in the pot and reduce them over medium heat until only 2 cups are left (solids and liquids together). Please measure.

Transfer this reduction to the pot containing the basic cream sauce. Whisk it gradually into the latter. Strain the mixture into a 2-quart pot or *sauteuse,* squeezing the vegetables against the strainer to extract all their essence.

Bring the sauce back to a high boil so as to rebind (rethicken) it. It will be light. Start adding the heavy cream, about ¼ of a cup at a time, and continue stirring and boiling. Once you have added half the cream, add the saffron. Then finish adding the cream. The sauce will be ready when it coats your spoon or spatula by a good ⅛–⅙-inch thickness. Reduce the heat to a bare simmer and let stand until you have made the tomalley/coral butter and shelled the lobster.

Cream the remaining butter and gradually add to it all the tomalley and coral of the lobster. You will obtain a lobster butter that resembles green buttercream. Shell the lobster pieces. Place them in a clean, pretty pan. Gradually pour half the sauce into the tomalley butter, whisking well. Reverse the process and whisk the heated tomalley into the bulk of the sauce. Reheat the sauce just below the boiling point. As the protein thickens, you will see your sauce take on an added degree of thickness. Do not boil it or it will thicken too much and become chalky to the palate. Strain the sauce over the lobster pieces. Reheat well. Heat the last ounce of Grand

Marnier and pour it flaming into the lobster pan. Correct the seasoning. You will need pepper, but not too much salt. Serve sprinkled with parsley over a bed of rice.

TERRINE PROVENÇALE
[Provençal Terrine of Veal, Pork, Herbs and Pignoli Nuts]

SERVINGS: 12–16 **COST:** affordable **EXECUTION:** easy
TOTAL PREPARATION TIME: 1 hour for making, 1½ hours for baking, 4 hours for chilling
BEST SEASON: Year round
SUGGESTED WINE: Châteauneuf du Pape Blanc
REMARKS ON INGREDIENTS: Please use all dried herbs; they are more concentrated and more flavorful in a cold slice of terrine. This recipe will make a large amount of forcemeat and may be divided into two halves. One terrine may be frozen *unbaked* for later use. When baked frozen, it takes twice as long as the first terrine less 30 minutes.

One 2½-lb. smoked shoulder
of pork (daisy roll)
(1 kg 250)
1¼ lbs. veal meat, fat and
gristle free (600 g)
1¼ lbs. pork meat, fat and
gristle free (600 g)
2½ lbs. fresh, unsalted fatback
of pork (no salt pork)
(1 kg 250)
3 tsp. dried basil
2 tsp. each: dried tarragon,
chervil, chives, and parsley

1 tsp. fennel seeds
½ tsp. each: dried marjoram,
rosemary, thyme, and savory
¼ tsp. each: dried mint and
oregano
1 TB salt (25–30 g)
1½ tsp. pepper from the mill
3 slices white bread, crusts
removed (75 g)
⅓ cup milk (1 small dl)
6 eggs
¼ lb. pignoli nuts (125 g)
4 bay leaves

TO PREPARE THE GARNISH:
Remove ½ pound smoked shoulder, ¼ pound veal and pork meat and ½ pound fatback from the bulk of the meats and dice them into

⅓-inch cubes. Salt and pepper these cubes lightly and sprinkle them evenly with 1 teaspoon of dried basil. Let stand in a bowl while you prepare the forcemeat.

TO PREPARE THE FORCEMEAT:

Grind the remainder of the smoked shoulder, the veal, pork, and fatback twice and mix well. This is best done by dipping your hand in cold water and kneading the meats together.

In a small bowl, put all the herbs, the salt, pepper, bread, and milk. Mix well. Beat the eggs. Add them to the herb mixture and mix with the ground meats until nice and homogenous. Add the diced meat garnish and the pignoli nuts. Mix well.

To test the salt level, cook a nugget of the forcemeat in a frying pan. Cool it fast in the freezer. Add more salt if necessary. The salt level depends on how salty the smoked shoulder is. This is a variable factor that depends on the brand used.

Correct the seasoning. Pack the forcement into two 1½-quart terrines. Top each terrine with two bay leaves.

Put to bake in a hot water bath in a 350° oven until a skewer inserted in the center of each terrine comes out clean and burns the top of the hand. The fat should also be clear at the top. For a nice brown top to build while baking, do not cover the terrines.

When the terrines are done, put a plate over each of them and top each plate with a heavy weight. Chill. Serve cold.

PROVENÇAL TOMATO COULIS
[A Basic Tomato Essence for Use in Provençal Dishes]

This is the very best tomato sauce base that can be obtained with fresh tomatoes. It is perfectly neutral and can be seasoned and transformed into any type of tomato sauce desired. Prepare large quantities of this and freeze or can it. It is very inexpensive in September and October.

WITH FRESH TOMATOES:

Remove the stem end of the tomatoes. Do not peel them, but squeeze all the seeds and water out of them. Put the tomatoes in a large kettle. For each 5 pounds of fruit add:

1 TB fine salt	*2 TB olive oil*
1 tsp. fine sugar	*1 tsp. dried basil*

Bring to a boil and simmer for 4 full hours. Strain through a tamis or conical strainer. Store or use.

WITH CANNED TOMATO PUREE:
Empty five pounds of commercial, unseasoned tomato purée into a kettle. Add:

1 quart water	*1 TB olive oil*
2 tsp. salt	*½ tsp. dried basil*
½ tsp. fine sugar	

Simmer together 1 to 1½ hours. Store or use.

FONDUE DE TOMATES A LA PROVENÇALE
[Basic Stewed Tomatoes for Provençal Dishes]

These stewed tomatoes are used in many egg dishes (omelettes, scrambled eggs) and on vegetables (artichokes, eggplants), and are a delicious sauce for noodles and all types of pasta. They freeze well and can also be canned.

¼ cup olive oil (½ small dl)	*peeled, seeded, and cut into*
2 large onions, chopped fine	*large chunks (2 kg 500)*
2 cloves garlic, mashed	*Salt and pepper*
⅓ cup freshly chopped parsley	*2 TB basil leaves, fine scissored*
5 lbs. fresh sun-ripened tomatoes,	*½ tsp. sugar*

Heat the olive oil in a large pot; add the onions and sauté them until they are translucent. Add the garlic and parsley and continue sautéing until the onions take on a light golden color.

Add the tomatoes and mix well. Bring to a simmer and add salt and pepper, basil, and sugar. Simmer until most of the moisture has evaporated and the fondue looks thick with only a few tomato pulp lumps left. It should not be too thick nor too runny. This quantity yields a full quart. You may cook as much as you like at once, just multiply the other ingredients with each lot of 5 pounds of tomatoes.

CREPES D'AVIGNON
[Crêpes Filled with Cheese Soufflé and Tomato Coulis]

SERVINGS: 6 COST: affordable EXECUTION: difficult
TOTAL PREPARATION TIME: 2 hours
BEST SEASON: September–October, when fresh, sun-ripened tomatoes are plentiful
SUGGESTED WINE: Châteauneuf du Pape Rouge
REMARKS ON INGREDIENTS: Please use Swiss Gruyère and true freshly grated Parmigiano-Reggiano; the Grana cheese is second best. Do not use American-made, pre-grated, so-called Parmesan.

CREPE BATTER:
¾ cup sifted flour (90–100 g)
3 eggs
1 cup milk (2¼ dl)
½ tsp. salt
½ tsp. dried basil
¼ cup melted butter, cooled
SAUCE AND TOPPING:
2 TB olive oil
2 large onions, chopped
3 cups tomato coulis (page 331)
(6¾–7 dl)
1 cup veal or chicken stock
(2¼ dl)
Large pinch each: basil, chives, chervil, tarragon, and oregano

¼ tsp. crushed fennel seeds
Bouquet garni
Salt and pepper
2 cloves of garlic, crushed
⅔ cup freshly grated Parmigiano-Reggiano (125 g)
CHEESE SOUFFLE FILLING:
3 TB butter (40 g)
3 TB flour (25 g)
1 cup scalded milk (2¼ dl)
Salt and pepper
Nutmeg
3 eggs, separated
⅔ cup Swiss Gruyère, grated fine and packed (200 g)
3 TB Gruyère, diced fine (50 g)

TO MAKE THE CREPES:

Make a well in the flour, add the eggs and mix until the mixture shreds from the whisk in heavy strands. Gradually whisk in the milk; add the salt. Stir well and strain into a clean bowl. Add the basil and whisk in the melted, cooled butter.

Heat a crêpe pan and make a dozen crêpes. Keep them hot over a hot water bath.

TO PREPARE THE SAUCE:

Sauté the onion in olive oil. Add the tomato *coulis,* stock, herbs, fennel seeds, *bouquet garni,* garlic, salt, and pepper and cook until reduced to 3 cups. Strain. Correct the seasoning.

TO MAKE THE SOUFFLE BATTER:

With the butter, flour, and scalded milk, make a basic white sauce. Season it with salt, pepper, and nutmeg. Add the egg yolks, one by one, then both cheeses (grated and diced). Whip the egg whites. Mix one-quarter of their volume into the base and fold in the remainder.

TO PUT THE DISH TOGETHER:

Fill 12 crêpes with a large serving spoon of the batter. Cut each end of the crêpes to prevent drying out of the edges. Put the filled crêpes into a buttered baking dish and cover with buttered parchment paper. Bake in a 325° oven for 15 minutes.

Open the oven, spoon the hot tomato sauce over the crêpes. Sprinkle with the parmesan, turn the oven heat to broil, and broil until the parmesan melts. Serve promptly.

FILET DE BOEUF DES ECHANSONS
[*Fillets of Beef for the Echansons of the Echansonnerie*]

SERVINGS: 6 COST: expensive EXECUTION: medium-difficult
TOTAL PREPARATION TIME: 2 hours plus 24 to 48 hours for marination
BEST SEASON: Best in winter, the sauce is good in cold weather.

SUGGESTED WINE: Châteauneuf du Pape

REMARKS ON INGREDIENTS: Any roast of beef can be used if fillet is too expensive: sirloin strip, rib, sirloin tip, eye of the round can all be used. The better the wine, the better the sauce. The homemade meat glaze may be replaced by a small dose of commercial meat extract, see below.

1 bottle excellent Châteauneuf
*   du Pape, red*
1 large onion, chopped fine
4 shallots, chopped fine
10 crushed juniper berries
1 tsp. dried basil
A large pinch each savory,
*   rosemary, and thyme*
½ tsp. each dried tarragon
*   and chervil*
1 TB chopped parsley stems
4 cloves

Dash of allspice
1 carrot, diced fine
10 peppercorns, crushed
1 lemon, sliced
Olive oil
4½ lbs. of tenderloin of beef
*   (1 kg 500)*
1 quart excellent brown veal
*   stock (1 litre)*
7–8 oz. unsalted butter
*   (200–225 g)*

Empty the wine into a large saucepan. Bring to a boil. Add onions, shallots, juniper berries, and all the herbs, the parsley stems, the cloves, taking care to crush the buds into the wine before adding them to the pot, the allspice, and carrot. Bring back to a boil and simmer 20 minutes, adding the peppercorns during the last 10 minutes of cooking. Cool completely.

Trim the meat completely of all fat and gristle, down to the bare muscle. Empty the marinade into a 2-quart glass or pyroceramic baking dish. Set the meat in the marinade. Top with the lemon slices and a few drops of olive oil. Cover with a plastic wrap. Marinate 24 hours at room temperature or 48 hours in the refrigerator.

The longer the meat marinates, the more it will taste like venison. When you are ready to roast and prepare the sauce, proceed as follows: remove the meat from the marinade. Pat it dry. Rub it well with olive oil. Set it on a roasting pan and let it reach room temperature before roasting.

Pour the veal stock into a flat pan and reduce it quickly to ⅓ cup of very heavy meat glaze. Set aside.

Put the beef to roast in a preheated 400° oven. It will take no more than 35 to 40 minutes, but adjust the roasting time to the exact weight of your piece of meat (20 minutes for the first pound and 15 minutes for each additional pound).

While the meat cooks, quickly reduce the marinade to about ⅓ cup of liquid surrounding all the vegetables of the marinade. Blend with the meat glaze. If you do not have any glaze, blend with approximately ½ to ⅔ teaspoon commercial meat extract. You may need more later.

When the meat is done, remove it from the oven and let it rest 10 minutes. Meanwhile, dissolve any brown meat juices in the roasting pan with 2 to 3 tablespoons of the marinade. Return this deglazing to the bulk of the marinade.

Bring the reduced marinade to a high boil. Whisk in about 6 ounces of butter. Taste the sauce. Correct the seasoning. If it is too acid, add some salt or meat extract very carefully. If it is too salty, add a few drops of lemon juice.

Strain through a very fine strainer, pushing on the vegetables to release all the flavors. Serve with the beef.

For vegetables, use fennel (see page 347).

ESCALOPES D'AGNEAU A LA PROVENÇALE
[Lamb Scaloppine Marinated and Breaded]

SERVINGS: 6 COST: moderately expensive EXECUTION: medium-difficult

TOTAL PREPARATION TIME: 3 hours

BEST SEASON: Year round

SUGGESTED WINE: Châteauneuf du Pape Rouge

REMARKS ON INGREDIENTS: Use as small a leg of lamb as you possibly can locate. A New Zealand leg slowly defrosted in the refrigerator does very well here. There will be a shank left over for a good bean soup or even enough odd little cubes of meat for 2 *brochettes* that can be broiled for a dinner for two persons. Also, shank and cubes can be turned into a small lamb fricassée.

SCALOPPINE:	BREADING AND COOKING:
1 whole small leg of lamb	*Flour*
(4 lbs. or 2 kg)	*2 eggs*
Olive oil	*2 tsp. oil*
Lemon juice	*2 tsp. water*
Dried thyme	*Salt and pepper*
Dried rosemary	*Dry breadcrumbs*
	⅓ tsp. fennel seeds
	½ cup butter (110 g)

Remove all fat from the leg of lamb so that the bare meat of the leg shows completely. Bone the leg, taking care to separate each and every one of the muscles forming the leg.

Remove all traces of fat, gristle and superficial conjunctive membranes. Cut each muscle *against the grain* into *escalopes* ⅓ inch thick. Flatten them with a meat bat.

With 1 tablespoon lemon juice and 3 tablespoons olive oil, make a small dressing. Season it with as much dried thyme and rosemary as you like, but be discreet. Marinate the scaloppine in the mixture for one or two hours.

Prepare the breadcrumbs. Put them in the blender with the fennel seeds and blend well together so that the taste of the fennel thoroughly permeates the breadcrumbs. Let the breadcrumbs and fennel stand together while the lamb is marinating.

Remove the lamb from the marinade. Pass each *escalope* between the first two fingers of your left hand; squeeze to discard any excess liquid. Flour the meat.

Beat the eggs, oil, water, salt, and pepper and brush the mixture on the scallopine. Coat the meat with the fennel-flavored crumbs.

Panfry the *escalopes* in half butter, half olive oil until a golden color on both sides. Add one or two tablespoons of butter to the marinade; heat it well. Add salt and pepper and dribble over the cooked *escalopes.*

For vegetables you may want to consider the artichoke hearts (see page 299) and the julienne of peppers and zucchini (see page 348).

TIAN D'AGNEAU ET DE POMMES DE TERRE AUX HERBES
[Baked Leg of Lamb on a Bed of Potatoes]

SERVING: 6–8 COST: moderately expensive EXECUTION: easy
TOTAL PREPARATION TIME: 2½ hours
BEST SEASON: April through September
SUGGESTED WINE: Châteauneuf du Pape rouge
REMARKS ON INGREDIENTS: This recipe is but a variation of the multiple versions of lamb baked on a bed of vegetables that exist in the classic and provincial food lore of France. The presence of the herbs and garlic makes it typically Provençal.

Olive oil
5 medium potatoes, preferably
* Maine (1¼ lbs. or 600 g)*
3 large onions
6 cloves garlic
½ cup chopped parsley
Salt and pepper

1½ quarts excellent brown
* veal stock (1¼–1½ litres)*
3 medium, sun-ripened tomatoes
One 4-lb. leg of lamb
Dried thyme, rosemary, and
* savory*
4 TB butter (50–55 g)

Rub an earthenware or large pyroceramic dish with olive oil. Peel and slice the potatoes into paper-thin slices. Keep them immersed in cold, lightly salted water while you prepare the onions.

Peel and slice the onions into thin slices. Heat a couple of table-spoons of olive oil in a frying pan and brown the onion slices on both sides. Remove the onions to a plate.

Chop 3 cloves of garlic fine (but do not mash them here). Mix with the chopped parsley and brown in a bit of olive oil.

Build your *tian* as follows: one layer of potatoes, salt and pepper, all the onions in one layer, the browned garlic and parsley, a second layers of potatoes, salt and pepper. Pour just enough stock in the *tian* to cover the potatoes and bake 30 minutes in a 400° preheated oven.

Meanwhile, slice the tomatoes into ⅓-inch-thick slices. Keep ready to use on a plate.

Completely remove the skin and fat from the whole surface of the leg of lamb, exposing the muscles. Cut the last three cloves of garlic into slivers. Cut little slits in the surface of the meat and slide one sliver of garlic into each slit. Use all the garlic on all sides of the lamb. Rub the leg with olive oil and sprinkle with a mixture of thyme, rosemary, and savory to your taste.

After the potatoes have baked 30 minutes, set the lamb on the bed of potatoes and arrange the tomato slices in a border around the dish. Sprinkle the tomatoes with mixed thyme, rosemary, and savory, and dot the tomatoes with the butter. Return the dish to the oven and bake one more hour, basting the meat regularly with the juices in the dish until a meat thermometer inserted in the center of the leg registers 135°. If the potatoes appear too dry, do not hesitate to add a bit of warm stock.

Remove the dish from the oven and let stand 10 minutes before carving.

ESCALOPES DE VEAU AU ROQUEFORT
[*Veal Escalopes with Roquefort Sauce*]

SERVINGS: 6 COST: expensive EXECUTION: easy
TOTAL PREPARATION TIME: 1 hour
BEST SEASON: Preferably during the cold months because of its hardy taste. But the best Roquefort will be available from late winter through late summer.
SUGGESTED WINE: Châteauneuf du Pape rouge
REMARKS ON INGREDIENTS: Buy a whole veal top and cut the *escalopes* yourself. *Escalopes* bought already cut in stores are a waste of money since they are cut with the grain of the meat.

The Roquefort should be white and uniformly veined with blue mold. Beware of grayish-yellow cheese with a pungent smell. Please, no substitutes here.

1 whole veal top, about 3 lbs. (*1 kg 250*)	*1 cup excellent brown veal stock* (*2¼ dl*)
10 walnut halves, chopped fine	*1 cup heavy cream* (*225 g or* (*2½ dl*)
1½ oz. excellent Roquefort, mashed fine (*45 g*)	*Olive oil*
3 TB unsalted butter (*45 g*)	*Salt*
	Pepper from the mill

Cut, against the grain, from the width of the veal top, enough ⅓-inch-thick slices of veal to obtain two large slices per person. Flatten each with a meat bat until it is about as wide and 1½ times as long as your hand. Keep ready to use on a plate.

Chop the walnuts fine and mash the Roquefort into them to obtain a paste. Then, mash the butter into the walnut and cheese mixture to obtain a compound butter. Set aside.

Mix the veal stock and the heavy cream together. Reduce to 1 cup. While the mixture reduces, whisk at regular intervals.

To cook the dish: heat ⅛ inch of olive oil in a large frying pan until the oil almost smokes. Sear the *escalopes* on one side. Turn over, salt and pepper the seared side, and remove from the pan as soon as the meat juices are beading on the surface of the meat. If you have to, proceed in two batches. The meat already cooked will lose some juices while the second batch cooks; do not discard them.

When the *escalopes* are cooked, keep them warm and quickly make the sauce. Discard the cooking oil. Add any juice that escaped from the meat to the frying pan and let it caramelize. Add the reduced cream and stock mixture and scrape the pan well to dissolve all the cooking juices. Turn the heat off and add the Roquefort butter to the sauce. Roll the *escalopes* in the sauce to coat them lightly, and serve.

For a vegetable, consider fennel and peas (see page 347), and green gnocchi (see page 243).

CANARD AU PISTOU
[Duck with Basil Sauce]

SERVINGS: 6 COST: expensive EXECUTION: medium-difficult

TOTAL PREPARATION TIME: 3–4 hours

BEST SEASON: September and October when it is already cold enough for a heavy meat and fresh basil is still available. This can be made year round with fresh-frozen basil leaves.

SUGGESTED WINE: Châteauneuf du Pape rouge

REMARKS ON INGREDIENTS: The *pistou* here is not 100 percent Provençal, since it is made with butter, but it finishes the sauce better than olive oil would. It will in any case please the American palate, which is shy of an olive taste, more than a true *pistou.*

Three 4½-lb. ducks (2½ kg each)	*1 quart brown veal stock (see page 10) (1 litre)*
3 TB olive oil, or 4 TB butter (45–50 g)	*1¼ cups dry white wine (2½ dl)*
1 carrot, diced into ¼-inch cubes	*1 TB tomato paste*
1 onion, diced into ¼-inch cubes	Bouquet garni
	½ cup unsalted butter
4 TB flour (30–35 g)	*2 cloves garlic*
	1 cup packed basil leaves
	Salt and pepper

Remove the ducks' wingtips. Put them in a roasting pan together with the necks, hearts, and gizzards of the birds. Roast in a preheated 400° oven until nice and brown.

Meanwhile, heat the oil or butter in a 2-quart saucepan, add the carrots and onions, and sauté until the onion starts turning a golden color. Add the flour and continue cooking until the flour is hazelnut brown and the onions have turned russet brown. Take the pot off the heat, whisk in the brown veal stock, and return to the heat to thicken. As soon as the sauce boils and has thickened, remove the duck giblets from the oven. Discard the fat in the roasting pan completely and add the white wine. Transfer the duck giblets to the saucepan containing the simmering sauce and scrape all the brown meat juices in the roasting pan well to dissolve them in the white wine. Add the white wine to the sauce together with the to-mato paste and the *bouquet garni.*

Let simmer one hour, skimming as much as possible. After one hour, strain the sauce into a 1-quart saucepan and continue skim-ming until about 1¼ cups of very clean sauce are left. Strain the sauce into a small, clean pot. Cream the butter in a bowl. Place ¼ cup of the sauce in the blender container. Add the garlic and all but 9 of the basil leaves. Blend until smooth. Cool completely and then strain into the creamed butter. Whisk together to homogenize.

All the operations described up to now can be done ahead of time. When you are ready to cook the duck, preheat the oven to 325°. Season the ducks in the cavity with salt, pepper, and three basil leaves each. Roast the ducks for 2½ hours, tilting them forward several times during the baking to let their juices run into the roasting pan and build a good gravy.

When the ducks are done, keep them warm. Empty the juices in the roasting pan into a 4-cup measuring cup. Let the juices settle. Then, separate the gravy from the fat, using a baster to suck up the meat gravy that is at the bottom of the cup.

Add these meat juices to the already-prepared sauce. Simmer to-gether for 10 minutes; then whisk the *pistou* butter into the sauce. Correct the seasoning. Serve the duck with the *pistou* sauce. For a vegetable consider the *Julienne Provençale* (see page 348) and green gnocchi (see page 343) with *Fondue de Tomates* (see page 332).

POULET SAUTE AUX GNOCCHI
[*Sautéed Chicken with Gnocchi*]

SERVINGS: 6 COST: inexpensive EXECUTION: easy
TOTAL PREPARATION TIME: 2 hours
BEST SEASON: Year round, but hearty for the cold months

GNOCCHI:

½ lb. Maine potatoes (250 g)

½ egg, beaten (2 TB)

1 tsp. salt

½ cup sifted flour (60 g)

¼ lb. spinach leaves, chopped
    very fine (125 g)

1 TB butter

Salt and pepper

Freshly grated nutmeg

SAUTEED CHICKEN:

6 beautiful, sun-ripened
    tomatoes, peeled and seeded
    (750 g)

Olive oil

Salt and pepper

1 rasher of bacon, ⅛ inch thick,
    diced small

One 3½–4-lb. roasting chicken,
    cut into 8 serving pieces

2 dozen small silverskin onions,
    peeled

1 dozen garlic cloves, peeled

1 small lemon

⅓ tsp. each: dried rosemary,
    marjoram, and thyme

½ cup brown veal stock or
    chicken broth

TO MAKE THE GNOCCHI:

Boil the potatoes in their jackets for 25 minutes. Peel and strain them through a strainer. Cool completely. Beat one egg with 1 teaspoon of salt. Sift the flour. Keep ready to use.

Chop the spinach leaves very, very fine. Sauté them in the butter with salt, pepper, and nutmeg until the mixture is dry and shiny with butter and all the spinach water has evaporated. Cool completely.

Knead together the potatoes, half the egg, flour, and cooled spinach until a ball forms.

Bring a large pot of water to a boil. Shape hazelnut-size nuggets of dough with a teaspoon and drop in the simmering water. If the dough is too soft and falls apart, add a little more flour, but be careful or the gnocchi may become rubbery.

Cook the whole batch of gnocchi. They are ready when they come floating to the surface of the water. Remove them to a lightly oiled or buttered dish and keep warm.

TO SAUTE THE CHICKEN:

Chop the tomatoes coarsely. Heat 1 tablespoon olive oil in a 1½-quart saucepan and toss the tomatoes in it. Salt and pepper them.

Let them cook until the fondue obtained is well bound and not too fluid.

Chop the rasher of bacon. Place it in a cold *sauteuse* pan with 1 tablespoon olive oil. Let the bacon crisp; remove it to a little cup with a slotted spoon. In the same *sauteuse,* brown the chicken pieces on all sides; salt and pepper them after browning. Remove to a plate.

In the same pan and the same fat, brown the small onions and the garlic lightly. Discard the fat. Return the chicken dark meat to the *sauteuse.* Pepper, cover, and cook 15 minutes.

After 15 minutes, cut the lemon into sixteen ⅙-inch-thick wedges and add. You should leave the rind on and discard both ends of the lemon. Add also the white meat and the herbs. Continue cooking another 10 minutes. If at any time the chicken starts to stick, add a little of the broth.

FINAL PREPARATION:

As soon as the last 10 minutes of the chicken cooking time are up, add the gnocchi, tomato fondue, and bacon to the pan. Simmer together another 5 minutes. Correct the seasoning of the sauce carefully and serve in a pretty, country-style casserole. As a fresh vegetable, serve a good green salad.

POIVRONS FARCIS A LA BROUSSE
[Peppers Stuffed with Cheese]

SERVINGS: 6 COST: inexpensive EXECUTION: easy

TOTAL PREPARATION TIME: 1½ hours

BEST SEASON: September and October, when the peppers are nice and ripe

SUGGESTED WINE: Cassis, Châteauneuf du Pape Blanc

REMARKS ON INGREDIENTS: Although far from being the real French Brousse, ricotta is its closest equivalent in the United States. Use the very best available brand. Also use true Parmigiano-Reggiano and for goat cheese, use the small Banon, wrapped in brown chestnut leaves.

3 red peppers	*3 small zucchini, shredded*
3 green peppers	*¼ cup dry breadcrumbs*
1 large onion, chopped fine	*1 lb. fresh ricotta cheese*
Salt and pepper	*½ cup each: Parmigiano-*
4 TB olive oil (½ small dl)	*Reggiano and Banon cheese,*
¼ cup chopped parsley	*grated fine*
2 cloves garlic, mashed fine	*1 egg*
½ tsp. dried oregano, crumbled	*1–2 TB wine vinegar, accord-*
fine	*ing to taste*

Cut a lid in each of the peppers. Remove the stem and all the seeds and membranes.

Chop the onion very fine. Heat 2 tablespoons olive oil in a frying pan and add the onion. Add a bit of salt and pepper and sauté the onion until lightly browned. Add the chopped parsley and the garlic together with the oregano and the shredded zucchini. Add more salt and pepper. Toss together and cover to draw the zucchini juices out. When the zucchini juices are flooding the pan, raise the heat and let evaporate. Let cool.

Mix well the breadcrumbs, the ricotta, Parmigiano, goat cheese, and the egg. Mix this composition with the cooled zucchini hash. Taste for seasoning. There should be enough salt, but you may want to add some pepper. Use coarse-grated black pepper.

Heat the remaining 2 tablespoons of olive oil in a braising pot or *sauteuse* pan. Stuff the peppers with the cheese mixture. Stand them in the pan, salt and pepper, cover, and bake in a 325° oven until the peppers are done, or about 1 hour. This will vary with the vegetable. The red peppers may be done before the green. In this case, remove them first.

When the peppers are done, cool them. There will be a lot of cooking juices. Reduce them by half and add 1 or 2 tablespoons wine vinegar. Serve warm, lukewarm, or even cold.

These may be used as a first course or as a main course for a weekday supper. In the latter case, you may want a small portion of gnocchi (see page 343) and a green salad to round out the meal.

PATES A LA FONDUE DE POIVRONS
[Pasta with Fresh Pepper and Tomato Purée]

SERVINGS: 6 COST: inexpensive EXECUTION: easy

TOTAL PREPARATION TIME: 2 hours

BEST SEASON: September and October, when the peppers are plentiful and ripe

REMARKS ON INGREDIENTS: Please use only freshly grated Parmigiano-Reggiano. Use the pasta or macaroni of your choice, homemade or store bought.

9 red, ripe, sweet peppers
9 green sweet peppers
½ cup olive oil (1 generous dl)
3 cloves garlic, mashed
4 cloves garlic, sliced fine
4 TB parsley, chopped fine
1 cup tomato coulis *(see page 331) or ordinary tomato purée (2¼ dl)*

1 cup broth of your choice (2¼ dl)
Dash of cayenne
Salt
Pepper from the mill
1 lb. pasta of your choice (egg noodle or macaroni type) (500 g)
4 TB unsalted butter (55 g)

Remove the stem of the peppers. Cut them in quarters. Remove all the seeds and slice the peppers into ¼-inch julienne strips.

Heat ¼ cup olive oil in a deep pot. Add 3 cloves of garlic, mashed, and 2 tablespoons parsley. Cook in the oil until brown. Add the julienne of peppers, the tomato *coulis* or purée, the broth, salt, pepper from the mill, and the dash of cayenne. Stir well. Cover and let the peppers mellow and completely lose their water. As soon as they have done so, remove the pot lid and simmer until the mixture forms a thick purée in which the pepper pulp has fallen apart and the pepper skins are clearly visible. Strain to discard the skins. Correct the seasoning.

Heat the remaining olive oil in a large frying pan. Slowly cook the garlic slivers and then discard the garlic. Replace it with the remaining parsley; let it brown.

Meanwhile, add a few tablespoons of olive oil to plenty of violently boiling water. Boil the pasta *al dente*.

To the frying pan containing the garlic-flavored oil and the browned parsley, add the butter. Let it turn a golden brown. Immediately transfer the pasta from the water it cooked in to the frying pan. Toss well. Correct the seasoning. Pour half of the pepper sauce into the pasta and mix well. Put the remainder of the sauce in a bowl and pass around with a large bowl of freshly grated Parmesan.

FENOUIL AUX PETITS POIS
[Fennel and Baby Peas]

SERVINGS: 6 COST: moderately expensive EXECUTION: easy
TOTAL PREPARATION TIME: 30 minutes
BEST SEASON: November through February, when the fennel bulbs
  are available
REMARKS ON INGREDIENTS: Only baby peas. Unfortunately the
  frozen ones, when frozen without that gooey butter sauce, are
  better than any fresh peas in the shell, unless you grow your
  own. If only the baby peas in butter sauce are available, rinse
  that magnificent goo away with warm water.

2 TB butter, unsalted (30 g)	Salt and pepper
3 leaves of Boston lettuce, cut into chiffonade	Pinch of sugar
	3 TB olive oil
1 large onion, sliced thin	2 fennel bulbs, cut into ⅓-inch
½ lb. shelled baby peas (250 g)	strips

Melt the butter in a 1½-quart pot. Mix the lettuce, onion, and peas together and add. Add salt and pepper and the pinch of sugar.

Cover and cook until the peas are tender and discolored. They must be almost overcooked.

Heat the olive oil in a frying pan. Sauté the fennel, adding a pinch of salt and pepper until the fennel mellows and starts losing its juices. At this point, mix fennel and peas. Keep covered for another five minutes to blend the flavors. Correct the seasoning and serve.

JULIENNE PROVENÇALE
[Julienne of Peppers and Zucchini]

SERVINGS: 6 COST: inexpensive EXECUTION: easy
TOTAL PREPARATION TIME: 1 hour and 15 minutes with the salting of the zucchini
BEST SEASON: Best flavor in September and October, but can be prepared year round
REMARKS ON INGREDIENTS: Do not peel the zucchini. If you peel the peppers, which is time-consuming, the dish can accompany any special piece of meat.

3 small zucchini	Pepper from the mill
Salt	2 TB olive oil
4 ripe red peppers	2 TB butter
2 green peppers	1 tsp. flour
Pinch each: dried rosemary, thyme, and savory	

Cut the zucchini into ¼-inch-thick slices, lengthwise. Then into a julienne about ¼ inch wide. Salt the julienne and let stand 30 minutes.

Cut the peppers into quarters, discarding all seeds and stems as well as the internal membrane. If you wish you can now peel the peppers. Peeled or not, cut them into ¼-inch julienne strips. Keep ready on a plate.

Mix the herbs well and crumble them together. Add a few turns of the mill of pepper. Keep ready for use. Drain the zucchini of its water, rinse, and pat dry.

Heat the olive oil in a large frying pan. Add all the vegetables at once, salt, and the mixture of herbs and pepper. Stir over high heat until the vegetables start losing their juices. Turn the heat down.

Mix the butter and flour. Stir it through the vegetables until the vegetable juices have bound with the flour. Correct the seasoning and serve.

EPINARDS AUX RAISINS ET AUX PIGNONS
[Fresh Spinach with Light Raisins and Pignoli Nuts]

SERVINGS: 6 COST: the pignoli are expensive EXECUTION: easy
TOTAL PREPARATION TIME: 30 minutes
BEST SEASON: Summer, when the spinach is fresh, young, and not
    too strong

3½ lbs. fresh spinach	*preserved without sulfur*
(1 kg 500)	*dioxide, preferably*
2 TB olive oil	*2 TB butter*
Salt and pepper	*¼ lb. pignoli nuts*
½ cup light raisins (sultanas),	

Wash the spinach very carefully. Remove the stems and pat the leaves as dry as possible. Chop the spinach as fine as possible. *Do not blanch it* in water.

Heat the olive oil in a frying pan. Add the spinach, salt and pepper and toss until the juices come out. Immediately add the raisins and continue cooking over medium heat until both have cooked and most of the juices have evaporated.

In another little pan, heat the butter. Sauté the pignoli until they turn a golden color. Add the pignoli-butter mixture to the spinach. Serve promptly. A good vegetable for veal and chicken.

ARTICHAUTS A LA FONDUE DE TOMATE
[Artichoke Hearts with Tomato Fondue]

SERVINGS: 6 COST: expensive EXECUTION: easy, but time consuming

BEST SEASON: September through May for baby artichokes. Best in
September and October, when both artichokes and tomatoes
can be used fresh. Can be made year round with frozen artichoke hearts and preserved tomato fondue.

REMARKS ON INGREDIENTS: Baby artichokes, no more than 2 inches
long by 1½ inches wide, are available in all Italian neighborhood vegetable markets. They come from California and are
every bit as good as the purple Mediterranean artichokes.

3 dozen California baby artichokes	1 clove garlic, mashed
2 quarts cold water	2 TB chopped parsley
¼ cup lemon juice	2 cups tomato fondue or 1½ cups coulis (see pages 332 and 331), or, if need be, tomato purée
2 TB oil of your choice	
2 TB flour	
2 TB olive oil	
	Salt and pepper

Remove all the leaves of the artichokes until they are about 1 inch
wide and the whole artichoke can be eaten easily. Cut the stem off.
Round off the bottom with a stainless steel knife. Cut the tip of the
artichoke leaves so the vegetable looks like a small barrel. Keep immersed in water well acidulated with lemon juice.

Mix the 2 quarts cold water with the lemon juice, oil, and flour.
Bring to a boil, stirring occasionally. Keep at a violent boil and cook
half of the artichokes 7 to 8 minutes. Remove them to a bowl and
salt them lightly. Repeat with the other half of the artichokes.

Heat the olive oil; brown the garlic and parsley in it. Add the
tomato fondue. Correct the seasoning and allow the mixture to simmer with the artichokes for about 5 minutes. Serve promptly.

TIAN D'AUBERGINES A LA PUREE D'AIL
[Gratin of Eggplant with Tomato Fondue and Garlic Purée]

SERVINGS: 6 COST: moderately expensive EXECUTION: medium
difficult

TOTAL PREPARATION TIME: 3 hours

BEST SEASON: September and October, when fresh tomatoes are
plentiful

REMARKS ON INGREDIENTS: This is a variation on a classic of
Provençal cookery. Use, if you can find them, the small Italian-
style eggplants found in Italian neighborhoods, or the pale-
green Puerto Rican eggplants.

*1½ lbs. small eggplants, cut
lengthwise into ⅓-inch slices
(750–800 g)*
Salt and pepper
Olive oil
1 onion, chopped fine
*2 lbs. tomatoes, peeled, seeded,
and cut into chunks (1 kg)*
1 clove garlic, chopped fine
1 TB basil leaves, scissored
¼ tsp. thyme

1 bay leaf
4 large whole heads of garlic
*Brown veal stock or other stock
of your choice*
4 TB butter (55 g)
3 TB flour (25 g)
2½ cups scalded milk (5 dl)
1 egg
Flour
*½ cup grated Gruyère cheese
(100 g)*

Place the eggplant slices in a baking dish, salt them, and let them
lose their strong juices for about one hour.

While the eggplants disgorge, heat 1 tablespoon olive oil in a
nice heavy pot. Sauté the onion until a golden color. Add the
tomatoes, 1 clove garlic chopped fine, the basil leaves, and the herbs.
Salt and pepper and let cook until the fondue looks nice and thick.

Meanwhile, crush each remaining garlic clove, peel it and put it
in a small pot. You should use all the cloves of the 4 heads of garlic
listed in the ingredients. Add the veal stock and cook over medium
heat until the garlic falls apart. Reduce them to a heavy purée. Strain
through a conical strainer and reserve for later use.

While the eggplants are curing and the tomatoes and garlic are cooking, prepare a cream sauce by making a white roux with the butter and flour and binding it with the scalded milk. Let cook 15 minutes, stirring occasionally. Blend the cream sauce and garlic purée as soon as the latter is ready. Beat one egg and gradually add some of the hot sauce to it. Then reverse the process and pour the egg and sauce mixture back into the bulk of the sauce. Correct the seasoning.

Remove the eggplant from its dish. Rinse it under clear water and pat it dry. Put some flour in a paper bag and add the eggplant slices. This is the fastest way to flour them evenly.

Heat a few tablespoons of olive oil in a large frying pan and fry the eggplant slices until golden brown on each side. Drain on paper towels.

Build the gratin as follows: line a 2-quart rectangular baking dish with one layer of eggplant slices. Top with the tomato fondue. Top the fondue with whatever is left of the eggplant slices. Pour the sauce evenly over the vegetables. It should be about ½ inch thick. Sprinkle with the cheese and bake in a 350° preheated oven until the top is a light golden color.

POMPE A L'HUILE
[Olive Oil Christmas Bread]

SERVINGS: 6 COST: inexpensive EXECUTION: easy

REMARKS ON INGREDIENTS: Orange flower water imported from
France is available in all so-called gourmet stores. Middle-
Eastern and Greek specialty stores also carry an excellent grade.

2 cups unsifted flour (300 g)   ½ tsp. salt
¼ cup lukewarm milk or water   3 eggs
   (small ½ dl)   ½ cup olive oil (1 generous dl)
4 TB sugar (30–35 g)   1 tsp. orange flower water
1 envelope dried yeast   ¼ tsp. dried, grated orange rind

Make a well in the flour. Add the milk or water. Sprinkle the yeast on it; let the yeast moisten well. Then mix in with a fork 1 tablespoon sugar and about 2 tablespoons of flour gathered from the edges of the well. Let the mixture bubble for at least 30 minutes.

Then, mix two eggs with the salt and the last 3 tablespoons of sugar and beat until a foam starts to develop. Add the egg mixture, the olive oil, the orange flower water, and the orange rind to the well. Slowly gather the flour from the edges of the well until all the flour has been absorbed. At this point, pull the dough to develop the gluten until the mass turns into a ball that almost pulls off the table or counter top.

Transfer the dough to a lightly oiled bowl and let double in bulk. Return to the countertop and knead again 2 or 3 minutes. Let rise again until double in bulk.

Butter or oil a 10-inch cake pan. Roll out the dough to fit into it. Cover the whole bottom of the pan. Dock (slash) the top of the bread with a crisscross pattern of 2 lines ½ inch deep in each direction. Let rise until at least 1½ inches high. Beat the last whole egg and brush over the bread. There will be too much egg; keep the remainder for a breading. Slash again into the already marked lines, this time about ¼ inch deep. Bake in a 375° preheated oven for 20 to 25 minutes. Unmold and cool on a cake rack.

TARTE AUX POMMES CITRONNEE
[Apple and Lemon Pie]

SERVINGS: 8 COST: moderately expensive EXECUTION: easy
TOTAL PREPARATION TIME: 1½ hours, including the pastry
BEST SEASON: Follow the apples: Gravenstein, September; Cortland, October–December; Newton, December–February; Granny Smith, July–September

*1 recipe for ordinary pastry (see
    page 13), or better yet,
    ½ recipe for semi-puff pastry
    (see page 17)
5–7 apples, depending on the
    size
1–2 oz. dark or light rum*

*Rind of 1 lemon, grated
One 12 oz. jar lemon or lime
    marmalade (725 g)
Juice of one lemon
2 TB unsalted butter (30 g)
Pinch of salt*

Roll out the pastry ⅛ inch thick. Set it in a lightly buttered 9-inch pie plate. Refrigerate while you prepare the apples. Preheat the oven to 375°. Peel the apples and slice them into 8 slices each. As soon as peeled and sliced, marinate the apple slices in the rum (you may use up to 2 ounces of rum). Toss well to make sure that all the apples are in contact with the rum. Add the lemon rind and toss again.

Empty the jar of marmalade in a small pot. Melt it over low fire. Add the lemon juice, butter, and salt. Arrange the apples in the pie plate in one layer of concentric circles. Strain half the marmalade over this. Arrange the remainder of the apples in a second layer of concentric circles, but reverse the direction of the apple slices this time. Mix the remainder of the marmalade, rinds and all, and spoon it over the apples without straining.

Bake the pie on the bottom rack of the oven for 20 minutes. Then, raise it to the top rack and continue baking at least another 25 to 30 minutes until the marmalade starts to caramelize lightly. Cool and serve in the pie plate.

TARTE A L'ORANGE
[Orange Tart]

SERVINGS: 8 COST: moderately expensive EXECUTION: watch the
    glazing of the oranges
TOTAL PREPARATION TIME: 2½ hours with the pastry
BEST SEASON: January to April, when the citrus fruit is fresh, plenti-
    ful, and not so expensive

½ recipe for semi- or full-
    puff pastry (see page 14)
6 TB soft, unsalted butter
    (65–70 g)
Pinch of salt
½ cup sugar plus 2 TB (155 g)
2 TB flour (15 g)

3 eggs
2 egg yolks
Rind of one orange,
    grated fine
⅔ cup orange juice (2
    small dl)
Juice of one lemon

2 TB Grand Marnier or	Water
Cognac	½ cup strained orange
3 thin-skinned oranges	marmalade

Preheat the oven to 425°.

Roll out the pastry ⅛ inch thick. Set it into a lightly buttered pie plate. Refrigerate it for 30 minutes. Line the pastry with foil. Fill the foil with dried beans and bake the pastry 15 to 20 minutes on the second lowest oven rack. Remove the beans and with a fork, scrape off any wet dough (there is always at least one layer) until you can see the dry pastry. Turn the oven down to 375°.

Cream the butter. Gradually add the salt and ½ cup sugar. Turn the mixer down to low and add the flour. Add the whole eggs one at a time. As soon as they are all incorporated, raise the speed of the mixer to medium and add the egg yolks, the orange rind and juice, the lemon juice, and the Grand Marnier. The custard may not look smooth. *Do not worry,* it will homogenize while baking.

Put the pie plate on the upper rack of the oven and pour the custard into the pastry. Bake 15 minutes or until the custard is set. Do not let it brown. Cool the pie completely. You may unmold it onto a platter if you wish.

With a lemon zester, cut 8 ridges down the sides of the orange to obtain crinkle-cut edges for the orange slices. Cut the oranges into ⅛–⅙-inch slices. Use a very sharp knife and cut evenly with the part of your blade close to the handle. (No machine will do that well, neither Cuisinart nor Mandoline.) Remove all pits and pith at the center of the fruit slices.

Put ⅓ inch of water in a frying pan with 2 tablespoons sugar. Allow the sugar to melt. Add the orange slices and cook them until they start caramelizing in the sugar syrup. Turn over at regular intervals. Do not let them caramelize too deeply or the oranges will be bitter, tacky to the teeth and difficult to eat. When the orange slices are done put them to cool on a lightly buttered pastry sheet. Arrange them on the custard so they just overlap one another and form concentric circles.

Heat the marmalade, strain it, and brush a very thin layer of it over the orange slices.

Careful. This is not easy to cut. Use a sharp, serrated blade.

CONFITURES DE CANTALOUP
[Cantaloupe Jam]

This is for those underripe cantaloupes that taste no better than turnips when eaten raw. Do not use super-ripe melons for jam. This yields eight 1½-cup jars.

5 lbs. cantaloupe pulp, diced	*1 bottle pectin*
into ½-inch cubes	*5 ounces Kirschwasser*
7 lbs. sugar	*Paraffin*
Grated rind of two lemons	

Mix the fruit and sugar in a large container that cannot oxidize. Add the grated lemon rind. Let stand 24 hours.

Transfer to a kettle. Bring to a violent rolling boil. Let cook to the "jam stage" on the sugar thermometer. Add the pectin to the center of the boil. Remove from the heat and add the Kirsch. Cool to lukewarm. Ladle into sterilized jars (wash them in the sani-cycle of your dishwasher). Spoon ⅓ inch of paraffin on top of the jam. Cool and store.

MACARONS AUX PIGNONS
[Pignoli Macaroons]

This is a modernized recipe. Years ago, one pounded the almonds with the sugar for two hours at least—or so it seemed to my young arms. Expensive but worth it.

One 8-oz. cake or can of	*1 cup sugar (250 g)*
almond paste (not marzi-	*Rind of one lemon, grated*
pan) (250 g)	*fine*

2 *egg whites*   ½ *lb. pignoli nuts*
Pinch of salt   (*250 g*)
1 *TB butter*

Preheat the oven to 325°. Grate the almond paste into a bowl. Mix with the sugar and the lemon rind. Gradually add the egg whites and a pinch of salt. Spread the pignoli on a paper.

Lightly grease 2 pastry sheets. Cover each with parchment paper, which you will also grease very lightly if it is not silicone treated (check the box). Rinse your hand in cold water. Use your hand to roll and shape 24 small balls of almond paste. As soon as the ball is shaped, place it on the pignoli and flatten it to about 1½ inches thick. The pignoli will impress themselves into the almond cookie. Set the cookies on the two sheets (1 dozen per sheet) and bake 25 to 30 minutes in the preheated oven.

To remove the cookies, roll the paper around the edge of a counter or table. The cookies will come off the paper easily; pluck them up quickly and put them on a rack to cool.

INDEX

Madeleine Kamman

Madeleine Kamman, born in Paris and educated in languages at the Sorbonne, started her cooking career in 1940 in her aunt's restaurant in the heart of France, the lovely Touraine. She has been teaching cooking since 1962 and operates her own professional cooking school in Massachusetts, together with a restaurant that has become Boston's most exclusive dining spot. She has written for several publications, including Boston Magazine, Family Health, Cuisine et Vins de France, La Revue de Vin de France *and, most recently,* The Boston Globe. *She has appeared several times on "Today" and regularly on WCVB's "Good Morning Show" in Boston. Her two previous books are* The Making of a Cook (1971), *a selection of the Cook Book Guild, and* Dinner Against the Clock (1973), *a selection of the Cook Book Guild and a Tastemaker Award winner. Ms. Kamman is a member of many food and wine societies, including the Escoffier Society and The American Culinary Federation. She is married to a consulting engineer and is the mother of two lively sons.*